Books are to be returned on or before
the last date below. AC 14/5/12.

Book damaged on Issue

14/9/07

CD

DUE
2 3 FEB 2008

DUE
- 4 APR 2008

DUE
2 1 APR 2008

DUE
2 3 JUN 2008

DUE
- 2 SEP 2008

DUE
2 7 APR 2010

14/4/11
AC

DUE
- 7 JUN 2011

DUE
2 5 JUN 2012

LIBREX–

Other titles in this series

Relationship Marketing:
A Consumer Experience Approach
Steve Baron
Nick Ashill
Janet Carruthers

ISBN 1-4129-3121-5 £70.00
ISBN 1-4129-3122-3 (pbk) £19.99
Publication November 2008

Business-to-Business Marketing

Ross Brennan
Louise Canning
Raymond McDowell

SAGE Publications
Los Angeles • London • New Delhi • Singapore

SAGE Publications Ltd
1 Oliver's Yard
55 City Road
London EC1Y 1SP

SAGE Publications Inc.
2455 Teller Road
Thousand Oaks, California 91320

SAGE Publications India Pvt Ltd
B 1/I 1 Mohan Cooperative Industrial Area
Mathura Road, New Delhi 110 044
India

SAGE Publications Asia-Pacific Pte Ltd
33 Pekin Street #02-01
Far East Square
Singapore 048763

British Library Cataloguing in Publication data

A catalogue record for this book is available from the
British Library

ISBN 978-1-4129-1969-2
ISBN 978-1-4129-1970-8 (pbk)

Library of Congress Control Number: 2006928778

Typeset by C&M Digitals (P) Ltd, Chennai, India
Printed in Great Britain by The Cromwell Press Ltd, Trowbridge, Wiltshire
Printed on paper from sustainable resources

Contents

Acknowledgements

We are grateful to the following companies that granted permission for the reproduction of their copyright material in this book.

**Figure 2.1*: Reprinted from Anderson, M.G. and Katz, P.B. (1998) 'Strategic sourcing', *The International Journal of Logistics Management*, 9 (1), Figure 8, p. 7. Republished with permission, Emerald Group Publishing Limited.

Table 2.1: Bevilacqua, Maurizio and Petroni, Alberto (2002) 'From traditional purchasing to supplier management', *Internal Journal of Logistics: Research and Applications*, 5(3), Table 3, p. 247. With permission from Taylor & Francis Limited (http//www. tandf. co.uk/journals) and the author.

Table 2.3: Reprinted from Smeltzer, L.R. and Carr, A.S., *Industrial Marketing Management*, 32, (6) Table 1, p. 487. With permission from Elsevier.

Figure 3.1: Ford, D., Gadde, L.E., Håkansson, H., Lundgren, A., Snehota, I., Turnbull, P. and Wilson, D. (1998) *Managing Business Relationships*, Figure 2.1, p. 18. Copyright John Wiley & Sons Limited. Reproduced with permission.

Figure 3.2: Håkansson, H. (ed.) (1982) *International Marketing and Purchasing of Industrial Goods*. Figure 2.2, p. 24. Copyright John Wiley & Sons Limited. Reproduced with permission.

Figures 5.1, 5.2, 5.3, 5.4: Website material reproduced from http://dbuk.dnb.com with permission from D&B (UK).

Figure 7.1: ANDERSON, JAMES C., NARUS, JAMES A., BUSINESS MARKET MANAGEMENT, 2nd Edition, © 2004, p. 319. Reprinted by permission of Pearson Education, Inc., Upper Saddle River, NJ.

**Table 7.1*: Reprinted from Jackson, D.W., Keith, J.E. and Burdick, R.K. 'The relative importance of various promotional elements in different industrial purchase situations', From *Journal of Advertising*, vol. 16, no. 4 (Winter 1987): 20. Copyright © 1987 by American Academy of Advertising. Reprinted with permission of M.E. Sharpe, Inc.

Table 7.2: Reprinted with permission from the Association of the German Trade Fair Industry.

Table 7.3: Reprinted with permission from the Association of the German Trade Fair Industry.

Figure 7.3: Reprinted with permission from the Institute for Operations Research and the Management Sciences.

Table 7.4: Reprinted from Blythe, J. (2002) 'Using trade fairs in key account management', *Industrial Marketing Management*, 31 (7), Table 10, p. 633. With permission from Elsevier.

Figure 7.3: Reprinted from Gopalakrishna, S. and Lilien, G. (1995) 'A three-stage model of industrial trade show performance', *Marketing Science*, 14 (1), Figure 1, p. 25. With permission of the Institute for Operations Research and the Management Sciences.

Table 8.1: Reprinted with permission from the author.

Figure 8.2: Reprinted from *Harvard Business Review,* 7 (8), Shapiro, B.P., Rangan, V.K. and Sviokla, J.J. (2004) 'Staple yourself to an order', p. 164 (no figure number in orginal). With permission from Harvard Business School Press.

Figure 8.3: Reprinted from Möller, K. and Rajala, A. (1999) 'Organising marketing in industrial hi-tech firms', *Industrial Marketing Management*, 28(5), Figure 5, p. 530. With permission from Elsevier.

Chapter 8 end of chapter case study adapted from Möller, K. and Rajala, A. (1999) 'Organising marketing in industrial hi-tech firms', *Industrial Marketing Management,* 28 (5), pp. 528–31. With permission from Elsevier.

Table 9.3: Ford, D., Gadde, L.E., Håkansson, H., Lundgren, A., Snehota, I., Turnbull, P. and Wilson, D. (1998) *Managing Business Relationships,* Table 9.3, p. 247. Copyright John Wiley & Sons Limited. Reproduced with permission.

Table 9.3: Ford, D., Berthon, P., Brown, S., Håkansson, H., Naude, P., Ritter, T. and Snehota, I. (2002) *The Business Marketing Course,* Table 4.1, p. 81. Copyright John Wiley & Sons Limited. Reproduced with permission.

Figure 9.4: Ford, D., Berthon, P., Brown, S., Håkansson, H., Naude, P., Ritter, T. and Snehota, I., (2002) *The Business Marketing Course,* Figure 10.8, p. 226. Copyright John Wiley & Sons Limited. Reproduced with permission.

Table 11.1: Reprinted from Cespedes, F.V. and Corey, E.R. (1990) 'Managing multiple channels', *Business Horizons,* 33 (4), Figure 3, p. 74. With permission from Elsevier.

Table 11.2: Reprinted from Shipley, D. and Prinja, S. (1988) 'The services and supplier choice influences of industrial distributors', *Service Industries Journal,* 8 (2) Table 3, p. 18. With permission from Taylor & Francis Limited (http://www.tandf.co.uk/journals) and the author.

Figure 11.2: Reprinted from Cespedes, F.V. and Corey, E.R. (1990) 'Managing multiple channels, p. 72 (figure 1), 1990, with permission from Elsevier.

Figure 11.3: Reprinted from *Business Horizons,* 33(4), Cespedes, F.V. & Corey, E.R., Managing multiple channels, p. 73 (figure 2), 1990, with permission from Elsevier.

Figure 11.4: Reprinted from (1995) Tamer-Cavusgil, S., Yeoh, P.L. and Mitri, M. 'Selecting foreign distributors', *Industrial Marketing Management,* 24 (4), Figure 1, p. 300. With permission from Elsevier.

Figure 12.4: Reprinted from *Industrial Marketing Management*, 30(3), Shipley, D. & Jobber, D., Integrative pricing via the pricing wheel, p. 303 (figure 1), 2001, with permission from Elsevier.

Figure 12.5: Reprinted from *Industrial Marketing Management*, 30(3), Shipley, D. & Jobber, D., Integrative pricing via the pricing wheel, p. 308 (figure 4), 2001, with permission from Elsevier.

Figures

Tables

Abbreviations

ARA	actor bonds, resource ties and activity links
ARPU	average revenue per user
B2B	business to business
B2C	business to consumer
CRM	customer relationship management
CRP	continuous replenishment programme
DMU	decision-making unit
EBIT	earnings before interest and taxes
EDI	electronic data interchange
ERP	enterprise resource planning
EU	European Union
GATT	General Agreement on Tariffs and Trade
GDP	gross domestic product
ICT	information communications technology
IMP	Industrial Marketing and Purchasing Group
ISIC	international standard industrial classification
IT	information technology
JIT	just-in-time
MRO	maintenance, repair and operating supplies
OEM	original equipment manufacturer
NACE	EU classification system for economic activities
NAICS	North American industrial classification system
PR	public relations
R&D	research and development
RFI	request for information
RFQ	request for quotations
SBU	strategic business unit
SIC	standard industrial classification
SWOT	strengths, weaknesses, opportunities, threats
TCO	total cost of ownership
USP	unique selling proposition
USSIC	United States standard industrial classification
VAR	value-added reseller
WTO	World Trade Organization
WWW	World Wide Web

Preface

As you have probably already gathered from the front cover, this book was written by Ross Brennan, Louise Canning and Ray McDowell. At the time of writing, we are all business-to-business marketing specialists in marketing departments within university business schools – Ross works at Middlesex University in London, Louise at the University of Birmingham in the English West Midlands, and Ray at the University of the West of England in Bristol. We decided to write this book because we felt there was a genuine gap in the market and that we three, working as a team, had the right blend of academic and practical experience to fill that gap.

For many years the global market for business-to-business marketing textbooks has been dominated by American works. The principal reason for this is that the American market for these textbooks is far and away the biggest in the world, so that writing primarily for that market makes excellent economic sense. However, and here we speak from our lengthy experience in teaching business-to-business marketing at undergraduate and postgraduate levels, students from outside the USA often complain that the American textbooks they are asked to use are not wholly appropriate. The case studies, the examples, the references to business and wider culture all reflect an American bias. More than this, however, American textbooks usually treat business-to-business marketing as no different, in any fundamental way, than the marketing of consumer goods (Brennan and Skaates, 2005). The details of the marketing mix may be different but the fundamental marketing process – research, segment, target, and then develop a marketing mix for each target market segment – remains the same.

Meanwhile, over in Europe the last three decades have seen something of a revolution in thinking about business-to-business marketing (and purchasing). Business-to-business marketing is not something that is done *by* marketers to passive organizational buyers. Frequently, two organizations transact business between themselves over a period of many years, so that it makes sense to talk about an inter-firm *relationship*. Organizations invest in these relationships and make adaptations for each other so that they can work better together (Brennan and Canning, 2002) and within these relationships people get to know, like and trust each other. Each organization is involved in many such relationships, and each relationship is connected to many others, so that it makes sense to start talking about the whole system as a *network* (Håkansson and Snehota, 1995). Business-to-business marketing involves the explicit analysis and management of these relationships and networks (Ford and McDowell, 1999).

It seems as though this gives us two conflicting views of what business-to-business marketing is. On the one hand it is about developing marketing mixes tailored for the needs of selected target markets based on an understanding of organizational buying behaviour; on the other hand it is about managing inter-firm relationships and seeking to establish influential positions within industrial networks. Textbooks in the field have tended to adopt one or other of these approaches (Brennan and Skaates, 2005). However, as the authors discussed the rationale for this book, it seemed clear to us that business-to-business marketing is not about one of these approaches *or* the other, it is about *both*. And so the idea of this book was born – a book that acknowledges that business-to-business marketing involves both the processes of marketing mix management and of relationship/ network management.

Chapter 1 provides some essential background by defining the domain of business-to-business marketing, and then Chapters 2 and 3 address the question of buying and selling processes in organizational markets. Chapter 2 focuses on what we know about organizational buyers and buying teams, while Chapter 3 extends this analysis by examining the interaction between buyers and sellers in a business relationship. In Chapter 4, dealing with marketing strategy, we discuss the important concept of customer value and look at the ways in which marketers seek to organize the strategic effort to enhance the value that they deliver to customers. We also introduce the important topic of marketing ethics in Chapter 4. Chapters 5 and 6 deal with key analytical processes in business-to-business marketing; first, gathering the research that is needed to make marketing decisions (Chapter 5), and second, dividing the market into relatively homogeneous segments in order to develop a targeted marketing strategy (Chapter 6).

The first half of the book, Chapters 1–6, has laid the foundations so that in the second half, Chapters 7–12, we can move on to discuss the practicalities of business-to-business marketing management. In Chapter 7 we look at integrated marketing communications in business-to-business markets. Chapter 8 is complementary to Chapter 7 since it looks at marketing communications methods that are deployed at the level of the inter-firm relationship, rather than at the level of the market or market segment. And while Chapter 8 concentrates on communication within inter-firm relationships, Chapter 9 then addresses the more general issue of how to manage the firm's portfolio of customer relationships. A business-to-business marketing organization has two key portfolios to manage – the portfolio of customer relationships, addressed in Chapter 9, and the portfolio of products, which is addressed in Chapter 10. Having addressed the issues of managing marketing communications, customer relationships and the product portfolio in Chapters 7–10, in Chapters 11 and 12 we examine the management of routes to market (also known as channel or distribution management) and business-to-business pricing decisions.

Our book does not contain a separate chapter on e-marketing in business-to-business markets, since the availability of the Internet and other technologies has affected virtually all aspects of business-to-business marketing, such that e-marketing is covered at many different points within the book. This includes, to mention a few, the use of IT to facilitate distribution channel coordination, the use of electronic communications media in marketing communications, the impact of IT on organizational buying behaviour, and the effects of online auctions on business-to-business buying, selling and pricing decisions.

We are grateful to all of those colleagues and students who have added over the years to our knowledge of business-to-business marketing. In particular Peter Turnbull, Stuart Hanmer-Lloyd and David Ford have contributed greatly to our understanding of the field. Naturally, any errors or deficiencies in the book remain entirely our own responsibility.

A website to accompany the book can be found at http://www. sagepub. co.uk/brennan.

The website includes a lecturer's manual that gives access to power point slides and links to case studt organizations and key sources of B2B marketing intelligence

Ross Brennan
Louise Canning
Ray McDowell

References

Brennan, R. and Canning, L.E. (2002) 'Adaptation processes in supplier–customer relationships', *Journal of Customer Behaviour*, 1 (2): 117–44.

Brennan, R. and Skaates, M. (2005) 'An international review of the business to business marketing curriculum', *Marketing Education Review*, 15 (Fall): 77–89.

Ford, D. and McDowell, R. (1999) 'Managing business relationships by analyzing the effects and value of different actions', *Industrial Marketing Management*, 28 (5): 429–42.

Håkansson, H. and Snehota, I. (eds) (1995) *Developing Relationships in Business Markets*. London: Routledge.

Companion website

A website to accompany the book can be found at:
  http://www.sagepub.co.uk/brennan.

The website includes a lecturer's manual that gives access to power point slides and links to case study organizations and key sources of B2B marketing intelligence.

1 Business-to-Business Markets and Marketing

Learning outcomes

After reading this chapter you will:

- know what are the defining characteristics of business-to-business markets;
- be able to differentiate between business-to-business markets and consumer markets;
- understand how the characteristics of business-to-business markets affect the practice of marketing management;
- appreciate the changing balance between the agricultural, manufacturing and service sectors in the world's major economies;
- understand the nature and significance of derived demand in business-to-business markets;
- be able to explain the significance of an industry concentration ratio;
- understand the nature and the significance of the accelerator effect in business-to-business markets; and
- be able to apply two complementary classification schemes to the categorization of business products.

Introduction

Lying behind every consumer purchase in a modern economy there is a network of business-to-business transactions. The hair stylist who provides the client with a new look uses hair products that were manufactured by a cosmetics company from materials bought from chemical manufacturers, equipment that was manufactured by an electrical products manufacturer using components purchased from a range of electrical engineering companies, and then arranges the client's next appointment using the salon's Wi-Fi network that was designed and installed by a computer systems firm around equipment bought from various IT vendors. Even an apparently simple transaction at the supermarket is only made possible by a web of supporting business-to-business transactions. When you buy a few items of confectionery or some vegetables (in a healthier frame of mind) from your local supermarket, you may give some thought to the supplier of the product itself, but perhaps less to the shop-fitting company that designed and supplied the shelving, the geo-demographic consultancy firm that helped the supermarket decide where to locate its store, the IT systems company that installed the point of sale equipment, and many other businesses that made the simple transaction possible. This book is concerned not with the final consumer transaction – buying the services of a hair stylist, or buying some confectionery or vegetables – but with the network of business-to-business transactions, largely invisible to the final consumer, that underlie it.

In this chapter our aims are to clarify just what is meant by business markets, to explain why it is considered necessary to distinguish them from consumer markets, and to show how business products and markets can be classified. We begin by discussing the nature of business markets. In order to emphasize the message that business markets involve both goods and services we spend a little time looking at the industrial structure of modern economies, to see how influential the service sector has become. The subsequent section deals with the core idea of this chapter, namely that business markets can be differentiated from consumer markets along a number of dimensions. Those dimensions can be summarized as market structure differences, buying behaviour differences and marketing practice differences. The chapter then moves on to look at the ways in which business products can be classified. An approach based on the uses to which products are put is contrasted with an approach based on customer perceptions of the risk and the effort (including cost) involved in acquiring a product. The chapter concludes with a case study of the steel industry. The difficult business conditions of the steel industry in recent years have led to industry consolidation. The case study looks at the supply side of the industry by examining the merger of British Steel and Koninklijke Hoogovens in 1999 and the subsequent fortunes of the merged company, Corus. Despite over-capacity in the world steel industry, we see how Nissan encountered difficulties in buying all the steel it needed in 2004, leading to cut-backs in car production.

The Nature of Business Markets

The key distinguishing feature of a business-to-business market is that the customer is an organization rather than an individual consumer. Organizations and consumers often buy the same products. For example, both organizations and individual consumers buy DVD players, laptop computers, cleaning services, automobile repair services and light fittings. Therefore, one cannot distinguish unambiguously between a business market and a consumer market on the basis of the nature of the product. It is true that there are certain products that are often bought by organizations and never by individual consumers, such as management consultancy services for a corporate merger, or – more prosaically – industrial cranes. On the other hand, it is difficult to think of anything that an individual consumer buys that would not be bought by some organization.

A brief observation on terminology is necessary at this point. The generally accepted term for the marketing of goods and services to organizations is 'business-to-business marketing'. This gradually superseded the older term 'industrial marketing' in the 1980s and 1990s. Industrial marketing is often considered to be a term that is exclusively applied to primary and secondary industries – primary industries include agricultural and the extractive industries like coal and iron ore mining, while secondary industries are those that manufacture tangible products such as cars, planes and furniture. In many modern economies the primary and secondary industries account for a relatively small share of economic activity, and it is the tertiary sector of the economy (the service industries) that contribute most to measures of national income (of which Gross Domestic Product (GDP) is probably the best known).

The expression business-to-business marketing is synonymous with 'business marketing'; these will be the two terms that we use throughout this book to refer to our subject matter. However, two other expressions are worth mentioning: 'B2B' and 'organizational marketing'. The term B2B is clearly just a contraction of business-to-business. What makes it important in its own right is that it is the ubiquitous term on the World Wide Web for business-to-business marketing and selling, to be contrasted with B2C, which stands for 'business to consumer'. The term 'organizational marketing' has been advocated by some authors (Wilson, 1999) as superior to 'business marketing' because it explicitly includes *all* organizations, while 'business marketing' seems to exclude organizations that are not 'businesses'. This may be a legitimate distinction, since charitable organizations, other non-profit organizations and governmental organizations have different fundamental objectives from private enterprise businesses. However, the expression 'organizational marketing' has not yet proved popular, and we will stick to the conventional terms 'business-to-business marketing' and 'business marketing'.

It is important not to suppose that business-to-business marketing is synonymous with marketing goods and services to the manufacturing industries. Figure 1.1 shows a time series for employment in the UK economy, broken down by industry sector, over the period 1978–2003. There has been a prominent trend over this period away from manufacturing employment and towards service sector employment. In 1978 there were 6,920,000 people employed in UK manufacturing industries, and by 2003 this had declined to 3,455,000 – a decline of just over 50 per cent in 25 years. Over the same

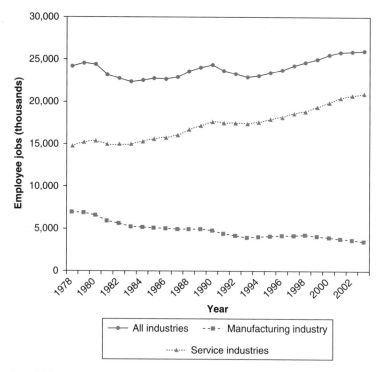

Figure 1.1   UK employment by industry sector (Economic Trends Annual Supplement, 2004).

period, service sector employment increased from 14,802,000 to 20,928,000 – an increase of 41.4 per cent. The absolute number of jobs created in the service sector considerably exceeded the number of jobs lost in manufacturing, so that total employment in the UK increased over the period. Manufacturing jobs made up 28.6 per cent of British jobs in 1978 and 13.3 per cent of all jobs in 2003; over the same period service sector jobs increased from 61.2 per cent to 80.5 per cent of the total.

In itself this trend is a matter of widespread debate for UK economists and politicians (Hadjimatheou and Sarantis, 1998; Julius and Butler, 1998). In particular, an unresolved debate revolves around the question of whether manufacturing industry is especially important (for example, because it has a high propensity to export and exhibits more rapid productivity growth than the service sector), or whether it is a normal part of the developmental process for an advanced economy to see a shift of activity away from manufacturing and into the service sector. This has important economic policy implications: should the government try to slow down or reverse the decline in manufacturing? However, from the perspective of marketing professionals, the trend away from manufacturing industry and towards the service

Table 1.1 Industry sector employment trends in selected countries, 1990 and 2000

	Total civilian employment (thousands)	Agriculture (%)	Industry (%)	Services (%)
Australia				
1990	7,850	5.6	25.4	69.0
2000	9,048	4.9	22.0	73.1
Canada				
1990	12,572	4.2	24.6	71.2
2000	14,910	3.3	22.6	74.1
Germany				
1990	27,946	3.4	39.8	56.8
2000	36,978	2.7	33.4	63.9
Ireland				
1990	1,115	15.0	28.6	56.4
2000	1,664	7.9	28.6	62.8
Japan				
1990	62,500	7.2	34.1	58.7
2000	64,620	5.2	31.7	63.2
New Zealand				
1990	1,472	10.6	24.6	64.8
2000	1,779	8.7	23.2	67.7
Sweden				
1990	4,508	3.3	29.1	67.5
2000	4,159	2.4	24.6	72.9
United Kingdom				
1990	26,577	2.1	29.0	68.9
2000	27,677	1.5	25.4	72.8
United States				
1990	11,7914	2.8	26.2	70.9
2000	13,5208	2.6	22.9	74.5

Row values may not total 100% due to rounding.
Sources: OECD, 1993, 2003.

sector should be seen as an important element of the marketing environment, which suggests that the opportunities to market goods and services to the UK manufacturing sector may decline, and will certainly grow more slowly than opportunities in the service sector of the economy. In passing, it is worth observing that the decline in manufacturing employment in the UK has also been associated with a decline in the manufacturing share of GDP (Hartley and Hooper, 1997); although manufacturing productivity has grown faster than service sector productivity, it has not grown fast enough to compensate for the very substantial decline in manufacturing employment seen over the last few decades.

The trend away from manufacturing and towards the service sector is much more than just a UK phenomenon, as Table 1.1 shows.

Over the ten-year period from 1990 to 2000 virtually all of the world's major economies saw a decline in manufacturing employment and an increase in service sector employment. A decline in employment in agriculture is also evident from Table 1.1. From the marketing point of view it is interesting to observe not only these trends, but also the different structural characteristics of these economies. Despite declines in agricultural employment, this sector remains a large-scale employer in Ireland, New Zealand, and, to a lesser extent, Australia and Japan. It is important to distinguish between percentages and absolute numbers, however. The UK, with the smallest proportion of the workforce employed in agriculture, nevertheless had more than twice as many agricultural workers in 2000 as either Ireland or New Zealand. Germany and Japan – two of the world's largest economies – have retained a large, if declining, manufacturing sector. Understanding such trends in the economic environment is a useful foundation for the more complex research and analysis that goes into preparing an international marketing strategy.

Business Markets: Defining Characteristics

Having established that it is not the nature of the product that is bought and sold that differentiates business markets from consumer markets, we move on to examine what are regarded as the defining characteristics of business markets. Many authors have sought to identify the *dimensions* by which business markets can be distinguished from consumer markets, and then the specific *characteristics* of business markets and consumer markets on each of these dimensions. Table 1.2 provides a synthesis of these dimensions and characteristics. The table is organized into three columns. The first column identifies the dimension against which business and consumer markets are thought to differ, the second column provides the characteristic expected of a business market, and the third column the characteristic expected of a consumer market.

Table 1.2 is also divided into three major sections, entitled respectively market structure differences, buying behaviour differences and marketing practice differences. In general, it is underlying structural differences between business and consumer markets that bring about important differences in buying behaviour. Marketing practice in business markets differs from that in consumer markets because of the underlying differences in markets structure, and because of the differences in buying behaviour. For example, it would be wrong to assert that business markets differ from consumer markets because the most frequently used promotional tool in the former is personal selling, while in the latter it is advertising. The extensive use of personal selling in business markets can be traced to the market structure and buying behaviour characteristics commonly found in business markets, which are usually not found in consumer markets. Specifically, in many business markets demand is concentrated in the hands of a few powerful

Table 1.2   Differences between business and consumer markets

Market structure differences

Dimension	Business marketing	Consumer marketing
Nature of demand	Derived	Direct
Demand volatility	Greater volatility	Less volatility
Demand elasticity	Less elastic	More elastic
Reverse elasticity	More common	Less common
Nature of customers	Greater heterogeneity	Greater homogeneity
Market fragmentation	Greater fragmentation	Less fragmentation
Market complexity	More complex	Less complex
Market size	Larger overall value	Smaller overall value
Number of buyers per seller	Few	Many
Number of buyers per segment	Few	Many
Relative size of buyer/seller	Often similar	Seller much larger
Geographic concentration	Often clustered	Usually dispersed

Buying behaviour differences

Dimension	Business marketing	Consumer marketing
Buying influences	Many	Few
Purchase cycles	Often long	Usually short
Transaction value	Often high	Usually small
Buying process complexity	Often complex	Usually simple
Buyer/seller interdependence	Often high	Usually low
Purchase professionalism	Often high	Usually low
Importance of relationships	Often important	Usually unimportant
Degree of interactivity	Often high	Usually low
Formal, written rules	Common	Uncommon

Marketing practice differences

Dimension	Business marketing	Consumer marketing
Selling process	Systems selling	Product selling
Personal selling	Used extensively	Limited
Use of relationships	Used extensively	Limited
Promotional strategies	Limited, customer-specific	Mass market
Web integration	Greater	Limited
Branding	Limited	Extensive, sophisticated
Market research	Limited	Extensive
Segmentation	Unsophisticated	Sophisticated
Competitor awareness	Lower	Higher
Product complexity	Greater	Lesser

Sources: Chisnall, 1989; Dwyer and Tanner, 2002; Ford et al., 2002; Lilien, 1987; Simkin, 2000; Webster, 1991; Wilson, 1999, 2000; Wilson and Woodside, 2001.

buyers (market structure), who employ teams of purchasing professionals to do their buying (buying behaviour). In most consumer markets demand is dispersed widely throughout the buying public and no single consumer has any real buying power (market structure), and buyers are not trained professionals (buying behaviour). Personal selling makes sense in the first set of circumstances (concentrated demand, powerful buyers, trained professionals), since organizational buyers expect to hear a well-argued case specifically tailored to the needs of their organization, and the costs associated with employing a sales executive are justified by the high potential value of each order. Advertising makes sense in the second set of circumstances (dispersed demand, no powerful buyers), primarily because the relatively low value of a typical transaction only justifies low selling costs. Of course, specifically tailoring the message to the needs of the individual consumer, which was once effectively impossible, is becoming more and more feasible with the deployment of sophisticated IT and customer relationship management (CRM) software (Evans et al., 2004). Indeed, such technologies may bring about a degree of convergence between marketing practices, based around the Internet and CRM, between consumer markets and those business markets that have relatively dispersed demand.

Market structure differences

Derived demand

> Bread satisfies man's wants directly: and the demand for it is said to be direct. But a flour mill and an oven satisfy wants only indirectly, by helping to make bread, etc., and the demand for them is said to be indirect. More generally:-
>   The demand for raw materials and other means of production is *indirect* and is *derived* from the direct demand for those directly serviceable products which they help to produce. (Marshall, 1920: 316, italics in original)

It is the convention in marketing to treat demand by consumers as *direct* and demand from businesses as *derived*. This idea originated with the economist Alfred Marshall (Eatwell et al., 1987). At its simplest, it is supposed that consumers only buy goods and services to satisfy their wants, whereas businesses only buy things to facilitate the production of goods and services. In this case, consumer demand is wholly *direct* while business demand is wholly *derived*. The word derived indicates that the demand for something only exists so long as there is a demand for the goods or services that it helps to produce. Businesses do not 'want' fork-lift trucks or computerized logistics system in the same way that consumers want fashion clothing or computer games. The demand for fork-lift trucks and logistics systems is derived from the demand for the products that they help to deliver. Of course, many industries have no contact at all with final consumers. For example, steel manufacturers (see case study at the end of this chapter) sell their products to other businesses, such as shipbuilders, car manufacturers and building firms. So we have a chain of derived demand. For example, final consumer demand (direct demand) for cars and diesel fuel creates a derived demand for steel (to manufacture cars), ships (to transport crude oil), and many other goods and services besides. The derived demand for ships in turn creates a derived demand for steel, as well as a whole range of other products and services. The derived demand for steel creates many more forms of derived demand, including raw materials, transport services, and general business services such as accountancy and management consultancy. The whole chain of derived demand is driven by the direct demand of consumers. The metaphor of a river is often used to describe the chain of derived demand, with 'downstream activities' being those that take place in close proximity to the consumer and 'upstream activities' being those that take place far away from the consumer.

While it is convenient to think of consumer demand as direct and business demand as derived, the stark dichotomy is probably a little misleading (Fern and Brown, 1984; Simkin, 2000). Consumers do not generally buy washing machines because they 'want' a washing machine; rather it is because of the valuable services the machine provides. The consumer may 'want' clean clothes, or to be accepted socially by sending out their children looking smart, or to look good in a clean white shirt for a job interview. The machine is a means to an end, not the end itself, so that arguably the demand for the machine is derived. Equally, one can envisage a manager in a business organization using company funds to buy a particularly attractive painting for the office; while this would no doubt be justified in terms of creating the right ambience for effective working, it is easy to see it as a direct demand based on the intrinsic merits of the painting. Nevertheless, there is little doubt that the great majority of business expenditure represents derived demand. Firms do not buy such things as office buildings, factories, warehouses, raw materials, logistics support, cleaning services, lubricants and backhoe loaders for the pleasure that they give, but for their ability to facilitate the delivery of goods and services to customers.

The accelerator effect

The most straightforward implication of derived demand in business markets is that marketers must be aware of developments, both upstream and downstream, that may affect their marketing strategy. In particular, it is downstream demand that 'drives' the level of derived demand in a specific business market. Of course, this is intuitively obvious – if the demand for new housing increases then clearly, perhaps after a time lag, the (derived) demand for housing materials such as steel and wood will also increase. In due course, and probably after a longer time lag, the (derived) demand for capital equipment used in the construction industry, such as backhoe loaders and cement mixers, may well also rise. However, what is less obvious is that the percentage change in derived demand may be much larger, or much smaller, than the percentage change of original demand. This is a phenomenon that can occur in capital equipment industries, and is known as the accelerator effect. The illustration in Box 1.1 shows the basic arithmetic of the accelerator effect.

Box 1.1   *An illustration of the accelerator effect*

- Suppose that a house-building firm knows that it needs to own one backhoe loader for every 50 houses that it builds per year. Each backhoe loader is depreciated over five years. The company usually builds around 500 houses per year, and so owns a stock of 10 backhoe loaders. This means that it buys two new backhoes each year to replace machines that reach the end of their economic life.
- Now, suppose that because of a house-building boom the firm experiences a growth in demand to 600 houses per year. Let us assume that the managers of the house-building firm expect this increase in production to be permanent. They need to increase their stock of backhoe loaders to 12, as well as replace two worn-out machines. Rather than buying two backhoe loaders, this year they buy four.
- The increase in demand for houses experienced by the building firm was 20 per cent (that is, $100 \div 500$), but the increase in purchases of backhoe loaders by the firm was 100 per cent (four instead of the usual two).
- The accelerator effect in this case is five (the 100-per-cent increase in demand for capital equipment divided by the 20-per-cent increase in demand for houses).
- Notice that if the managers of the house-building firm expect the demand for housing to remain constant from now on, then this will be a one-time-only increase in the demand for backhoe loaders. The long-term demand for backhoe loaders will increase by 20 per cent, exactly in line with the permanent increase in demand for houses. In subsequent years the firm will replace, on average, 2.4 ($12 \div 5$) machines each year.
- What if the managers of the building firm expect their sales of houses to return to their previous level of 500 per year? The firm would temporarily own two more backhoes than it needed, and for one year only its demand for backhoes would fall to 0.4. The accelerator then works in reverse, and is entirely symmetrical, since sales of houses have declined by 16.7 per cent, and demand for backhoes has declined by 83.3 per cent, giving an accelerator of five (after allowing for rounding error).

The example in Box 1.1 is hypothetical and not intended to be realistic. It illustrates the principle of the accelerator only. A purely hypothetical example is needed because in practice things are never so clear-cut, and the underlying acceleration principle can be difficult to discern. In practice, managers will be cautious about investing in new equipment at the first sign of an increase in demand for their own products, since they cannot be sure that the new demand will be enduring. In the short term managers are very likely to spend a little more on maintaining old equipment (so continuing to use equipment even though it has been fully depreciated on the balance sheet) rather than investing in new equipment, to get a better picture of the trend in demand. Naturally, managers can choose to lease equipment rather than to buy it new – although this in itself does not make the accelerator principle incorrect, since the equipment leasing company has to get its equipment from somewhere. For the accelerator principle to work with full effect we have to assume that capital equipment is being worked to full capacity; otherwise the building firm in our illustration could have chosen to work its existing backhoe loaders more intensively rather than buy new machinery.

Despite these various objections, there is considerable evidence that the acceleration principle plays a substantial role in explaining the demand for capital equipment. Almost all macro-economic models of the economy include a version of this principle to explain capital investment, indicating that the principle is valid (Eatwell et al., 1987). The key implication of the principle for business marketers is that, in capital equipment markets, the future trend in demand cannot be predicted straightforwardly from forecasts of demand in downstream markets. Changes in downstream demand can lead to much larger percentage changes in demand for capital equipment. The fact that this is very unlikely to happen with the simple arithmetic precision of our illustration, for the various practical reasons discussed, makes the forecasting job much harder. One task for the business marketer working in such an industry is to understand both the scale of underlying accelerator principle for the industry, and the moderating influences on the accelerator exerted by conditions in the market and the behaviour of managers in customer organizations.

Market concentration in business-to-business markets

Business-to-business markets in general are characterized by high concentration of demand compared to consumer markets. However, the degree of demand concentration varies from market to market, and it is important to have some means of comparing markets to establish just how highly concentrated they are. The standard measure that is used is the concentration ratio. A concentration ratio is defined as the combined market shares of the few largest firms in the market – what is known as the 'oligopoly group' of firms in the market. Quoted concentration ratios are usually based on the top three, four, or five firms; that is to say, the concentration ratio is the sum of the market shares held by the top three, four, or five firms. The 'five-firm concentration ratio' is the most common method of describing the extent to which a market is dominated by a few firms. For purposes of economic analysis and economic policy concentration ratios are important because it is supposed that the higher the concentration ratio, the more likely it is that firms in an industry will collude to raise prices above those that would be found in a truly competitive market. Economists also theorize that where concentration ratios are relatively high, industry will be less innovative and production volumes less stable. Empirical economic research has generally shown that prices do tend to be higher, and innovation less dynamic, in highly concentrated industries (Eatwell et al., 1987).

The perspective taken by economists, when studying concentration ratios, is generally that of the *customer* of the industry in question and the *economic efficiency* of the structural conditions of the industry. To the business marketer it is the perspective of the industry *supplier* that is generally most relevant, along with the implications of the industry structure for *sales and marketing strategy*. While economists are generally most concerned about the *monopoly power* that businesses have over their customers because of the concentration of market share, business marketers are usually more interested in the *monopsony power* that businesses have with respect to their suppliers because of the concentration of buying power. The degree of monopsony power in the supply market is symmetrical with the degree of monopoly power in the customer market; those firms that control large shares of the customer market are also the largest customers for suppliers to the industry. So we can use the concentration ratio (concentration of market share) as a proxy for the concentration of buying power within an industry.

Illustrating concentration ratios

The concentration of market power in consumer markets is widely known and understood. For example, anyone who has studied consumer marketing in the UK knows that although there are many brands in the laundry detergent market, the market is in fact dominated by just two producers: Lever Faberge Ltd and Procter & Gamble Ltd. In 2003 the brands owned by Procter & Gamble Ltd had a combined share of 46.1 per cent of the UK market, while Lever Faberge brands had a combined share of 34.1 per cent (Euromonitor, 2004b). At the company level this market is highly concentrated, since two firms control around 80 per cent of the market, and can be reasonably referred to as a *duopoly*. Clearly, any business wanting to supply products or services to the UK laundry detergent market must take this factor into account when developing a sales and marketing strategy. If your aim is to obtain a substantial share of the business to supply the UK laundry products market, then it is essential to do business with at least one of the industry leaders. To have any chance of achieving this you must become very familiar with the business of those companies and adapt your products and services so that they exactly match their requirements, which may well involve specific investment in new technology or new systems. Throughout this book we will frequently return to the implications of this for the theory and practice of business marketing.

Tables 1.3 and 1.4 show the top five company market shares in two other consumer markets, the Western European market for beer and the German market for audio products. From these we can calculate the five-firm concentration ratio for each sector, which is 38.7 per cent for the beer market and 51.8 per cent for the audio products market. It is equally possible to calculate the three- and four-firm concentration ratios from the data; for example, the three-firm concentration ratio in the Western European beer market is 29.5 per cent. Both of these industries fall into the normal range of concentration ratios. While the German audio products market is more concentrated than the Western European beer market, both show typical levels of industrial

Table 1.3   Western European market for lager beer: volume company shares 2002

Company	%
Heineken NV	13.2
Interbrew NV SA	8.7
Carlsberg A/S	7.6
Scottish & Newcastle Plc	5.8
Grupo Mahou-San Miguel	3.4
Five-firm concentration ratio	**38.7**

Source: Euromonitor, 2004c.

Table 1.4   German market for audio products: volume retail company shares 2002

Company	%
Sony Deutschland GmbH	16.5
Panasonic Deutschland GmbH	10.1
JVC Deutschland GmbH	8.7
Pioneer Electronics Deutschland GmbH	8.7
Philips GmbH	7.8
Five-firm concentration ratio	**51.8**

Source: Euromonitor, 2004a.

concentration. Neither shows nearly as great a concentration of demand as the UK laundry detergents market, however. Business marketers aiming to develop a marketing strategy to supply products or services to either of these industries clearly need to be aware of the buying power of the top companies listed in Tables 1.3 and 1.4. However, there is great deal of scope to develop sales and marketing strategies based on other segments of these markets, rather than simply focusing on the major players. It is also noteworthy that while the beer market is dominated by relatively local producers, that is to say, by European companies, the German market for audio products is dominated largely by the local subsidiaries of Japanese firms.

Other market structure differences
An understanding of derived demand, the accelerator effect and concentration ratios provides a basis for analysing many of the structural differences between typical consumer and business markets. Table 1.2 listed a number of other dimensions, along which lines experts have proposed that there are systematic differences between business and consumer markets. Demand elasticity is one of these dimensions. First, it is argued that businesses have less freedom simply to stop buying things than consumers, so that business demand is likely to be less price elastic (that is, less responsive to price

changes) than consumer market demand. Second, and for similar reasoning, it has been suggested that there will be more instances of reverse (or 'perverse') price elasticity of demand in business markets than in consumer markets. Both of these hypotheses about demand elasticity arise from the nature of derived demand and assumptions about the availability of substitutes for the inputs to critical business processes. Businesses need critical inputs if they are to continue trading.

For example, if a computer manufacturing firm cannot gain access to the latest generation of microprocessors, then it cannot build machines that will sell and the very existence of the company is at risk. Should the purchasing professionals at this company see the price of microprocessors rising, then they may take this to mean that there is a shortage of supply (price tends to rise in markets where demand outstrips supply) and may therefore *increase* their orders in the short term in the hope of guaranteeing a sufficient supply of microprocessors to keep the business functioning. In effect this is a case of reverse elasticity, where a rise in price triggers an increase in demand. Even if the purchasing team at the computer firm do not believe that there is likely to be a shortage of microprocessors, price changes are unlikely to affect the volume that they purchase to any great extent. The volume of microprocessors that the company buys is primarily driven by their computer sales forecasts, and not so much by component prices. The expectation is that demand for microprocessors will be inelastic with respect to price.

From Table 1.2 we can see that business markets have been described as more heterogeneous, more fragmented and more complex than consumer markets. All of these characteristics are reflections of the enormous diversity of organizational forms found in business markets. Of course, the point is not that consumers are all alike. Rather, it is that organizations are even more diverse than consumers. For example, most private firms employ fewer than ten people, while many household-name firms employ tens of thousands of people at multiple locations across several continents. A local decorating business employing three or four people has almost nothing in common with, say, a global automobile manufacturer.

Buying behaviour differences and marketing practice differences

In this section we will discuss these aspects of the differences between business markets and consumer markets only quite briefly. The reason for this is that buying behaviour and marketing practice are the subject matter of the remainder of the book, and we wish to avoid repeating ourselves excessively! In the following chapters you will find detailed discussions of organizational buying behaviour and business-to-business marketing practice.

In essence, organizations tend to have more professionalized buying processes than consumers, often involving formal procedures and explicit decision-making practices, which in many organizations are implemented by managers who are specifically employed as purchasing professionals. Transaction values can be very high. As a result, sellers tend to tailor their product offerings to the needs of the buyer, seeking to offer complete solutions to their business problems rather than just to sell them a product. The conventional tools of consumer mass marketing are not very appropriate under these circumstances. Promotional messages must be tailored to the specific needs of the customer. Sales executives (and, for the most important customers, Key Account Managers) are employed to develop and manage the relationship between the buying and selling organization. All of these aspects of buying behaviour and business marketing practice will be explained in much greater detail in subsequent chapters of the book.

Classifying Business Products and Markets

We have emphasized that the key difference between business marketing and consumer marketing is the nature of the customer rather than the nature of the product. In business markets customers are organizations. There are indeed many products that are purchased by organizations that one cannot envisage being bought by consumers, such as management consultancy services and heavy engineering equipment. Equally, there is a vast array of products bought both by organizations and by private consumers, such as personal computers and health insurance services. This raises the question of whether one can classify business products separately from consumer products, or whether a single classification system will function equally well for both.

The standard approach to classifying business products is to use a classification system that is quite separate from the usual consumer product classifications (Copeland, 1924; Kotler, 1972; Murphy and Enis, 1986). This classification is based on the use to which the products are put, and the extent to which they are incorporated into (or 'enter') the final product. Many things that organizations buy, such as office cleaning services, are not incorporated into the final product at all. Some things, such as the DVD drives that a computer manufacturer buys from an optical drive manufacturer, are incorporated directly and completely into the final product. The distinction between 'entering goods' and other types of purchase is based on the idea that something incorporated into the buying organization's final product contributes directly to the finished product quality and so directly to the customer's business reputation. Other purchases affect the buyer's own customer less directly, and so do not have such an immediate potential influence on the buying organization's business performance. The system of classification is as follows:

- *Installations* are major investment items such as heavy engineering equipment, which are treated as investment items by the customer, so that the costs involved in acquiring them are depreciated over their expected economic life. Customers are expected to plan such investments carefully, perhaps involving the use of extensive financial analysis including discounted cash flow analysis, and scenario planning.

- *Accessory equipment* consists of smaller items of equipment such as hand tools. Larger items of accessory equipment may be treated as investment items and depreciated on the financial statements, while smaller items will be treated as expense items. The economic life of accessory equipment is usually shorter than that of installations.
- *Maintenance, repair and operating (MRO) supplies* are individually minor items of expenditure that are essential to the running of the organization. These would include such things as office supplies (for example stationery), lubricants and abrasives.
- *Raw materials* are unprocessed basic materials such as crude oil, coal and metal ores (the steel industry – see the case study at the end of this chapter – is a major buyer of coal and iron ore). These products are often traded on international exchanges (such as the London Metal Exchange) and are particularly prone to price fluctuations arising from the forces of supply and demand.
- *Manufactured materials and parts* include raw materials that have been processed (such as finished steel and prepared timber) and component parts (such as computer DVD drives and automobile windscreens) that are ready to be incorporated directly into the finished product.
- *Business services*, are often subdivided into maintenance and repair services and business advisory services.

From this classification of business products one can easily derive a commonly cited classification of industrial manufacturing organizations into original equipment manufacturers (OEMs) and others. OEMs are manufacturing businesses that buy component parts from other firms to incorporate into a finished product that is then sold under their own brand name to other businesses or to consumers. Car manufacturers (such as VW/Audi, Ford and Toyota) and computer manufacturers (such as Dell, Compaq and Fujitsu Siemens) are classic OEM businesses. One can then distinguish between the OEM market (sales of component parts to OEMs for incorporation into the final product when it is first manufactured) and the after-market (sales of component parts to the owner of the product *after* it has been sold by the OEM). In the after-market, for example, car owners may need to replace a shattered windscreen, and computer owners may choose to upgrade the RAM capacity of their desktop machine. OEM customers are by definition business customers. They usually buy in large quantities, and are typically large and powerful buying organizations. Customers in the after-market may be either organizations or consumers. Both organizations and consumers buy vehicles and computers, for example, for which they will buy spare parts or upgrades. The OEM market is therefore an exclusively business-to-business market, while the after-market includes both businesses and consumers.

In contrast to the standard classification system for business products that we have cited above, Murphy and Enis (1986) argued that only one classification system was needed for products, and that it could apply equally well to business and consumer products. They proposed a fourfold classification of products based on the buyer's evaluation of the effort involved in acquiring the product and of the risk of making a poor decision. Effort and risk are considered to be the costs incurred by the buyer when making a decision; effort is a variable that includes the amount of money, energy and time that the buyer is willing to expend to acquire a given product.

- *Convenience products* involve very little effort and negligible risk for the buyer. The maintenance, repair and operating supplies described previously would generally be classified as convenience products.
- *Preference products* involve a little more effort than convenience products but substantially more risk. In general, this means that they are a little more expensive than convenience products, but that the buyer perceives a much greater chance of making the wrong decision. Minor items of accessory equipment as described above would generally also be classified as preference products; Murphy and Enis also mentioned business travel as a characteristic preference product.
- *Shopping products* involve a great deal more effort and perceived risk than convenience or preference products. This would include major items of accessory equipment, manufactured materials and parts (that is, products that enter the final product completely), and market research services. Buyers are willing to spend a considerable amount of time and energy on acquiring these products because of their relatively high price and risk associated with possibly making the wrong decision.
- *Specialty products* are the highest ranked in terms of both buyer risk and effort. Installations (such as major new items of engineering plant) and highly specialized business services (such as the services of a top management consultancy firm) would fall into this category. The main distinction between specialty products and shopping products is effort, rather than risk. Buyers are prepared to invest great amounts of time and energy in seeking to make the right choice about these high-value purchases.

The two principal classification systems described above should be regarded as complementary rather than as alternatives. The first of them concentrates on the nature of the product, the way in which products are used and whether they enter the final product or not. It is a seller-orientated classification scheme. The Murphy and Enis classification is buyer-orientated, classifying products on the basis of dimensions that are considered meaningful to buyers. Although they are logically distinct, there is clearly a degree of consistency between them. For example, 'installations' will almost certainly fall into the category of 'specialty products', and MRO supplies almost certainly into the category of 'convenience products'. The Murphy and Enis classification has the advantage of explicitly treating goods, services and ideas equally. In classifications of business products it is all too easy to relegate services to a single undifferentiated category, with the implication that services are relatively unimportant compared to goods. However, as we saw earlier in the discussion of Table 1.1, the service sector is a much larger employer than the manufacturing sector in the world's major economies, so it is important not to think of the marketing of business services as somehow less important than the marketing of industrial products.

Chapter Summary

- Business marketing is concerned with the marketing of goods and services to organizations. The key distinguishing feature of business marketing is the nature of the customer, rather than the nature of the product. Although there are products that are bought only by organizations and not by final consumers, there are many products that are bought by both organizations and consumers.

- Modern economies are becoming increasingly service orientated. The service industries accounted for close to 75 per cent of employment in such countries as Australia, Canada, the UK and the USA in 2000 – and the trend is towards even higher levels of service sector employment.

- Business markets can be distinguished from consumer markets along a wide range of dimensions, but those dimensions can be conveniently grouped into market structure, buying behaviour and marketing practice. At the most fundamental level, it is structural differences that tend to drive differences in buying behaviour and in marketing practice. In particular, demand in business markets is derived rather than direct, and levels of demand concentration in business markets are typically much higher than in consumer markets. As a result, buyer power in business markets can be much greater than in consumer markets. In turn, this often means that business marketers prefer relational marketing strategies, developing solutions tailored to individual customers rather than conventional marketing mix strategies.

- A common classification for business products is installations, accessory equipment, MRO supplies, raw materials, manufactured materials and parts, business services. A key distinction is made between products that are incorporated into the final product (entering goods) and those that are not. Original equipment manufacturers combine components bought from other suppliers into a finished product that is sold to end-users.

The after-market comprises sales of parts for repair and upgrade to products that are already owned by an end-user. Business products can also be classified using the customer-orientated categories of convenience, preference, shopping and specialty products. This classification scheme is based on the risk and the effort that buyers perceive in acquiring a given product.

Questions for discussion

1 Why do we not differentiate between business markets and consumer markets on the basis of the type of product purchased?

2 Draw up an elementary chain of derived demand for the personal computer industry.

3 What is the accelerator effect and why is it important in business-to-business markets?

4 Are business markets fundamentally different from consumer markets?

5 What is a five-firm concentration ratio? What difference does it make to the business marketer whether this ratio is 30 per cent or 70 per cent?

Case study: Snapshots of the steel industry

The steel supplier

British Steel, 1999

The end of the millennium saw British Steel struggling to achieve financial success. In his Chairman's statement Sir Brian Moffat remarked: 'The past year was increasingly challenging for British Steel due mainly to the disruptive effects of the economic crises in the Far East and the continuing strength of sterling.' Indeed, the Group suffered an operating loss of £174 million on a total turnover of £6259 million, while only a year before it had achieved an operating profit of £265 million on turnover of £6947 million. In British Steel's most important market, the UK, market share was down to 55 per cent from 57 per cent, while there were contrasting fortunes in the main steel-using industries. Output stagnated in the electrical and mechanical

Case study

engineering sector, and declined by 5.5 per cent in the metal goods sector, but UK car production was up by 3 per cent, while the construction sector was stable. Other European markets showed an overall decline of 3 per cent in demand for steel. Even though the use of steel was not in decline, a surge in steel imports during 1998 had built up stocks. Demand for steel was suppressed as users chose to bring down their steel stocks before placing new orders. The USA market was growing, but Asian markets were still depressed following a severe Asian financial crisis.

Steel is a capital-intensive industry with extensive international trade. Producers strive to keep their production facilities working at high utilization levels. This means that geographical fluctuations in demand often lead to rapid changes in sales patterns as producers pursue market opportunities in order to keep their plants busy. In 1998/99 the decline in steel demand in their home markets caused Asian steel producers to look for export markets, primarily turning to the USA and Europe. As the elementary economics of supply and demand suggest, if there is excess capacity in an industry then competition is expected to drive prices down. World demand for steel declined in 1999, meanwhile there was an estimated 30 million tonnes of excess capacity, and international competition brought about the expected result as steel prices declined sharply. To aggravate the problem for British Steel, the period 1995–2000 saw a steady strengthening of sterling against the world's other major currencies. This directly reduced export earnings (since foreign currency earned was worth less in terms of sterling), improved the competitive strength of overseas competitors in the UK market (since they could charge lower sterling prices and obtain the same amount of revenue in their own currency), and adversely affected British Steel's UK manufacturing customers (so tending to reduce UK demand for steel).

British Steel responded to these adverse circumstances by striving to improve its marketing and purchasing operations. On the marketing side, British Steel was working with customers to develop new steel products that delivered improved manufacturing performance to their customers. For example, in partnership with a forging company an improved type of steel for manufacturing connecting rods was developed, which significantly improved machinability. On the purchasing side, British Steel reorganized its purchasing operations around networked supply hubs and continued to reduce the number of suppliers with which it worked. Substantial cost reductions were achieved.

The birth of Corus, 1999

In October 1999 British Steel merged with the Dutch company Koninklijke Hoogovens to form Corus. Industry commentators regarded this as an inevitable consolidation within the European steel industry to deal with the combined pressures from depressed demand, intense international competition and declining global steel prices. Over the course of the next few years

Corus became the focus of intense public and political scrutiny as it implemented the rationalization programme that was the main justification for the merger of the two companies. The main impact was on employment in the UK, where thousands of job losses were to follow in already depressed industrial regions such as south Wales and northern England.

Corus 2003

In 2003 Corus had an operating loss of £208 million on a turnover of £7953 million, compared to an operating loss of £446 million on a turnover of £7188 million in 2002. Sales turnover improved both because of improved sales volume and because of increased prices; average revenue per tonne of carbon steel increased from £285 in 2002 to £305 in 2003. In the UK, still the most important market for the merged company, there was a slight decline in the number of cars manufactured, but this was offset by growth in the construction industry. Sterling had weakened against the Euro, so that British manufacturing industries were having greater success in exporting to Europe, with consequent benefits for British steel manufacturing. Other European markets saw a decline in steel use, in particular from the domestic appliance industry, as a general decline in economic confidence caused European consumers to cut back in this area. Elsewhere in the world the USA experienced a decline in demand for steel and there was a small increase in Japan because of strong export growth achieved by Japanese manufacturing companies. However, the driving force behind the world steel market was undoubtedly China, with an estimated 20 per cent growth in steel demand during 2003. Chinese demand for steel in 2003, at 203 million tonnes, was estimated to be 21 per cent of global steel demand. Because of the strong demand for steel from China, the competitive pressures felt by British Steel in 1999 from Asian steel producers looking for alternative export markets in Europe were diminished. In the longer-term, a worry for other world steel producers was that the Chinese economy would inevitably, sooner or later, slow down from its hectic growth and that the massive increase in steel manufacturing capacity developed in China would be available to serve other world markets. One forecast suggested that by 2010 China would have a steel producing capacity of 63 million tonnes in excess of domestic steel demand.

Principal steel-using industries

- Aerospace
- Automotive (components industry and car manufacturing)
- Construction
- Consumer products (including domestic appliances)
- Energy and power generation
- Engineering
- Rail

Case study

- Packaging
- Shipbuilding

The steel user

Nissan 2004

In late 2004 Nissan Motor had to stop production at three of its four assembly plants in Japan because of steel shortages. In order to improve efficiency Nissan had cut the number of main Japanese steel suppliers it used from five to two, leaving it more dependent on the remaining two. While demand for cars was booming, Nissan did not have enough steel to maintain production. As a result, the production of up to 40,000 Nissan cars was delayed, just as Nissan was about to launch several new models in Japan. Sales revenue and profitability were adversely affected. Because the two preferred suppliers were already operating at full capacity, Nissan had to look elsewhere for high-quality steel. Indeed, across a large part of the region there was a scramble to obtain sufficient steel, with a construction boom in China, buoyant demand for ships from the shipyards of Japan and South Korea, and growing levels of production at other major car manufacturers such as Toyota. Steel producers in the region were already working to increase production capacity, but the construction of new steel manufacturing facilities takes some time. The steel industry has only limited flexibility to respond to fluctuations downstream in the chain of derived demand because it is so capital intensive. Building new steel manufacturing capacity is a massive undertaking with lengthy lead-time and heavy investment costs.

Case study questions

1. Explain how the chain of derived demand affects the demand for steel.
2. Explain the differences between marketing an industrial raw material such as steel and a fast-moving consumer good (such as washing powder) in terms of market structure differences, buying behaviour differences and marketing practice differences.

Sources: British Steel, 1999; Corus Group, 2003; The Economist, 2004, 2005.

References

British Steel (1999) *British Steel, Report and Accounts*. London: British Steel.
Chisnall, P.M. (1989) *Strategic Industrial Marketing*. Hemel Hempstead: Prentice Hall.
Copeland, M.T. (1924) *Principles of Merchandising*. Chicago: A.W. Shaw.
Corus Group (2003) *Corus, Report and Accounts*. London: Corus Group.

Case study

Dwyer, F.R. and Tanner, J.F. (2002) *Business Marketing: Connecting Strategy, Relationships and Learning* (2nd edn). Boston: McGraw Hill.

Eatwell, J., Milgate, M. and Newman, P. (eds) (1987) *The New Palgrave: A Dictionary of Economics*. London: Macmillan.

Economic Trends Annual Supplement (2004). London: TSO.

Euromonitor (2004a) *German Market for Audio Products*. London: Euromonitor.

Euromonitor (2004b) *Laundry Care*. London: Euromonitor.

Euromonitor (2004c) *Beer in Western Europe*. London: Euromonitor.

Evans, M., O'Malley, L. and Patterson, M. (2004) *Exploring Direct & Customer Relationship Marketing* (2nd edn). London: Thomson.

Fern, E.F. and Brown, J.R. (1984) 'The industrial/consumer marketing dichotomy: a case of insufficient justification', *Journal of Marketing*, 48 (Spring): 68–77.

Ford, D., Berthon, P., Brown, S., Gadde, L.E., Håkansson, H., Naude, P., et al. (2002) *The Business Marketing Course: Managing in Complex Networks*. Chichester: Wiley.

Hadjimatheou, G. and Sarantis, N. (1998) 'Is UK deindustrialisation inevitable?', in T. Buxton, P. Chapman and P. Temple (eds), *Britain's Economic Performance* (2nd edn). London: Routledge.

Hartley, K. and Hooper, N. (1997) 'Industry and policy 1: theory and competition policy', in P. Curwen (ed.), *Understanding the UK Economy*. Basingstoke and London: Macmillan.

Julius, D. and Butler, J. (1998) *Inflation and Growth in a Service Economy*. London: Bank of England.

Kotler, P. (1972) *Marketing Management: Analysis, Planning, and Control*. Englewood Cliffs, NJ: Prentice-Hall.

Lilien, G.L. (1987) 'Business marketing: present and future', *Industrial Marketing and Purchasing*, 2 (3): 3–21.

Marshall, A. (1920) *Principles of Economics* (8th edn). London and Basingstoke: Macmillan.

Murphy, P.E. and Enis, B.M. (1986) 'Classifying products strategically', *Journal of Marketing*, 50 (July), 24–42.

OECD (1993) *United Kingdom*. Paris: OECD.

OECD (2003) *United Kingdom*. Paris: OECD.

Simkin, L. (2000) 'Marketing is marketing – maybe!', *Marketing Intelligence and Planning*, 18 (3), 154–8.

The Economist (2004) 'Not-in-time manufacturing', *The Economist*, 4 December, pp. 73–4.

The Economist (2005) 'Forging a new shape'. *The Economist*, 10 December, pp. 71–2.

Webster, F.E. (1991) *Industrial Marketing Strategy* (3rd edn). New York: Wiley.

Wilson, D. (1999) *Organisational Marketing*. London: International Thompson.

Wilson, D. (2000) 'Why divide consumer and organizational buyer behaviour?', *European Journal of Marketing*, 34 (7): 780–96.

Wilson, E. and Woodside, A. (2001) 'Executive and consumer decision processes: increasing useful sensemaking by identifying similarities and departures', *Journal of Business & Industrial Marketing*, 16 (5): 401–14.

2 Buyer Behaviour

Learning outcomes

After reading this chapter you will:

- know how the nature of a company's activities and its business strategy affect its dealings with supply markets;
- understand differing purchasing orientations and their contribution to a customer's acquisition of supplier resources and capabilities;
- be able to explain the buying process and reasons why this process can vary;
- be able to describe the membership and characteristics of the decision-making unit;
- be able to explain how and why individual needs can sometimes override rational decision-making;
- know about the job of the purchasing professional;
- understand the contribution of IT to purchasing activities; and
- understand the implications of these factors for the business marketer.

Introduction

Few customers, private or organizational, are self sufficient, able to maintain their existence by satisfying their needs without drawing on the capabilities of suppliers and without purchasing products marketed by those companies. To function and to achieve objectives requires that an organization has access to supply markets from which it can obtain products to support its own activities. Behaviour associated with gaining access to necessary supply markets and products is affected by a variety of factors. Some of these are external to an organization, such as general macro-environmental forces as well as influences that are more peculiar to the sector and market in which the organization operates. In addition to these external dynamics, purchasing is affected by what goes on inside a firm. So consideration has to be given to how organizational characteristics, as well as group and individual factors, affect purchase behaviour and decisions (Webster and Wind, 1972). The central themes in this chapter lie in understanding what goes on inside a business and how organizational, group and individual forces influence the purchasing behaviour of business customers, and the implications for the business marketer of the way in which organizational customers deal with supply markets as a result of these forces.

Organizational Factors Affecting Purchasing Decisions

Organizations are not faceless and monolithic; rather they consist of human beings who repeatedly make decisions and take particular courses of action regarding purchasing. So the organizational factors discussed here inform the purchasing behaviour of managers in customer companies.

The nature of company business

We can think about our customers in terms of the industry sector or market in which they operate and how the dynamics in these industries influence their purchasing behaviour. However, it is possible to operate at a more general level by thinking about the 'technology' associated with our customers' businesses. By this we mean the way that a customer organizes their own activities in order to perform transformation processes that represent the essential components of their value-adding activities (Woodward, 1965). A company can be categorized according to whether its activities are essentially based on unit, mass or process production technology.[1] This classification system could be criticized because it is derived from the manufacturing and engineering industries, while in the previous chapter we saw the growing importance of the service sector. Nevertheless the categories can be used – irrespective of whether a customer organization might be viewed as essentially a manufacturing, engineering or service business – to generate some understanding of the nature of the key product capabilities that customer companies might purchase and of the expectations that might be placed on suppliers.

Unit production involves the design and supply of products that are tailored to specific customer requirements. The bespoke products are typically associated with major capital investment projects, with a company's production activity being triggered by, and adapted to meet, the requirements of the individual customer. The technological complexity and scale of such projects affects the supply needs and purchasing behaviour of organizations whose business activities essentially revolve around competing for and supplying such major investments projects. A company will have the technical competence and operational capabilities to design and produce some components/parts that are an essential part of the final product and to assemble/configure and install the finished product.

However, the company also has to draw heavily on the design and production capabilities of suppliers that provide the materials, components or equipment that are central to the finished project as well. The unit production company typically requires the involvement of such suppliers in its design and production/assembly phases and requires coordination amongst its various key suppliers to ensure the completion and financing of these major projects. Companies whose business is geared around unit production include organizations such as General Electric. The company's Energy Division competes for multi-million-dollar projects worldwide to provide power generation installations and distribution systems, requiring it to work with a variety of subcontractors in order to assemble the finished systems. Other businesses, such as those supplying organizations with bespoke and complex information communications technology (ICT) systems, again work in a similar way. British Telecommunications Plc (BT), for example, supplies and operates the ICT system used by the financial services company National Australia Group (NAG). The system draws on BT's information communications expertise, but to assemble and operate this bespoke system it has to draw from the technological capabilities of other parties (BT, 2005). The complexity, scale and bespoke nature of such products means that purchasing lies within the remit of the team assembled to oversee the project, with managers that are responsible principally for the technical content of the final product assuming a key role in dealing with suppliers.

In contrast to unit production businesses, a *mass production* company is involved in the design and supply of high-volume, standard products. Production efficiency and a low cost base are central to the ability of mass production companies to compete. This efficiency is in part determined by the equipment used and the integration of the various sections that make up the company's primary production activities. The materials and components used to make up a finished product also contribute to the company's cost base. To maximize the efficient use of its resources, a company's production activities will be characterized by a high degree of inflexibility, requiring that the supply of materials and components used in primary operational activities be precise, regular and consistent. To this end the company would expect key suppliers to adjust logistical and administrative procedures to suit its requirements, to link these procedures with its own operations and to invest in systems such as just-in-time delivery and extranets. The importance attached to the stable and secure flow of materials and components to support the buying organization's primary production activities often results in the company seeking to have some influence over the behaviour and activities of businesses that are not immediate suppliers but are nevertheless part of its supply chain.

A mass production company's ability to compete is determined not only by its low cost base but also by the regular introduction of new products into its target market. The company's key material and components suppliers would be expected to contribute to the buying organization's new product development activities. When new products are being developed, a supplier will have regular contact with the buying organization's design and technical managers. However, once a supplier's material or component proposal is accepted and becomes part of the customer's product specification, then the principal point of contact is with the purchasing function. Companies that operate in this way with their supply markets are quite diverse, ranging from high-volume car manufacturers to food processors such as Heinz and Nestlé. For food processors, efficient operations are central to the company's ability to remain cost competitive. A key contributor to a food processor's product costs lies not in the food that it provides to consumers but in the packaging that contains and preserves that food. In addition to this, the packaging acts as an important marketing tool for the food company. So the packaging supplier makes a significant contribution to the food processor's finished product, with companies simultaneously trying to reduce packaging costs and develop innovative designs. For example, if you think about olive oil, you might picture it in tin cans or bottles. Oil is particularly vulnerable to light and air, such that the oil's properties quickly deteriorate. So glass bottles are not ideal for olive oil. Packaging supplier Tetra Pak has worked with one of its customers, the Spanish oil producer Arteoliva, to eliminate this problem by developing a carton package for the customer's oil products. Having developed a packaging product that worked, all that remained was to convince retailers and consumers of the added value offered by the new packaging form; that is, an oil with a longer shelf life but one which retains its health-giving properties (Tetrapak, 2004).

While the ideas of mass production have obvious resonance when we think about companies producing tangible consumer goods, they can be extended to service businesses. If we take the retail sector, for example, and think about large chains such as Wal-Mart, Tesco, Sainsbury, Carrefour and Ikea, then these firms operate on the same principles, where the key to business success is the ability to keep costs per square metre to a minimum. Supply continuity is important and retailers will, for example, work with key suppliers to maximize the efficiency of retail operations.

As with mass production, the *process production* company is involved in the manufacture of high-volume products, with low cost, operational efficiency and therefore supply continuity being central to the organization's performance. A key distinction is that the process producing firm does not assemble finished products but rather its business centres on the processing of raw materials for use in other supply chains. The company will typically consume high volumes of necessary materials, with those that have a standard specification being sourced via commodity markets. Others, which may be unique to the buying organization's requirements, will be purchased from specialized suppliers. Consumption volume, the importance of supply continuity and the effect of raw material prices on the processor's business performance means that although a company might have buyers responsible for purchasing specific commodity materials, corporate management will also have some involvement in purchasing activities. The equipment used as part of the organization's primary processing activities is central to the business's performance. Equipment purchases are infrequent, but they represent complex capital investment projects, with suppliers becoming involved with the buying company's project team at the early stages of investment project. Businesses involved in process production include steel manufacturers such as Corus (see the case study in Chapter 1) and utilities companies such as NPower.

Business strategy

In addition to thinking about a customer's operational 'technology', vendors could also consider the customer's business strategy as this can give some indication of the way in which the customer will deal with supply markets. A firm's generic strategy defines the organization's competitive domain and how it will position itself against competitors. Decisions made at the business level regarding a firm's competitive strategy are guided by and also inform actions and decisions at the functional level, including purchasing. So, for example, a firm that adopts a *product leadership* strategy relentlessly pursues innovation in order to offer customers leading-edge products that consistently enhance the value derived by its customers in their use of the company's products (Treacy and Wiersema, 1993). Product leadership requires that a company has excellent technical and creative abilities and that it is able to use its own experience and learning capability to drive a rapid rate of product innovation and obsolescence. Hewlett-Packard, for example, derives over 50 per cent of its annual sales from products that have been in the market for less than two years (Barnholt, 1997). As well as managing its own internal product development processes, the involvement of suppliers in those processes is also key to the firm's ability to pursue a product leadership strategy. Business marketers striving to supply such companies will need an intimate knowledge of the customer's business, the ability to offer design and product expertise to contribute to the company's development activities and sufficient responsiveness to support the customer's pursuit of innovation.

An alternative strategy is that of *cost leadership*, where a company competes by providing reliable products with minimal inconvenience to customers and at competitive prices (Treacy and Wiersema, 1993). Clearly, businesses adopting this strategy must contain costs to enable them to satisfy customer requirements at the lowest possible cost. A company might rethink the design and implementation of business processes, eliminating activities that are redundant and reconfiguring others such that use of resources is more efficient. Business marketers dealing with such companies would expect procurement of products to be organized around keeping costs to a minimum. Cost containment and ways to improve this would be an ongoing and central feature of dealings with suppliers. For example, efficient ground services such as aircraft refuelling and luggage handling are important for any airline. However these airport services are essential for low-cost companies such as easyJet and Ryanair to enable fast turnaround and maximize the flying time of aircraft.

Most companies have some form of social responsibility policy that guides the behaviour of managers and also affects dealings with suppliers. As part of their compliance process, the toy retailer Woolworths requires suppliers to confirm that their operations ensure the safe and fair treatment of employees and minimal environmental damage. For other companies, social responsibility is a central part of their strategy. For example, the business of the small German brewer Neumarkter Lammsbräu is built around the production and marketing of ecological beer. This has required the company to work closely over a number of years with, for example, raw materials suppliers to ensure the suppliers' material production complied with its own ecological policies.

Purchasing orientation

A company's approach to acquiring resources and capabilities from external supply markets, its purchasing orientation, is guided by the expected contribution of purchasing to that organization's performance. Purchasing orientations will differ between industries and between firms within the same sector. In fact, a single organization will vary its orientation depending on the product to be sourced. Anderson and Katz (1998) identify four different orientations, whilst Dobler and Burt (1996) propose three. The basic principles that underpin these two different taxonomies are essentially the same. For simplicity and clarity, the discussion that follows uses Dobler and Burt's (1996) classification of purchasing orientations; namely buying, procurement and supply management.

The *buying orientation* uses purchasing practices whose principal purpose is to achieve reductions in the monetary value spent by a company on bought-in goods and services. Decisions are driven by attempts to get the *best deal* for the buying organization and to *maximize power* over suppliers in order to do this. Suppliers are selected based on their ability to meet quality and availability requirements and to offer the *lowest purchase price* or to meet *target prices* set by the purchaser. The buying organization sets target prices for its suppliers by determining the price at which it can sell its own products to its target market. The company then works back from this, calculating what proportion should come from items that it obtains from suppliers and which ones go into its finished product. The supplier is then presented with a maximum price that it cannot exceed if it wants to win the customer's business.

Having and being able to use a powerful negotiating position to broker deals that serve mainly the interests of the customer company is an important factor in the buying orientation. The customer might centralize purchasing decisions, thereby consolidating volume requirements and enhancing its negotiating position. As well as consolidating company supply needs, a customer can enhance their negotiating power by using multiple sources of supply for the same product category and by playing suppliers off against each other. The buying decisions have a short-term focus with orders being awarded to suppliers that offer the best prices, quality and availability. As we will see in our subsequent discussions, companies that have web-based search and purchasing capabilities can make use of the internet in order to identify and transact with sources of lowest-cost supply across the globe.

For many companies, the cost of bought-in goods and services can account for up to 70 per cent of net sales. A saving of €10 in purchasing costs has the same effect on company profitability as an increase in sales revenue of €60. The recognition that purchased items and therefore the purchasing function can have such a dramatic effect on an organization's financial performance has led to many firms trying to 'buy better'. The emphasis shifts from getting the 'best deal', to optimizing the purchase resource, to increasing productivity. This is the *procurement orientation* and use of this approach changes the way that purchasing managers deal with suppliers and with other functions inside their own company.

In striving to increase productivity a firm will not select and review suppliers according to specification conformance and lowest priced offer, but will base the evaluation and decision on *total cost of ownership* (TCO). TCO looks at the true cost of obtaining a product from a given supplier and involves a company measuring costs that are most significant for that product in terms of its acquisition, possession, use and subsequent disposal. TCO varies depending on the category, value and volume of product purchases. Obvious targets for using a TCO approach are products that are used over an extended time period, such as capital equipment and purchases of raw materials, manufactured parts and MRO items that involve large financial sums and/or ongoing, repetitive buying activities (Ferrin and Plank, 2002). Being able to identify the main cost drivers of different product categories requires that purchasing managers work with and have access to information from other functions inside the company (that handle and use the different products) and from product suppliers.

For an example of how one company used TCO in a purchase decision, see Box 2.1.

Box 2.1 *Life cycle costing pays dividends for logistics business*

For a logistics firm, its fleet of trucks represents a major capital investment. One company used life cycle costing (another term for TCO) in its decision to switch to a new vehicle supplier. As well as the purchase price of vehicles, it estimated operating cost per mile, productivity and the resale value of different manufacturers' vehicles. It switched supplier when it estimated that it could save up to $7000 per lorry with an alternative vehicle. The new fleet of trucks is costing the company less to run. Fuel spend is down by 30 per cent and as its mechanics get used to the new vehicles, the company expects servicing costs to fall too (even the windscreens on the new truck are easier to replace). In addition to such measurable costs, the company has seen other improvements that it hadn't included in its calculation. Drivers have reported a better ride and a quieter cab. Since the firm uses teams to run its vehicles, being able to sleep while your driving buddy is at the wheel is important. The firm believes that the better cab has contributed to lower driver turnover, which is important when you rely on a core group of drivers to help to run your business.

Source: Adapted from Fleet Equipment, 2003.

Rather than providing suppliers with target prices as a condition for awarding contracts, companies adopting a procurement orientation are more likely to use *target costing*. The principle is the same as that already described, in that the company will work back from the price at which it can sell its own products to target customers. However, by setting a target cost instead of a target price the company gives a supplier considerable scope to determine how this might be realized. Instead of meeting prescribed quality, availability and price specifications, the supplier can look at the customer's acquisition, possession, use and disposal (TCO) of the product that it is being asked to supply and look at ways in which these might be rethought in order to meet the buyer's cost target.

Reducing total ownership costs requires willingness and a capacity to share information and to align more closely activities between supplier and buyer organizations. The purchase-and-supply process and the handling of goods can be improved by the use of extranets and JIT (just-in-time) delivery systems such that administrative and material flow costs are reduced. The investment and coordination needed to achieve such improvements mean that when dealing with suppliers and making purchase decisions the buyer has to take a longer-term perspective, and negotiations might be informed by efforts to satisfy the needs of both parties rather just those of the buying organization.

Some firms broaden the scope of their dealings beyond immediate suppliers and customers in the knowledge that their own performance is linked to the activities of other companies in the same value chain. A *supply management orientation* is driven by efforts to *maximize value* along that chain. This typically results in:

- companies assessing core competencies and key capabilities to determine what activities they will perform themselves;

- the outsourcing of activities to which companies do not add value;
- the purchase of 'product systems' that are central to the buying organization's own operations or finished product;
- larger organizations driving change along a supply chain; and
- the restructuring of supply markets such that a company will rely on a small number of direct suppliers and a larger network of second- and third-tier suppliers.

The purchasing function and how it handles a company's supply chain become key strategic contributors to the firm's performance. The firm might be involved with fewer direct suppliers but their contribution will be much more important in terms of product expertise, involvement in the company's development activities, and in the case of systems suppliers, coordination of activities with second- and third-tier suppliers. The purchasing task is obviously more complex with this approach and those with supply management responsibilities have to work closely with other managers across a variety of functions in their own company and in other firms in the supply chain. The importance of key suppliers means that manager behaviour in dealing with those suppliers is guided by the need to ensure the long-term viability of both parties.

Segmenting purchase categories

All organizations buy a range of products. These products vary in their importance to the company, so the purchasing orientation adopted is likely to vary too. To determine what approach to take in dealing with supply markets, a company might segment its purchases by product category. Figure 2.1 shows how purchases can be grouped according to complexity and business risk (Anderson and Katz, 1998). Complexity includes factors such as the technical complexity of the product, the extent of necessary supply chain coordination and whether TCO needs to be considered. Business risk is based on the potential of a purchase to affect the company's revenue-generating capability or corporate performance. The complexity and business risk of product categories will vary depending on the industry in which a company operates and the firm's own activities.

Marketing implications of a customer's purchasing orientation

Knowing the purchasing orientations of customers and the way in which supplier products might be categorized by them can help business market managers decide which customers to target and how to formulate solutions for the supply needs of those customers. If a customer adopts a supply management orientation and a supplier's product is classed as strategically important (high complexity and high risk), then the supplier has the scope to become a key contributor to the customer organization's strategy. Obviously this requires that the supplier has the technical, financial and human resources to operate with the customer in this way.

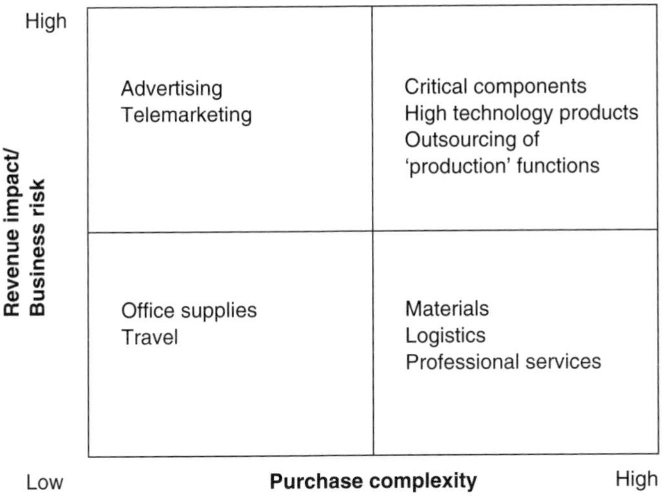

Figure 2.1 Segmenting purchasing decisions (Anderson and Katz, 1998: 7)

For less important products such as MRO items a customer might adopt a buying orientation. This means that a company supplying such items has little scope to do much other than concentrate on internal efficiency and deliver according to the buyer's price and contract specification. However, this does not stop some companies from trying and succeeding to shift their position and the way in which the buyer might deal with them. See Box 2.2 to learn how one company has successfully done this.

Box 2.2 *Not just a spare part*

Beverage can manufacturers produce several millions of cans each day and have to maximize plant availability 24/7. One MRO supplier worked with its beverage can customer to see how parts supply and equipment maintenance could be made more efficient. The supplier assisted the customer's improvement initiatives by providing product substitution on some items (including buy–back of obsolete stock) and identifying duplicate inventory (as part of the customer's product standardization and consolidation measures). For larger items, such as the motors used to run the beverage can production equipment, the supplier even took over responsibility for managing the customer's stock of motors. The MRO company's motor expertise and experience of dealing with motor suppliers meant that it was able to predict what the beverage company needed before it knew itself and it succeeded in reducing the customer's motor inventory cost by 70 per cent. The MRO supplier is considered a strategic partner by the customer, to the extent that senior executives from both companies communicate with each other on a regular basis.

Source: Adapted from Avery, 2003.

Purchase Process

Decision-making

When a customer buys a product, the purchase is not necessarily a single act or isolated event; rather it consists of a number of linked activities, namely the decision-making process. In business markets, buying consists of the following activities:

- *Need/problem recognition.* Purchases are triggered by two factors. One is the need to solve specific supply 'problems' such as the identification of under-capacity. This would trigger the purchase of extra 'production' capability in the form of operations equipment, temporary staff or the subcontracting of the production activity. Others might relate to ways in which the organization can improve its operational performance or pursue new market opportunities. If the company has to develop new products to realize those opportunities, then it will look to its supply markets for help in doing this.
- *Determining product specification.* Based on the satisfaction of supply need, the company then draws up a specification for the item. The specification could include any or all of the following:

  - what the product will be required to do (functional);
  - its physical properties (technical or material);
  - how the product should be produced (process); and
  - outputs that the customer expects from using the product (performance).

  Depending on what is being purchased the specification will obviously vary, as will the range of functional managers from across an organization that contribute to determining the specification parameters. For vendors, this stage in the buying process can be critical. If the company has contact with managers involved in agreeing the specification, then it has some scope to influence that specification and potentially lock out competing suppliers.
- *Supplier and product search.* Here the buyer will look for organizations that can meet its product need. This search centres on two basic issues, finding a product that will match the buying firm's specification and organizations that can satisfy the company's supply requirements. The amount of effort invested in this stage will depend on the cost and importance of the purchase as well as how familiar the buyer already is with the supply market.
- *Evaluation of proposals and selection of suppliers.* Evaluation of proposals will vary depending on the complexity and risk attached to the purchase decision. The importance attached to the various choice criteria amongst members of the decision-making unit will also vary. Evaluation will

Table 2.1 Supplier selection and evaluation

Criteria	Weighting	Supplier 1	Supplier 2	Supplier 3
Financial stability				
Total cost				
Technological capabilities				
Geographic locations				
Cultural compatibility				
After-sales technical support				
Flexibility				
TQM				
JIT purchasing				

Source: Adapted from Bevilacqua and Petroni, 2002: 247.

normally consider the compatibility of a supplier's proposal against the buying company's product specification and an assessment of the supplier organization itself. The importance attached to and the nature of the assessment of the supplier organization will be determined in part by the customer's purchasing orientation and therefore the expected contribution of suppliers to the buying company's own business. So evaluation can relate to the product specification as well as how a customer wants to engage with potential suppliers. See Table 2.1 for an illustration of what the format of product and supplier evaluation might look like.

- *Selection of order routine.* Once a supplier has been chosen then the purchasing manager will normally be responsible for negotiating and agreeing processes for order delivery and payment.
- *Performance feedback and evaluation.* This can be a formal process in which user departments regularly complete evaluation sheets designed by the purchasing team. The results will typically feature as an agenda item at meetings between the supplier and customer organizations. Alternatively, evaluation might be more informal, featuring as part of the daily exchanges between the companies.

Variations in the purchase process

The stages in the decision-making process might not be followed sequentially, some of the stages might be omitted altogether, and the time and effort invested in completing the various stages will vary. A key cause of variation in the process is the degree of risk associated with the purchase decision. Risk is an inherent feature of exchange in business markets, where managers have to deal with *uncertainty* and possible *negative consequences* surrounding purchase and supply decisions (Mitchell, 1995). For the business customer the decision-making process can vary depending on the buying organization's familiarity with and experience of the product to be purchased, such

Table 2.2 Organizational buying process – buygrid framework

Buying stages	New task	Buy classes Modified re-buy	Straight re-buy
Problem recognition	yes	possibly	no
Product specification	yes	yes	no
Product and supplier search	extensive	limited	no
Proposal evaluation and supplier selection	extensive	limited	no
Selection of order routine	yes	possibly	no
Performance feedback and evaluation	yes	yes	yes

Source: Adapted from Robinson et al., 1967.

that it is faced with three different buying situations; namely new task, modified re-buy and straight re-buy (Robinson et al., 1967). These different situations are derived from the 'newness' of the task that the buyer has to deal with, and will affect the extent to which current or alternative suppliers are considered in order to solve the purchasing problem, as well as the amount of information sought and used to guide the decision at hand. Table 2.2 illustrates the effect of the purchase situation on the decision-making process.

Table 2.2 illustrates what is known as the buygrid framework. This framework links different buying situations with the use of information and choice of suppliers. It is attractive to managers and researchers alike because of its simplicity and intuitive appeal. The buygrid does, however, consider only one factor likely to affect the buying process (task newness) whilst ignoring others, such as the importance of the purchasing to the organization, and market conditions, such as the range of suppliers from which the company can choose and the purchasing power held by the customer organization relative to its supply market (Bunn, 1993). By extending the range of factors likely to affect the decision process, further variations in it become apparent, such that the customer's *approach* to solving the supply problem can mean that:

- in a new-task buying situation, a judgemental or strategic buying approach might be used;
- a modified re-buy might consist of either a simple or complex buying approach; and
- for straight re-buys, the company might use casual or routine low priority purchasing approaches. (Bunn, 1993).

New task

In a new-task situation the organization is faced with a purchasing decision that is completely different from previous experiences. This means that the organizational customer needs large amounts of information so that those involved in making the purchase decision can consider alternative ways of solving the supply problem. The uniqueness of the task can also lead to the company considering a number of potential suppliers. Such new-task buying situations can be split into those in which a *judgemental buying approach* is used, whilst in others a *strategic buying approach* is more likely (Bunn, 1993).

The judgemental buying approach is typically associated with the highest degree of uncertainty. The product might not be of major strategic importance to the firm, but the buying company is in a position where it has difficulty in articulating a precise product or performance specification for its purchasing problem. This difficulty can be the result of the company's lack of prior experience in solving similar supply needs. It can also be because the sought-after solution is technologically complex, with the products available from various suppliers being difficult to evaluate. Such a situation will trigger a moderate degree of search effort both in terms of the breadth and depth of information sought from suppliers as well as the number of suppliers considered to solve the purchasing problem. The fact that the firm has difficulty in clarifying the necessary product/performance specification means that analytical tools normally used to evaluate supplier proposals are not likely to be used, and neither are the formal procedures normally followed for higher-risk purchasing decisions. Instead, the purchase decision will be based on the personal judgement of a small group of managers.

The strategic buying approach, as it suggests, is associated with buying decisions that are strategically important to the business customer. This could be because the purchase represents a key contribution to the customer company's operational activities or to their own products, and/or because the purchase involves significant financial outlay for the company. The potential effect of such purchase decisions on the company's performance means that they can feature as part of corporate planning activities and require a long-term perspective with regard to the management of the business's supply needs. It also means that considerable effort is invested in obtaining and evaluating information regarding suppliers and their proposed solutions, and in negotiating with those suppliers.

Guidelines for the business marketer in new-task buying situations
Suppliers that encounter customers dealing with new-task buying situations can try to build a strong position by becoming involved in the decision-making process at an early stage. This involvement can include obtaining information on the nature of the purchasing problem the customer is seeking to address, identifying specific product/supply requirements and formulating proposals to match those requirements.

Companies that already deal with the buying organization ('in-suppliers') have an advantage over other firms during their dealings with the customer, since they are likely to encounter the new purchasing problems that it is trying address. The key for the in-supplier is to monitor the changing needs of the customer and to be able to support the company in such new-purchase situations.

Modified re-buy

Situations involving repeat purchases in which the customer deviates in some way from previous purchase decisions to satisfy essentially the same supply need are classed as modified re-buys. Various factors can trigger this deviation, but the principal cause is normally the company's dissatisfaction with its existing supplier. Such repurchase situations can be either simple or complex.

A *simple modified re-buy* involves the purchase of a product and involvement with a supply market with which the customer is already familiar, so information search can be quite limited. Previous experience and product sourcing also means that the purchase lends itself to the use of standard buying procedures. The product may be of some strategic importance to the buying organization with only a limited set of choice alternatives open to the company. This results in the sourcing of the product featuring as part of the firm's long-term planning of supply needs and management of relationships with vendors.

A *complex modified re-buy* is characterized by purchase situations in which the customer is faced with little uncertainty and a large choice of possible suppliers, which in turn enhances the negotiating position of the buying organization. This type of purchase situation is the one most likely to exhibit all stages of the decision-making process. A key feature of this is the search for large amounts information, the use of sophisticated analysis techniques to evaluate proposals and the adherence to established purchase procedures. A significant proportion of complex modified re-buys involve the purchase of products that originate from previously negotiated contracts. The clarity of the product specification and the choice set of possible suppliers mean that the buying organization can readily evaluate costs and prices on a repeated basis. The clarity of the decision is arguably suited to competitive bids and therefore offers potential scope for the use of online auctions.

Guidelines for the business marketer in modified re-buy situations

A modified re-buy occurs because the customer sees potential benefits from re-scrutinizing alternative supply solutions. An in-supplier's principal objective is to move decision-makers from a modified to a straight re-buy, reducing or eliminating these perceived benefits. To do this the in-supplier should invest significant effort in understanding and satisfying the customer's purchase requirement and in the event of problems occurring, should act to resolve these immediately. Conversely, the out-supplier has to try and keep the customer in the modified re-buy situation as long as possible to enable the customer to evaluate alternative supply solutions. Having some idea of the factors that led the customer to re-scrutinize alternatives can be helpful, particularly if the out-supplier can offer performance guarantees in relation to these factors.

Straight re-buy

As the term suggests, this type of situation involves purchases in which the customer sources products in order to satisfy a recurring need. Purchases are normally of minor importance and are typically associated with products used to facilitate the customer's operational activities. The company's familiarity with the supply market and required product specification means that little effort is invested in searching for new information or alternative sources of supply. Prior buying experience means that the customer will have clearly developed purchase criteria and might also draw from a narrow range of suppliers to satisfy supply needs. In straight re-buy situations a customer might adopt two different approaches, namely *casual* and *routine low priority*.

A *casual re-buy* can be used for a range of low-value and low-importance items that are purchased incidentally. Little effort is invested in the decision process, with the emphasis being to process the order rather than search for and evaluate information, consider alternative suppliers and reach a purchase decision using formal purchasing procedures.

A *routine, low-priority* re-buy might involve the sourcing of products that are of some importance to the buying organization, and compared to the casual purchase it represents more of a repetitive buying decision. Customers perceive little distinction between the products available from various sources and for low-value items they are likely to continue using their same supplier. However, to ensure that technical improvements are not overlooked, a customer may periodically consider alternative supply sources. The automatic and habitual buying procedure adopted lends itself to e-procurement.

Guidelines for the business marketer in straight re-buy situations

In-suppliers have to ensure that there is no reason for the customer to switch to alternative suppliers. Regular contact might be necessary to ensure that the customer has no complaints or to identify and quickly resolve any problem areas. A company could also look at ways of reducing the customer's buying effort, such as automated reordering. For the out-supplier, this type of buying situation is particularly challenging. Without any causes of dissatisfaction, the customer will be reluctant to switch. Offering a lower price will not necessarily tempt the buyer. One approach that the supplier could adopt to move the purchase to a re-buy situation is to use TCO and the ways in which it could reduce this cost for the customer company.

Buying Teams

Few purchase decisions are made by individual managers. The decision-making process involves a range of managers that represent the buying team or 'decision-making unit' (DMU). Members of the buying team assume six different roles, as follows:

- *initiators*, requesting the purchase item and therefore triggering the decision-making process;
- *deciders*, making the actual purchase decision. These members might not have formal authority but have sufficient influence such that their decision carries considerable weight within the buying team. The fact that they do not have formal authority can make it difficult for the business marketer to identify such members of the team;
- *buyers* (purchasing managers) selecting suppliers and managing the buying process such that the necessary products are acquired. A buyer might not select the actual product to be purchased, but can greatly influence the parameters of that decision;
- *influencers*, contributing to the formulation of product and supply specifications, and recommending which vendors to consider or which products best satisfy the organization's needs. Influencers will also contribute to the evaluation of offerings from potential suppliers;
- *users*, frequently initiating the purchase as well as actually using the product. They may be involved in the specification process prior to purchase and once the product has been supplied will evaluate its performance; and
- *gatekeepers*, controlling the type and flow of information in to and out of the company and members of the buying team (Webster and Wind, 1972).

As Figure 2.2 illustrates, members of the DMU may be drawn from a wide variety of different departments in the firm.

To influence purchase decisions successfully the business marketer needs to know who the key members of the DMU are and what their specific concerns or requirements are in relation to the decision at hand. This enables the marketer to formulate solutions to satisfy these individual needs and minimize the perceived risk of DMU members. If the decision involves new purchases or modified re-buys, the marketer has to have contact with members of the DMU at an early stage of the decision process. By doing this the supplier might be able to influence key decisions (such as product specification) that could subsequently determine supplier selection decisions.

Depending on the product to be bought and the buying situation, the DMU will be more or less formal and will draw from the expertise and authority of various functions and levels of responsibility within an organization. Business marketers can use these two factors in order to determine which managers across a range of departments might assume the different roles in the DMU and the type of information likely to be used to guide decisions. Trying to determine influential DMU members can be challenging for the business marketer. As well as assuming that those in senior management

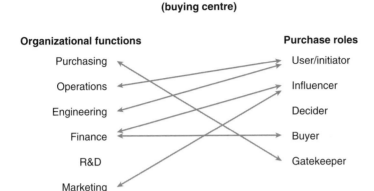

Figure 2.2   The decision-making unit

positions might exert considerable influence, the business market can try to identify employees who:

- work in boundary-spanning roles;
- have close involvement with the buying centre in terms of flow of activities;
- are heavily involved in communication across departments in the buying organization; and/or
- have direct links with senior management (Ronchetto et al., 1989).

Understanding of the DMU has to be linked to the dynamic nature of the decision-making process and not just the product category and buying situation. We already know that buying is a dynamic process and that, depending on what is being purchased, it can take some time before a product finally satisfies the needs of the buying organization. This affects what happens inside the DMU in terms of composition and behaviour, such that the involvement of managers and their degree of influence in the DMU is unlikely to be continuous throughout the decision-making process. The dynamic nature of the decision-making process and buying team means that the business marketer has to determine:

- what happens to the structure of the DMU during different phases of the buying process;
- the effect that the change in structure will have on the communication and influence patterns inside the unit; and
- the information needs of DMU members at any given point in time (Ghingold and Wilson, 1998).

The effect of risk on buying teams

Although few purchases might be made by a single individual in an organization, the extent to which procurement is a 'team effort' will vary. In some cases, organizational policy might dictate that purchases must be handled by committees. This is frequently what happens in the public sector when procurement of particular products or those above a certain monetary value must be reviewed and approved by committees before the purchase can go ahead. In many instances, however, the use of buying teams is determined by the degree of risk attached to the purchase decision. Risk is an inherent feature of business markets, where managers have to deal with *uncertainty* and possible *negative consequences* (Mitchell, 1995) surrounding purchase decisions. The risk that managers may perceive in relation to purchase decisions takes a variety of forms. It could be linked to *financial* or *performance* issues. For example, managers in the buying organization will experience heightened levels of risk if the purchase involves a significant monetary sum or the organization stands to incur costs should the item bought fail to perform as promised. *Social* risk can become an issue if the approval of significant reference groups such as co-workers or immediate superiors is important to the purchasing manager.

Normally perceived risk will be heightened in new task buying or more complex modified re-buy situations. As the level of risk increases:

- the buying centre composition changes, both in terms of the number of members and the authority of those members;
- the buying team actively searches for information and uses a wide range of sources, including personal contacts (possibly from other companies that have made similar purchases), to guide the decision process;
- members of the buying team invest effort in the process and consider each stage of it more deliberately; and/or
- suppliers with a proven track record tend to be preferred by the buying team.

Business Buying and the Individual Manager

Personal factors

It should be clear from much of the discussion in this chapter that buying activities are performed and decisions made by people, not the organizations that they represent. As human beings, we have different personalities and learned experiences and we are not necessarily wholly rational or objective in our decisions. The business marketer needs to understand what makes managers tick to try to influence the behaviour of key players in the buying company.

As we have just discussed, risk can influence business buying and this is indeed an important influence on the various managers that contribute in some way to buying decisions. Experience goes some way to reducing the level of perceived risk in purchase decisions and some managers, who are risk tolerant, are more able to deal with the uncertainty of some buying situations. Others, however, are inherently risk averse and will deal with this perceived uncertainty by sticking to known and trusted sources of supply or by amassing vast quantities of information and involving numerous other people in the purchase decision. As well as being affected by perceived risk and the ability to handle this, an employee's behaviour in purchase situations is influenced by the rewards that they accrue from buying decisions. All employees are rewarded for the roles that they perform in organizations. Some of these rewards are intrinsic, such as feelings of satisfaction and friendship, and others extrinsic, such as the bonuses and promotions given by organizations. Rewards are not of equal value to individuals and the importance that a manager attaches to various intrinsic and extrinsic rewards will shape that manager's behaviour with regards to buying activities.

We know that employees involved in buying activities can represent different functions and levels of responsibility in the customer company. They will have varying educational backgrounds, qualifications, employment histories and their contribution to the organization will differ. These factors will influence the criteria that a manager holds as important when evaluating products and suppliers, and the mental processes that a manager uses to handle information related to this. By mental processes we mean the type of information that a manager looks for, selects and then recalls when assessing products and suppliers.

The purchasing professional

Many organizations will have a department that is responsible for overseeing the sourcing of the company's supply needs. From what we have discussed in this chapter it should be clear that the scope of the purchasing manager's responsibilities will vary and that organizational factors contribute significantly to this variation. Generally speaking however, purchasing managers have to be familiar with a firm's specific needs and must be able to use negotiating techniques and pricing methods so that purchase costs can be minimized. They have to try to build good relationships with suppliers whilst ensuring that a firm gets the best value for its money.

Depending on the size of an organization, the purchasing department might have a senior buyer. Their job would be to oversee the work of individual buyers, direct all purchasing operations, negotiate large contracts and assume ultimate responsibility for the performance of the buying team. Where there are numerous buyers in a company they will typically specialize in dealing with certain product categories. By doing this the managers can get to know the supply market intimately. Whether the buyers are senior or junior managers, whether they work as part of purchasing team or have sole responsibility for acquiring their organization's supply needs, there are generic tasks that they have to perform and skills that they need to enable them to do this.

Buyer tasks:

- consulting with colleagues in other departments;
- determining the necessary parts, materials, services and supplies;
- calculating needed volume;
- searching for suppliers and requesting quotations;
- negotiating contracts; and
- monitoring the performance of the organization's various suppliers.

Buyer skills:

- keeping detailed and accurate records;
- collecting and analysing information;
- using maths;
- working under pressure;
- making decisions using experience and personal judgement;
- managing and supervising people;
- working well with suppliers and colleagues;
- negotiating and bargaining.

For a picture of what the work of a purchasing manager might look like, see the case study at the end of this chapter.

The Effect of Information Technology on Purchase Behaviour

Securing supplies incurs significant cost to the buying company, not only in relation to the price paid for those supplies but also the time spent by employees and management in handling the buying process (de Boer et al., 2002). This includes searching for and selecting potential suppliers, negotiating and agreeing contracts, and raising and processing orders, as well as handling and paying for items received. Electronic procurement uses Internet technology to support the purchasing process, enabling companies to greatly reduce this process cost. The cost reduction (and therefore reduced employee/management effort) can be achieved in a number of ways, with companies using Internet technology to improve communication with external markets and coordinate activities in the buying organization itself, as well as to link specific supply chains with the company's internal systems.

Communicating with external markets
In recent years, most industries have witnessed a dramatic growth in the number of transactions conducted via electronic marketplaces. Electronic

marketplaces are essentially online markets where companies are able to exchange information, do business and collaborate with each other. Buyers and sellers might want to simply find new exchange partners by conducting searches via a web portal, use the portal in order to be networked with other companies in similar geographic areas or related industries so that the order process between the buyer and seller becomes more efficient.

Electronic marketplaces can be grouped according to their main stakeholders and operators. Many are run by *independent* third parties and can be accessed by buyers and sellers in a particular industry or region. Others operate as *industry consortiums*, in which a limited number of companies either combine their supply capabilities in order to deal with a large customer base and make the sales process more efficient, or combine their product requirements in order to deal with known suppliers and so improve the efficiency of the purchasing process.

Purchase-oriented electronic markets represent a popular form of industry consortium in which large companies combine purchase processes and common product requirements, and build a business system to handle these. Electronic markets can be either horizontal or vertical. *Horizontal marketplaces* are used by buyers for items that do not contribute directly to the company's own products; rather they are used indirectly and would normally be classed as MRO items. So, for example, a company based in Europe might use www.cc-chemplorer.com whilst others based in Australia and New Zealand could visit www.corprocure.com.au to search for and source MRO items. Companies participate in *vertical marketplaces* in order to buy and sell items that contribute directly to a product chain. So a business that operates leisure attractions might visit www.amuse–exhibition.com in order to search for and purchase ride and slide equipment for use in a theme park. Companies that supply and buy components for use in the electronics industry could use www.converge.com, which has a network of over 6,500 trading partners, including companies such as Apple, Cisco, Intel, IBM, Packard Bell and Phillips. Such marketplaces typically offer a range of exchange facilities to participants, including auctions, reverse auctions, bulletin boards, exchange, catalogues, catalogues with online ordering and commodity exchanges. Two of the principal forms of transactions that can be facilitated by electronic marketplaces are auctions and catalogue purchasing.

Auctions

Any auction is based on the common principle that it represents a form of exchange in which competitive bidding drives a sale or purchase. An 'English' auction is normally used for the sale of unwanted items, whereby the seller offers an item for sale to a range of interested buyers, with the sale going to the buyer who makes the highest bid. A 'Dutch' auction on the other hand is the reverse; the buyer offers the opportunity to satisfy a product requirement to a range of interested suppliers, with the order going to the company that makes the lowest priced bid. Auctions have long been a feature of business markets and have normally been used for the sourcing of commodity items by business customers. Auctions conducted via electronic marketplaces operate under the same principles. However, the fact that the bidding process operates in real-time (even though buyers and sellers do not need to meet face-to-face), along with the fact that the auctions can be conducted on a global scale and can offer participants significant reductions in transaction costs, has led to a growth and broadening in the use of this market mechanism.

The range of specialized auction sites through which buyers and sellers can transact is extensive, with online auctions operating across a wide variety of industries and product categories. Companies operating in the chemicals industry could make use of www.chemexpo.com whilst others operating in the European food industry (as a processor, retailer or restaurant for example) could participate in fish auctions via www.pefa.com. The UK supermarket chain Tesco uses online auctions for direct and indirect purchases, but is selective in their use, specifically targeting high-value purchase items (Cushing, 2002).

If the switch in general to auctions via electronic marketplaces has attracted considerable attention, then reverse ('Dutch') auctions have become a key point of interest and a trading mechanism for business buyers. In reverse auctions a buying organization hosts the online auction and invites suppliers to bid on announced request for quotations (RFQ). In many ways the reverse auction is simply an electronic form of the competitive tendering process that has long been used to award contracts in numerous business buying situations. Before the bidding can start:

- the buyer must clearly articulate the product specification, quality requirements, delivery lead time, location and transportation needs, order quantity and service issues;
- some communication may take place between the buyer and interested suppliers in order to further clarify details of the RFQ; and
- potential suppliers have to go through a qualification process to ensure that they have the capability to meet the tender conditions should they be awarded the contract.

The buying organization might use an intermediary to manage the entire reverse auction process or it could use the facilities available in vertical marketplaces related to its own industry. For example, companies involved in the aerospace sector might handle reverse auctions via the service available on www.aeroexchange.com. Irrespective of whether a buying organization handles the process itself or delegates this to an intermediary, the fact that reverse auctions require high-value orders for the mechanism to work effectively (by offering suppliers the opportunity to win major contracts) means that purchasing professionals who are experts in the particular supply market and the auction process must control and be closely involved in this purchasing method. The high value of transactions typically conducted via reverse auctions means that they frequently form part of a company's strategic procurement activity. It is normally assumed that items purchased in this way are commodity or indirect products. For example, if a manufacturer wanted to buy 25,000 kg of cement at a good price, then it might try using an online reverse auction to do this. Many large multinational organizations have streamlined purchasing activities across disparate locations and have combined common supply needs across their businesses in order to get the best possible price and cost for items bought. The pharmaceuticals giant Glaxo SmithKline makes strategic use of such reverse auctions to purchase items ranging from hotel rooms to laboratory furniture. See Box 2.3 for more detail.

Box 2.3 *GSK cuts better deals for accommodation and furniture*

GlaxoSmithKline has a massive purchasing operation – 800 buyers worldwide and an annual spend of $12 billion. The company is driven by best-value purchasing strategies; that is, ensuring that GSK gets the best possible price and cost for everything that it buys. The company has used reverse auctions to help them realize cost savings on items ranging from hotel rooms to laboratory furniture.

Hotel rooms. GSK spends $80 million each year on 420,000 hotel room nights in 39 different countries using 1226 different hotels. Over a period of two and a half weeks GSK held 95 auctions and 113 electronic sealed bids with 3 people working on the project. The company believes that it has made savings of between 5 and 35 per cent as a result.

Lab furniture. Four suppliers participated in a bid to satisfy GSK supply needs and to hit a cost target of $500,000. Auction results produced 32 bids (equivalent to 8 sourcing cycles with 4 suppliers) and the price dropped to $250,000 in 48 minutes.

Source: Adapted from Hannon, 2004a.

Reverse auctions are being used by companies not only to purchase commodity and indirect products, but also to secure suppliers for items that contribute directly to their own products and to award contracts for equipment and major capital investment projects. Sun Microsystems spent some time identifying products that would make good targets for reverse actions. This mechanism now accounts for 25 per cent of its procurement budget, with the company purchasing both indirect/MRO items as well as direct products such as custom cables and printed circuit boards via reverse auctions (Hannon, 2004b). Another company, Bechtel Telecommunications, has used reverse auctions to source services and equipment that it needs in order to handle major capital investment projects such as the expansion and upgrading of a telecoms operator's network (McCall, 2002).

This form of trading offers opportunities and risks to both buyers and sellers (see Table 2.3 for a summary of these). For the moment, we will move

Table 2.3   Reasons for reverse auctions and the risks involved

Suppliers' reasons	Buyers' reasons
• new business • market penetration • cycle time reduction • inventory management	• reduced purchase price • lower administrative costs • inventory levels
Suppliers' risks	Buyers' risks
• low price focus threatens long-term relationships • competitive bargaining tool for buyer • offering unrealistic prices	• undermine relationship trust • reduced buyer commitment makes supplier less willing to make relationship investments • insufficient suppliers can cause non-competitive auction scenario

Source: Adapted from Smeltzer and Carr, 2003: 487.

on from online auctions to discuss other approaches to organizational buying. However, in Chapter 12 the theme of online auctions will be discussed further, from the point of view of business-to-business pricing decisions.

Catalogue purchasing

The catalogue idea is pretty straightforward, whether it is a printed or electronic version. It involves an organization that is effectively acting as an intermediary collating a wide range of items within a particular product category from a range of suppliers. The catalogue lists the items and provides detailed product specifications as well as current market prices. Buying organizations will normally use catalogue purchasing to handle a wide range of casual and routine re-buys of direct and indirect product/MRO items. Using a catalogue reduces search and information collection costs for the buying organization. Paper systems do consume considerable company time with users of the items having to initiate a product request and those with the buying authority completing order forms, faxing and/or calling the supplier. Many customer companies have reduced the time (and therefore cost) needed to handle such purchasing by switching to electronic catalogues, moving their own purchasing process online (which in turn enables the company to connect with the electronic catalogue) and devolving responsibility for initiating the catalogue purchase to users of those items.

For smaller companies, purchasing might be limited to browsing and purchasing items from a range of catalogues available via horizontal or industry-specific electronic marketplaces. In larger organizations, where firms have rethought business processes and sought to coordinate and integrate purchasing across the full spectrum of products, the investment in electronic procurements systems has allowed transactions for high-volume, low-priority re-buys to become part of automated stock replenishment systems, with more causal/routine repurchasing devolved to the user. For this latter type of buying, the purchasing manager retains control of the range of products available from any one catalogue and negotiates the terms and conditions of supply. However, once these have been determined, the routine purchasing activities associated with sourcing catalogue items is transferred to employees. The employee can log on to the company's online procurement system and, depending on their job title and expenditure limits, will be able to browse certain supplier catalogues, view and compare items and prices from those catalogues that have already been negotiated by the purchasing manager, trigger an order and track the fulfilment/receipt process.

Internal coordination of buying activities

The range of products bought, the different functional areas that have some purchasing authority and the geographical dispersion of many decision-makers presents many large organizations with a major challenge in trying to operate a more efficient purchasing process in which the business has a clear idea of product and volume requirements and the costs associated with satisfying those needs. In recent years there has been a growth in investments in electronic procurement systems to enable large organizations to coordinate and integrate purchasing across their full spectrum of products requirements. Texas Instruments (TI), for example, has to deal with large fluctuations in demand for its products. To cope with the consequent adjustments in production capacity, the company draws heavily on temporary workers. TI has centralized its sourcing of contract labour and now uses an electronic system to purchase labour, streamlining the process and developing an online repository for contractor data. The firm expects to save 5–8 per cent on its annual contract labour and consulting services as a result of the online system (Hannon, 2002).

Inter- and intra-firm coordination

For companies whose purchasing orientation centres around supply management, the ability to minimize waste and costs along its supply chain is critical. To do this, companies will align their administrative and operational activities and the flow of materials between the various parties in the supply chain. Information technology is essential to the firms' capacity to do this. CHEP is one company that tracks the movement of its products using electronic tagging. See Box 2.4 for more information.

Box 2.4 *Keeping a close eye on things*

CHEP provides pallet and plastic container pooling services to customers in the consumer goods, meat, home improvement, beverage, raw materials and automotive industries. One of the key challenges is knowing where their products are as they move between companies. CHEP's research investment has resulted in a Radio Frequency Identification (RFID) programme which allows retailers such as Wal-Mart, Tesco and Metro, and manufacturers such as P&G and Gillette, to keep an eye on their products. The pallets (which are used to move goods around in bulk before they reach a retail store shelf) are tagged so that as they, and the products that they carry, are distributed, companies can track the movement of goods from production facilities, through distribution centres to retail outlets. The system is designed to make the flow of goods more efficient.
Source: Based on a press release issued by CHEP at *www.chep.com*, accessed 01 February 2005.

Chapter Summary

- Organizational buying is affected by a number of factors. The successful vendor understands these and tailors its marketing activities accordingly.

- Key areas that have attracted much attention are the buying process and the decision-making unit (DMU) and how these vary depending on the purchase situation.

- The buygrid (new task, modified re-buy, straight re-buy) is a useful tool for classifying organizational buying decisions, although an important limitation of the buygrid is that it focuses only on the newness of the buying decision.

- The buying process and DMU, while clearly important, have to be placed in the broader context of the company's purchase orientation and overall business strategy. Being familiar with purchase orientation and business strategy allows the vendor to accurately meet the supply expectations of the buying organization.

- What should be clear from this chapter, and is further elaborated in the next, is that the supply expectations of the buying organization do not necessarily centre on product exchange. Rather, depending on the importance of the product and supplier to the company, the buying organization might also have certain relationship expectations of suppliers. This must also be taken into consideration by the vendor when formulating marketing strategies to influence the buying decisions of its customers.

Questions for discussion

1   How do the buying and procurement orientations differ? How will this affect the way in which an organizational customer might deal with suppliers?

2   How will total cost of ownership affect the way in which a business marketer prices its products?

3   Describe the decision-making process enacted by organizational customers, identifying how and why this process might vary.

4   Why would a customer want to use online catalogues and reverse auctions to buy products? Do these two forms of e-procurement pose threats to suppliers?

Case study: Getting wired can make a supply manager's life more manageable

In recent years the global household appliances industry has witnessed a rash of mergers and acquisitions as companies seek to extend the geographic scope of their activities, capitalize on growth opportunities in some countries and take advantage of low-cost production facilities in others. Whatever their target markets and wherever their operational activities, there are common issues that household appliance companies have to address to compete effectively. These issues include:

* regular product innovation and short development cycles to stimulate and capture consumer demand;
* strong global brands; and
* efficient production, purchasing and distribution operations that ensure a low cost base but also enable firms to respond to variations in consumer preferences.

In order to reduce their cost bases many household appliance firms have relocated production to countries with lower cost levels and they search international supply markets for materials and components suppliers that can meet their procurement requirements and are competitively priced. Cost reductions have also been achieved by firms using global product platforms within product categories such as cookers, refrigerators and washing machines. This allows a greater standardization of components, fewer product variants and simpler production. It also gives the appliance company a more powerful negotiating position for large-scale purchasing and reduces inventory levels.

Case study

Clearly, coordination between functions within an appliance company and with various members along its supply chain (from raw material producer to retailer) is important to ensure cost efficiency and also to meet end consumer requirements effectively. It also presents the producer with quite a headache given the disparate locations around the world where these various parties might be found. IT can go some way to relieving this headache. Enterprise Resource Planning (ERP) systems have helped household appliance companies to implement supply chain strategies that ensure trading partners are never out of stock of high-volume dishwashers, refrigerators and washing machines that appeal to a broad range of consumers. For low-volume items these systems can help a firm build-to-order; all inventory is removed and production is on a pure pull basis.

For those with purchasing responsibilities, web-enabled technology is critical to supply management and is likely to continue to be so in the future. Let us think ahead a few years from now: imagine that you are the supply manager for A-One Appliances and see how you might use this technology in a typical day's work …

You're at your desk by 7.45 a.m. and in between sipping your coffee and biting into a croissant, you switch on your computer. Almost immediately a listing of customer orders appears on your screen that A-One Appliances has received overnight. As you browse the report, you spot that Diane Cain from Birdsville in South Australia ordered a fire-engine red refrigerator – at 1.45 in the morning!

Having finished your breakfast and gone through last night's orders, you proceed to review supplier stock and work-in-process levels. You notice that your distributor's sheet steel stock level is flagged as critical because of the volume of last night's orders. You click on the button for that supplier and see that the steel mill (which supplies your sheet metal distributor) doesn't have enough work in process to satisfy your next-day requirements. The distributor has the problem in hand, having launched a buy-side spot auction to fulfil your next-day supply needs and having posted an electronic note to let you know of this action.

Another electronic flag notifies you that Diane Cain's fire-engine red order will incur substantial set-up costs at the metal paint shop unless delivery can be delayed by a week. You click on the screen for Diane's fridge model in the decision support menu, enter figures for the new cost and see straight away that your company will lose a couple of hundred dollars if you keep to the five-day delivery promise. You notify the marketing and customer service group who email Diane with a rebate offer if she agrees to wait 10 days for the fridge. An hour later you've placed a 7-day hold on the fire-engine red order. Diane took the $200 rebate.

Having dealt with Diane's order, your attention switches to an embryonic project on production outsourcing. Your company has some of the leading global brand names, investing heavily in new product development and in designs that attract strong interest from consumers. For some of firm's less strategically important brands, A-One Appliances is testing the outsourcing of production. You reach up from your desk and switch on the camera positioned on top of your computer ready for a virtual conference at 9.15 a.m. with A-One Appliances finance and design managers as well as representatives from some of your company's suppliers. The main purpose of the meeting is to introduce a project that will connect selected suppliers to produce a new range of washing machines. A-One Appliances won't actually build anything, rather it will design, market and service the machines. As the supply manager, you'll be the virtual 'plant manager', making use of Internet-based technologies to monitor manufacturing and sourcing activities through your chosen 'lead' supplier for the new product line.

Your virtual meeting ends at 11 a.m. and you spend the next hour or so gathering market intelligence via the Internet on major commodities used in A-One's product lines. This allows you to check to ensure that first tier suppliers are competitive and to monitor new technology developments outside of your existing supply base. Your data-mining agent identifies a newly published report on the Indian sheet steel industry. You download the information into your commodity management system, triggering an email to your tier-one suppliers to note the new data. Going through the report yourself, you notice details of a new Malaysian supplier of metal stampings and you send them an email requesting that they complete your online RFI (Request for Information) that you maintain on all stampers worldwide.

At 12.15 p.m. you take part in a 'virtual tour' of an electronic component plant in China. A rep for the potential low-cost supplier is going to walk the plant floor with a video camera, feeding voice and images back to your desktop and answering questions from you and the manufacturing engineer who will also be sitting in on the tour. If the two of you like what you see then you'll schedule an in-person visit.

You take a break from your computer screen, popping out to a nearby deli-bar for some lunch and a stroll in the park next door.

At 1.15 p.m. you sit on an interview panel tasked with choosing two recruits for the company's graduate scheme. By 3.30 p.m. you're back at your desk and as the company's online office and MRO catalogue contracts are due for renewal next month, you take a quick look at companywide office and MRO buying activity before leaving your office at 4.30 p.m. This time you're heading up a cross-functional meeting on centralizing and improving your company's approach to buying office equipment.

At 6.00 p.m. you pack up your computer and head for home, taking your notes in preparation for the video conference scheduled later tonight at 9.00 p.m. with another potential supplier – this one in is Taiwan.

Case study questions

1. Explain what is meant in the case study by the expression 'all inventory is removed and production is on a pure pull basis'. What are the implications for suppliers to the industry?

2. How realistic is the picture painted in the case study of the future of purchasing? Explore www.cips.org (The Chartered Institute of Purchasing and Supply) to help you answer this question.

Sources: Based on material from Electrolux, 2006; Maruca, 1994; Slone, 2004. Anonymous (2000) A day in the life of a WIRED supply manager. *Purchasing*, 128, 4: S 44–8.

References

Anderson, M.G. and Katz, P.B. (1998) 'Strategic sourcing', *The International Journal of Logistics Management*, 9 (1): 1–13.

Avery, S. (2003) 'Buyers get back to basics', *Purchasing*, 132 (4): 30–31.

Barnholt, E. (1997) 'Fostering business growth with breakthrough innovation', Research-Technology Management, March–April: 12–16.

Bevilacqua, M. and Petroni, A. (2002) 'From traditional purchasing to supplier management', *Internal Journal of Logistics: Research and Applications*, 5 (3): 235–55.

de Boer, L., Harink, J. and Heijboer, G. (2002) 'A conceptual model for assessing the impact of electronic procurement', *European Journal of Purchasing and Supply Chain Management*, 8: 25–53.

BT (2005) 'Renewed outsourcing contracts saves National Australia Group £13.5m over five years', online source: www.btglobalservices.com.

Bunn, M.D. (1993) 'Taxonomy of buying decision approaches', *Journal of Marketing*, 57 (January): 38–56.

Cushing, C. (2002) 'Online auction sharpens Tesco's purchasing moves', *Computer Weekly*, 10 October, p. 16.

Dobler, D.W. and Burt, D.N. (1996) *Purchasing and Supply Management* (6th edn). New York: McGraw-Hill.

Electrolux (2006) *Acceleration – Annual Report 2005*, online source: www.electrolux.com, accessed 11 May 2006.

Ferrin, B.G. and Plank, R.E. (2002) 'Total cost of ownership models: an exploratory study', *Journal of Supply Chain Management*, 38 (3): 18–29.

Fleet Equipment (2003) 'Low life cycle costs of Kenworth T600s pay dividends to Zimmerman truck lines', 29 (11): 32 (Anonymous).

Gadde, L.-E. and Håkansson, H. (2001) *Supply Network Strategies*. Chichester: Wiley.

Ghingold, M. and Wilson, D.T. (1998) 'Buying centre research and business marketing practice: meeting the challenge of dynamic marketing', *Journal of Business and Industrial Marketing*, 13 (2): 96–108.

Hannon, D. (2002) 'Electronics giant centralises contract labour buy online', *Purchasing*, 131 (3): 12.

Hannon, D. (2004a) 'GSK closes the loop using e-sourcing tools', *Purchasing*, 133 (10): 14–16.

Hannon, D. (2004b) 'Sun shines by combining two supplier strategies', *Purchasing*, 133 (8): 43–6.

Case study

McCall, M. (2002) 'Bechtel puts the "e" in procurement', *Wireless Week*, 8 (37): 25.

Maruca, R.F. (1994) 'The right way to go global: an interview with Whirlpool CEO David Whitwam', *Harvard Business Review*, 72 (2): 134–45.

Mitchell, V.W. (1995) 'Organizational risk perception and reduction: a literature review', *British Journal of Management*, 6: 115–33.

Purchasing (2000) 'A day in the life of a WIRED supply manager', *Purchasing*, 128 (4): S44–8 (Anonymous).

Robinson, P.J., Faris, C.W. and Wind, Y. (1967) *Industrial Buying and Marketing*. Boston: Allyn & Bacon.

Ronchetto, J.R., Hutt, M.D. and Reingen, P.H. (1989) 'Embedded patterns in organizational buying systems', *Journal of Marketing*, 53 (October): 51–62.

Slone, R.E. (2004) 'Leading a supply chain turnaround', *Harvard Business Review*, 82 (10): 114–21.

Smeltzer, L.R. and Carr, A.S. (2003) 'Electronic reverse auctions: promises, risks and conditions for success', *Industrial Marketing Management*, 32, 481–8.

Tetrapak (2004) 'Sealing in olive oil's goodness', online source: www.tetrapak.com.

Treacy, M. and Wiersema, F. (1993) 'Customer intimacy and other value disciplines', *Harvard Business Review*, January–February: 84–93.

Webster, F.E. and Wind, Y. (1972) 'A general model for understanding organizational buying behaviour', *Journal of Marketing*, 36 (2): 12–19.

Woodward, J. (1965) *Industrial Organization: Theory and Practice*. Oxford: Oxford University Press.

Note

1. The discussion in this section is based on material from Gadde and Håkansson 2001.

3 Inter-firm Relationships and Networks

Learning outcomes

After reading this chapter you will:

- appreciate that the traditional approach to business marketing based solely upon influencing organizational buying behaviour assumes that the marketer is active while the customer is relatively passive;
- recognize that value creation in business-to-business exchange comes from a clear understanding of the relationship between buyer and seller;
- know what is meant by relationship concept and what variables affect business-to-business relationships;
- appreciate the range of tasks involved in continually managing a relationship; and
- recognize the impact that the network concept has upon business-to-business marketing and the strategic imperative of network thinking.

Introduction

Arguably, the greatest change in the marketing discipline in the last 40 years has been the renewed emphasis upon the relationship between marketer and customer as the basis of understanding and sustaining value creation in exchange, an emphasis that the 'marketing mix' approach underemphasized. This realignment originated in the business-to-business context (see, for example, the challenges to the prevailing orthodoxy evident in the work of the IMP Group of researchers (Håkansson, 1982; Turnbull and Valla, 1986; Ford, 1990, 1997, 2001)). However, the refocusing has also extended to the consumer context, driven most notably by the emerging literature on consumer services (Gummesson, 1987) and has been hailed as a 'paradigm shift' (Grönroos, 1997) in marketing theory and practice. This chapter recognizes the central role that relationships play in business markets and discusses how marketing theory and practice has developed in the light of this recognition.

The chapter commences with a reappraisal of the earlier coverage of organizational buying behaviour, identifying the deficiencies of a marketing approach based solely upon an analysis of buying centres and attempts by the marketer to influence the buying behaviour of the customer. It then proceeds to re-examine the basis for business marketing, arguing that successful business-to-business marketing comes from an understanding of value-creating exchange. In exploring exchange, a selection of key theoretical perspectives is introduced, along with the key variables that they use, to indicate the contribution they make to our understanding of relationships. Business marketing means constantly appraising relationships in terms of these variables and making changes within relationships cognisant of the effects upon the variables and the relationship at large. These are enduring tasks for the business marketer.

Though the relationship between marketer and customer assumes the greatest import in the coverage, the chapter goes further than the level of the relationship. It extends the relationship concept to incorporate the network of relationships that surround any single relationship; the strategic understanding of a relationship comes from an understanding of the network within which it is embedded and that affects it directly or indirectly. While managerial action typically takes place at the level of a relationship, strategic thinking also takes place at the network level so that it can be enacted at the level of individual relationships.

Inadequacies of traditional approaches to business marketing

Traditional approaches to business-to-business marketing, often subsumed under the '4Ps' (standing for product, price, promotion and place) or 'Marketing Mix' labels, tend to make several assumptions:

- Essentially, the marketer and customer operate separately, wholly independently, and at odds with each other. Marketers market and customers purchase, and as a consequence each has essentially conflicting interests in exchange. Ideally, the marketer wants to obtain the best price possible for his or her goods, which are preferably standard offerings. Ideally, the purchaser wants to obtain the lowest price possible for goods/services that require no further customization. These opposing positions mean that each purchase decision and the associated transaction assume great importance in the dealings each has with the other.
- The marketer is active while the customer is relatively passive. The traditional approach tends to assume that the marketer is the active party in a business-to-business exchange, bringing offerings to the attention of customers. In this respect the customers are relatively passive recipients of the offerings created by the active marketer.

- The marketing process typically involves the study of the buying behaviour of business customers, as detailed in Chapter 2, as a precursor to attempts by the marketer to influence that behaviour in their own favour. The marketer establishes the customer need via traditional research activities. It is the marketer that creates an offering that meets this need and then attempts to influence the customer's decision-making to ensure the evoked set of offerings from which the customer chooses will have this offering at the head of the list.

The traditional marketing approach has been criticized more generally for being overly prescriptive, with the implementation of marketing in practice often lacking a clear conceptual basis because the concept itself has become more of an ideology than a well supported, clearly elucidated set of principles that benefit the firm (Brownlie and Saren, 1992). However, in the business-to-business context the traditional approach to marketing embodied in the 4Ps has been criticized more specifically for lacking relevance to the way in which business markets actually work (Arndt, 1979; Håkansson, 1982; Ford, 1990). While there is no doubt that success in any market comes from a strong understanding of customers and their needs, in business markets customers are often as active as suppliers, with the process involving substantial interaction between the two over time rather than a cool detachment.

Furthermore, there is often a clear understanding that the economic well-being of both parties depends substantially upon the relationship. The weighted average duration of relationships with suppliers where there is a technical development activity has been reported as 13 years (Håkansson, 1982) with 70 per cent continuing for more than 5 years, and 29 per cent for more than 15 years. Ford et al. (2002) report that of the top 17 suppliers to vehicle manufacturers, accounting for about 33 per cent of their purchase costs, only two have been supplying for less than 5 years, while 10 have been supplying for more than 15 years. As these figures would indicate, the parties often work together, customers are very active in the exchange and the process of determining and fulfilling the need is an interactive one.

To all intents and purposes, the neoclassical economics notion of markets involving discontinuous transactions between large numbers of buyers and sellers operating relatively anonymously with lots of choice, and on the basis of full information upon which to make such choices, does not hold. Instead, the situation comes closer to what Arndt (1979) has called 'domesticated markets', where control is established over the exchange by parties cooperating through negotiated ways of working so that choice is foregone, in the expectation that greater value will accrue to the parties through non-market exchange.

The relationships between retailer Marks and Spencer (M&S) and its suppliers in the UK provide just one clear example for questionning the assumptions that underlie the traditional approach – see Box 3.1.

Box 3.1 *Marks and Spencer supplier relationships*

As a retailer, M&S knows that its ability to add value for its customers comes primarily from the nature of the offerings it can secure from its suppliers, many of whom either produce only for M&S or produce offerings that are unique to M&S. On the food side, it has relationships with suppliers such as Bowyers, a division of Northern Foods, for the supply of prepared cold foods, where it accounts for a large proportion of Bowyers turnover. On the garment side, there are businesses in the UK that have grown over the last 30 years on the strength of their relationship with M&S. M&S was a major customer of companies such as William Baird for men and women's clothing, Courtaulds for a variety of clothing (leisurewear, swimwear, fitness clothing, knitwear, lingerie and underwear), bed linen and soft furnishings, and Coats Viyella for hosiery. It has even been the sole customer for some companies, including Desmond & Son for items such as men's and women's trousers, pyjamas and leisurewear.

M&S itself plays a substantial role in the exchange value created with its suppliers. As a customer, it is very active indeed. For instance, in its relationship with Bowyers, its food technologists work with Bowyers to come up with recipes specifically for M&S. It plays equally active roles in the relationships it has with its garment manufacturers. Its close relationship with suppliers such as Courtaulds and Coats Viyella over the years had led to innovations such as the non-iron shirt and machine-washable silk sweaters (Christopher and Peck, 2001). The strong relationship with Coats Viyella meant it could also use electronic data interchange (EDI) technology to pioneer the electronic return of daily garment sale numbers from M&S stores, enabling its supplier to dye semi-finished goods overnight to enable next-day replenishment (Oxborrow, 2000), thus ensuring that availability at M&S was second to none.

The strong role M&S has played in its relationships with suppliers and the dedicated production that they have made available over time spawned the soubriquet, 'the manufacturer without factories'. Of late, of course, with the increasing moves to off-shore sourcing, some of its major suppliers have seen their business with M&S contract or disappear completely. However, those suppliers that remain with M&S continue to work very closely with it, day in, day out.

Matching the Uncertainties and Abilities of Both Parties

Success in business markets comes from the recognition that the customer and marketer together create value in exchange by each providing solutions to each other's problems. Drawing in part on organizational buying behaviour literature, Håkansson et al. (1976) proposed that a business buyer faces particular kinds of uncertainties either concerning the basis of the need itself, or the nature of changes in the marketplace, or the transaction associated with meeting the need or each of these. Successful business marketing involves cultivating the ability to reduce these uncertainties.

Customers face uncertainties
Need uncertainty relates to the difficulties of knowing exactly what or how much to buy. For example, a customer just may not really know how much

material is required, perhaps because the level of demand from its own customers is highly uncertain. Alternatively, the customer may not be certain as to which materials technology will be most demanded by customers or integrate best with its own manufacturing processes. The lack of knowledge upon which to make a decision is fundamental here and thus need uncertainty is typically higher for new-buy tasks. It is also typically higher when the need itself is more important, so the need uncertainty of a critical component will be higher, as will equipment central to the production of the product.

Market uncertainty arises from the degree of choice a buyer perceives in the supply base and the difficulty in knowing which supply choices to make. The degree of difficulty is a function of how different the alternative suppliers are from each other and how dynamic those differences are. Increased knowledge is the route to reducing the difficulty but comes at a cost: increased time and effort in evaluating the different suppliers before purchase commitments are made. Worse perhaps, when a buyer has made a commitment in a relationship with a supplier it comes with an opportunity cost since there is always the prospect that a better relationship could be had with another supplier, which is precluded by the commitment to the current relationship.

Transaction uncertainty refers to the degree of exposure that the buyer is faced with once a transaction has been agreed. The integrity of a product may be affected in transit, damaging it irreparably or leading to additional delays in fixing the damage, or delivery may be late. For example in high street fashions, where the sales window for a season may only be four to six weeks, a delivery delay of two or three days is significant; the retailer literally cannot sell what is not in the store. Delay problems are particularly significant when coordinated production schedules are involved, such as with JIT systems, so transaction uncertainty would be naturally higher here. The extent of transaction uncertainty is also related to how well the buyer and seller know and communicate with each other. If they and their systems communicate well then the degree of uncertainty is reduced. However, different language, culture and technological infrastructure raise the uncertainty. Standardization of the transaction process should reduce the scope for transaction uncertainty.

Supplier abilities can reduce customer uncertainties

The *problem-solving abilities* of a supplier in meeting the customer need and/or their ability to transfer the solution create the basis for a successful match as far as the customer is concerned. If a supplier can demonstrate a superior knowledge of the need then it is in the best position it can be. However, this requires a clear customer orientation and a strong recognition that reduced need uncertainty comes from a strong focus on solving the customer's problems, rather than merely a focus on what the supplier's products can do. Further, if a supplier can demonstrate convincingly that it can reduce the customer's market uncertainty then again it is in the best position it can be. This might actually involve recognizing the difficult choice that the supplier faces and attempting to reduce the extent of the customer's exposure. This could be achieved, for example, by limiting contract lengths, or by the use of pilot projects or trials. Not only do arrangements like this limit how exposed the buyer is in the first place, they give the supplier the opportunity to demonstrate its *transfer ability*, reducing transaction uncertainty at the same time.

Customer abilities can reduce supplier uncertainties

As we have indicated, the primary task for the business marketer is to ascertain the nature and extent of the customer's uncertainties and their own abilities to provide solutions to those uncertainties. While this is already a wider activity than understanding and influencing organizational buying behaviour, there is another dimension to this task that is truly relationship-based. The happy situation for the customer of having their uncertainties reduced does not necessarily reduce uncertainties for the supplier. Ford et al. (1998) indicate that the specific uncertainties faced by suppliers revolve around the capacity that they must plan for (*capacity uncertainty*) and the sorts of application that the market will demand (*application uncertainty*). In addition, suppliers are subject to *transaction uncertainty* in the same way as buyers. As with the customer, the supplier may be subject to none or more uncertainties, to differing degrees, through time. The relative needs and uncertainties of buyers and sellers are presented in Figure 3.1.

What a customer can bring to resolve the uncertainties faced by the supplier are its demand abilities or transfer skills. Historically in the UK, M&S

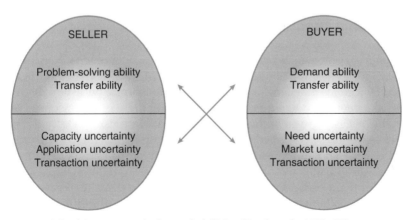

Figure 3.1 Matching uncertainties and abilities (Ford et al., 1998: 18)

has demonstrated strong ability to understand the clothing preferences of British women – an important *demand ability* and a substantial strength in its relationships with its suppliers. The capacity and application uncertainties of their suppliers diminished with the strong year-on-year stability of M&S demand ability. However, many of the problems M&S has faced within the last five years on the High Street stem from its reduced demand ability. In the competitive womenswear market it has struggled to demonstrate that it has this ability at a time when other stores, most notably Next Plc and international brands such as The Gap, are showing stronger ability in this respect and with equivalent transfer abilities.

The basic tasks then for the business marketer (in conjunction with the business purchaser) are to establish the respective uncertainties and abilities as a prelude to determining the likelihood of the success of their respective value-creating activities. This undoubtedly incorporates an understanding of the organizational buying behaviour of the customer, but extends beyond that.

The need to match uncertainties and abilities in order to achieve business marketing success provides a clear indication that relationships matter (Ford et al., 1998). The relationship constitutes the context within which value-creating activities take place and thus the next level of management activities for both parties involves the relationship. Consequently, anyone interested in business marketing needs to have a clear understanding of relationships – in order to understand individual customer relationships and what drives them, as well as to understand clearly how to manage such relationships successfully. Knowing what relationships to focus upon, what is possible in such relationships, the resource requirements for initiating changes in any relationship and the implications of such changes upon the relationship, the wider portfolio of customer relationships and beyond are just the sort of concerns that a business marketer must have. It is to the bases of relationships that our attention is now turned.

Relationship Theories and Variables

Relationships between organizations are complex phenomena. Regardless of the size of the organizations, and the number of people involved, there is a range of variables that can characterize a relationship. A wide variety of variables have been used to study relationships and there is no consensus on the set that is necessary and sufficient to explain a relationship. Despite the lack of consensus, however, relationship-based theories provide us with a set of perspectives that can be drawn upon when trying to understand any relationship, each of which tends to emphasize different relationship aspects.

Some of these perspectives more readily explain discrete exchange transactions while others extend the focus across a series of individual transactions to the relationship more broadly. Some emphasize the political and economic dimensions of relationships, while others focus more upon the social. In one case, a perspective incorporates both a transactional layer and a relationship layer and provides the means by which political, economic and social dimensions can all be located through the interactions that take place in relationships. Table 3.1 lists the various perspectives. As we will see, all have a contribution to make to our understanding of relationships over- all. That does not mean that every one provides prescriptive advice for all situations that a firm faces. Rather, depending upon the particular issues in a relationship at particular times, it is possible to draw lessons from whichever perspective has most to offer on that subject.

Exchange risk and its management

All forms of commercial activity involve risk. It is a fact of life. Previously in this chapter we talked about the uncertainties faced by firms. These are sources of risk, and organizations spend much time trying to eradicate uncertainty or reduce their exposure to it. Perception of risk is a function of the possible negative outcomes and the probability of those outcomes aris- ing. There are many sources of risk. For a buying company they might include: late delivery, poor quality, inadequate level of service, unsatisfac- tory product performance, price increases since order placement or adverse reaction from one's own management.

In the exchange between two organizations, uncertainties for one party arise from having to rely upon the other to undertake its part in the exchange in a way that delivers the value the first party considers is fair in the exchange. To use a simple example: when a supplier acts to make available the goods that have been negotiated with a customer, it is subject to risk until the goods have been paid for and the money safely transferred. Should a customer default before then, despite the recourse to law, the supplier's business is affected negatively. Similarly, a customer that has negotiated to receive goods of a particular quality, at a particular time, in a particular quantity and at a negotiated price is at risk of any one of these failing to be as expected.

Of course, the parties in relationship exchange may not necessarily react in the same way to the same level of uncertainty because they may have differ- ing attitudes to risk. Indeed, a basic assumption of Principal-Agent Theory is that there is such a difference and that the parties have different goals in the exchange. This assumption stems from the concern with establishing the contractual basis in agency transactions. The perennial difficulty for a com- pany (principal) that is forced to retain an agent to work on its behalf (for instance, in a foreign market) is that there are unknowns and unknowables. These hidden elements are *hidden characteristics* of the agent, such as their actual abilities; *hidden actions,* such as the way in which they undertake the tasks on the principal's behalf and *hidden intentions,* such as whether they really have the principal's interests at heart. These constitute risks that have

Table 3.1 Key relationship variables

Principal variable(s)	Level of emphasis	Major theoretical source	Theory type	Typical reference sources
Risk and its management	Individual transactions Agent	Principal Agent	Political–economic	Arrow, 1985; Bergen et al., 1992
Distribution of transaction costs	Individual transactions	Transaction cost economics	Economic	Williamson, 1979
Dependence; power and its exercise; switching costs	Transactions or Relationship	Resource dependence	Political	Pfeffer and Salancik, 1978
Social embeddedness; trust and commitment	Relationship	Social exchange	Social	Granovetter, 1985
Interaction processes	Individual exchanges and Relationship	Interaction	Social/interactional	IMP Group (Håkansson, 1982; Ford, 1990, 1997, 2001)

to be managed. Principal-Agent Theory argues that the *contract* is the basis for the management of the exchange risk because it is through the contract that risk is distributed between the parties. In this respect, it has much to offer the business marketer.

The extent to which the contract is more or less formally stated will depend upon the parties' attitude to risk within the relationship and their propensity to cooperate. A weakly stated contract and a laissez-faire approach to its operation and enforcement may be as much as is required in some relationships. This approach may be more useful in such relationships where perhaps both parties have a similar attitude to risk, where there is substantial uncertainty and where both parties know that they need to work flexibly, sharing information fully, in order to achieve objectives. The relationship itself brings obligations to the parties (Sako, 1992) without the need for a strongly worded contract. Achieving the objectives in this context is not helped by an overly fastidious attention to the details of the contract and the parties may have sufficient trust that the counterpart will not behave in a way that is obviously self-seeking.

In some relationships it may even be the case that the contract is little more than a gentlemen's agreement. In other relationships, however, where there is uncertainty and inadequate information, or power asymmetry, or dissimilar attitudes to risk, then more formally stated contracts that are followed to the letter may be the order of the day. The recent case of the relationship between M&S and William Baird paints a salutary lesson in relationship contracts. William Baird took M&S to court claiming damages over the latter's decision to stop buying from it after 30 years, in contravention of what it saw as an implied contract. The High Court in the UK ruled that M&S was not liable for damages because the fact that M&S had singularly refrained from introducing a formal contract with William Baird with the express purpose of agreeing future dealing indicated that it had no such intention. This (lack of) action itself indicated that there was no agreement between the two as to the relationship. Thus M&S had broken no contract since what had gone before signified no agreement.

Where greater formality is sought in a relationship then several questions need to be borne in mind when it comes to drafting a contract:

- Can performance as stipulated in the contract be stated more or less behaviourally, as a set of specific activities and the way they must be undertaken, or does performance equate to specific outcomes of the activities? Here the distinction is between the 'what', that is the purpose of the contract, or the 'how', that is the way in which the 'what' should be produced. In some exchange situations it is clear what the outcome should be. A physical product such as a component part has clear properties that enable contractual integrity to be established if the component performs to the properties promised in the exchange. In exchanges where the offering is much less tangible, such as in specialist advice or design services, and the outcome itself is not wholly prescribed there may need to be much greater reliance on behaviour-based contract forms to ensure that contractual integrity is achieved.

- Who controls the contract and thus has greater potential to influence the terms? Essentially, the party with the greater relative power is in the strongest position to specify terms and enforce them. Alongside this question is the related issue of the incentives for the weaker parties to engage in the contract. If the contract is the means by which risk is distributed then attempts to pass greater risk to the weaker party may find that party unwilling to enter an exchange where it feels disadvantaged. Where it does enter the exchange the weaker party is unlikely ever to step outside the confines of the contract; it is more likely to work to the letter of the contract. So, for example, a small architect's practice working for IKEA in the UK found that it often had to engage in extra design activity as a result of changes initiated by the client. While having a client such as IKEA was a major boon to the practice, and in the early years this accounted for upwards of 30 per cent of turnover in several successive years, the contract rates were such that all the extra design activities were damaging the profitability of the contract. The practice had no alternative but to invoke a Change Request process under the terms of the contract, where all requests had to be approved by the client's Project Manager and were billed at cost. It had to stick to the letter of the contract in order to ensure it was not adversely affected.
- Even when the basis for the contract is established and the control and engagement issues are dealt with, there are the operational elements to be considered. The nature of the standard operating procedures within the contract may also need to be established. In more formal contracts there needs to be clarity about what is expected from each party, what the specific outcomes are, the relative roles in the contract, and what constitutes acceptable behaviour by the parties. If necessary, there will need to be specific coverage of the procedures for dispute resolution when and if it arises.

Principal-Agent Theory tends to place the focus upon the contract and the demands of the current transaction. The issues mentioned above tend to be more salient, with greater uncertainty and inadequate information. The theory has less to tell us when market forces have a greater role in affecting relationships. When there is great market choice then typically there is less uncertainty and sufficient information so that price-based mechanisms deal with the risk.

Allocating exchange costs

All transactions incur costs. Bruhn (2003) points to costs arising from initiating, handling, controlling, modifying and terminating contracts, as well as opportunity costs. Initiation costs incorporate searching, information access and evaluation as well as the efforts in actually reaching a decision, such as negotiation activities. Control costs include monitoring activities to ensure the counterpart is keeping its part of the bargain and extend to the actions required to enforce the bargain in order to remedy any perceived inequity. The levels of these transaction costs are directly linked to the nature of market conditions. In perfect economic market conditions, where everyone has equal access to all information needed for a transaction and where the costs for managing the transaction are the same for all, the mechanism for ensuring the most economically efficient transaction is the open market itself. Here price-based competition will ensure efficient transactions. Of course, when markets are not perfect there is unequal access to information and the costs of managing a transaction are not the same for all possible exchange partners. According to transaction cost theory, the task for companies is to find an exchange partner and a way of working with that partner that creates the most economically efficient transaction possible. That is, the imperative is to establish the sources and nature of transaction costs and to minimize them.

The following three factors affect transaction costs:

- *Uncertainty* concerns the completeness of information. The level of uncertainty can be affected by many factors and extends from general market structure knowledge right down to the specific details of the transaction and what it involves. Where there are unknowns the level of uncertainty is inevitably greater.
- *Asset specificity* is the relative amount of assets or resources that need to be committed *specifically* to the transaction. There is a range of asset types, including: site assets, brought about by co-location or geographical consolidation; physical assets, such as special tools or equipment required in the transaction; human assets, where unique skills arise as a consequence of the transaction; and other dedicated assets, where particular investments are made at the behest of a particular exchange partner. For example, a manufacturer may need to invest in tooling for the production of designs for a specific customer. Equally, a customer may have to change its own production processes in order to use the inputs from a specific supplier most efficiently. Both of these constitute transaction specific investments.
- The *frequency* of the transaction has implications for costs because the more often it happens then the greater the transaction costs.

As the level of these three factors rises, so transaction costs rise (Williamson, 1979). The issue becomes what structure should be adopted by the firm to manage the transaction costs. As transaction costs rise the simple market solution becomes less efficient and relationships – so-called 'bilateral forms of governance', incorporating cooperation between the exchange parties over the long term – become appropriate. Long-term cooperation should reduce uncertainty levels. Although levels of asset specificity may rise, this will be considered less risky when doing business with a trusted partner.

It is useful to think about transaction costs in the management of business relationships. They help to explain the diversity of relationships that exist, since the combination of different levels of the three factors above leads to a multitude of unique relationships. Transaction cost analysis helps us to understand how relationships change and develop in response to changing levels of uncertainty, asset specificity and transaction frequency. Firms need to give explicit attention to the level of asset specificity in business relationships.

Dealing with relative power dependence

Dependence is inevitable as a consequence of exchange. Requiring access to the resources held by others creates dependence. Of course, there is dependence on both sides of an exchange: buyers are dependent upon suppliers for the goods they provide, whilst the suppliers are dependent upon the economic value that comes from supplying customers. The issue is the relative extent of dependence since more often than not levels of dependence are asymmetrical. A customer may be relatively more dependent upon a supplier of a critical or scarce resource because the customer's value-adding activities require that *specific* resource or because there are few other suppliers. This puts the supplier in a position of strength with respect to the customer. Of course, it can happen the other way round. IKEA has a relative power advantage over its UK architectural service suppliers, for example.

From the point of view of either party to an exchange there are several major tasks that must be undertaken:

- Establish the relative levels of dependence and thus the degree of autonomy of the firm.
- Understand the behavioural consequences of that interdependence, including the potential for the exercise of power. For the stronger party this typically concerns the extent to which it needs to exert its power over the weaker party. If the weaker party is compliant then the stronger party may feel no need to exert explicit dominance. For the weaker party the major concern will be the extent to which the stronger party will seek to dominate the exchange and enforce its will.
- Consider the consequences of actions that may change the levels of relative dependence. This typically revolves around switching costs – the costs incurred by leaving the relationship and establishing are relationship with a new partner.

The social dimensions of relationships

The emphasis thus far in our consideration of relationship variables has been economic. The central role of business relationships is to manage economic exchange. The general assumption is that the parties to an exchange are essentially self-seeking, seeing exchange as a necessity but seeking to control it. While one cannot ignore the self-seeking view, it must also be said that companies do not always behave completely selfishly. They know that the world does not merely operate at the economic level. Relationships also have a social dimension. They are, after all, social constructions and the parties to exchange exist embedded within a wider social structure (Granovetter, 1985).

This is not to dismiss the economic dimension, nor is it to underplay the inherently selfish motivations that may surround exchange management. However, exchange parties may recognize that their self-interest is best served by cooperation in exchange. That is, it is best achieved when they behave equitably and in the mutual interests of both. The economic value created within the relationship can only be maximized when the two parties cooperate with each other. The social exchange view throws relief upon processes that create equitable conditions. Foremost amongst these are the concepts of trust and commitment:

- *Trust* is seen to be central to a relationship (Young and Wilkinson, 1989; Moorman et al., 1993; Morgan and Hunt, 1994), encapsulating the confidence a party has with the reliability and integrity of a counterpart, and building expectations. The reliability and integrity comes from displays, in words as well as deeds (Ganesan, 1994), of consistency, competence, honesty, fairness, helpfulness, responsibility and benevolence (Morgan and Hunt, 1994). High levels of trust in a relationship enable the parties to focus on the long-term benefits of the exchange (Ganesan, 1994).
- *Commitment* goes hand-in-hand with trust since it is by a company's behaviours as manifestations of its commitment that trust can be established and maintained. It is essentially a state of organizational mind or intention, where the relationship has significance for a party and where it wishes it to endure. Morgan and Hunt (1994: 23) characterize commitment as '… an exchange partner believing that an ongoing relationship with another is so important as to warrant maximum efforts at maintaining it'. 'Maximum efforts at maintaining it' involve clear manifestations of the commitment. This could include financial commitments to show willing, or may involve doing something special for a counterpart that is not available to other counterparts such as product or service customization. In all cases the larger the scale of commitment, the stronger the signal that is communicated.

Social exchange theory makes a clear contribution to our understanding of exchange relationships by showing that factors other than the pure economic may apply and by indicating the role that factors such as trust and commitment play in moderating the impact that power dependency plays in relationships.

Business marketing: an interaction perspective

While the previous perspectives provide an understanding of elements of inter-organizational exchange relationship behaviour, they do not focus attention upon the dynamic processes of interaction over time that are the stuff of relationships between business-to-business companies. Relationships unfold through a whole series of actions and reactions of the parties involved. Managing relationships at the behavioural level necessitates an understanding of the processes of interaction so that the consequences of relationship action can be recognized. The Industrial Marketing and Purchasing Group (IMP) Interaction approach (Håkansson, 1982) provides a comprehensive conceptual framework within which to locate a whole host of relationship actions.

- It considers the exchange to embody more than the basic exchange of a market offering for money, extending, as it does, the nature of exchange to cover all forms of interaction between the relationship parties (financial, product, informational and social).
- It adopts a view of exchange that is inherently dyadic, where both parties to the exchange have the potential to act. As Ford et al. (1998) put it, the process of handling company interdependence 'is not simply about cooperation. It involves the manager working *with* other companies, but it also involves working *against* them, *through* them and often *in spite* of them' (p. 1, italics in original).
- It embodies the politico-economic perspective in respect of the structure of power in an exchange relationship while at the same time focusing upon the processes by which the interaction takes place.

The basic tenet of the interaction approach is that enhanced understanding of business-to-business markets is derived from the recognition that the exchange process between companies is not typically characterized by an active seller and a passive buyer. While this state of affairs frequently exists in mass consumer markets, in business markets the buyer may be as active as, or more active than, the seller. Consequently, the exchange '*process is not one of action and reaction; it is one of interaction*' (Ford, 1997: xi, italics in original). Rather than a large number of individually insignificant customers who are all relatively homogeneous in their needs, customers in business markets come in all sizes with widely differing product/service requirements 'and marketers seem to talk about them individually so that each seems to be more or less important to the seller' (Ford, 1997: xi). The relative importance leads to distinctive differences in the ways that a business marketer deals with each customer and therefore relationships can differ substantially.

Some relationships may be complex and long term and bring mutual benefits to the parties, while others may be short term and manifestly dominated by one party. Some may be characterized by trust and cooperation, while others are riddled with conflict and deception. Some may be close while others are more distant. Over time, a single relationship may be characterized in all these ways, sometimes at the same time. The Interaction Model, proposed by the IMP Group of researchers (Håkansson, 1982; Ford, 1990, 1997, 2001) and based upon their empirical studies (see Figure 3.2), captures the diversity and complexity of the relationships witnessed in business markets. It depicts a relationship in terms of the short-term and long-term interaction process between two organizations and the individuals who represent them. It does this within a wider environmental context and the atmosphere within which the interaction takes place; an atmosphere that affects the interaction on the one hand and is affected by it on the other hand.

The interaction process

The parties in a business-to-business exchange interact with each other. In understanding this interaction over time a distinction can be made between what happens in any individual interaction and what happens at the level of the relationship itself, as an aggregation of and gestalt of these individual interactions (what the IMP Group have termed interaction 'episodes'). The prevailing aspects of the relationship affect, and are affected by, the individual episodes.

The interaction may be of several types:

- *Product/service.* This is often the reason for exchange in the first place; the relationship builds around this central element. The nature of the product/ service offering inevitably affects the interaction between two companies. For those situations where there is a relatively simple customer need for a standard offering, the degree of interaction is likely to be low and type of interaction is likely to be narrow. On the other hand, where there is substantial uncertainty as to the nature of the requirement or the ability of a supplier to provide it, the degree of interaction is likely to be higher and the nature of interaction broader (Håkansson et al., 1976).
- *Financial.* The amount of money involved in the exchange is also likely to affect the interaction. Financial exchange indicates the relative importance of the relationship and thus the imperative for more or less interaction. The interaction may concern anticipated or actual financial exchange.
- *Informational.* It is not always product or money that is exchanged. There is often a large amount of informational contact. For example, technical details may be discussed by research, production or engineering staff from both companies in respect of new product or process initiatives (Cunningham and Homse, 1986). Commercial material such as terms and conditions may be discussed as part of ongoing negotiations between relationship parties. Equally, one party may impart information about planned changes within its organization or its vision for the future of the industry. All of these have no specific reference to money or product/ service but are nonetheless important elements of the interaction process. The content of the information and its width and depth, the number of

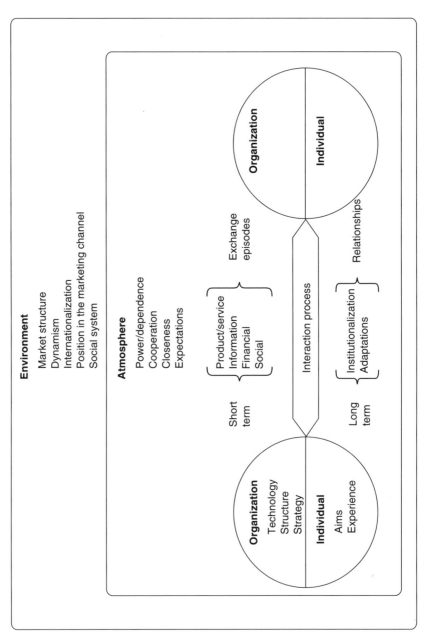

Figure 3.2 The IMP Group interaction model of business-to-business marketing (reproduced from Håkansson, 1982: 24).

people involved in the information exchange, the formality of the process and the use of personal or impersonal communication channels all give an indication of the nature of the relationship between the parties.

- *Social exchange.* This plays an important part in maintaining a relationship between economic transactions and seems particularly important in reducing the uncertainties between parties that come from cultural or geographical distance (Håkansson and Ostberg, 1975). Over time social contact between relationship participants creates 'bonds' between the actors that cements the relationship, building the sort of trust that comes from personal experience of interaction (Håkansson and Snehota, 1995a).

Relationships

Interaction episodes over time create a relationship with a history. Each new episode adds to this history such that a relationship assumes an essence that is more than an individual episode. As a result of the elements of interaction above, relationship partners come to know each other better and develop clear expectations of the relative roles and responsibilities of each other. This constitutes a degree of *institutionalization;* they don't really have to think about every step they take with each other. An analysis of the *contact patterns* between the partners that come from the exchange elements above provides an indication of the nature of the relationship: close, distant, cooperative, conflict-ridden, predictable or wildly fluctuating. Furthermore, as a relationship unfolds one or other party may make *adaptations* in the exchange elements or the process of exchange (Hallén et al., 1991), adaptations that constitute irretrievable investments unique to that relationship.

The participants in the interaction process

Obviously, a relationship requires parties to the relationship; without the parties there is no relationship. The parties are the two organizations and the individuals (at least two people) from those organizations. It is the organizations, or more precisely, the individuals, who interact. Consequently, the process of interaction between two firms and the relationship that ensues will depend upon the characteristics of the firms and the individuals themselves. The IMP interaction model posits that the organizational factors include physical characteristics of the firms in terms of *size, structure,* and *technological resource base.* They also include less tangible factors such as *organizational strategy* and the *experience of the firms.* The model also posits that the *personalities, experience and motivations of the individuals* working for the firms will also very directly affect the interaction between two firms.

Size has a strong bearing upon relative power in a relationship (El-Ansary and Stern, 1972; Stern and Reve, 1980) and, consequently, establishes the pecking order in interaction. The dominant party on the basis of size has greater capacity to call the shots.

The forms of *structure* adopted by the parties and the degree of centralization of authority, formalization and standardization of rules, or levels of specialization of jobs, all affect interaction. They do this to the extent that they allow for more or less interaction of different types between people from different levels and departments within the firms. Where structures are heavily centralized, roles strongly ascribed, staff very specialized and procedures always followed, one might expect the levels of interaction to be low and the substance of the interaction to be narrow. Conversely, where there is little centralized control and less formality there is greater likelihood of wider interaction concerning a wider range of subjects.

Interaction brings together the *technological resource bases* of the two relationship parties and so these bases provide the conditions under which interaction occurs. The technological systems extend beyond equipment-based resources or technology infrastructure. They also include the knowledge bases of the individuals working in the two firms. If the systems match well then the basis for smooth interaction exists. However, if there is a substantial gap between the systems then the basis for smooth interaction is not there. In practice, companies may well get involved in activities to bring their technology systems closer into alignment. For example, a supplier might establish supply capabilities close to a customer's plant or adopt logistics systems (such as more warehousing and extra delivery vehicles) that ensure continuity of supply (Frazier et al., 1988; O'Neal, 1989a, 1989b). It might even go as far as to deploy staff on a customer's premises to facilitate a customer's activities (Wilson, 1996).

In a further example, if the production technology of the seller is geared towards long continuous runs of the same product yet a buyer needs varied, and relatively small, batches of product then interaction between them may revolve around alternative forms of production. Take the case of a supplier of blow-moulded plastic bottles to the food industry and a dairy customer. The supplier had spent a few happy years providing the dairy with its needs for one, two and four-pint bottles. The moulds and production testing equipment of the supplier were geared to produce these. The customer sourced its needs for six-pint bottles from the supplier's sister plant, which involved greater transport distance. The interaction between the supplier and the customer was heavily affected by the need to source from two separate plants because of the cost implications (for example, greater product mileage and duplication of order processing). The issue was resolved when the supplier added a new moulding machine, new moulds, and product-testing equipment. It could then meet the need for one-, two-, four- and six-pint bottles, all from the same plant within the vicinity of the customer plant, and could respond more quickly and flexibly to the demand for all of these product variants. As a result the customer felt happy to source its total requirement from the single plant. This is an example of an adaptation involving technological realignment affecting the relationship positively.

What either party seeks to gain overall and, perhaps more importantly, through its relationships affects its interaction. If it sees value through exchange, for instance by joint development of products or sharing of expertise, then its interaction will follow suit in terms of willingness to engage and the commitments it may be prepared to make. Where a company perceives that it can attain its goals independently of a counterpart then this is less likely to lead it to make substantial commitments to that relationship and its interaction will be affected accordingly.

The previous relationship experiences of organizations may affect their propensity to become more or less involved with other relationships. Those that feel strong commitment to one or several close and deep relationships has left them exposed financially, or subject to perceived negative behaviours from the counterparts, may be less inclined to attain such closeness in future relationships. At the same time, since relationships require a set of skills to manage them, those companies that have managed to build the sorts of relationships that they consider appropriate are likely to feel suitably equipped for other relationships.

Ultimately, it is the interactions between individual participants that create and sustain a relationship. Even when resources such as information or process technology are shared and underpin a relationship, people are still involved in bringing these resources to bear and performing the activities that use the resources. The personalities of these people affect the relationship. Some individuals find it easier to approach new people (a necessary activity for creating the bonds between people that initiate relationships). Further, some individuals are more forthcoming than others; again, a trait that may be appropriate to relationships. This is not to say that relationships only require extravert personalities. On occasions, the levels of application and single-mindedness that are characteristic of introverts may be more appropriate for a relationship. For instance, these traits are likely to be necessary to overcome obstacles in a relationship such as operational fulfilment problems or to achieve changes in the basis of exchange such as new process or product development activities. Regardless of the benefit of either set of traits, the point is that individual personality undoubtedly affects relationships. Individual experiences in general and relationships in particular will also affect the way an individual interacts, as will the individual's motivation to interact. These varied personal characteristics alongside the characteristics of the role the individual fills, the functional affiliation he or she has, and the level he or she occupies within the organization all affect the interaction that takes place and thus the relationship that ensues.

The interaction environment

The external environment in which a dyadic relationship unfolds is likely to affect the behaviour of the firms in the relationship (Achrol et al., 1983). These effects can be seen in a variety of ways. *Market structure* affects a relationship in terms of the availability of and scope for switching to alternative relationship partners (Anderson and Narus, 1984). Where there are few alternatives there is a strong tendency for a company to seek close and stable relations with a counterpart buyer or seller. Where firms operate in a dynamic or internationalizing marketplace they may seek to reduce the uncertainty that goes with this *dynamism* through their supplier or customer relationships. This might involve greater interaction in the form of information or social exchanges.

An individual relationship's *position in the manufacturing channel* or the characteristics of the wider *social system* may also be significant, particularly where the strategies of companies elsewhere in the supply chain are able to influence the behaviour of a firm in that dyadic relationship. A relationship's 'embeddedness' in the network that surrounds it (Håkansson and Snehota, 1995a) creates constraints upon the freedom to act on the part of the relationship parties – something that has been called the 'burden' of relationships (Håkansson and Snehota, 1995b).

The atmosphere affecting and affected by the interaction

Interaction over time leads to a relationship that is more than the individual episodes. The relationship is dynamic in that it is affected by the individual episodes. However, the passage of time in the relationship brings a degree of stability. This establishes an atmosphere for the relationship within which relationship participants act. Within the IMP model this atmosphere can be described in terms of the power–dependence relationship between the companies, the degree of cooperation/conflict and the overall closeness/distance in the relationship, as well as in terms of the companies' mutual expectations.

In a relationship the stronger party has great potential to affect the activities of the weaker party. The strength may come from ownership of resources needed by the other party and/or where the other party is strongly dependent on its counterpart. With power asymmetry comes the potential for conflict, though this depends upon the stronger party exercising the power that its strength brings. If it does use its power in ways that are considered by the weaker party to affect it negatively then this may give rise to conflict when the weaker party objects. The extent to which the weaker party does object depends on how weak/strong it feels; it may just accept there is nothing it can do about it.

While there will always be moments of conflict in a relationship, there may be greater incentive for companies to cooperate (Anderson and Narus, 1990), the self-interest of each party being best served by mutual action (Heide and John, 1990). Parties might act jointly to develop tools and design products (Drozdowski, 1986); to undertake value analysis or cost targeting (Dowst, 1988); to design quality control and delivery systems (Treleven, 1987); and to engage in long-term planning (Spekman, 1988). Inevitably, trust also affects the atmosphere of the relationship. With repeated interaction comes the ability of each party to more strongly ascertain the trustworthiness of its counterpart and for trust to affect the atmosphere of the relationship.

The IMP interaction model: criticisms and lessons

Whilst the IMP interaction model has been acknowledged for its contribution to the understanding of inter-firm relationships, there have been some criticisms of it. Theory is often developed from individual examples such that law-like generalizations are not readily derived. This means that there is a lengthy list of concepts (Seyed-Mohamed and Wilson, 1989) and these concepts can lack clarity or overlap (such as with adaptation and adaptation processes (Brennan and Turnbull, 1995)). Criticisms are not generally levelled at the central proposition that the relationship is central to the understanding of business marketing.

The IMP interaction model captures the various elements that may affect the relationship interaction process in the short- and long-term as well as clearly showing that the interaction itself may affect the parties to the relationship, either directly or through the atmosphere surrounding the relationship. In this way, organizations adapt to the relationships they have, and as a result may be changed. When it comes to drawing from the model to help with the management of relationships there are several preliminary points that must be made:

- Relationships are two-way. Even if one party is dominant and can obtain its own way, the fact that it has to use the resources provided by another means that there is still an interactive process unfolding and the relationship is the outcome of the interactions between the two. This means that managers need to consider the aspirations, potential and behaviour of both parties to the exchange if they want to obtain clarity about the way the relationship is and could be.
- Relationships in general are complex and can be described using a multitude of variables, some of which may be of more explanatory use in some relationships than others. In one relationship it might be the power a supplier has over a customer on the basis of its provision of a scarce resource that explains much of the interaction in the relationship. In another, the common history and levels of trust between the partners over time might explain it better. In yet another, despite a history of cooperation, changes in the wider marketing environment may drive impending changes in the relationship. The situational diversity and the range of variables that could explain any individual relationship mean that simple prescriptions for action are not easy to obtain. Rather, managers have to reflect upon the relationship that confronts them, understanding its entirety in its natural setting. Only from that understanding, aided by the analytical tools that this book provides, will sensible development of the relationship result.
- Whether a relationship is long term or short term, at any particular point there is a history leading to that point. The history both makes it what it is and sets the jumping-off point for the future. Understanding the history of a relationship is a prerequisite for establishing what it can be in the future.

Business Marketing as Network Analysis and Management

Beyond relationships to the network

Relationships are the primary basis for exchange, and are thus central to business marketing. It is through relationships that companies achieve objectives. However, the decisions taken in relationships and their motivations do not necessarily originate at the level of the relationship (Ford and McDowell, 1999). Often for the business marketing organization there are considerations that extend across the whole portfolio of customer relationships in which it is involved. How it behaves within any one relationship will be conditioned by these other relationships. Further, how it behaves in any one relationship will be conditioned not just by its customer relationships at large, but potentially by its own supply relationships; it may be affected by the links that its suppliers have with their suppliers. Beyond that, it may even be affected by the links with other agencies, governments, banks, universities and industry associations. All of these have the potential to affect the single relationship because of 'connectedness' (Cook and Emerson, 1978) – all of these relationships are connected to the wider network within which they are 'embedded' (Granovetter, 1985). As Ford et al. (2002: 29) argue, 'This network is the arena in which the business marketer must operate. The relationships in the network enable the company to grow and develop, but they are also a constraint on that development and may restrict its activities.'

This points to the fundamental issue for the firm, surrounded as it is by a network of relationships, that its relative value strategically is a function of its position in the network. This requires a different strategic mindset from the traditional one that sees the firm as atomistic, independently deciding upon its own strategic future and having the freedom to pursue that course. The network view means that it has to accept that it is interdependent and embedded, and that this limits both its ability to think and act independently. Thus, the task for the firm, managerially, is to analyze the network in order to establish its network position and engage in relationship behaviour that will enhance that position. This will inevitably involve acting within existing relationships in ways that may achieve this. It might also involve activities aimed at forging new relationships.

Network analysis to establish current position

Given the complexity of individual relationships that we have depicted in the previous section, managers or practitioners would find the application of an analytical framework such as the interaction model in its entirety overly cumbersome. In any event, that level of analysis is unnecessary to obtain some knowledge of the relative positioning of firms in a network. Rather, it is possible to employ the sort of shorthand analysis that Håkansson and Snehota (1995a) have used to great effect. This analysis recognizes that there are three important components that networks bring together from all those organizations within the network: what Hakansson and Snehota call the substance of relationships. The three components are the *actors* who engage in relationship behaviour, the *resources* that are created or used in relationships, and the *activities* that are undertaken in relationships. To distinguish the different kinds of interconnection, while at the same time recognizing that they are relational, they are referred to in terms of actor bonds, resource ties and activity links – which is why the activity of examining each of these can be called *ARA Analysis*.

Actor bonds

It is people within organizations who initiate relationships and typically create and control resources and activities, and it is often easiest to start with an identification of as many companies and people within them that have connections with other actors in the network. The nature of the connections may be economic or social. It is also easiest to start with one's own organization and work out from there.

Activity links

Relationships start operating to achieve their purpose when activities are undertaken that deliver that purpose, whether it is design activity from a supplier or requests for information from a customer. Typically, an activity cycle between two companies would commence with an order and end when it is delivered. However, depending upon the nature of a relationship it may be that other activities are worthy of note in a network diagram, such as a joint research project or combined promotional activity. The consequence of mapping the links between the parties in the network is an indication of the range of activities that are taking place and the relative role that the focal company has in this.

Resource ties

Resources are used to undertake activities by actors, but may also be created as part of the relationship exchange. The resources may be used by actors on their own (such as equipment within their own firms required to perform specific tasks) or may be combined with the resources from other parties to create a shared resource. IT makes the sharing of data resources increasingly easy for companies. So, for instance, there may be design inputs from a variety of network actors making use of a shared design system.

By establishing the variety of linkages between the firms in a network in terms of these types of interconnection it becomes possible for a focal company to establish where the critical mass in terms of the ARA components lies. This then enables it to determine where it lies in relation to others in the network in positional terms, whether it has a strong presence and is central to the direction things are going, or whether it is relatively weakly joined and on the periphery of network developments.

Initiating changes towards a new network position

On the basis of the analysis of network position, a focal company is better able to consider how it changes network position. This is likely to involve it in attempts to forge stronger relationships with partners that are in stronger network positions, or may lead it to wind down or forsake some of the relationship linkages that it already has. This may seem obvious: to get stronger it just involves forging relationships with positionally strong actors. That is, move from the periphery to a position closer to the centre. However, in examining their own network positions, stronger network parties are unlikely to welcome relationship advances from any party that does not maintain or further enhance their existing positions. Furthermore, stronger network players are likely to be highly sought after. However, in the pharmaceutical or biotechnology sectors, for example, some smaller players can certainly do this if they bring forward a new drug or treatment platform.

Parties to exchange also need to be aware of the costs of attempting to forge lots of relationships. First of all, relationships are not free and as with any investment decision the firm needs to be sure it will obtain value for the not inconsiderable costs it will incur. At the same time there is also a level beyond which it becomes cognitively difficult to consider the links with counterparts and have clarity about what is obtainable from those relationships.

More often network positional change has to be achieved more gradually using existing relationships to forge the sort of actor bonds, activity links and resource ties that will strengthen the parties involved. Furthermore, by acting with a relationship partner, or a chain of partners, it becomes possible to exert greater change in position than acting alone. Indeed, an important asset of network thinking is that achieving an improved positioning may not actually involve specific actions on the part of the focal party. Rather, it may involve encouraging changes in another network party or parties for the benefit of both it and the focal company. For instance, by encouraging a supplier to innovate with new materials technology it becomes possible that the value-adding activity of the focal company is enhanced with its customers, making the network positions for both focal company and supplier improved.

Chapter Summary

- As well as an understanding of the behaviour of the buying company, business marketers also have to understand the relationship between the buying company and the selling company.

- Relationships are two-sided: treating customers as passive recipients of the attentions of the marketer is a naive view of business marketing and inherently flawed.

- Any ability a marketer has to influence the buyer is predicated on the nature of the relationship between the two parties and so must involve a clear understanding of what is possible within the relationship. This means that rather than being solely preoccupied with the buying centre the marketer must analyze the relationship at large.

- A variety of theoretical viewpoints can be drawn upon to understand a relationship. However, it doesn't matter which perspective the marketer draws from, so long as by doing so a clear understanding of what is happening in the relationship is derived. Decisions about the future of a relationship can only come about from such an understanding.

- The business marketer strives for deep understanding of the current state of the relationship, of its likely future development and of the process of value creation within the relationship.

- Success in any individual relationship will depend upon the business marketer's understanding of that relationship within the wider network of relationships within which the company is embedded. Strategic business marketing focuses on a clear understanding of the network and on creating individual relationship strategies that establish the most favourable network position for the company.

Questions for discussion

1. Why is an understanding of the buying behaviour of the customer insufficient for successful business marketing?

2. Explain the uncertainties and abilities that buyers and sellers bring to an exchange situation.

3. Explain how Principal-Agent theory can help our understanding of exchange risk.

4. Identify the three factors that affect the level of transaction costs and how they do so.

5. Why doesn't a stronger exchange partner always exercise its power?

6. To what extent are parties to exchange only concerned with economic value?

7. What are the four main elements of the IMP interaction model? What has it got to offer that other perspectives may not?

8. Why does a business marketer need to have a network view?

Case study: ## Surface Inspection – ensuring quality, tile after tile after tile

As with many lifestyle furnishing products, people demand more and more choice from ceramic tiles. Floor tiles and wall tiles both now come in an increasing range of colours and styles to cater for these diverse customer tastes. Of course, when their selections are splashed across their wall or on their floor, they expect uniformity of pattern, colour and texture. They certainly don't want marked variations in colour, blemishes or apparent flaws. Maintaining consistency of quality in tiles has traditionally been difficult and has typically relied upon human checking. Of course, operationally this has implications for throughput rates, which has meant that the process is only as fast as the speed at which one or more quality inspectors have been able to work.

With greater complexity in tile design, and a wider range of colours being used in any single tile, human checking gets even slower; the quality of checking also deteriorates because the task gets more difficult and attention can only be maintained by inspectors for short periods of time. Change in the prevailing light conditions also has an effect.

Tile batch production itself has been increasingly mechanized over the years, with manufacturing lines incorporating pressing, drying, glazing and decorating processes before tiles get fired in the kiln. The ability to remove flawed tiles at the earliest point possible is desirable. This reduces the costs incurred in glazing a tile biscuit that has a problem, or decorating a tile where there are glaze deficiencies, or firing a tile that will be later rejected or marked as second or third quality at best. It also ensures that the kiln is used to fire a greater number of first-quality tiles. Some of the tile manufacturers are large internationally known companies (Dal Tile, Graniti Fiandre, H&R Johnson, Interceramic, Pilkingtons, Porcelanosa, Villeroy & Boch) that have

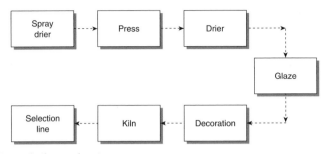

Figure 3.3   Typical tile production process

invested heavily in capacity where the benefits of investment cannot be achieved if the process faces discontinuities with quality checking.

Thus, inevitably, attention in the industry has turned to the use of technology to undertake tile inspection, the great bottleneck in production. Technology has the potential to enable inspection at tolerances that were hitherto not possible and to achieve greater consistency in quality, tile after tile after tile. And, of course, the technology can work 24/7, if required, and doesn't need a tea break. While production occurs in many locations, Spain and Italy continue to be the largest exporters of manufactured tiles, with the areas around Sassuolo in Italy and Castellón, Spain, being the source of much of the world's production.

Surface Inspection in the UK is a world leader in automatic, visual tile inspection technology, with over 350 systems installed with companies in Europe and the Americas and with over 40 per cent of that being repeat business. Its Master Series equipment, incorporating a ProcessMaster® and FlawMaster® can handle checking at various stages of the tile production process (see Figure 3.3) in order to remove substandard tiles at the earliest (and thus most cost effective) opportunity. The current range of Surface Inspection machines can provide a throughput of 750 million per hour and can handle tiles up to 600mm × 1200mm. Efforts are continuing to increase the rate further and the complexity of tiles that can be checked reliably.

The £6.5 million turnover company, with its staff of 60 people, only undertakes the design and assembly of the machines, relying then upon the expertise of several suppliers with whom it works closely in making the various components (conveyors, lighting, camera equipment, processors, machine casing and so on). The relationship with the provider of the camera equipment is particularly important and Surface Inspection is very protective of the intellectual property created by their close relationship. Surface Inspection completes the product development process by assembling the machine at its Bristol location in the UK before shipping to customers. When the machine is in place, the Surface Inspection engineers install the necessary software, incorporating its protected analysis algorithms, and fine tune for the local conditions. These local conditions vary enormously but the tile production environment is generally quite a hostile one, with lots of variations in heat and dust in the manufacturing plants.

Case study

Surface Inspection considers it has benefited substantially from its contacts with the industry itself when it comes to product development activity. In the early days, when the technology was developing, a German customer that had faith in their visual inspection approach allowed the company to put machines into their production line while they perfected them, enabling software debugging to be undertaken and re-specification of the mechanical performance of the equipment. Similar contacts with a nearby UK customer allowed ready access to production testing facilities. On the basis of a long-term loan of a machine to this customer, it can secure access to a test rig at short notice in a real production environment. This same customer had sufficient faith in the Surface Inspection solution to take an equity stake in the company in its early days. Its reward has been a 6 per cent increase in first-quality tiles.

In an overall market estimated to be worth €95 million in 2003, it is understandable that competition for inspection internationally would be on the increase. However, while there have been a lot of entrants to the market over the 17 years that Surface Inspection has been on the scene, the number of firmly established players in the market has not increased substantially (from four in 1987 to five major players currently). These major competitors include another UK company, Axiom, a company from Germany, Massen, and two companies from Italy, System and Italvision. While these companies also undertake automatic visual inspection of ceramic tiles, they may have interests in other industries as well. System of Italy provides process control equipment more generally, and storage and handling equipment for the logistics sector, as well as a range of equipment for the tile production process (handling, decorating, selection line, palletizing and storage). Massen uses its machine vision technology in the automotive, textile, and flexible circuit board sectors as well as ceramics, and for more general applications such as sorting and in-line measurement.

Like Surface Inspection, some of the competitors have been refining their technology through successive upgrades of their installed systems. This enables them to build upon the knowledge that is gleaned from machines having to work continuously in the harsh environment of tile manufacturing facilities where they have to cope with the effects of heat, noise and dust. Other companies are more recent entrants, seeking to prove themselves and their technology. In some cases the technology has emerged from the development activities of a variety of players working together. For example, an Italian company, Examina, recently came about as a result of EU research programmes involving the collaboration of a variety of parties, including:

- tile manufacturers (Ceramiche Atlas Concorde of Italy and EmilCeramica of Italy);
- specialist research institutes (Istituto di Elaborazione della Informazione (IEI), Italy – image processing for quality control expertise); and
- software companies (Macs Tech, Italy – neural networks and vision technology, system integration and project management; and Cromemco, Germany – parallel computing specialists).

The company claims that its system is able to process 30 × 30cm tiles in less than 300 ms, allowing a line speed up to 60 metres per minute. Whether it will manage to establish a presence in the market remains to be seen.

Surface Inspection itself has benefited from its own product collaborations in the past. A development project with a Spanish customer (Errece) has led to the creation of an integrated Selection Line product that can inspect and then separately stack and pack tiles of different quality (SelectMaster®). It is also currently working in a research consortium incorporating 13 EU partners from six countries, straddling industry and academia (Monotone) to improve production in the ceramic tile industry in the EU. While the EU (with Italy and Spain) currently leads in production of tiles, China and Brazil are narrowing the gap very quickly. The project started in 2000 and aims to improve quality (especially colour tones) and reduce waste in order to prevent the gap narrowing.

Given the leaps that are being made by the competition, the development required to stay ahead of the game may necessitate further collaboration for Surface Inspection and it may mean that it has to develop closer relationships than it has up to now. This includes being able to decide who to collaborate with, in which projects, and how deeply to become involved.

Sources:

www.surface-inspection.com
www.tile-inspection.com
www.axiom.mvhi.com/en/index.php
www2.massen.com/frameset.php?PageName=willkommen&Language=en&Issue=1
www.system-group.it
www.italvisionsrl.it/ita/index2.html
http://web.tiscali.it/examina/english/index.htm

Case study questions

1. Why do relationships increasingly matter in this marketplace?
2. Attempt to depict the network for tile surface inspection and evaluate the network position of Surface Inspection.
3. Using the ARA analytical model described in the text, recommend some changes for Surface Inspection that will further enhance its network position.

The assistance of Stewart Coe, Marketing Director, Surface Inspection Ltd, in the preparation of this case study is gratefully acknowledged.

Case study

References

Achrol, R., Reve, T. and Stern, L. (1983) 'The environment of marketing channel dyads: a framework for comparative analysis', *Journal of Marketing*, 47 (4): 55–67.

Anderson, J. and Narus, J. (1984) 'A model of the distributor's perspective of distributor–manufacturer working relationships', *Journal of Marketing*, 48 (Fall): 62–74.

Anderson, J. and Narus, J. (1990) 'A model of distributor firm and manufacturer firm working partnerships', *Journal of Marketing*, 54 (January): 42–58.

Arndt, J. (1979) 'Toward a concept of domesticated markets', *Journal of Marketing*, 43 (Fall): 69–75.

Arrow, K. (1985) 'The economics of agency', in J. Pratt and R. Zeckhauser (eds), *Principals and Agents: The Structure of Business*. Boston, MA: Harvard Business School Press.

Bergen, M., Dutta, S. and Walker, O. (1992) 'Agency relationships in marketing: a review of the implications and applications of agency and related theories', *Journal of Marketing*, 56 (July): 1–24.

Brennan, R. and Turnbull, P. (1995) 'Adaptations in buyer–seller relationships', in P. Turnbull, D. Yorke and P. Naudé (eds), Proceedings of the 11th IMP Conference, Manchester, September.

Brownlie, D. and Saren, M. (1992) 'The four Ps of the marketing concept: prescriptive, polemical, permanent and problematical', *European Journal of Marketing*, 26 (4): 34–47.

Bruhn, M. (2003) *Relationship Marketing*. Hemel Hempstead: Prentice Hall.

Christopher, M. and Peck, H. (2001) 'Moving mountains at Marks & Spencer. Case prepared for Council of Supply Chain Management Professionals', online source: www.cscmp.org/ Downloads/CaseStudy/ms.pdf.

Cook, K. and Emerson, R. (1978) 'Power, equity and commitment in exchange networks', *American Sociological Review*, 43: 721–39.

Cunningham, M.T. and Homse, E. (1986) 'Controlling the marketing–purchasing interface: resource development and organizational Implications', reproduced in D. Ford (ed.) (1997) *Understanding Business Markets: Interaction, Relationships and Networks*, London: Dryden.

Dowst, S. (1998) 'Quality suppliers: the search goes on', *Purchasing* (January 28): 9A4A–12

Drozdowski, T. (1986) 'At BOC they start with the product', *Purchasing* (March 13), 62B5–1.

El-Ansary, A. and Stern, L. (1972) 'Power measurement in the distribution channel', *Journal of Marketing Research*, 9: 47–52.

Ford, D. (ed.) (1990) *Understanding Business Markets: Interaction, Relationships, Networks*. London: Academic Press.

Ford, D. (ed.) (1997) *Understanding Business Markets: Interaction, Relationships, Networks* (2nd edn). London: Dryden.

Ford, D. (ed.) (2001) *Understanding Business Marketing and Purchasing* (3rd edn). London: International Thomson.

Ford, D., Berthon, P., Brown, S., Gadde, L.E., Håkansson, H., Naudé, P., Ritter, T. and Snehota, I. (2002) *The Business Marketing Course*. Chichester: Wiley.

Ford, D., Håkansson, H., Lundgren, A., Snehota, I., Turnbull, P. and Wilson, D. (1998) *Managing Business Relationships*. Chichester: Wiley.

Ford, D. and McDowell, R. (1999) 'Managing business relationships by analyzing the effects and value of different actions', *Industrial Marketing Management*, 28 (5): 429–42

Frazier, G., Spekman, R. and O'Neal, C. (1988) 'Just-in-time exchange relationships in industrial markets', *Journal of Marketing*, 52 (October): 52–67.

Ganesan, S. (1994) 'Determinants of long-term orientation in buyer-sellers relationships', *Journal of Marketing*, 58(2), 1–19.

Granovetter, M. (1985) 'Economic action and social structure: the problem of embeddedness', *American Journal of Sociology*, 91 (3): 481–510.

Grönroos, C. (1997) 'From marketing mix to relationship marketing – towards a paradigm shift in marketing', *Management Decision*, 35 (4), 322–39.

Gummesson, E. (1987) 'The new marketing – developing long-term interactive relationships', *Long Range Planning*, 20 (4): 10–20.

Håkansson, H. (ed.) (1982) *International Marketing and Purchasing of Industrial Goods: An Interaction Approach*. Chichester: Wiley.

Håkansson, H., Johanson, J. and Wootz, B. (1976) 'Influence tactics in buyer–seller processes', *Industrial Marketing Management*, 5 (5): 319–32.

Håkansson, H. and Ostberg, C. (1975) 'Industrial marketing: an organizational problem?', *Industrial Marketing Management*, 4 (2/3): 113–23.

Håkansson, H. and Snehota, I. (1995a) *Developing Relationships in Business Networks*. London: Routledge.

Håkansson, H. and Snehota, I. (1995b) 'The burden of relationships or who is next?', Proceedings of the 11th Annual IMP International Conference, Manchester, 7–9th September.

Hallén, L., Johanson, J. and Seyed-Mohamed, N. (1991) 'Inter-firm adaptation in business relationships', *Journal of Marketing*, 55 (April): 29–37.

Heide, J. and John, G. (1990) 'Alliances in industrial purchasing: the determinants of joint action in buyer–supplier relationships', *Journal of Marketing Research*, 27 (1): 24–36.

Morgan, R. and Hunt, S. (1994) 'The Commitment–trust theory of relationship marketing', *Journal of Marketing*, 58 (July): 20–38.

Moorman, C., Deshpande, B. and Zaltman, G. (1993) 'Factors affecting trust in market research relationships', *Journal of Marketing*, 57 (Jan), 81–101.

O'Neal, C.R. (1989a) 'JIT procurement and relationship marketing', *Industrial Marketing Management*, 1 (1), 55–64.

O'Neal, C.R. (1989b) 'The buyer–seller linkage in a just-in-time environment', *Journal of Purchasing & Materials Management*, 25 (1): 34–41.

Oxborrow, L. (2000) 'Beyond needles and thread: changing supply chains in the UK', article available from the Harvard Center for Textile and Apparel Research (www.hctar.org/pdfs/ GS03B.pdf).

Pfeffer, J. and Salancik, G. (1978) *The External Control of Organizations: A Resource–Dependence Perspective*. New York: Harper and Row.

Sako, M. (1992) *Prices, Quality and Trust – Inter-Firm Relations in Britain and Japan*. Cambridge: Cambridge University Press.

Seyed-Mohamed, N. and Wilson, D.T. (1989) 'Exploring the adaptation process', *Research in Marketing: An Interactive Perspective*, Proceedings of the 5th IMP Conference, Pennsylvania State University.

Spekman, R. (1988) 'Strategic supplier selection: understanding long-tern buyer relationships', *Business Horizons*, 31(4): 75–81.

Stern, L. and Reve, T. (1980) 'Distribution channels as political economies: a framework for comparative analysis', *Journal of Marketing*, 44 (3), 52–64.

Treleven, M. (1987) 'Single sourcing: a management tool for the quality supplier', *Journal of Purchasing and Materials Management*, 23 (Spring): 19–24.

Turnbull, P. and Valla, J.P. (1986) (eds) *Strategies for International Industrial Marketing*. London: Croom Helm.

Williamson, O. (1979) 'Transaction-cost economics: the governance of contractual relations', *Journal of Law and Economics*, 22 (October): 233–61.

Wilson, E. (1996) 'Theory transitions in organizational buying behaviour research', *Journal of Business & Industrial Marketing*, 11 (6): 7–19.

Young, L. and Wilkinson, I. (1989) 'The role of trust and co-operation in marketing channels: a preliminary study', *European Journal of Marketing*, 23(2), 109–22.

4 Business-to-Business Marketing Strategy

Learning outcomes

After reading this chapter you will:

- know what shareholder value, customer value, supplier value and relationship value are, and what role they play in the formulation of business marketing strategy;
- understand how business marketing strategy is closely linked to an understanding of organizational buying behaviour;
- be able to explain the similarities and differences between the formal, planned approach to strategy and the resource-based view of strategy;
- understand the role played by the relationships and networks of which the firm is a part in the formulation of business marketing strategy;
- appreciate the impact of new information and communications technologies on strategy;
- be able to apply several different ethical frameworks to the analysis of decisions in business marketing; and
- understand the significance of international climate change agreements for business-to-business strategic decision-making.

Introduction

Strategy is one of those words that is used commonly in the business world, but which cannot easily be defined. Mintzberg et al. (1998) argue that strategy needs five definitions – the five Ps for strategy:

- Strategy as a *plan*: a direction, a guide, a path for getting the organization from where it is now to where it wants to be in the future. This is the organization's *intended* strategy, that is, what it set out to achieve.

- Strategy as a *pattern*: meaning that strategy is a consistency in behaviour over time. This is the organization's *realized* strategy, that is, what it actually achieved. In practice it is likely that the realized strategy will be neither identical to the intended strategy, nor completely different from it. As Mintzberg et al. (1998: 11) put it: 'The real world inevitably involves some thinking ahead as well as some adaptation en route.'
- Strategy as a *position*: the locating of particular products in particular markets. Companies seek to establish a position in the market that is both unique and valued by customers.
- Strategy as a *perspective*: a company's fundamental way of doing things. While strategy as position is outward-looking, to the external marketplace, strategy as perspective is inward-looking, to the overall purpose of the organization. These approaches are complementary. Market positions must be consistent with the fundamental purpose and values of the organization. For example, construction equipment manufacturer Caterpillar (see Box 4.1) aims to be the global leader in customer value in its field, while 'sustaining the quality of the earth'. In positioning Caterpillar products in the marketplace, the company will seek to deliver excellent customer value while taking account of environmental impacts.
- Strategy as a *ploy*: finally, strategy can refer to clever manoeuvres designed to outwit competitors – ploys.

Box 4.1   *Vision and mission at Caterpillar*

Vision

Be the global leader in customer value.

Mission

- Caterpillar will be the leader in providing the best value in machines, engines and support services for customers dedicated to building the world's infrastructure and developing and transporting its resources. We provide the best value to customers.
- Caterpillar people will increase shareholder value by aggressively pursuing growth and profit opportunities that leverage our engineering, manufacturing, distribution, information management and financial services expertise. We grow profitably.
- Caterpillar will provide its worldwide workforce with an environment that stimulates diversity, innovation, teamwork, continuous learning and improvement, and rewards individual performance. We develop and reward people.
- Caterpillar is dedicated to improving the quality of life while sustaining the quality of our earth. We encourage social responsibility.

Source : www.cat.com.

In the rest of this section we examine the meaning of strategy in a little more detail. Then we move on, in the next section, to argue that the fundamental purpose of business and marketing strategy is to create value, and we explain the various forms of value that are important in strategic decision-making. The primary focus is upon customer value, something that we have already seen is central to Caterpillar's business purpose. Following the discussion of value, we take a look at different approaches to marketing strategy formulation – the rational planning approach, the resource-based view, and the relationships and networks view. In the final two sections of the chapter we discuss two key issues in business marketing strategy. The first of these, ethics and corporate social responsibility, has already been raised in the Caterpillar example. The other issue – the impact of new technology on business marketing strategy – is a pervasive issue that affects just about every business-to-business-marketer. The impact of new technology is also addressed elsewhere in this book when we deal with specific aspects of business-to-business marketing, such as the impact on buying behaviour, the effect on marketing communications and the impact of online auctions on pricing strategy. In this chapter we look at a general framework for analysing the effects of new technology on marketing strategy.

The meaning of strategy

Buzzell and Gale (1987: 18) defined strategy as 'The policies and key decisions adopted by management that have *major* impacts on financial performance. These policies and decisions usually involve significant resource commitments and are not easily reversible.' They made the distinction, which is today widely accepted, between *business unit strategy* and *corporate strategy*. Business unit strategy is concerned with how an individual business competes with its rivals, with what it does and what it could do to stay in business and to beat the competition. Corporate strategy is concerned with decisions made in an organization comprising multiple businesses (often called strategic business units, or simply SBUs). Questions of corporate strategy concern the overall shape of the corporation, which SBUs should form part of the overall portfolio, and the way in which key resources (such as investment capital) should be divided between them. Strategic marketing management is concerned with business unit strategy, also known as competitive strategy.

Strategy is concerned with strategic decision-making. McDonald (1996) identified four characteristics of strategic decisions. First, they are concerned with the long-term orientation of the organization rather than day-to-day management issues. Second, strategic decisions define the scope of the organization's activities, selecting what it will do and what it will not do. The third and fourth characteristics of strategic decisions both concern the *matching* of the organization's activities – they have to be matched to the external environment and they have to be matched to its resource capacity. There is no point in setting objectives and devising strategies that are unconnected to the realities of the business environment; nor is there any point in pursuing strategies that cannot be implemented using the available resources. Jain (2000) identified the following salient features of strategic marketing:

- *Emphasis on long-term implications.* Since strategic marketing decisions take a long-term perspective, this makes it more likely that changes in the external business environment will affect such decisions. That is why monitoring the business environment is such a central element of strategic marketing planning.
- *Corporate inputs.* Day-to-day tactical marketing decisions can often be made without reference to the broader activities of the firm. Strategic marketing decisions have much wider-reaching implications however, and so require a whole-firm perspective. Jain suggests that in making strategic marketing decisions, managers need to consider the corporate culture, the corporate stakeholders and corporate resources.
- *Varying roles for different products/markets.* Strategic marketing means looking at the whole of a company's portfolio of products and markets, and managing the portfolio to achieve the company's overall goals. The result could be that decisions are made not to invest in certain products or markets in order to release resources to be invested elsewhere in the portfolio, where the opportunities are judged to be greater.

Lambin (1997: 8–10) differentiated between *strategic marketing* and *operational marketing*. The role of strategic marketing is to 'lead the firm towards attractive economic opportunities; that is, opportunities that are adapted to its resources and know-how and offer a potential for growth and profitability'. On the other hand, operational marketing 'is an action-oriented process which is extended over a short- to medium-term planning horizon and targets existing markets and segments'. In other words, operational marketing (which is synonymous with tactical marketing) is concerned with doing what we already do as effectively and efficiently as we can. Strategic marketing is concerned with identifying important changes taking place in the market and in the business environment, and working out how the organization should respond.

The Purpose of Strategy: Value and Value Creation

Michael Baker (1992: 20, italics in original) argued that marketing 'is concerned with the *establishment of mutually satisfying exchange relationships in which the judgements as to what is satisfying depend upon the perception of the parties to the exchange'*. We see much to commend in this definition of marketing. In recent years, both marketing practitioners and marketing scholars have focused on *value* as the fundamental determinant affecting satisfaction in exchange relationships. The purpose of marketing exchanges is to create value for all parties to the exchange. This is such a simple idea that it can easily be overlooked. In a straightforward, simple, voluntary exchange of a product for money between two parties, value is created because the buyer values the product at more than the selling price (otherwise they would not buy) and the seller values the product at less than the selling price (otherwise they would not sell). The economic value created through the exchange is the amount that the buyer would have been prepared to pay over and above the selling price (this is the *consumer surplus* in economic jargon) plus the difference between the actual price and the minimum price that the seller would have been prepared to accept (the *producer surplus*).

Many business-to-business exchanges are as simple as this: for example, as when a small shopkeeper goes to the cash-and-carry to stock up on confectionery and snack items, or when a builder buys cement, glass, bricks and other materials from a builders' merchant to build a conservatory for a client. However, it is a particular characteristic of business-to-business exchanges that the process of value creation can become complex, involving several parties and multiple interconnected exchanges (Ulaga, 2001). It is only in a very abstract sense that the value-creation processes involved in developing a major new construction project – such as the development of the new Terminal 5 at Heathrow airport – can be analyzed as a simple exchange of goods for money. Ultimately the many contractors and subcontractors involved in the project believe that they will derive enhanced economic value from their involvement, and the ultimate client, BAA (British Airports Authority), believes that the investment in the project will generate enhanced economic value for them. However, the value created in the project is long-term and subject to a considerable degree of uncertainty because of factors internal to the project (such as unexpected delays or cost overruns) and factors external to the project (such as the international political debate about climate change and the long-term trends in demand for air travel). For this reason, paying explicit attention to the value created through exchange processes is often a matter of particular concern to business marketers.

Customer value

Customer value: give–get definitions
In an influential paper on customer value, Zeithaml (1988) explored the concepts of perceived price, perceived quality and perceived value. She found that customers thought of value in four ways: value is low price; value

is whatever I want in a product; value is the quality I get for the price I pay; and value is what I get for what I give. Zeithaml (1988: 14) proposed this definition of customer perceived value: 'Perceived value is the consumer's overall assessment of the utility of a product based on perceptions of what is received and what is given ... value represents a tradeoff of the salient give and get components.' She made the point that different consumers will often have different salient give and get components and will weight components differently. Both the give (sacrifice) and the get (benefit) components included a range of different attributes; in particular, the sacrifice components include monetary and non-monetary elements.

Many subsequent authors have used Zeithaml's definition as the essence of their own definitions of customer value. The give–get or trade-off definition is at the heart of many conceptual and empirical enquiries into customer value (Anderson and Narus, 1999; Blois, 2003; Christopher, 1996; Desarbo et al., 2001; Kothandaraman and Wilson, 2001; Lapierre, 2000; Ravald and Grönroos, 1996; Ulaga, 2001). However, there are differences of detail in the definitions used. Christopher (1996) made customer value a *ratio* of perceived benefits to total costs of ownership, and argued that both benefits and costs should be measured relative to competitive offers. Ravald and Grönroos (1996) and Kothandaraman and Wilson (2001) also proposed a ratio model, but put price (or perceived price) in the denominator rather than total costs of ownership. Blois (2003) preferred a *subtractive* functional form (value equals benefits minus sacrifices). Therefore, while there is substantial agreement that customer (perceived) value is a trade-off between benefits and sacrifices, there is some disagreement about the nature of the functional relationship, and some definitions include only price in the denominator while others include all of the customer (perceived) sacrifices of ownership.

Two further approaches to customer value are noteworthy because, while being generally consistent with the give–get approach, they introduce potential terminological confusion. Reddy (1991) talks about 'product value', but it is clear that his focal concept is what other researchers have called *customer value*. This is a simple point of terminology. The concept at issue is *the value of the seller's product (or market offering) to the customer*; Reddy chooses to call this product value, whereas most researchers call it customer value. The approach advocated by Anderson and Narus (1999) differs from other give–get definitions in a rather more important way, since price is excluded from the definition of value. They define customer value as the benefits that the customer receives minus the costs that the customer incurred *other than the purchase price*. The implications of this are interesting: 'In this concept of value in business markets, raising or lowering the price of an offering does not change the value that offering provides to a customer firm. Rather, it changes the customer's incentive to purchase that offering' (Anderson and Narus, 1999: 7). Whereas, of course, in other give–get formulations of customer value, changing the price does change perceived value.

The real test of a conceptual definition arises when one has to operationalize it in order to develop measurement tools. Desarbo et al. (2001) and Lapierre (2000) have done substantial empirical studies of customer value in industrial markets. However, their operational definitions of customer value were rather different. Both used give–get conceptual definitions of customer value, but Desarbo et al. used narrower definitions of 'give' and 'get' than Lapierre. Desarbo et al. (2001: 846) defined customer value as the 'trade-off between (customer-perceived) quality and (customer-perceived) price', while Lapierre defined customer value as the difference between benefits and the sacrifices, explicitly including all monetary and non-monetary costs among the sacrifices. Lapierre found that 'a value proposition implies much more than a trade-off between product quality and price' (2000: 130), which appears to contradict the definition of customer value used by Desarbo et al.

Flint and Woodruff (2001) distinguished between customer-received value and customer-desired value. Received value is the value that customers actually experience through specific product–customer interactions, while desired value is the value that customers want to receive from products/ services and their providers. Desired value is defined as 'the entire bundle of product attributes, and resulting consequences, both positive and negative, and monetary and non-monetary, that the customer wants to have happen' (p. 323). The purpose of their paper was to identify the factors driving changes in customer-desired value, on the argument that being able to predict changes in customer-desired value would be of profound competitive value.

Customer value: means–end chain definition

Woodruff (1997) identified a number of common aspects in the definition of customer value: that it is linked to product use, is a customer perception rather than an objective phenomenon, and that it involves a trade-off between what the customer receives and what the customer gives up. However, he argued that customer value should be conceptualized as a means–end chain, with desired product attributes (at the first level) leading to the achievement of desired consequences in use situations (at the intermediate level) and then to the fulfilment of customer goals and purposes (at the highest level). Woodruff's contention was that there was too much emphasis on product attributes, with a consequent neglect of the delivery of customer value at the higher levels of the means–end chain. He defined customer value in those terms as: 'a customer's perceived preference for and evaluation of those product attributes, attribute performances, and consequences arising from use that facilitate (or block) achieving the customer's goals and purposes in use situations' (p. 142). Parasuraman (1997) suggested that the nature and determinants of customer value may change depending on the stage in the customer life cycle; pre-purchase, post-purchase and long-term criteria for customer value assessment may be different.

Woodruff's approach suggests a longer-term perspective, in which the customer has the opportunity to evaluate the performance of the product and its impact on lifestyle. The distinction between Woodruff and the give–get approach is perhaps one of timescale. The means–end chain definition of value seems more suited to high-involvement purchases while give–get is more suited to low-involvement purchases. However, this is not what one finds in Woodruff and Gardial (1996). Their definition of value follows Woodruff (1997): 'Customer value is the customers' perception of what they want to have happen (i.e., the consequences) in a specific use situation, with the help of a product or service offering, in order to accomplish a desired purpose or goal' (p. 54). Clearly, they believe that they are presenting a complete approach to customer value, which is equally applicable to all product categories.

Perceived customer value for an organization
A substantial unresolved issue in the conceptualization of value is the nature of value for an organization (similar issues arise wherever there are multiple perspectives on the purchase decision, for example within households and informal friendship groups, but these contexts are not relevant here). When an exchange decision affects more than one person, how can we define perceived or subjective value for the organization? One solution is to assert that a superordinate organizational goal is the only relevant decision criterion, for example shareholder value. Such an assertion is subject to all of the criticisms associated with that decision criterion (for example, many organizations do not have shareholders; organizations should serve a plurality of interests), and presents prodigious computational challenges. Nevertheless, this would be the position of the value-based marketing enthusiasts (Doyle, 2000).

Walter et al. (2001) proposed that value rests in the perceptions of *key decision-makers* in the organization, which is clearly not a solution – unless it reduces to a shareholder value argument. Generally, directors and senior managers are key decision-makers. They are agents for the shareholders; if they do not pursue shareholder value maximization, then on what basis do they make their judgements about value? Blois (2003) focused on customer and supplier value in business-to-business markets but did not explain how the aggregate benefits and sacrifices to the organizations involved in the exchange are calculated from the benefits and sacrifices incurred by different stakeholders. Woodruff and Gardial (1996: 70) discussed the issue in the following terms: 'The desired end states of buying organizations might include longevity, a sense of unity or community, customer responsiveness, quality, or shareholder wealth.' However, this comes close to anthropomorphizing the organization. Organizations are abstractions and do not have desired end states. The desired end states that they mention seem likely to appeal very differently to different stakeholders in the organization. Customer responsiveness and quality are not desired end states at all; they are means to an end, namely, economic success.

Supplier value

Any exchange requires at least two parties, and for voluntary exchange to take place, both parties must believe that they will be better off as a result (Blaug, 1997). Marketing researchers tend to focus on customer value, because the theory and practice of marketing has focused primarily on converting the seller's products into cash. However, with the increasing emphasis on the supplier–customer relationship rather than just making the sale, the concept of supplier value has become of interest. Walter et al. (2001) argued that supplier value was a neglected, but important, topic since the supplier will only enter into or persist with a relationship so long as it yields net benefits. They defined supplier value as: 'the perceived trade-off between multiple benefits and sacrifices gained through a customer relationship by key decision makers in the supplier's organization' (Walter et al., 2001: 366). This is a simple transference of the give–get concept of customer value to the supplier. Since they conceive of the supplier as an organization, they refer to the key decision-makers in the organization as the judges of value.

Blois (2003) proposed the application of 'value equations' in business-to-business exchanges. He argued, following the subjective value theorists in economics (Blaug, 1992; Viner, 1925), that both parties to an exchange have a 'wants list', and consequently both parties can be considered to have a value equation for the exchange. Marketing literature has implicitly concentrated on the customer's value equation, but in order for an exchange to take place both parties to it must expect that the benefits of the exchange will exceed the sacrifices. Blois postulated value equations of the form:

$$B_c - Sa_c = V_c \qquad \text{Customer's value equation}$$
$$B_s - Sa_s = V_s \qquad \text{Supplier's value equation}$$

He provided illustrative lists of the likely components of benefits and sacrifices in business-to-business markets. These include both short-term and 'life cycle' benefits and sacrifices, and both easily measurable (in monetary terms) and intangible benefits and sacrifices. Blois then illustrated how, by simultaneously considering the value equations of both parties, it is possible to devise creative strategic marketing options.

Customer lifetime value, a.k.a. supplier value

A straightforward use of the term customer value is in the context of relationship marketing strategies. Such strategies have as their raison d'être the creation of customer loyalty and, consequently, the reduction of customer defections and the retention of customer business. Reichheld (1996) is a particularly strong advocate of the loyalty effect. The essence of this, by now well-known, argument is that customers vary considerably in terms of their profitability that understanding and managing customer profitability is the key to long-term corporate success (Rust et al., 2000), and that increasing customer loyalty will increase customer profitability. The focus of attention lies on the lifetime net present value to the business arising from doing business with a customer, which is termed 'lifetime customer value' by McDougall et al. (1997). They define lifetime customer value as the net present value of expected profits over the duration of the customer relationship.

It is immediately clear that 'lifetime customer value' is quite different from the 'customer-perceived value' discussed previously. The concept of lifetime customer value measures *value to the supplier*, not value to the customer. This illustrates the dangers of using terminology loosely. Clearly, lifetime customer value is an expression of *supplier value*, not of customer value.

Relationship value

In discussing customer value we saw that Desarbo et al. (2001) used a narrower definition than Lapierre (2000); the former defined customer value as the trade-off between quality and price, the latter as the difference between benefits and sacrifices. Lapierre's conceptual definition of benefits is broader than Desarbo et al.'s definition of 'quality', and this is carried forward into the operational definition. Consequently the two studies, while measuring something similar, are not measuring exactly the same thing. One interpretation is that Desarbo et al. measured the value of the product (or market offering) to the customer, while Lapierre measured the holistic value of the product and the relationship with the supplier to the customer. Of the ten benefit drivers identified by Lapierre, three were relationship related (for example, trust), and of the three cost drivers two were relationship related (for example, conflict).

Gassenheimer et al. (1998) used three bases for the analysis of value in relationships between firms: the economic (transaction cost analysis), the social (social exchange theory) and the distributive (distributive justice theory). They argued that most inter-firm exchange relationships required both economic and social value to endure. Their definition of economic value was of a financial give–get nature, while their definition of social value was as 'satisfaction with the exchange situation' (p. 325). Gassenheimer et al. argued that economic value tends to predominate where relational distance is high, and social value tends to predominate where relational distance is low. High relational distance is characterized by factors such as one-time exchange with no future obligation, intolerance of mistakes and asymmetrical dependence. Low relational distance is characterized by factors such as anticipated future exchange, mutual obligation, tolerance of mistakes and interdependence. Similarly, Ravald and Grönroos (1996) argued that in an enduring buyer–seller relationship, the relationship itself could provide some of the benefits and sacrifices perceived by both parties, over and above the value of the money, goods and services exchanged.

In the next section we move on to examine alternative approaches to strategy – the rational planning approach, the resource-based approach and the relationships/networks approach.

Approaches to Strategy

The rational planning approach

We saw in the introductory section of this chapter that strategy is concerned with big, long-term decisions that will have a substantial effect on the future of the organization. What we will here call the 'rational planning approach' to strategy development is the idea that a formal strategic planning process is the mechanism that is most likely to create a successful strategy. In the marketing field this will usually be known as strategic market planning, or simply marketing planning (McDonald, 1996). The aim of strategic market planning is to create a competitive advantage over rival firms. Michael Porter (1985) provided a two-fold classification of the forms of competitive advantage that can be achieved (differentiation of the product/service along a dimension valued by customers, or cost leadership) and a four-fold classification of competitive strategies depending on whether these competitive advantages applied across a whole market or only to a single market segment. Porter's classification gives us four strategic alternatives – differentiation, cost leadership, differentiation focus and cost focus. Porter (1980) was also responsible for formalizing the competitive environment into his famous 'five forces' (competitive rivalry, power of buyers, power of suppliers, threat of new entrants and threat from substitutes). In conceptualizing strategic planning as the process of analysing the competitive environment, identifying alternative strategic options open to the firm, and then choosing and implementing the option that best meets the firm's objectives, Porter was continuing an intellectual tradition associated particularly with Igor Ansoff (Ansoff, 1965). This is a prescriptive tradition (meaning that it provides guidance on what *should* be done), which advocates a series of logical, sequential steps through which organizations can arrive at their best strategy. The core components of these logical steps are:

- An 'external audit' examining both the competitive environment and the wider macro-environment to identify key opportunities and threats.
- An 'internal audit' examining the differential strengths and weaknesses of the organization compared to key competitors.
- A summary of the marketing audit in a SWOT (strengths, weaknesses, opportunities, threats) analysis.
- Identification of strategic alternatives – different possible strategies.
- Evaluation of strategic alternatives – testing the different possible strategies for their efficacy in achieving the organization's goals (which may be as conceptually simple as maximizing long-term shareholder value (Doyle, 2000)).
- Implementation of the strategy through the budgeting and operational planning systems, and control through a monitoring mechanism.

We refer to this as the rational planning approach because the underlying intellectual framework is an optimization routine employing rational choice theory. All of the possible alternative strategies are evaluated to see which provides the optimum results and the best strategy is chosen. There is, in fact, considerable evidence that business organizations do not and probably cannot rigorously pursue optimal choice decision-making processes (Gigerenzer and Selten, 2001; Simon, 1960), while Henry Mintzberg has shown that firms do not actually make strategy in this way (Mintzberg, 1973, 1976). Nevertheless, this in itself need not render the rational planning approach to strategy invalid since it could be seen as an ideal form to strive for, rather than a description of what organizations actually do. The key features of this approach are a series of prescribed logical steps, the identification of strategic alternatives and application of a choice routine to identify the best strategy, and the emphasis that is placed on analysing the competitive environment and responding appropriately by acquiring and deploying organizational resources. Over the last two decades, an alternative approach to strategy formulation based on the resource-based theory of the firm has become increasingly popular, and we turn to this alternative in the next section.

The resource-based view

The resource-based view of competitive advantage operates on the assumptions that firms are heterogeneous in terms of their control of important strategic resources and that resources are not perfectly mobile between firms. Firm resources are defined as 'strengths that firms can use to conceive of and implement their strategies' (Barney, 1991: 101). Resources can be classified as physical capital resources, human capital resources and organizational capital resources. Physical capital resources include physical technology, plant and equipment, geographic location and access to raw materials. Human capital resources include the training, experience, judgement, intelligence, relationships and insight of the individual managers and workers of the firm. Organizational capital resources include the formal reporting structure, the formal and informal planning, controlling and coordinating systems, the informal relations among groups within a firm, and those between a firm and other agents in the firm's environment.

Jay Barney (1991: 102, italics in original) has defined a sustained competitive advantage in the following terms:

> ... a firm is said to have a *competitive advantage* when it is implementing a value creating strategy not simultaneously being implemented by any current or potential competitors. A firm is said to have a *sustained competitive advantage* when it is implementing a value creating strategy not simultaneously being implemented by any current or potential competitors *and* when these other firms are unable to duplicate the benefits of this strategy.

Note that this definition includes potential competitors, not just current competitors – a sustained competitive advantage protects the firm against other firms considering a competitive market entry as well as providing an edge over firms already in the market. Barney makes it very clear that a sustained competitive advantage cannot be defined in terms of a specific period of calendar time; indeed, a sustained competitive advantage is one that cannot be nullified through the efforts of competing firms to duplicate it. A sustained competitive advantage will endure until some structural change takes place in the industry that renders it no longer relevant.

In order for a resource to be a potential source of sustained competitive advantage it must be *valuable, rare, inimitable,* and *non-substitutable.* These rather daunting-sounding characteristics are readily understood. Firms may have many unique attributes that do not assist them in exploiting opportunities or neutralizing threats. To be a *resource* an attribute must contribute to the firm's ability to deal effectively with the competitive environment – it must be *valuable.* An attribute that is found among most firms cannot be a source of sustained competitive advantage – to be a *resource* it must be *rare.* Even though an attribute may be both valuable and rare, if it is easily imitated by competitors then it will not provide a *sustained* competitive advantage, since current or potential competitors will duplicate it. To be a *resource* it must be inimitable, which may arise because of the unique historical circumstances under which it was created, because of the causally ambiguous link from the resource to enhanced value creation, or because of the social complexity of the attribute. Unique historical circumstances simply mean that a firm was in the right place at the right time and was therefore endowed with a unique resource (often called *path dependency* in the academic literature on the subject). A causally ambiguous link from the resource to enhanced value creation means that it is not possible to define precisely which resources provide a competitive advantage or why. Every firm comprises a very complex bundle of attributes and it is often not a simple matter – or perhaps not even possible – to identify exactly which characteristics of the firm make it more or less successful. Socially complex attributes, meaning characteristics of the firm that are embedded in its internal and external relationships, are a particularly difficult resource to imitate. This insight is one of the reasons why, in business-to-business markets, so much effort has been devoted to understanding inter-organizational relationships and networks. In turn, this effort has created a related but distinct view of strategy as the management of relationships and networks, which we will discuss in a subsequent section. Finally, to be a *resource* an attribute of the firm must be *non-substitutable*. Even if a characteristic of a firm – for example, the charismatic leadership of its Chief Executive Officer – is *inimitable*, it may still be the case that other firms can match its performance by implementing strategies that deliver similar benefits (for example, by having an excellent formal planning system that creates a clear, agreed mission that is shared by all of the employees). The less substitutable a resource is, the more effective it will be in creating a sustained competitive advantage.

To summarize, the resource-based view of the firm concludes that a firm can only build a sustained competitive advantage if it controls physical, human or organizational assets that are valuable, rare, inimitable and non-substitutable. In contrast to the rational planning approach, which focuses primarily upon the external environment and assumes that resources can be acquired and deployed to respond to environmental imperatives, the resource-based view advises organizations to concentrate on their unique resources and seek business opportunities that enable them to exploit these.

Like other theories, the resource-based view has been subject to criticism. Priem and Butler (2001: 28) argued that the resource-based view was tautological and of little practical relevance to managers. Tautological, because the resource-based view can be interpreted as saying that 'firms which control unique resources that enable them to exploit opportunities and neutralize threats will be able to implement strategies to exploit opportunities and neutralize threats better than other firms'. Of little practical relevance, because telling managers that they should aim to control valuable, rare, inimitable and non-substitutable resources is probably not telling them anything they do not already know, and does not help at all in explaining how to achieve this.

Barney (2001) has responded to these criticisms and, in particular, emphasized the practical relevance of the resource-based view. Managers experiencing a competitive disadvantage can use resource-based logic to identify the valuable and rare resources that competitors have, and establish whether these can be duplicated either by imitation or substitution. Resource-based logic encourages firms that are not currently exploiting all of their competitive advantages to look for resources they control that have the right characteristics to generate a sustained competitive advantage. By adopting a resource-based view, managers can seek to identify the resources that are generating their competitive advantage and, at a minimum, try to avoid damaging their resource advantage – this is a particularly delicate matter where the resource advantage is derived from cultural and social phenomena, which could be damaged unintentionally by some apparently unrelated managerial fad (for example, a new remuneration structure).

Strategy as the management of relationships and networks

While the rational planning approach to strategy and the resource-based view were both developed as generic approaches, equally applicable to businesses operating in consumer markets or business markets, the perspective addressed in this section arose directly out of research into business markets. It may well be the case that businesses marketing consumer goods and services could benefit from adopting a relationships and networks perspective, particularly in relation to the management of their supply chain. However, business-to-business marketing organizations, which interact with identifiable networks of heterogeneous suppliers and customers, certainly have the most to gain from the relationships and networks perspective on strategy.

Many of the important fundamental concepts have been introduced in the preceding chapters, in particular Chapter 3. Business marketing organizations do not deal with vast numbers of relatively homogeneous customers, each wielding relatively little market power. Rather, they deal with relatively small numbers of heterogeneous customers, some of whom wield considerable market power. In practice, suppliers and customers in business markets often do business together for many years, forming dyadic business relationships within which the parties to the relationship often make substantial relationship-specific investments that create structural bonds between the organizations in addition to the social bonds that are often created within business relationships. Each relationship has a unique atmosphere, which is the cumulative outcome of the exchange episodes (financial, product/service, information and social) that have taken place. Relationships are path dependent, and are connected together in networks that can be characterized in terms of *actors*, *resources*, and *activities*. One cannot hope to understand behaviours at the level of the individual relationship without understanding something of the network context within which it takes place. An action that takes place within a single relationship (for example, if a supplier prefers *not* to deepen its relationship with customer A) may only make sense in the context of other network connections (for example, if the supplier's parent company has decided to focus on developing relationships with customer B, who is a direct rival of customer A).

The relationships and networks approach to strategy has something in common with the resource-based view, in that the current resources of the firm are considered to be the key factor in determining its strategic behaviour. However, while the resource-based view focuses on three principal categories of resource – physical capital, human capital and organizational capital – the relationships and networks approach identifies the firm's *portfolio of relationships* and its *network positional resources* as the key factors in strategy formulation. The relationships and networks approach has very little in common with the rational planning approach to strategy; certainly there is no list of steps to be followed, and no suggestion of an optimization procedure. However, according to Ford and his colleagues (Ford et al., 2003: 5, emphasis in original) what clearly distinguishes this approach from both the rational planning approach and the resource-based view is: 'the Myth of Independence: A company *is* able to act independently. It can carry out its own analysis of the environment in which it operates, develop and implement its own strategy based on its own resources, taking into account its own competences and shortcomings.' To the contrary, from the relationships and networks perspective:

- Companies have a restricted view of the surrounding network.
- Firms have limited freedom to act independently, and the outcomes of their actions will be dependent upon the actions of other firms within the network.
- Strategizing is not simply concerned with competition. Business relationships have to be considered in their entirety, and there is no simple dichotomy between cooperative and competitive relationships. It is frequently the case that two firms will be simultaneously competing and cooperating within the same business relationship – for example, in the automotive industry, where it is quite common for competing automobile manufacturers to collaborate on the development of a new vehicle platform.

Within this perspective, much of the effort involved in developing strategy is concerned with identifying just how much freedom of action the individual firm has within the constraints of the industrial network. Strategy involves dealing with the actions of other network members, and achieving the organization's goals by 'working with, through, in spite of, or against them' (Ford et al., 2003: 6). No matter how strategically capable the organization may be, its own performance is irredeemably tied up with the performance of other members of the network. According to Håkansson and Snehota (1989: 190, emphasis added):

The performance and effectiveness of organizations operating in a network, by whatever criteria these are assessed, become dependent not only on how well the organization itself performs in interaction with its direct counterparts, but also on how these counterparts in turn manage their relationships with third parties. *An organization's performance is therefore largely dependent on whom it interacts with.*

When strategy is conceived as the management of relationship and networks, the primary focus ceases to be the internal allocation and structuring of resources, and becomes the way in which the organization relates its activities and resources to other parties in the network. The activities of strategizing involve far less analysis of a supposedly impersonal external/competitive environment, and far more explicit attention to the nature of the business relationships and the networks of which the organization is a part. Strategic action is concerned with the efforts of actors to influence their positions within networks (Johanson and Mattsson, 1992).

Ethics and Corporate Social Responsibility

In the final two sections of this chapter we discuss two key strategic issues that will also feature later in the book as we address specific aspects of business-to-business marketing. These are ethics and corporate social responsibility, and the impact of new technology.

Laczniak and Murphy (1993: x) defined marketing ethics as '*the systematic study of how moral standards are applied to marketing decisions, behaviors, and institutions*' (emphasis in the original). A number of authors have claimed that managers generally, and marketing managers specifically, should consider ethical matters in their decision-making. Petrick and Quinn (1997: 25) put forward five reasons why 'managers need to improve ethical decision making', of which four focused on the cost risks associated with unethical conduct, and the fifth on 'the benefits of increased profitability and intrinsically desirable organizational order'. Laczniak and Murphy (1993: 5) claimed that, in the long run, the relationship between good ethics and profitability is 'most likely positive'. Schlegelmilch (1998: 8) also noted that 'some ethicists and practising managers believe that good business ethics is, in the long run, synonymous with good business', although he cited others (Hoffman and Moore, 1990) who disagreed that ethical behaviour would always be in the best economic interests of the firm. Arjoon (2000) summarized recent evidence on the association between 'corporate social performance' and 'corporate financial performance', concluding that the balance of evidence is that there is a positive relationship between the two.

Four approaches to marketing ethics are generally distinguished: managerial egoism, utilitarianism (where judgement is based on anticipated consequences), deontological ethics (judgement based on the application of rules) and virtue ethics.

Managerial egoism

The basis for egoism is the pursuit of self-interest. For present purposes we will assume that the interests of the management of the organization are aligned with the interests of the owners, so that the ethical principle underlying managerial egoism is the maximization of shareholder value. This is also the principle underlying neoclassical economics and Adam Smith's 'invisible hand' of the market. By pursuing their own self-interest within a free market system, independent and rational economic agents also maximize aggregate economic welfare. This accords with Friedman's (1979) proposition that the only responsibility of the manager is to maximize returns for the shareholder, and his observation (Friedman, 1979: 90) that 'managers lack the wisdom and ability to resolve complex social problems'. Friedman's position depends upon the existence of a framework of laws that define the 'rules of the game'. However, Palmer (2001) argued that the ability of multinational firms to affect law-making through lobbying undermines the validity of Friedman's position.

According to Schlegelmilch (1998: 18–19), Friedman's appeal to free market principles and the duty of the manager to the shareholder is today rejected by 'most scholars and most managers' because 'companies are not operating in conditions of perfect competition, managers do exercise discretion, even individual companies are powerful and managers often see a positive relationship between "enlightened self-interest" and long-term profitability.' Similarly Koslowski (2000) argued that shareholder value is not the final purpose of the firm but an instrumental end. If the firm is to pursue its many legitimate purposes, such as making products, offering employment and contributing to the community, then a sufficient return on equity is a necessary condition. Yet Barry (2001: 58) defended the contention that the market system, operating on the basis of self-interest, will produce 'the optimal supply of virtue'. He defended the proposition that the reason for the existence of a firm is to increase long-term shareholder value. Recently Doyle has developed the parallel argument that the marketing function must demonstrate a clear link between marketing activity and shareholder value if it is to retain any influence in Board-level decision-making (Doyle, 2000). The proposition that managers should desist from making moral judgements and concentrate on maximizing returns within the framework of the law has been recently supported by Gaski (1999, 2001).

Utilitarianism

Utilitarianism is the best-known form of consequentialist ethical theory. Consequentialism refers to those ethical theories that judge whether an action is right or wrong on the basis of the consequences of the action. In the case of utilitarianism, the consequences of actions are evaluated in terms of the balance between utility and disutility (or happiness and unhappiness). In choosing between alternative courses of action, someone applying utilitarianism would evaluate the likely net utility resulting from each alternative and select the action with the highest value for net utility (or the lowest value for net disutility). Laczniak and Murphy (1993) argued that utilitarianism was attractive to managers because of its similarity to the analysis of costs and benefits associated with an investment decision, and, in principle, the simple decision criterion of 'choose the option with the maximum utility'.

In practice, however, utilitarianism is far from easy to apply. How is one to compare the utilities derived by different people? What is one to do when the outcome of a utilitarian analysis conflicts with what might be regarded as a basic rule of civilized behaviour? For example, suppose that the sales executive for a medium-sized manufacturing company concludes that by lying to a customer he could win a particular order and safeguard the jobs of 25 people for the next year; the customer would be no worse off, and the competitor that would otherwise have won the contract is already operating near full capacity. A utilitarian analysis says 'lie', but most companies and professional associations have codes of conduct that explicitly state that lying is forbidden. This brings us to duty-based or deontological approaches to marketing ethics.

Deontological ethics

In contrast to the consequentialist approach of utilitarianism, deontological or duty-based approaches to ethics focus on the ethical nature of actions, rather than on the consequences of those actions. Many religious people adopt a deontological approach to ethics, based on the religious faith that they hold. For example, to Christians the Ten Commandments are a list of duties and forbidden activities that guide ethical decision-making in both everyday life and in business. However, deontological ethical systems need not be based on religious teachings. The approach proposed by Immanuel Kant has proved very influential in Western philosophy.

The duty-based approach to ethical decision-making is popular in business and marketing. Professional associations for marketing and sales managers, and large employers, typically have codes of conduct that members or employees are expected to abide by – such that serious contravention of the code of conduct would constitute grounds to be expelled from the professional association, or to be dismissed from employment. Box 4.2 provides illustrations from two professional associations (the American Marketing Association and the Chartered Institute of Marketing) and one global IT firm (Texas Instruments).

Box 4.2: *Codes of conduct*

American Marketing Association

Code of Ethics

Responsibilities of the Marketer
Marketers must accept responsibility for the consequences of their activities and make every effort to ensure that their decisions, recommendations and actions function to identify, serve and satisfy all relevant publics: customers, organizations and society.

Marketers' professional conduct must be guided by:

1. The basic rule of professional ethics: not knowingly to do harm.

2. The adherence to all applicable laws and regulations.

3. The accurate representation of their education, training and experience.

4. The active support, practice and promotion of this Code of Ethics.

Chartered Institute of Marketing

Code of Professional Standards (extract)

A member shall at all times conduct himself with integrity in such a way as to bring credit to the profession and the CIM.

A member shall promote and seek business in a professional and ethical manner.

Members shall at all times act honestly in their professional dealings.

Texas Instruments

We are honest by: representing ourselves and our intentions truthfully

- Offering full disclosure and withdrawing ourselves from discussions and decisions when our business judgment appears to be in conflict with a personal interest.
- Respecting the rights and property of others, including their intellectual property.
- Accepting confidential or trade secret information only after we clearly understand our obligations as defined in a non-disclosure agreement.

> - Competing fairly without collusion or collaboration with competitors to divide markets, set prices, restrict production, allocate customers or otherwise restrain competition.
> - Assuring that no payments or favours are offered to influence others to do something wrong.
> - Keeping records that are accurate and include all payments and receipts.
>
> *Sources*: www.marketingpower.com; www.cim.co.uk; www.ti.com.

In discussing utilitarianism we explained that a utilitarian analysis could, in principle, find that it was ethically correct for a sales or marketing executive to lie to a customer. However, it can be clearly seen from Box 4.2 that such behaviour would certainly break the code of conduct of a professional association to which the executive belonged, and may well also breach the ethical standards set down by an employer – Texas Instruments insists that its employees are always honest, for example.

Virtue ethics

The ethical theories outlined above provide, in principle, criteria that can be used to choose between alternative courses of action. By contrast, virtue ethics stresses the cultivation of virtuous principles and the pursuit of a virtuous life. The foundation of morality is said to lie in the development of good character traits as virtues (Arjoon, 2000). Virtue theory has been criticized on the grounds that it seems to provide no clear-cut rules and principles for use in ethical decision-making. This is because attention is focused on the cultivation of the virtues, from which sound ethical behaviour is expected to flow.

New Technology and Business Marketing Strategy

It is, of course, widely accepted that the new information and communications technologies that have emerged during the last three decades have had, and will continue to have, a substantial effect on marketing practice (Chaffey, 2003; Hoffman and Novak, 1996). Rather than deal with new technology as a separate and distinct aspect of marketing, we take the view in this book that it will be integrated into marketing practice, affecting various aspects of the marketing manager's job in different ways. We discuss these impacts of new technology under the various different functional aspects of marketing addressed in subsequent chapters. However, there is also an overall strategic impact of new technology, which is discussed briefly here.

There are three aspects to this overall strategic impact. First, buying organizations are using new technology extensively in their buying processes, and this affects the structure and processes of the buying centre, which in turn affects business marketing strategy. Second, the adoption of new technology is expected to influence the way in which inter-organizational relationships are formed, develop and are managed – this

Table 4.1   A classification of business-to-business e-commerce tools

	External	*Internal*
Communication orientated	*Extra-organizational*	*Intra-organizational*
	Tools that enhance communication between firms, e.g. Extranet	Tools that enhance communication within firms, e.g. Intranet
Transaction orientated	*Extra-organizational*	*Intra-organizational*
	Tools that facilitate exchange between firms, e.g. Internet, EDI	Tools that facilitate exchange within firms, e.g. Online transactions database

Source: Adapted from Osmonbekov et al., 2002.

affects relationship management strategy. Third, new technology has created new, online market forms – this affects the context within which business marketing strategy is conducted.

Table 4.1 provides a classification of e-commerce tools. The adoption of e-commerce tools alters the structure of the buying centre and the processes that take place within it (Osmonbekov et al., 2002). In general, using e-commerce tools for business procurement can be expected to lead to a smaller buying centre, involving fewer hierarchical levels and fewer functional areas but with increased participation by individual buying centre members. Within this smaller buying centre, technical personnel will tend to have greater influence owing to their mastery of the technology, but the widespread availability of improved information combined with improved opportunities for communication by various different means will tend to reduce conflict and improve coordination within the buying centre. Overall, it is to be expected that buying centre efficiency will improve, with the adoption of e-commerce tools, in terms of both cost savings and better decision-making. Marketing and sales executives will have to develop more focused marketing communications strategies, addressing the needs of a smaller set of decision-makers while recognizing that buying centre members are likely to participate more actively in the process and therefore demand more and better information. The greater influence from technical personnel means that communications messages and product benefits will have to be framed in more technical language. At the same time, buying centre members will have easy access to a wide range of emerging information sources, such as industry-specific information clearing houses and objective online third party rating services. Marketers should take account of the wider and easier access of a more technically astute buying centre to external information that may be perceived to be more 'objective' in developing marketing and selling strategies.

The Internet is the most ubiquitous of the new technological tools affecting business-to-business marketing and purchasing. Most people in developed countries are familiar with the Internet, and many have used it to make personal purchases (commonly referred to as B2C e-commerce). However, it is widely acknowledged that B2C e-commerce is dwarfed by business-to-business Internet transactions, or B2B e-commerce.

Chapter Summary

- Strategy concerns decisions that have a major effect on the performance of the firm. It can be subdivided into corporate strategy (concerning the overall design of a corporation comprising multiple business units) and business unit strategy (concerning the competitive strategies of individual businesses). Marketing strategies are devised and implemented at the business unit level.

- The overall aim of business strategy in profit-seeking firms is to increase long-term shareholder value. The key contribution that marketing strategy in business-to-business firms should make is to understand, analyze and deliver customer value. Customer value is defined as the trade-off between what a customer has to give up and what the customer receives in a business transaction or relationship.

- Three approaches to marketing strategy were discussed in the chapter: the rational planning approach, the resource-based approach, and strategy as the management of relationships and networks. The rational planning approach proposes that good strategy results from a systematic, planned approach to strategy development. The resource-based approach focuses on key internal resources of the firm as the source of enduring competitive advantage. The relationships and networks view of strategy contends that network positional resources are the key to success in business markets.

- Business strategists are increasingly convinced that sound business and marketing strategies must be built on sound ethical principles – that long-term economic performance is enhanced by ethical corporate behaviour. In addressing ethical issues in business-to-business marketing, four perspectives may be used: managerial egoism (what is best for the company), utilitarianism (evaluating the costs and benefits to all stakeholders), the deontological approach (abiding by codes of conduct), or virtue ethics (learning and applying sound judgement based on integrity).

- New technology affects many aspects of business-to-business marketing at the strategic and operational levels. The organizational buying process, the development of business-to-business relationships and the variety of market forms in business markets are all being affected by technological change.

Questions for discussion

1. How can customer value be defined?

2. What are the key differences between the resource-based view of business marketing strategy and the conventional strategic market planning approach?

3. Is the Internet completely revolutionizing business-to-business marketing and purchasing?

4. What kind of ethical issues might a business-to-business marketer or salesperson have to take into account when engaged in (a) a major account sales negotiation; (b) a substantial international market research project; and (c) bidding for a government contract in a foreign country?

5. You are a sales executive for an engineering company. Yesterday one of your clients told you – in confidence – about an important government initiative that could revolutionize their industry. Today you are hoping to close a big deal with a different client in the same industry. It is obvious that they have not heard about this government initiative yet, and if you let them in on the secret they would be impressed and it might help secure the deal. You remember that you learned about several different approaches to ethical decision-making when at Business School – how do they help you when deciding whether or not to pass on the information?

Case study: The Carbon Trust

The global environmental challenge

Strategic Approach – Manage the Impact of Climate Change

Climate change is a fact. It is happening now and it will have an impact on every business in every sector. Carbon emissions, a by-product of burning fossil fuels, are the prime cause of climate change. Around one half of the UK's carbon emissions come from the business sector. Every business has a part to play in combating climate change by reducing its carbon emissions.

Case study

The commercial implications of climate change go beyond the simple, though vital, need to reduce energy use. As the regulatory framework surrounding carbon emissions expands, this will have fundamental consequences for business performance and company valuation.

Carbon management is key. For businesses this is not only about controlling emissions, but also about understanding and managing the effects that climate change will have on their relationships with customers, shareholders and the community.

The immediate challenge, then, is to reduce your carbon emissions. The potential reward is that you will save energy and money in the short term, and that you will put your business on a sounder footing in the long term.

Source: www.carbontrust.co.uk/ceo.html.

There is now widespread awareness of the hypothesis that we are in the midst of a gradual, general increase in global temperatures – what is commonly known as 'global warming'. Although gradual in terms of normal human timescales, this increase is rapid in geological terms, and possibly unprecedented. The evidence seems to be consistent with the theory that the current rise in global temperatures has been substantially caused by human activity. In particular, the last two centuries have seen human beings consuming carbon-based energy (particularly coal and oil) in very large quantities. What is undeniable is that human consumption of coal and oil results in the production of large quantities of carbon dioxide. What is more controversial is the hypothesis that the release of all of this carbon dioxide into the Earth's atmosphere has been the principal cause of global warming during the last two centuries.

Nevertheless, the scientific consensus is that humankind bears direct responsibility for a large part of global warming. The implications of this are difficult to predict, and vary from the mildly alarming to the catastrophic. The scientific consensus is also that there is massive inertia in the Earth's climatic system, so that whatever we do now will only gradually begin to undo the damage wrought by the last two centuries of burning carbon. Glaciers and possibly polar icecaps will continue to melt, sea levels will continue to rise, low-lying land will be flooded, and the incidence of severe weather events will increase over the next few decades, regardless of what we do now. But if we do nothing, and the burning of carbon fuels continues to increase relentlessly, then the consequences will eventually be far worse.

The British Government is a signatory to the United Nations Framework Convention on Climate Change (signed at the Rio Earth Summit in 1992) and has agreed to legally binding emission reduction targets by ratifying the Kyoto Protocol of 1997. The Carbon Trust is an independent company that was set up by the government to help to put into practice Britain's obligations under the Kyoto Protocol. The Carbon Trust offers impartial advice to businesses to help them cut carbon emissions and capture the potential of low carbon technologies. Funding is provided from governmental sources – the Department for Environment, Food and Rural Affairs, the Scottish Executive, the National Assembly for Wales and Invest NI. In January 2005 The Carbon Trust launched a high-profile, integrated marketing communications campaign to raise awareness among businesses about how they can play a role in combating climate change and what the benefits would be.

Key features of the global climate change challenge

- Recent temperatures are warmer than any since direct measurements began. All of the 10 warmest years on record have occurred since 1990. Recent years are probably the warmest seen for more than 100,000 years.
- Mountain glaciers are in retreat. The Arctic ice cap is shrinking. The Larsen Ice Shelf in Antarctica is breaking up.
- Many areas of the world have seen fewer long cold spells of weather and more long hot spells.
- Insurance data shows that losses from catastrophic weather events have risen globally by a factor of 10 since the 1950s, after accounting for inflation.
- The most respected estimates suggest that global temperature will rise by 1.5–5.8 degrees Celsius by the end of the century.
- Many species of plants and animals will die out because their eco-systems will be disrupted; possibly as many as a quarter of the world's known species.
- We can expect more intense tropical cyclones, intensified droughts and floods associated with El Niño in the Pacific, and greater variability of the Asian summer monsoon.

The responsibility of business

Is the responsibility of private businesses solely to maximize the returns they make for their owners, the shareholders, or do they have a wider responsibility to society? Many people – the most prominent in recent years has been the eminent late American economist Milton Friedman – have argued that the sole objective of a private enterprise should be to maximize shareholder value. Others have argued that businesses are an integral part of wider society and must contribute, as responsible corporate citizens, to the wider aims of that society.

One enduring line of argument in this debate is whether there is any contradiction between shareholder value maximization and making a contribution to wider society. Might it not be the case that those businesses that cultivate socially responsible strategies are also the most profitable? There is no simple answer to this question. When a company gets caught out in unethical practice, and sees its brand equity and share price damaged as a result of public disapproval, it seems obvious that ethical practice is closely related to profitability. But we cannot know how many companies have quietly got away with unethical practices and enhanced their profits as a result. The few, high-profile cases of companies that are caught out may represent proof that unethical behaviour (like crime) 'doesn't pay', or they may simply indicate that most unethical companies 'get away with it'.

In the case of reducing human consumption of carbon-based energy, appeals can be made both to profitability/shareholder value and to good corporate citizenship. The case can be made that reducing the use of carbon-based fuels is good business sense. If a company can reduce its use of fuel without any adverse effect at all on its business operations, then this argument is a powerful one. So the simple message of increased energy efficiency (turning off lights and heaters when they are not needed, closing windows to avoid heat loss, and so on) is a good starting point. This is a clear-cut case, since there is little or no expenditure associated with the cost savings. Going beyond this to change business processes in order to increase energy efficiency requires greater justification. For example, improving building insulation or replacing the ageing business vehicle fleet with newer, more fuel-efficient replacements involves an investment in order to reap the energy-saving reward. The Carbon Trust can facilitate the analysis of such decisions, and point to any government initiatives that might provide financial incentives and so sway the decision in favour of energy efficiency, but ultimately this boils down to a private investment decision, which the company must decide is profitable or not. Conventionally, however, a company will only include the *private* costs and benefits of the decision in its investment appraisal. Once a company goes beyond this and includes an allowance for the wider impact of its decision, then it is adopting the message of corporate social responsibility. For example, should the company decide to replace its ageing fleet of vans sooner than expected (and despite an unfavourable investment appraisal) because of the damage that the emissions from their old and unsophisticated engines are doing to the environment, then it is engaging in an act of corporate social responsibility.

Only when a business forgoes a preferred alternative and consciously chooses an ethical but less profitable alternative can it be said to be pursuing corporate social responsibility. In the case of carbon emissions, this means taking action to reduce emissions even though an alternative course of action would be more profitable. The job of the Carbon Trust is not only to persuade businesses to do things that they really ought to do anyway in order to improve their profits (like cut energy running costs and make profitable investments in energy saving technology) but to persuade them to go beyond this and make investments for the good of the planet.

Case study questions

This exercise is best done as a debate, with one team being allocated to each side of the argument.

1. Make the case for the proposition that the only legitimate purpose for a commercial business in a free enterprise system is to maximize the returns to shareholders. What is the role of the Carbon Trust from this point of view?
2. Make the alternative case that all business organizations have a wider social responsibility that goes beyond the pursuit of shareholder value. What is the role of the Carbon Trust from this point of view?
3. On which side of the argument do your sympathies mainly lie? Explain why.

Sources: Carbon Trust, 2004; www.carbontrust.co.uk; Turner, 2003.

References

Anderson, J.C. and Narus, J.A. (1999) *Business Market Management: Understanding, Creating, and Delivering Value*. Upper Saddle River, NJ: Prentice-Hall.

Ansoff, H.I. (1965) *Corporate Strategy*. New York: McGraw-Hill.

Arjoon, S. (2000) 'Virtue theory as a dynamic theory of business', *Journal of Business Ethics*, 28: 159–78.

Baker, M.J. (1992) *Marketing Strategy and Management*. Basingstoke: Macmillan.

Barney, J.B. (1991) 'Firm resources and sustained competitive advantage', *Journal of Management*, 17 (1): 99–120.

Barney, J.B. (2001) 'Is the resource-based "view" a useful perspective for strategic management research? Yes', *Academy of Management Review*, 26 (1): 41–56.

Barry, N. (2001) *Ethics, Conventions and Capitalism*. London: Institute of Economic Affairs.

Blaug, M. (ed.) (1992) *Carl Menger (1840–1921)*. Aldershot: Edward Elgar.

Blaug, M. (1997) *Economic Theory in Retrospect*. Cambridge: Cambridge University Press.

Blois, K. (2003) 'Using value equations to analyse exchanges', *Marketing Intelligence and Planning*, 21 (1): 16–22.

Buzzell, R.D. and Gale, B.T. (1987) *The PIMS Principles: Linking Strategy to Performance*. New York: Free Press.

Carbon Trust (2004) *The Climate Change Challenge 1: Scientific Evidence and implications*. London: Carbon Trust.

Chaffey, D. (2003) *E-business and E-commerce*. London: FT/Prentice Hall.

Christopher, M. (1996) 'From brand values to customer value', *Journal of Marketing Practice: Applied Marketing Science*, 2 (1): 55–66.

Desarbo, W.S., Jedidi, K. and Sinha, I. (2001) 'Customer value analysis in a heterogeneous market', *Strategic Management Journal*, 22: 845–57.

Doyle, P. (2000) *Value-Based Marketing*. Chichester: Wiley.

Flint, D.J. and Woodruff, R.B. (2001) 'The initiators of changes in customers' desired value', *Industrial Marketing Management*, 30: 321–37.

Ford, D., Gadde, L.E., Håkansson, H. and Snehota, I. (2003) *Managing Business Relationships* (2nd edn). Chichester: Wiley.

Friedman, M. (1979) 'The social responsibility of business is to increase profit', in T.L. Beauchamp and N. Bowie (eds), *Ethical Theory and Business*. Englewood Cliffs: Prentice Hall.

Gaski, J.F. (1999) 'Does marketing ethics really have anything to say? A critical inventory of the literature', *Journal of Business Ethics*, 18: 315–34.

Gaski, J.F. (2001) 'Normative marketing ethics redux, incorporating a reply to smith', *Journal of Business Ethics*, 32: 19–34.

Gassenheimer, J.B., Houston, F.S. and Davis, J.C. (1998) 'The role of economic value, social value, and perceptions of fairness in interorganizational relationship retention decisions', *Journal of the Academy of Marketing Science*, 26 (4): 322–37.

Gigerenzer, G. and Selten, R. (eds) (2001) *Bounded Rationality*. Cambridge, MA: MIT Press.

Håkansson, H. and Snehota, I. (1989) 'No business is an island: the network concept of business strategy', *Scandinavian Journal of Management*, 4 (3): 187–200.

Hoffman, M.W. and Moore, J.M. (1990) *Business Ethics*. New York: McGraw Hill.

Hoffman, D.L. and Novak, T.P. (1996) 'Marketing in hypermedia computer-mediated environments: conceptual foundations', *Journal of Marketing*, 60 (July): 50–68.

Jain, S.C. (2000) *Marketing Planning and Strategy* (6th edn). Cincinnati: South-Western College Publishing.

Johanson, J. and Mattsson, L.G. (1992) 'Network positions and strategic action – an analytical framework', in B. Axelsson and G. Easton (eds), *Industrial Networks: A New View of Reality*. London: Routledge. pp. 205–17.

Koslowski, P. (2000) 'The limits of shareholder value', *Journal of Business Ethics*, 27: 137–48.

Kothandaraman, P. and Wilson, D.T. (2001) 'The future of competition: value-creating networks', *Industrial Marketing Management*, 30: 379–89.

Laczniak, G.R. and Murphy, P.E. (1993) *Ethical Marketing Decisions: The Higher Road*. New Jersey: Prentice Hall.

Lambin, J.J. (1997) *Strategic Marketing Management*. Maidenhead: McGraw-Hill.

Lapierre, J. (2000) 'Customer-perceived value in industrial contexts', *Journal of Business & Industrial Marketing*, 15(2/3): 122–40.

McDonald, M. (1996) 'Strategic marketing planning: theory, practice and research agendas', *Journal of Marketing Management*, 5 (1): 5–27.

McDougall, D., Wyner, G. and Vazdauskas, D. (1997) 'Customer valuation as a foundation for growth', *Managing Service Quality*, 7 (1): 5–11.

Mintzberg, H. (1973) *The Nature of Managerial Work*. New York: Harper & Row.

Mintzberg, H. (1976) 'Planning on the left side and managing on the right', *Harvard Business Review*, 54 (July–August): 49–58.

Mintzberg, H., Ahlstrand, B. and Lampel, J. (1998) *Strategy Safari*. London: FT/Prentice Hall.

Osmonbekov, T., Bello, D.C. and Gilliland, D.I. (2002) 'Adoption of electronic commerce tools in business procurement: enhanced buying center structure and processes', *Journal of Business & Industrial Marketing*, 17 (2/3): 151–66.

Palmer, E. (2001) 'Multinational corporations and the social contract', *Journal of Business Ethics*, 31: 245–58.

Parasuraman, A. (1997) 'Reflections on gaining competitive advantage through customer value', *Journal of the Academy of Marketing Science*, 25 (2): 154–61.

Petrick, J.A. and Quinn, J.F. (1997) *Management Ethics: Integrity at Work*. Thousand Oaks, CA: Sage.

Porter, M.E. (1980) *Competitive Strategy: Techniques for Analyzing Industries and Competitors*. New York: Free Press.

Porter, M.E. (1985) *Competitive Advantage: Creating and Sustaining Superior Performance*. New York: Free Press.

Priem, R.L. and Butler, J. (2001) 'Is the resource-based "view" a useful perspective for strategic management research?', *Academy of Management Review*, 26 (1): 22–40.

Ravald, A. and Grönroos, C. (1996) 'The value concept and relationship marketing', *European Journal of Marketing*, 30 (2): 19–30.

Reddy, N.M. (1991) 'Defining product value in industrial markets', *Management Decisions*, 29 (1): 14–19.

Reichheld, F.F. (1996) *The Loyalty Effect: The Hidden Force Behind Growth, Profits, and Lasting Value*. Boston, MA: Harvard Business School Press.

Rust, R.T., Zeithaml, V.A. and Lemon, K.N. (2000) *Driving Customer Equity: How Customer Lifetime Value is Reshaping Corporate Strategy*. New York: The Free Press.

Schlegelmilch, B. (1998) *Marketing Ethics: An International Perspective*. London: International Thompson Business Press.

Simon, H.A. (1960) *The New Science of Management Decision*. Englewood Cliffs, NJ: Prentice-Hall.

Turner, A. (2003) *The Inaugural Carbon Trust Lecture* (public lecture). London: Carbon Trust.

Ulaga, W. (2001) 'Customer value in business markets', *Industrial Marketing Management*, 30: 315–19.

Viner, J. (1925) 'The utility concept in value theory and its critics', *The Journal of Political Economy*, 33 (4): 369–87.

Walter, A., Ritter, T. and Gemunden, H.G. (2001) 'Value creation in buyer–seller relationships', *Industrial Marketing Management*, 30: 365–77.

Woodruff, R.B. (1997) 'Customer value: the next source for competitive advantage', *Journal of the Academy of Madrketing Science*, 25 (2): 139–53.

Woodruff, R.B. and Gardial, S.F. (1996) *Know Your Customer: New Approaches to Understanding Customer Value and Satisfaction*. Cambridge, MA: Blackwell.

Zeithaml, V.A. (1988) 'Consumer perceptions of price, quality, and value: a means–end model and synthesis of evidence', *Journal of Marketing*, 52: 2–22.

5 Researching Business-to-Business Markets

Learning outcomes

After reading this chapter you will:

- be able to explain why accuracy, timeliness, relevance and uniqueness are valuable characteristics of marketing information;
- understand how the fundamental characteristics of business-to-business markets affect the market research process;
- know how to apply market research sampling techniques in business markets;
- know why survey response rates tend to be low in business-to-business market surveys, and what techniques can be used to improve response rates;
- be able to use a standard industrial classification as a basis for sample selection in business markets; and
- understand how the relationship between a market research agency and a business-to-business client organization can affect the success of a research project.

Introduction

In the preceding three chapters we have looked at how organizations buy, at how inter-firm relationships are becoming ever more important in business markets, and we have examined key aspects of strategy in business markets, in particular how business marketers must deliver superior value to customers. In general terms it is clear that business marketers must be concerned with questions such as:

- What are the buying criteria and buying processes of customers and potential customers?

- How important are inter-firm relationships in their target markets?
- What are the strategic plans, positioning strategies and target markets of those customers with whom they seek to develop partnering relationships?
- How do customers and potential customers define value?

The only way to answer these (and many other) questions for specific markets and specific customers is to undertake market research. In the next chapter of the book we will address market segmentation in business markets, after which, in the succeeding chapters, we will look in more detail at the development of specific marketing plans – planning for integrated marketing communications, for effective distribution and logistics, for competitive pricing, and so on. All of these chapters also raise new research problems that require the application of systematic marketing research. Two examples of the use of systematic marketing research to cast light on important issues in business marketing are provided in Box 5.1; these examples deal with research concerning the size of the buying centre, and with appropriate techniques for industrial market segmentation.

Box 5.1   *Practical research in B2B markets*

The Buying Centre

In an American study (McWilliams et al., 1992) 440 questionnaires were sent to purchasing agents in 18 firms; 231 usable questionnaires were returned, for a response rate of 52 per cent. The study concerned the purchasing decision for component parts. The variables measured using the questionnaire were buying centre size, purchase situation (new buy, modified re-buy, straight re-buy) and purchase phase (need identification, establishment of specifications, identification and evaluation of buying alternatives, supplier selection). The study found that the mean size of the buying centre was four people, with a normal range of between three and five. The buying centre tended to be largest for new-buy purchasing situations and smallest for straight re-buys, with modified re-buys lying in between. The buying centre was smallest for the final stage of the buying process (supplier selection), and largest for the identification and evaluation of buying alternatives.

Market segmentation

In a study of the British car parts market (Dibb and Simkin, 1994) data were collected from 201 garages and retailers on every aspect of their supplier needs. The current segmentation methods used in the industry were studied and statistical analysis was used to generate a new approach to segmentation that was then evaluated for its usefulness to managers. Conventionally, car parts installers have been segmented into five types – specialist repairers, vehicle manufacturers' agents, retailers, menu/fast-fit and independent garages. If these installer types are true market segments then we would expect the members of each category to have similar buying needs (low within–group variability) and we would expect to see significant differences in buying needs between the installer types (high between–group variability). This proved not to be the case – the buyers in each installer category did not have relatively homogeneous needs. A new market segmentation method was created using the statistical technique of cluster analysis, revealing that there were seven distinct clusters or segments in this market.

The Value of Marketing Information

It seemed to me that too many people were accepting at face value, uncritically, the idea that information was becoming the most valuable commodity. Information was at the library. Anybody could check it out for nothing. Didn't that accessibility undermine its value? And information could be wrong, in which case it might have negative value – it might hurt instead of help. Even when the information that bombarded us every day proved to be correct, most of it was irrelevant anyway. And when information was relevant, its value was often ephemeral, decaying with the passage of time or if too many people had it. (Gates: 1996: 22)

Bill Gates, the founder of Microsoft, points out that accuracy, timeliness, relevance and uniqueness are important characteristics of information. In a world in which new media have made more and more information available ever more easily to businesses and consumers, this is perhaps a useful reminder. Few would doubt that the information generated through market research is important to marketing success. Baker and Hart (1989) and Hooley and Jobber (1986) have shown that the use of market research information is associated with above-average corporate performance. Baker and Hart (1989) found that companies that perform better than average are significantly more likely to gather market research than companies that perform below average – 52 per cent of above-average firms in their study conducted in-house market research (compared with 31 per cent of below-average companies), and 69 per cent of above-average companies used external market research agencies (compared with 47 per cent of below-average companies). Hooley and Jobber found that top-performing companies were significantly more likely than other companies to make use of a range of market research techniques. Baker and Hart's study showed that greater use of market research was a characteristic of better-performing firms, but did not differentiate between industrial and consumer marketing organizations. Hooley and Jobber identified industrial firms separately from consumer firms in their mail survey. They found that industrial firms were less likely to conduct market research than consumer firms (52 per cent of industrial firms, compared to 73 per cent of consumer firms) but that top-performing industrial firms were significantly more likely to conduct research than average-performing firms. They concluded that top-performing business-to-business firms have a strongly proactive approach to planning, put greater emphasis on product differentiation than average performers and demonstrate a strong commitment to customer orientation through above-average use of formal, objective market research. There is a positive statistical association between business-to-business firm performance and the use of formal, objective market research. This does not *prove* that greater use of formal market research causes improved business performance, since a statistical association alone cannot prove that one thing causes another. However, it does lend support to the hypothesis that one of the factors driving improved performance for business-to-business organizations is the use of formal market research.

Much attention in marketing research is paid to technical aspects, such as how to design measurement instruments, particularly questionnaires, and techniques for analysing data. These factors are very largely concerned with ensuring that information is accurate, while the other important factors mentioned by Bill Gates – timeliness, uniqueness and, perhaps most important of all, relevance – tend to be neglected. Of these factors, timeliness and relevance, and perhaps uniqueness to a degree, will depend largely on the effective management of the marketing research process. Getting 'accurate' (valid, reliable) data is largely a technical matter. Getting the 'right' (relevant) information, at the 'right time', is a managerial matter. Where marketing research is conducted by a specialist agency on behalf of a client organization, this managerial matter becomes one of so managing the relationship between the client and the agency as to maximize the likelihood of getting the right information, at the right time, and on budget.

Newman (1962: 106) argued that improvements in data gathering and analysis, laudable though they may be, did not address the important question of 'how to get the results of marketing research more into the decision-making act', while Andreasen (1985) suggested that poor communication and understanding between the researcher and the client are often at the root of disappointing research results. Moorman et al. (1992) reiterated the argument that the use of information is a topic deserving of greater attention since, as our technologies for gathering and disseminating information grow ever more sophisticated, it is through the effective use of this wealth of information that firms will gain a competitive edge.

In this chapter we will address the issues of accuracy, timeliness, relevance and uniqueness in the context of business-to-business market research. In the next section we return to a theme of Chapter 1 – the differences between consumer and business markets – and assess the implications of these differences for market research. Following this, we address issues affecting information accuracy, by looking at the pros and cons of different approaches to sampling, examining different survey techniques, and investigating the differences between qualitative and quantitative data gathering. We also introduce the concept of the standard industrial classification as a basic tool for business-to-business market research – subsequently, in Chapter 6, we will see how the standard industrial classification can be used for purposes of market segmentation. Having discussed these fairly technical issues associated primarily with data accuracy, we move on to look at the management of the market research process, and in particular the management of the relationship between the business-to-business client and their market research agency, to see how market research projects can be managed for data timeliness, relevance and uniqueness. In the closing section of the chapter we consider the impact of the Internet on business-to-business market research.

Market Research and the Nature of Business Markets

While there are many similarities between market research in business markets and consumer markets – for example, the statistical principles of sampling and the basics of sound questionnaire design remain the same – the characteristics of business markets introduce some differences. Of particular relevance are the following three aspects of business markets, which were discussed in Chapter 1:

- derived demand;
- accelerator effect; and
- concentration ratios.

You will remember that we define demand in business markets as 'derived demand', because organizations buy goods and services in order to pursue business goals and not for any intrinsic satisfaction to be derived from consumption. The accelerator effect occurs in capital goods industries, where relatively small changes in downstream demand can bring about much larger changes in the demand for investment goods. High concentration ratios are characteristic of business markets – meaning that only a few buying organizations make up a large proportion of the total buying power in an industry.

Because of derived demand, business marketing organizations cannot simply focus on their immediate customers but may also need to be aware of factors affecting demand further downstream. For example, a manufacturer of plastics that are used in the automobile and aerospace industries will try to keep abreast of developments in business and consumer demand for vehicles and for air travel, rather than simply looking at the immediate pattern of demand from automobile and aircraft manufacturers. This will provide a longer-term view of likely developments in the plastics market. The need to be aware of downstream patterns of demand is even more important where an accelerator effect is present, since a shift in downstream demand will have a multiplied effect on demand for capital goods. For example, the illustration used in Chapter 1 showed how a 20 per cent increase in demand for new houses could increase demand for construction equipment used in the house-building industry by 100 per cent in the short term. In general, business-to-business marketing organizations will rely on secondary sources of market research for purposes of keeping up to date with trends in markets that are downstream of their immediate customers. Primary market research would be too time-consuming and expensive. This tends to make secondary market research (that is, the use of existing data sources) particularly important to business marketers.

High concentration ratios affect market research in a different way. First, when conducting a primary market research project in an industry with a high concentration ratio it is important to include the 'vital few' buying organizations that constitute a high proportion of industry demand. Second, a few key buying personnel in those 'vital few' organizations are likely to receive a lot of requests to provide market research information. This tends to affect adversely the response rate to market research surveys, or to requests for market research interviews. As a result – as we will see later in the chapter – response rates to business-to-business market research surveys are often disappointingly low.

Research Fundamentals in Business-to-Business Markets

Sampling and sampling frames

The fundamentals of sampling theory are the same no matter what kind of market one is dealing with, and the statistical accuracy of estimates based on sample parameters is the same whether they are business-to-business or consumer markets. However, certain sampling techniques, not commonly used in consumer marketing, are used more frequently in business-to-business markets because of the structure of such markets, in particular because the relevant population is usually fairly small and some members of the population are much more important than others in terms of their buying power.

Table 5.1 shows the sampling techniques available for marketing surveys. A sample is a portion or subset of a larger group called a population. The population is the universe that is being sampled. In business-to-business marketing the population might include all business organizations in a particular country (for example, if one was conducting a national survey of business usage of mobile telephony) but more often would comprise all the organizations in a particular sector of the economy (such as 'all manufacturing industry', or 'all educational establishments'), or only those organizations in a particular industry (for example, providers of commercial cleaning services) or geographical area (all business within the boundaries of a specific city, county, or province, for example). In general, the aim of sampling

Table 5.1 Sampling methods

Probability sampling	*Non-probability sampling*
Simple random sampling	Convenience sampling
Stratified random sampling	Snowball sampling
Systematic sampling	Quota sampling
Cluster/multi-stage sampling	Focus groups

is to obtain a representative sample, meaning a sample that reflects the overall population in terms of important characteristics. For example, in taking a sample of 1000 businesses for a national survey of business use of mobile telephones, the size and industry distributions of firms in the sample should reflect the characteristics of the national economy – if 25 per cent of firms in the economy operate in the manufacturing sector, then around 250 of the firms in the sample should be in manufacturing.

In probability sampling, every member of the target population has a known, non-zero probability of being included in the sample. Probability sampling involves the selection of sampling units from a sampling frame. The sampling frame is a list of the units (such as firms, managers, or industry associations) that are eligible to be included in the survey. Ideally, the sampling frame should be a complete list of all of the members of the relevant population. Good sampling frames, including very nearly all members of the relevant population, are quite easy to find for business markets in developed countries. Commercial information providers, such as Dun & Bradstreet, make it their business to maintain databases of firms that are as complete and accurate as possible. In simple random sampling, every unit within the sampling frame has an equal chance of being selected for the sample. The difficulty with this method is that there is no guarantee that the sample will be representative; the sample may, by chance, contain a higher percentage of one kind of business organization than is found in the sampling frame and in the population. To avoid this problem stratified random sampling is often used, where the population and sampling frame are divided up into meaningful groups or 'strata' and then samples are taken from each of the strata according to their representation in the population. For example, company size and industry sector are typical strata in business-to-business sampling.

Table 5.2 shows how stratified random sampling is applied. A sample of 10,000 firms is to be taken. The sample is stratified using company size and industry sector. The proportions with which those strata are represented in the population are shown in the table. In order to calculate the subsample size in each cell of Table 5.2, it is necessary to multiply the column proportion by the row proportion, and multiply the result by the desired sample

Table 5.2 Illustrating stratified random sampling

		Company size categories			
	Proportion in population (%)	1–9 employees (%) 85	10–99 employees (%) 10	100 or more employees (%) 5	Total (%) 100
Primary industries	5	425	50	25	500
Manufacturing industries	25	2125	250	125	2500
Service industries	70	5950	700	350	7000
Total	100	8500	1000	500	10,000

size (in this case 10,000). So the desired subsample size for medium-sized firms (10 per cent) from the manufacturing industries (25 per cent) is:

$$10\% \times 25\% \times 10,000$$

or

$$0.1 \times 0.25 \times 10,000$$

which equals 250, as shown in the table.

Systematic sampling can also be used as an alternative to simple random sampling. Suppose that we want to take a sample of size 400 from a single industry sector; we have a list of all of the firms in the industry, of which there are 3600. We need a sample of one-ninth of the firms (400 divided by 3600). To obtain this we need a random starting number between 1 and 9; let us say that through a random process (even as simple as pulling numbers out of a hat) we get the starting number 2. Our sample will then comprise the firms in the list in places 2, 11, 20, 29, 38, and so on. This method can only be used when we are sure that there is no systematic variation within the sampling frame.

The final approach to probability sampling is cluster sampling. This can be used where there are naturally occurring units in the population. Naturally occurring units include such things as firms, trade associations, factories, schools and departments within firms. For example, if we wish to investigate the use of mobiles phones by sales executives in the IT industry, we could choose to select a random sample of sales *departments* (rather than a random sample of sales executives) and then conduct a survey with all of the members of the selected departments. The main advantage of this sampling technique over other probability sampling methods is its convenience. It would be difficult to obtain an accurate list of all of the sales executives in a geographical area in order to take a simple random sample; it is easier to get a list of all of the IT companies.

The main distinction when non-probability sampling is used is that the units in the population do not have a known, non-zero probability of being selected for the sample. Non-probability sampling may be used either with the aim of consciously building a representative sample, for reasons of convenience, or because in the researcher's judgement some units in the population *must* be included in the sample.

A convenience sample is simply a group of respondents who are ready and available to complete the survey. For example, a building supplies company may ask customers (generally, the owner-managers of small building firms) as they leave the premises to complete a customer satisfaction survey. Such a survey has limited validity.

In snowball sampling, the researcher relies on previously identified members of the target population to identify other sample members. Such an approach might be used in researching the organizational buying DMU, for example. Remember, from Chapter 2, that membership of the DMU is not strictly defined and is often not aligned with a particular organizational department or unit. It is quite likely that the only people who really know who was involved in a major buying decision are the members of the DMU. Once you have identified one member of the DMU (such as the purchasing executive who coordinated their efforts) you can ask this person to identify other members, who in turn may point you in the direction of further people who were also involved (remembering, also, that the DMU can extend to people outside of the buying organization).

Quota sampling divides the relevant population into subgroups, such as manufacturing and service firms, and small, medium and large firms. As with stratified random sampling, the proportions of these categories in the population are used to define their proportions in the sample – the sample size for each category is simply the desired overall sample size multiplied by its proportion in the population. The key difference with quota sampling is that the members of each subsample are not selected randomly.

Finally, focus groups represent a form of non-probability sampling that is often used for purposes of exploratory market research. Suppose that the Carbon Trust (see Chapter 4), in pursuing its mission to improve energy efficiency and reduce carbon emissions in British industry, wants to conduct a large-scale survey of the reasons why firms do not develop and implement energy efficiency plans. Unless similar research has been conducted before, it is difficult to see how one could begin to construct a meaningful questionnaire. There are so many possible reasons why firms may not seek to become more energy efficient (general inertia, energy costs being an insignificant part of the budget, it not being seen as a managerial priority, fear that it would involve high start-up costs, and so on) that one cannot know a priori which are genuinely relevant to business attitudes. Focus group discussions – that is, discussions with small groups (6–10 people) guided by a professional facilitator – with executives who are responsible for energy management are a way of establishing the genuine concerns of the relevant target population. The data (generally qualitative) gathered through focus groups can be very useful in itself. Often, once the key issues have been clarified through the use of focus groups a questionnaire will be developed for administration to a much larger sample in order to generate statistically valid, quantitative results.

Response rates

The purpose and logic of sampling are straightforward. A sample is designed to be representative of the target population, so that results achieved for the sample can be generalized (within known statistical limits) to the whole population. An ideal example is a miniature version of the population. However, even assuming that the sample is selected sufficiently well that it is indeed representative of the population, there is no guarantee that the effective sample of those who actually respond to the survey will conform to the original sample. The two issues that arise here are, first, what is the response rate from those who are selected for the sample and, second, are those who respond representative of the whole sample (and so of the population)? For example, if we send a questionnaire to 500 firms in the manufacturing industry and receive 113 usable replies, then we have a response rate of 22.6 per cent. How certain can we be that the 113 firms that replied are representative of the 500 firms in the original survey, and hence of the overall population of manufacturing businesses?

The first practical consideration associated with non-response in surveys is the effect on important subsamples. Suppose that we wish to investigate differences between large firms and small firms, and between firms from the north and those from the south of the country. With our original sample size of 500, subdividing the sample into four categories (large/north, small/ north, large/south, small/south) would result in around 125 firms in each category (assuming for simplicity that there is an equal number of large and small firms, and an equal number of firms in the north and in the south). With our effective sample size of 113, then we would expect to have around 28 firms in each category. If we make statements such as '60 per cent of small manufacturing firms in the north want … ', then it is important to remember that the statement is not based on a sample of 113, but on a much smaller subsample. It is important, therefore, to take account of the expected response rate to a survey at the planning stage of a market research survey.

There is considerable evidence that response rates in business-to-business market surveys are low and falling (Diamantopoulos and Schlegelmilch, 1996; Faria and Dickinson, 1992; Greer and Lohtia, 1994). Diamantopoulos and Schlegelmilch (1996: 505, emphasis in original) said that: 'Undoubtedly, the most serious problem of the mail questionnaire is that of *non-response*, as it has implications for both the quality and quantity of the data obtained.' The problem of relatively low rates of response to industrial marketing surveys is not a new one; Stacey and Wilson (1969) suggested a typical response rate of 25 per cent to industrial surveys in the 1960s, while Rawnsley (1978) quoted response rates of between 12 per cent and 29 per cent during the 1970s. Clearly, business-to-business market researchers must strive to maximize the response rate.

Most of the research into improving survey response rates has concerned postal surveys. Diamantopoulos and Schlegelmilch (1996) investigated the criteria that affected response rates in business-to-business postal surveys. They concluded that there are eight main aspects that affect the response rate: survey sponsorship, the covering letter, the questionnaire, anonymity/confidentiality, contacts, postage, monetary incentives and non-monetary incentives.

- *Survey sponsorship:* Sponsorship by, or approval from, an organization with which the respondents are likely to feel some sympathy (such as a relevant trade association) is likely to increase the response rate; response rates tend to be higher when the survey is on behalf of a non-profit organization.
- *The covering letter:* An individually typed or printed covering letter, with a handwritten signature, is likely to improve the response rate over a standard photocopied covering letter. The covering letter should aim to appeal to the respondent on egoistic grounds (emphasizing the expertise of the respondent), social utility grounds (emphasizing the importance of the research) and altruistic grounds (emphasizing that the research project can only be completed with the cooperation of the respondent). It is not recommended that the respondent should be given a deadline for return of the completed questionnaire, since this could be perceived as an unreasonable demand on their time.
- *The questionnaire:* The questionnaire itself seems to be the most important factor affecting the response rate. The response rate will be higher where the topic is of interest to the respondent but lower where the respondent has to actively search for the requested information. A shorter questionnaire will, all other things being equal, attract a higher response rate than a longer questionnaire. Presenting questions in a format that makes them easy to answer – such as brief questions with pre-coded response alternatives – will improve response. On the other hand, the colour of paper used for the questionnaire seems not to affect the response rate! (Greer and Lohtia, 1994)
- *Anonymity/confidentiality:* Questionnaires may be anonymous, so that it is not possible to identify the respondent or the company to which they belong. Questionnaires may also be confidential, meaning that the information contained in any single questionnaire will never be revealed to anyone else by the researcher; usually this means that the researcher will only use the aggregated data from all of the respondents and will not

report data from single questionnaires alone. Both anonymity and confi-
dentiality are considered to improve the likely response rate. The promise
of anonymity/confidentiality should be included in the covering letter,
and the questionnaire should include a minimum of identification information (a questionnaire code number may be necessary to allow the
researcher to identify who has not responded in order to send a follow-
up request or to conduct non-response analysis).

- *Contacts:* It is generally felt that telephone pre-notification (that is, calling
  the respondents to tell them to expect a questionnaire) improves the
  response rate. Pre-notification by letter does not improve response. In
  terms of survey timing, the main advice is to avoid known holiday
  periods – for example, in Western Europe July/August is a traditional
  holiday period and survey response rates may be depressed at this time.
  Follow-up contact with recipients who have not yet returned their questionnaire is considered to be a good way of improving the overall
  response rate.
- *Postage:* The main advice here is to supply a stamped addressed envelope
  of the correct size in which the respondent can return the questionnaire.
- *Monetary incentives:* Monetary incentives for respondents are not commonly used in business-to-business market research surveys. There is
  evidence that monetary incentives can improve response rates in consumer surveys. However, in the business-to-business field there is insufficient evidence to support the use of monetary incentives to boost
  response rates and the consensus is that they are unnecessary.
- *Non-monetary incentives:* Wherever possible, respondents should be
  offered a summary of the study's results. This is the only incentive that
  appears to improve the response rate in business-to-business surveys and
  supports the idea that managers are more likely to respond to a questionnaire when it deals with a topic that they find intrinsically interesting.

Standard Industrial Classification

A standard industrial classification is a systematic method of classifying economic activity. In everyday language it is usually sufficient to talk about 'the
tourism industry' or 'the banking industry', but for the purposes of marketing
research and marketing planning it is important to have clearly agreed definitions of precisely what is included and what is excluded from a definition
of an industry. Fortunately governments – for their own purposes – have
constructed precise classification systems for economic activity. The original
purpose of these standard industrial classifications was to enable governments to gather consistent data about the amount and the growth rate of
economic activity in a country. Such information is essential to the conduct of
government economic and industrial policies. Governments need to know

which industries are growing, which are stagnant and which are declining. Originally, the use of standard industrial classification data for marketing purposes was a by-product of this essential government tool. Today, standard industrial classifications are as useful to industry as they are to governments.

For most everyday purposes it is perfectly acceptable to talk about 'the car industry' or 'the chemical industry'. In a normal conversation we do not normally need to be any more specific than that. However, it is certainly not good enough for market research purposes. If a client asks a researcher to study the growth rate of the car industry, and to profile the key firms in the industry, then the researcher will immediately set about refining the definition of the industry.

> 'So, when you say the car industry, do you just mean manufacturers of automobiles, or would you include such things as trucks and buses ... what about construction equipment like backhoe diggers? Is it only the vehicle manufacturers that are of interest, or are you interested in the suppliers of automotive components as well, like exhaust systems, instrument clusters and tyres? Would you say that car repair firms should be included, or not?'

And so might the conversation continue. The answers to these questions will depend upon exactly what it is that the client is trying to find out. If the objective is to establish the potential of the UK original equipment market for fuel injection systems for use in passenger cars, then the car industry will be defined quite narrowly as those very few firms that actually assemble passenger cars in the UK. But fuel injection systems can also be sold to firms supplying engines to car manufacturers and to car repair shops operating in the after-market. So the definition of the industry or industry sector is a matter of fundamental importance to the success of a business-to-business marketing research project. If we do not have a clear and agreed industry definition, then we could end up wasting time and energy researching things that are of no interest. Worse, we could end up *not* researching something that is regarded as central to a targeted marketing strategy.

In order to ensure a common understanding of industry definition, a rigorous classification of industries, sectors and subsectors is required. Marketing researchers can make use of the standard industrial classification system as used by governments, first, to ensure that industry sectors are defined rigorously, and second, to build lists of similar firms for purposes of primary market research. Although there are many standard industrial classification systems in use throughout the world, there is a fairly high degree of common ground between them.

The British standard industrial classification (UK SIC) is, for all practical purposes, identical to the equivalent NACE system devised by the EU. Both of these systems are identical to the International Standard Industrial Classification of the United Nations (ISIC) at the two-digit level – a detailed description of the UK SIC is provided in Appendix 1 (see page 141). In North

America, the old United States Standard Industrial Classification (US SIC) has now been officially replaced by the North American Industrial Classification System (NAICS), which is used throughout the USA, Canada and Mexico. A project is underway to harmonize the NAICS classification with the NACE (the 'NACE–NAICS industrial classifications convergence project', see http://unstats.un.org/unsd/class/intercop/convergence default.htm).

The principle behind any standard industrial classification system is to put every form of economic activity into a unique numeric (or alphanumeric) category. A SIC starts with a single letter or digit, which divides an economy into broad industry categories. Each successive digit in the classification then subdivides that industry into smaller and smaller industry sectors and subsectors. Take, for example, the NAICS. Categories 31–33 denote manufacturing industries. Category 334 is 'computer and electronic product manufacturing', a subdivision of manufacturing industry, while category 3346 is 'manufacturing and reproduction of magnetic and optical media', a further subdivision. The NAICS is a six-digit classification system, so that this process of successively dividing up larger units into their component parts continues until the sixth digit is reached (for example, 334611 indicates 'reproduction of software'). Appendix 1 shows in greater detail how alpha-numeric codes are allocated to industries within a standard industrial classification, using the UK SIC as an example.

For business-to-business marketing researchers, standard industrial classification systems are useful for two key purposes. These purposes are, first, to make an unambiguous definition of an industry or industry sector, and second, as a means of specifying a sampling frame from which a sample will be drawn for purposes of primary data gathering. Commercial information providers, such as Dun & Bradstreet and Reed Information Services, will provide either hard copy or electronic lists of firms within a specified range of SIC codes. Of course, in addition to marketing research, such lists are very commonly used for purposes of business-to-business direct mail campaigns. These points are illustrated fully in the case study of Dun & Bradstreet at the end of this chapter.

Using Market Research Agencies

Business-to-business marketing managers collect, analyze and act upon marketing information all of the time. Much of this information comes to them more or less automatically, in the form of internal reports from sales executives, industry association newsletters, the trade press, industry-specific sites on the Internet, and so on. Other forms of information necessitate primary information gathering of some sort, through focus groups, mail/email surveys, or one of the other methods discussed earlier in this chapter. In some cases this research might be done in-house, but often primary data gathering is carried out on behalf of the marketing manager by a professional market research agency. The marketing manager will prepare a research brief and then will work with colleagues to select a research agency to undertake the work (this, of course, is a business-to-business purchasing process and the team involved constitutes a 'DMU' or buying centre). Working effectively with a market research agency is one of the skills of a good marketing manager.

The client–agency relationship in business markets

Market research agencies are business-to-business professional services organizations. Logically, therefore, we can analyze the client–agency relationship using the same frameworks that we introduced in Chapter 3. This section may, therefore, serve two purposes: to reinforce and illustrate further the ideas from Chapter 3 and to provide guidance on how to get the most out of a B2B marketing research project when employing a research agency.

Peterson and Kerin (1980: 69) argued that: 'While guidelines have been offered for obtaining and evaluating commercial marketing research proposals … critical considerations involved in managing the interface between buyers and sellers of marketing research services go virtually uncharted.' There are relatively few studies that focus exclusively on the management of the client–agency relationship in business markets. Peterson and Kerin went some way towards filling the gap that they had identified, by soliciting three 'tips' from a sample of market research buyers and users on the best way to manage the relationship between a business-to-business marketing researcher and his or her research suppliers. Content analysis of the responses showed that buyers and suppliers agreed the three most important tips were:

- have a clear understanding of the problem prior to contacting the research supplier;
- get closely involved, at an early stage; and
- check past clients of suppliers, and evaluate their prior experience and industry familiarity.

Peterson and Kerin concluded that effective management of the client–agency relationship required the client to: 'Open lines of frank and honest communication with the research seller early in the research process and maintain them throughout project implementation. Provide whatever information you have which bears on the problem at hand' (Peterson and Kerin, 1980: 72).

Eborall and Nathan (1989) also focused exclusively on the client–agency relationship in business-to-business marketing research. They argued that:

> Market research is unique among professional and business services in that the competitive project tender is usually the basis for the client/agency

relationship. This means that the contact between the two parties may be sporadic rather than continuous, and that the loyalty, commitment and expertise of the agency will be built more slowly than it would otherwise.

The competitive tender approach is contrasted with an account-handling approach to supplier relationship management, which allows the incumbent supplier a degree of security and therefore encourages the development of client-specific knowledge and skills. Williamson (1975) has analyzed the rationale for the development of transaction-specific assets. In the case of the research agency–client relationship, time spent by the researcher on understanding the client organization and the background to the specific research problem can be regarded as relationship-specific investments – they have very little value outside of the relationship, and can be treated as sunk costs. Where the client insists upon employing a competitive tender approach to relationship management, there is no incentive for the agency to invest in this way (Jackson, 1985). And yet, it is the absence of such investment that is bemoaned by many researchers as the reason for:

- researchers often failing to solve clients' problems;
- researchers being unable to participate in the strategic decision-making process;
- low perceived value of market research information; and
- low status attached to the market research profession.

Deshpande and Zaltman (1987) explored the specific factors affecting the use of marketing research information in industrial marketing organizations. The purpose of the work was to extend the findings from earlier work (Deshpande and Zaltman, 1982, 1984) by extending the analysis from consumer firms to industrial firms. It was expected that differences would emerge between consumer and industrial firms, given the acknowledged differences between the consumer and industrial marketing research processes (Cox and Dominguez, 1979). The factors with the greatest influence on the use of marketing information in industrial firms were:

- research conducted for exploratory purposes (this is positively associated with information use in industrial firms, in contrast to a negative association in consumer firms);
- the degree of formalization in the organizational structure (again, the positive association for industrial firms contrasts with a negative association for consumer firms); and
- the degree of surprise in the research findings (the negative association found for industrial firms was also found for consumer firms but the negative effect of the surprise variable is lower for industrial firms).

Is it better for businesses commissioning market research to adopt an 'arm's length' approach towards research agencies, or should they seek to develop closer working relationships with a small number of agencies to whom they give a substantial amount of repeat business? According to Nowak et al. (1997: 488): 'Some clients believe in the benefits of partnering with their marketing research suppliers while others are still skeptical.' However, their research strongly suggested that a partnering approach to managing market research suppliers should be preferred to a transactional approach. Adopting more of a partnership approach towards market research agencies is positively associated with client perceptions of service quality, cost effectiveness, research quality, research timeliness and overall satisfaction. The conclusion is that the positive aspects of engaging in partnerships with research agencies – their better knowledge of your business and understanding of your research requirements – more than offset any negative aspects associated with complacency. A research firm that has developed a close relationship with a client is in a better position to know the client's needs and preferences and to provide more efficient service.

Secondary Research in Business Markets

The importance and usefulness of secondary research

Secondary market research is used in all areas of marketing but is particularly important in business-to-business markets. One reason is cost. Secondary research is relatively inexpensive, and marketing budgets are usually less generous in business-to-business marketing than in consumer marketing. Furthermore, since demand in business-to-business markets is derived, it is necessary to study markets beyond the immediate customer market. The marketer must know something about what is happening in the customer's market, and perhaps even in the market of the customer's customer.

This is best explained by example. In marketing instant coffee to consumers, one must try to understand why it is that they buy coffee and how their tastes may change. In marketing component parts to a manufacturer of industrial diggers, one must look beyond the immediate customer (for example, a construction firm) to the customer's customers. These might include the government (for example, with road building), commercial firms (for example, offices and industrial facilities) and private individuals (for example, house building). This makes the marketing research problem much more complicated and means that secondary sources must play a greater part. It would be much too expensive to research all of these downstream markets using primary research.

Another reason for the emphasis on secondary research in business-to-business marketing is the wide availability of excellent information sources at various levels of detail – from the level of an entire economy, down to the level of an industrial sector, a subdivision of an industry, or a single firm. Governments are very interested to gather data on business activity and much broad information on industry trends can be found in government sources (for example, the *Annual Abstract of Statistics*, the *Monthly Digest of Statistics*, *Economic Trends*, and the *Business Monitor* series of publications). For most industries there is an industry association, to serve the interests of the firms in that industry (see, for example, the *Directory of British Associations* – www.cbdresearch.com), that collects data on key trends in the industry. At the level of individual firms, commercial information providers such as Reed Information Services and Dun & Bradstreet publish directories containing information on such things as ownership structure, principal lines of business and key personnel (for example, *Key British Enterprises, Who Owns Whom, Kelly's, Kompass*). Firms are keen to be included in such directories, since their primary purpose is as a source of reference for potential buyers. Marketing researchers benefit from the wide availability of accurate and current information. Directories can provide a quick and accurate method of identifying firms that lie within a target market, together with details of their product range and key management personnel.

Using the Internet in business-to-business research

The Internet and, in particular, the World Wide Web have made available an unparalleled number of sources of information on a very wide range of topics. Naturally, many of these sources are of potential value to the business-to-business marketer. In Appendix 2 of this chapter (see page 143) we have compiled a list of a few of those sources that we regard as particularly useful. However, even with these sources – which are only drawn from credible information providers with well-established reputations – one has to be careful to examine the information critically, to ask how recent it is, how relevant it is to any specific marketing problem and whether the information may be biased in some way. Where information does not come from such well-known and credible sources, critical examination is of even greater importance. This is why some familiarity with the basic principles of sound research, such as sampling and levels of statistical error, is so important to the business marketing researcher. The Internet has provided us with ready access to a plethora of information providers, many of whom are more than happy to give – or sell – us information of dubious quality. Relying on the credibility of a trusted supplier (such as the *Financial Times* or Dun & Bradstreet) is one way to protect yourself from making decisions based on incorrect data, but it can never be a complete substitute for exercising your own critical faculty and asking searching questions about the quality of the original data, the analysis and the interpretation.

Chapter Summary

- The value of marketing information can be judged in terms of accuracy, timeliness, relevance and uniqueness.

- There is good evidence that more successful business-to-business marketing organizations make more use of formal market research than those that are less successful.

- Although many aspects of market research are the same in business and consumer markets – such as sampling theory – there are several practical differences that arise from the basic characteristics of business markets. As well as understanding their direct customers, business marketers need to be aware of developments further downstream in the chain of derived demand, at the level of their customer's customer and perhaps even beyond that.

- Probability sampling methods include simple random, stratified random, systematic, and cluster/multi-stage sampling. Non-probability sampling methods include convenience, snowball, and quota sampling. Focus groups (non-probability sampling) are often used to identify the factors that are important to a target group (for example, buying criteria considered important by industrial buyers) prior to undertaking a market research survey.

- Response rates to business marketing surveys are often low. Various methods are available to try to increase response rates.

- A standard industrial classification (SIC) is a systematic method of classifying economic activity, originally designed by governments, which is useful for specifying business market research samples from list providers and for defining an industry sector unambiguously.

- Where a market research agency is used to gather data, the management of the client–agency relationship will affect the usefulness of the data collected.

- While the Internet has made many more secondary market research sources readily available, it is important to use information from trustworthy sources and to use critical judgement in evaluating secondary research sources.

Questions for discussion

1. In what ways does the practice of business-to-business marketing research differ from consumer marketing research?

2. Imagine that you are describing the use of the Internet/WWW/email to a business marketing manager who retired in 1990 (and who has had a particularly sheltered life since – let's say, living in a log cabin without electricity or a telephone). To them, this sounds like the perfect marketing tool

for gathering primary marketing research, securing secondary market intelligence and communicating with business customers. 'Oh, well', you say, 'it's not quite as perfect as it sounds'. Why not?

3. While studying for an MBA part-time, sponsored by your employer, your boss asks you to ring up a competitive rival posing as a university student undertaking a course assignment to try to obtain important commercial information. As your boss says: 'Well, we are paying for the MBA, so we expect a return on the investment, and you are a university student after all, so that bit is true.' What do you do? (You might want to refer back to the material on ethical issues in Chapter 4.)

Case study: Dun & Bradstreet

Dun & Bradstreet is a global provider of business information. They can provide information to help you profile your customers, check the creditworthiness of your suppliers, identify likely prospects and build a list for purposes of a market research survey – among other things. Many of these services are invaluable for business-to-business market research purposes. Naturally, like all business-to-business services this is a competitive market, and D&B has rivals that provide alternative services – such as Reed Business Information and its Mardev service (www.mardev.com). However, to get a feel for how such information providers can assist with business-to-business market research projects we focus here on D&B (UK).

Figure 5.1 illustrates the three categories of business solution that D&B (UK) offers – credit risk management, supply chain management and new customer prospecting. For our purposes it is the third of these that is most relevant.

In Figure 5.2 we have clicked through the welcome page in Figure 5.1 to see in more detail what marketing services D&B (UK) can provide.

Notice how the products that D&B provides are again classified into a range of business solutions emphasizing the customer benefits rather than the product features – in this case we have the continuous cycle of knowing the customers, acquiring the customers, developing the customers and retaining the customers. D&B are telling their customers and potential customers that this information can be used to initiate, develop, build and maintain business-to-business relationships, of the sort that we discussed in Chapter 3. This emphasizes the practical importance of the theoretical concepts that were developed in that chapter. If we now click through to 'acquire new customers' then we arrive at Figure 5.3.

In Figure 5.3 we now have a list of the specific D&B products (databases and information services) that can assist with new customer acquisition. Amongst others, these include *WOW* (a database focusing on the ownership structure of companies, so that we can find out the ultimate holding

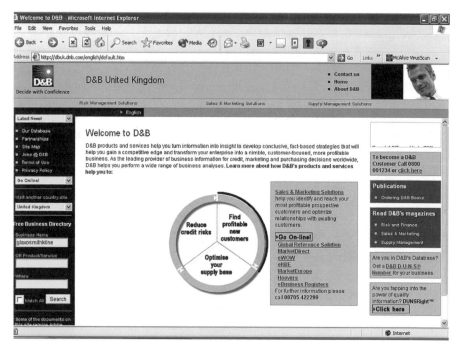

Figure 5.1 Dun & Bradstreet (UK) welcome page

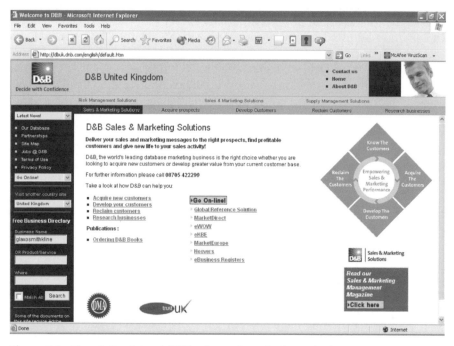

Figure 5.2 Dun & Bradstreet (UK) sales and marketing solutions

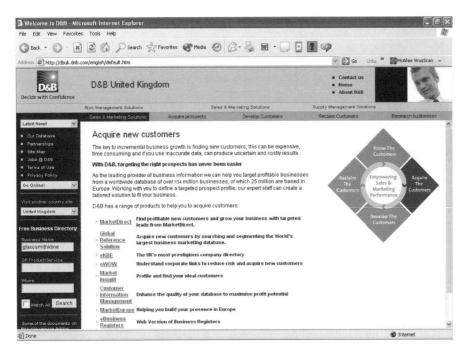

Figure 5.3   Dun & Bradstreet (UK) – acquiring new customers

company of a local subsidiary, or all of the subsidiaries of a large business), *KBE* (detailed information on the UK's largest firms) and databases with a wide geographical spread such as *Global Reference Solution*. Suppose that we are interested in building a database of prospective new customers in Europe, we click through to *Global Reference Solution*, bringing us to Figure 5.4.

Global Reference Solution clearly provides extensive information about a large number of firms (more than 100 million) throughout the world, and we can get a tailored list using a wide range of parameters such as location, company size, company turnover, legal status and industry sector in terms of standard industrial classification. This will provide us with the basic information we need either to conduct a pan-European market research study, or for a direct mail campaign with details of our products and services. Naturally, in order to get our tailored list (for the survey or the direct mail shot) we now need to specify exactly what we want to D&B and to pay for the information.

Sales & Marketing professionals
Now you can:

- Assess opportunities in any market sector in any country, or group of countries

Figure 5.4 Dun & Bradstreet (UK) – Global reference solution

- Create targeted marketing campaigns and build prospect databases by country, by sector or both
- Identify sales opportunities with other corporate family members of existing clients
- Align your sales resource around those client groups with the highest potential

And what information is available for each business?

Who? – runs the business – names of executives, partners, proprietors

What? – does the business do – line of business, SIC

Where? – does the business operate – trading address, telephone number

How? – large is the business – number of employees, sales ($)

How? – long has the business been trading

Which? – corporate family owns the business (where applicable)

Which? – other businesses operate from the same address

Case study questions

1. Explain in as much detail as you can the various ways in which the information supplied from a database such as *Global Reference Solution* can be used to help with B2B marketing and sales.
2. If you were responsible for marketing *Global Reference Solution*, what would be your key target markets? What benefits would you emphasize for those target markets?

Source: http://dbuk.dnb.com.

Appendix 1

The UK Standard Industrial Classification (2003)

At the highest level of aggregation the SIC is divided into sections that are indicated by a letter; manufacturing industry (section D) is divided into subsections, each with two letters. Each section contains a number of divisions, and each division is further subdivided into classes. Divisions are indicated by two digits – for example, within section G 'wholesale and retail trade; repair of motor vehicles, motorcycles and personal and household goods', we find division 50 'Sale, maintenance and repair of motor vehicles and motorcycles; retail sale of automotive fuel', division 51 'Wholesale trade and commission trade, except of motor vehicles and motorcycles', and division 52 'retail trade, except of motor vehicles and motorcycles; repair of personal and household goods'. Classes are indicated by three or four digits. In a few cases a fifth digit is used to indicate a subclass. The following material illustrates exactly what sections, divisions, classes and subclasses look like.

Sections of the UK SIC (2003)

This is a complete list of the sections in the UK SIC.

A   Agriculture, hunting and forestry
B   Fishing
C   Mining and quarrying
    CA   Mining and quarrying of energy-producing materials
    CB   Mining and quarrying except energy-producing materials
D   Manufacturing
    DA   Manufacture of food products, beverages and tobacco
    DB   Manufacture of textiles and textile products
    DC   Manufacture of leather and leather products
    DD   Manufacture of wood and wood products
    DE   Manufacture of pulp, paper and paper products; publishing and printing
    DF   Manufacture of coke, refined petroleum products and nuclear fuel
    DG   Manufacture of chemicals, chemical products and man-made fibres
    DH   Manufacture of rubber and plastic products
    DI   Manufacture of other non-metallic mineral products
    DJ   Manufacture of basic metals and fabricated metal products
    DK   Manufacture of machinery and equipment not elsewhere classified

DL   Manufacture of electrical and optical equipment
DM   Manufacture of transport equipment
DN   Manufacturing not elsewhere classified

E   Electricity, gas and water supply
F   Construction
G   Wholesale and retail trade; repair of motor vehicles, motorcycles and personal and household goods
H   Hotels and restaurants
I   Transport, storage and communication
J   Financial intermediation
K   Real estate, renting and business activities
L   Public administration and defence; compulsory social security
M   Education
N   Health and social work
O   Other community, social and personal service activities
P   Private households employing staff and undifferentiated production activities of households for own use
Q   Extra-territorial organizations and bodies

Illustrative classes of the UK SIC (2003)

We use two industries – a manufacturing industry (rubber and plastic products) and a service industry (financial intermediation) – to illustrate the SIC at the class level. Notice that subclasses are indicated by the use of the/character.

Subsection DH Manufacture of rubber and plastic products

25 Manufacture of rubber and plastic products
25.1 Manufacture of rubber products
25.11 Manufacture of rubber tyres and tubes
25.12 Retreading and rebuilding of rubber tyres
25.13 Manufacture of other rubber products
25.2 Manufacture of plastic products
25.21 Manufacture of plastic plates, sheets, tubes and profiles
25.22 Manufacture of plastic packing goods
25.23 Manufacture of builders' ware of plastic
     25.23/1 Manufacture of plastic floor coverings
     25.23/2 This code is no longer in use
     25.23/9 Manufacture of other builders' ware of plastic
25.24 Manufacture of other plastic products

Section J Financial intermediation

65 Financial intermediation, except insurance and pension funding
65.1 Monetary intermediation
65.11 Central banking
65.12 Other monetary intermediation
       65.12/1 Banks
       65.12/2 Building societies
65.2 Other financial intermediation
65.21 Financial leasing
65.22 Other credit granting
       65.22/1 Credit granting by non-deposit-taking finance houses and other specialist consumer credit grantors
       65.22/2 Factoring
       65.22/3 Activities of mortgage finance companies
       65.22/4 This code is no longer in use
       65.22/9 Other credit granting not elsewhere classified
65.23 Other financial intermediation not elsewhere classified
       65.23/1 Activities of investment trusts
       65.23/2 Activities of unit trusts
       65.23/3 Security dealing on own account
       65.23/4 Activities of bank holding companies
       65.23/5 Activities of venture and development capital companies
       65.23/6 This code is no longer in use
       65.23/7 Activities of open-ended investment companies
       65.23/8 Activities of property unit trusts
       65.23/9 Financial intermediation not elsewhere classified
Source: http://www.statistics. gov.uk./methods_quality/sic/downloads/UK_SIC_Vol2(2003).pdf

Appendix 2

Essential B2B intelligence sources

It would probably be impossible to compile a comprehensive list of valuable sources available to B2B marketers through the World Wide Web, and the list would be very long indeed. Rather than attempt the impossible, what we have striven to do is to make a comparatively small list of reliable providers of high-quality economic and business information that is likely to be of particular relevance to B2B marketers. The emphasis is on government sources, highly esteemed business newspapers, academic resources and reputable suppliers of commercial B2B marketing information.

Name of source	URL or other location information	Information available	Subscription? (a) Free – open access; (b) free – subscription required; (c) payment required
American Marketing Association	www.marketingpower. com	Wide variety of case studies, articles, reports and other information. Both B2C and B2B marketing.	(a), (c) – AMA is a membership organization; some information available to members only.
The Bulletin	http://bulletin.ninesm. com.au	General company, market and business information; Australia based.	(a), (c)
Business-China	http://business-china.com	General company, market and business information on China.	(a)
Business Week (Europe)	www.businessweek europe.com	General company, market and business information; European.	(a), (c)
Chartered Institute of Marketing	www.cim.co.uk	Wide variety of case studies, articles, reports and other information. Both B2C and B2B marketing.	(a), (c) – CIM is a membership organization; some information available to members only.
Dun & Bradstreet	www.dunandbrad. com; http://dbuk. dnb.com	Commercial market intelligence business offering a range of database services.	(c) – the site is open access, but market information is only available to paying customers.
The Economist	www.economist.com	General company and market information; UK based.	(a), (c)
Eurostat	http://epp.eurostat. cec.eu.int	Statistics and reports on all aspects of the EU economies; specific information available about many industries.	(a)

Name of source	URL or other location information	Information available	Subscription? (a) Free – open access; (b) free – subscription required; (c) payment required
Fifo Ost	www.fifoost.org	Wide-ranging information for business people interested in opportunities in the Eastern European economies.	(a)
Financial Times	www.ft.com	General company and market information; UK based.	(a), (c)
IMP Group	www.impgroup.org	Articles detailing the latest research developments in B2B marketing and purchasing; European and Australasian emphasis.	(a), (c) – free membership available but required only for those contributing material to the site.
Institute for the Study of Business Markets	www.smeal.psu.edu/isbm/	Articles and case studies dealing with the latest research developments in B2B marketing; USA based, global orientation.	(a), (c) – the ISBM provides a lot of free research information; it also offers a subscription service for corporations.
Mardev	www.mardev.com	Commercial market intelligence business offering a range of database services.	(c) – the site is open access, but market information is only available to paying customers.
The National Business Review	www.nbr.co.nz	General company, market and business information; New Zealand based.	(a), (c)
National Statistics Online	www.statistics.gov.uk	Statistics and reports on all aspects of the UK economy; specific information available about many industries; UK based.	(a)

Name of source	URL or other location information	Information available	Subscription? (a) Free – open access; (b) free – subscription required; (c) payment required
Reed Business Information	www.reedbusiness.co.uk	Information about B2B advertising media; European basis.	(a)
United Nations Statistics Division	http://unstats.un.org	Statistics and reports on all aspects of the world economy; specific information available about many industries; international basis.	(a)
US Census Bureau	www.census.gov	Statistics and reports on all aspects of the USA economy; specific information available about many industries; USA based.	(a)
The Wall Street Journal	http://online.wsj.com	General company, market and business information; USA based.	(a), (c)

References

Andreasen, A.R. (1985). '"Backward" marketing research', *Harvard Business Review* (May/June): 176–82.

Baker, M.J. and Hart, S. (1989). *Marketing and Competitive Success*. Oxford: Philip Allen.

Cox, W.E.J. and Dominguez, L.V. (1979) 'The key issues and procedures of industrial marketing research', *Industrial Marketing Management*, 8: 81–93.

Deshpande, R. and Zaltman, G. (1982) 'Factors affecting the use of market research information: a path analysis', *Journal of Marketing Research*, 19: 14–31.

Deshpande, R. and Zaltman, G. (1984) 'A comparison of factors affecting researcher and manager perceptions of market research use', *Journal of Marketing Research*, 21: 32–8.

Deshpande, R. and Zaltman, G. (1987) 'A comparison of factors affecting use of marketing information in consumer and industrial firms', *Journal of Marketing Research*, 24: 114–18.

Diamantopoulos, A. and Schlegelmilch, B. (1996) 'Determinants of industrial mail survey response: a survey-on-surveys analysis of researchers' and managers' views', *Journal of Marketing Management*, 12 (6): 503–31.

Dibb, S. and Simkin, L. (1994) 'Implementation problems in industrial market segmentation', *Industrial marketing management*, 23: 55–63.

Eborall, C. and Nathan, L. (1989) *Caveat Emptor, or Ours not to Reason Why? A Look at Client/Agency Relationships in Business Research*, paper presented at the Market Research Society Conference.

Faria, A.J. and Dickinson, J.R. (1992) 'Mail survey response, speed, and cost', *Industrial Marketing Management*, 21: 51–60.

Gates, B. (1996) *The Road Ahead: Revised and Updated*. London: Penguin.

Greer, T.V. and Lohtia, R. (1994) 'Effects of source and paper color on response rates in mail surveys', *Industrial Marketing Management*, 23: 47–54.

Hooley, G.J. and Jobber, D. (1986) 'Five common factors in top performing industrial firms', *Industrial marketing management*, 15: 89–96.

Jackson, B.B. (1985) 'Build customer relationships that last', *Harvard Business Review*, (November/December): 120–8.

McWilliams, R.D., Naumann, E. and Scott, S. (1992) 'Determining buying center size', *Industrial Marketing Management*, 21: 43–9.

Moorman, C., Zaltman, G. and Deshpande, R. (1992) 'Relationships between providers and users of market research: the dynamics of trust within and between organizations', *Journal of Marketing Research*, 24: 314–28.

Newman, J.W. (1962) 'Put research into marketing decisions', *Harvard Business Review*, 40 (2): 105–12.

Nowak, L.I., Boughton, P.D. and Pereira, A.J.A. (1997) 'Relationships between businesses and marketing research firms', *Industrial Marketing Management*, 26: 487–95.

Peterson, R.A. and Kerin, R.A. (1980) 'The effective use of marketing research consultants', *Industrial Marketing Management*, 9: 69–73.

Rawnsley, A. (ed.) (1978) *Manual of Industrial Marketing Research*. Chichester: Wiley.

Stacey, N.A.H. and Wilson, A. (1969) *Industrial Marketing Research: Management and Technique* (2nd edn). London: Hutchinson.

Williamson, O.E. (1975) *Markets and Hierarchies: Analysis and Antitrust Implications*. New York: The Free Press.

6 Business Market Segmentation

Learning outcomes

After reading this chapter you will:

- know what segmentation is and how the segmentation process unfolds in business markets;
- be able to segment business markets using several segmentation variables;
- know the criteria for successful segmentation;
- understand how segmentation information can be used to aid the process of targeting business prospects; and
- know how segmentation and the identification of target customers influences the establishment of differential positioning for those target markets.

Introduction

As we saw in Chapters 2 and 3, there is considerable variety in the purchase behaviour of organizational customers and in the nature of the relationships that may ensue between business-to-business marketers and their customers. These chapters have introduced an important reality for business-to-business marketers: all customers are unique. However, the fact that they are all unique does not mean that for the business-to-business marketer *all* individual relationships need be managed differently and uniquely. While individual and unique treatment is likely to be necessary for a number of strategically important customers within a business-to-business customer base (so-called 'segments of one'), it is also the case that there will be a substantial number of customers that do not really require a wholly customized offering. Many customers are happy to purchase a relatively standardized product and their behaviour to all intents and purposes is the same as many other companies that are happy to receive the same offering.

This understanding, that while all customers are different some may share similar needs and behaviours, is at the heart of segmentation. For it is through a process of segmentation that a business-to-business marketer can establish a degree of homogeneity in respect of the different customers in the marketplace. In this way notional groups of like-minded (or like-behaved) customers are created, for whom it becomes possible to talk meaningfully about a range of different market offerings. It enables the marketer to research the needs of specific groups (see Chapter 5), make choices about which groups in the market are worth the investment of marketing effort from the firm, and how exactly that effort needs to be managed.

Segmentation for its own sake is of little value; its value comes when it is used to make decisions about target markets and to establish specific competitive positions with respect to those targets that bring value to the firm. Ultimately, it is the success of differential competitive positioning within markets that creates success: doing things differently from competitors to establish advantage (such as more customized offerings or similar offerings at lower costs). In this chapter we deal with the trinity of activities associated with approaching the market in the first place in order to obtain that success – segmentation, targeting and positioning. Consequently, attention is paid firstly to segmentation. Then the outcome of the segmentation is considered in terms of target market selection. Finally, we move on to consider the establishment of positions within those target markets that are sustainable by the firm.

Principles and Value of Segmentation

As we saw in Chapters 2 and 3, there is great diversity in the needs and behaviours of business customers. At the most basic level, they are all unique. In principle, this would require completely unique market offerings for all customers in order to achieve greatest customer satisfaction. Satisfaction, after all, comes from meeting customer needs and expectations as precisely as possible. However, in the real world markets do not conform to the economists' notion of perfect competition, rather they are imperfectly competitive. This means that there is scope to differentiate the products of different suppliers and to identify different market segments, each with slightly different demand characteristics. Apart from anything else there will be many buyers out there that the marketer does not yet supply, or even know about, for whom the basis for individual treatment is not yet even known.

Of course, pushed to its opposite extreme it is entirely possible to produce a standard offering for customers that meets the needs of the maximum number of customers to an acceptable level. Typically, such standardization brings operating efficiencies for the firm. But, since it is designed to meet the needs of the average customer, by definition it does not meet the needs of others particularly well. This is a dangerous position to adopt since others will be only too willing to provide more satisfying offerings to these dis-affected customers. It has long been known that single over-generalized offerings to the whole market lead to problems for companies in achieving their objectives; 'cases where failure to recognize the reality of market seg-ments was resulting in loss of market position' (Smith, 1956: 5).

The difficult task of understanding customers and delivering market offerings involves adopting a position somewhere in-between the over-gen-eralized and the over-customized. It is in this territory that the value of seg-mentation to marketers can be seen. The pioneering view of segmentation put forward by Wendell Smith (1956: 6) was that it 'consists of viewing a het-erogeneous market ... as a number of smaller homogeneous markets in response to differing product preferences among important market seg-ments'. By seeing the market in terms of a set of different customer require-ments the marketer can establish clear target markets for the firm. Firms can make clearer choices about those segments that they want to serve, enabling them to more clearly match their own strengths and capabilities with the specific needs of particular segments.

The value of segmentation in aiding company capabilities to design more appropriate marketing programmes has long been understood (Yankelovich, 1964). Shapiro and Bonoma (1984) pointed to the value of industrial seg-mentation in three areas:

- facilitating better understanding of the whole marketplace including the behaviour of buyers and why they buy;
- enabling better selection of market segments that best fit the company's capabilities; and
- enabling improved management of the marketing activity.

A good understanding of the needs of the market in general makes it pos-sible for the successful marketer to identify groups of needs shared by cus-tomers. This enables the marketer to deal more effectively with more homogeneously identifiable groups of customers (and by definition the set of groups thus defined are much smaller than the number of individual cus-tomers). It makes it possible for the marketer to talk meaningfully about the behaviours of this more manageable number of groups (market segments) so that marketing activity can be undertaken more efficiently than would be the case without segmentation. It also makes it possible for the marketer to determine clearly how the company stands competitively with respect to the market segments, facilitating decisions to leave some segments of the mar-ket and pursue others, or to concentrate on meeting the demands of specific segments in ways that confer greater competitive advantage. This strategic use of segmentation means that the marketer can choose which customers to target, which ones to treat similarly and which ones to treat differently, even uniquely. A fundamental skill for superior business-to-business marketing then is knowing just which customers to treat similarly and which to treat differently.

Segmentation process

The process of segmentation involves an iterative (step-by-step) classification of the market in terms of sets of meaningful groupings, with each additional step in the iterative process defining further subdivisions. This means starting with the widest possible definition of the marketplace. Then on the basis of the application of a series of classification criteria, often called segmentation bases, a set of market segments is created. If the process has been done well, these are each clearly defined and the members of each segment share characteristics with respect to their market needs: 'homogeneous with respect to their response to a marketing mix', as Griffith and Pol (1994: 39) put it. It is their behaviour in response to market offerings that makes their association sensible for the purposes of marketing activity.

As far as the process is concerned, the most common difficulties that managers face are knowing the combination of descriptive or explanatory segmentation variables to use, and where to stop with a set of meaningful segments. These issues are addressed directly in the next sections.

Segmentation Bases

The process of segmentation requires the application of criteria that can support the classification activity. Even from the earliest writings on the subject, a range of such criteria have been proposed. For instance, in what appears to be the earliest published consideration of industrial segmentation bases, Frederick (1934) lists five factors that should be taken into account (industry, geographic location, channels of distribution, product use and company buying habits).

Many different variables have been used and we will consider a collection of them in this chapter in greater detail. However, there is agreement that the nature of the process described above means that there are different levels of segmentation. This involves moving from the use of more general or easily observable criteria at initial levels of the process (often using secondary data sources), through to more specific and less observable measures in the later stages. These often require specific knowledge of the personal attitudes or behaviours of customer representatives. The larger-scale analysis is often referred to as *macro-segmentation* while the finer level analysis is *micro-segmentation* (Choffray and Lilien, 1978). The nested set of segmentation bases proposed by Shapiro and Bonoma (1984) capture this movement from

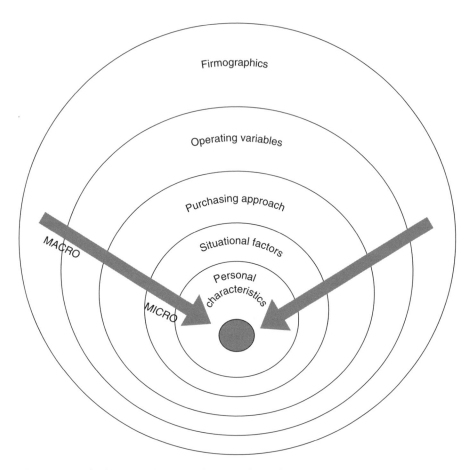

Figure 6.1 *The Segmentation Funnel – Nested use of segmentation bases (adapted from Shapiro and Bonoma, 1984).*

the macro-level to the micro-level, and this is illustrated in Figure 6.1. We will consider the range of criteria using the nested approach that they pioneered.

Firmographics

While Shapiro and Bonoma (1984) refer to demographics as the most general level of segmentation criteria, Gross et al. (1993) argue that a more fitting term in business-to-business markets is emporographics. Where demography is the study of the characteristics of human populations, such as size, growth, density and distribution, emporographics captures the fact that in the business-to-business context it is the characteristics of the firm that are the focus. However, we prefer the more prosaic term 'firmographics', which is increasingly widely used and makes the link to the firm more directly.

Shapiro and Bonoma (1984) highlight industry and company size as well as customer location as the major macro-factors providing a broad classification of customers. These enable a good first pass for many companies in segmenting. The expectation is that companies from the same industry, or of similar sizes or locations, share similar product needs or usage patterns.

Industry

For a company making automatic equipment for surface inspection, such as Surface Inspection Ltd (see the case study at the end of Chapter 3), a sensible first step in segmentation is to consider where such equipment would reasonably be used, now or in the future. To this end, the company has provided solutions in several industries, including checking paint quality in the auto industry and surface quality of ceramic tiles. The tile industry very quickly emerged as a particularly strong fit for the technological capability of Surface Inspection. This is an industry where the inspection process has traditionally been manual, laborious and subject to error, and where the opportunity costs of quality failure are great. For Surface Inspection, any company in this industry constitutes a prospect and thus the use of industry type is a very useful starting position for its segmentation.

Similarly, for any company, knowledge of an industry that may have use for its technology enables it to very quickly identify prospects. Of course, this requires a consistent definition of the activities of companies. Surface Inspection would be interested in all companies that make wall tiles, floor tiles and roof tiles, in a variety of shapes, designs and colours. Looking through a series of phone books (and it would involve lots of these for an international market) for such companies may generate leads but there would also be lots of wasted time and energy. The name of a company does not immediately give a clear indication of what it does. Likewise, a web search will certainly generate substantial leads but requires that customers have such a web presence in the first place. Many hits in this situation would also be of little relevance to Surface Inspection, as they would bring up distributors of tiles rather than manufacturers.

The use of SIC codes aids an industry-based segmentation approach because it provides consistent definitions of the activities of companies as a basis for categorization (see Chapter 5 for a lengthier explanation of SIC codes). Companies are classified according to the nature of their business by government or other agencies. For example, in the NAICS codes, establishments that use the same or similar processes to produce goods or services are grouped together by the US Census Bureau. NAICS codes replaced the earlier US SIC codes. These are now 6-digit (rather than the 4-digit industry classification codes used in the earlier US SIC scheme) to accommodate a larger number of sectors. There have also been changes to increase the number of service-based industries that have emerged and that were not easily included in the previous SIC.

Similar coding schemes exist outside North America. The UN uses its own 4-digit ISIC scheme for classifying all economic activities. In Europe, many countries have adopted the NACE codes, including Luxembourg, Denmark, Ireland, Portugal, Greece, Norway, Finland, Iceland, Switzerland, Poland, the Czech Republic, Bulgaria, Romania, the Slovak Republic, Hungary, Latvia, Yugoslavia, Lithuania, Croatia, Slovenia, Macedonia, Bosnia Herzegovina, the Russian Federation, Estonia and Latvia. Many countries also use a national coding scheme, though increasingly national schemes are making revisions to enable greater correspondence with international codes. For example, the national codes in use in a range of European countries are compatible with the NACE codes. These include the UK SIC code, the NAF code in France and the WZ code in Germany and Austria. Likewise, the ANZSIC codes in use in Australia and New Zealand have been devised to enable closer alignment with ISIC codes. The NAICS code revisions are also intended to achieve greater comparability with ISIC codes. The Eurostat Classifications Server (RAMON: www.europa.eu.int/comm/eurostat/ramon/) provides extensive coverage of a range of international classification schemes and correspondence between them.

As Table 6.1 shows, for Surface Inspection Ltd any company with a NAICS code of 327122 would be a suitable prospect. The US Census Bureau's website describes this category thus: 'This industry comprises establishments primarily engaged in shaping, molding, baking, burning, or hardening clay refractories, nonclay refractories, ceramic tile, structural clay tile, brick, and other structural clay building materials' (www.census.gov/epcd/naics02/, accessed, 17 April 2005). The use of the NAICS code thus helps to define a segment of value to the company. The codes can then be used to access databases or compendiums of company information. For example, the AMADEUS product available from Bureau van Dijk (www.bvdep.com/AMADEUS.html, accessed 18 April 2005) has information on 7 million public and private companies in 38 European countries and enables searches using NAICS codes.

Customer location

As well as knowing about the industries that may demand a company's output, it is possible to segment on where those prospects might be. The location of a customer will often affect the ease with which it can be reached by a company. That is, it may be influential in decisions about where a company makes a presence itself, how it deploys staff, or how it communicates with customers. The value of the ceramic tile manufacturing segment to Surface Inspection was indicated above. In terms of the location of companies engaged in such manufacturing, Spain and Italy assume great significance because of the number of tile manufacturers in those countries, particularly in the areas around Sassuolo in Italy and Castellón in Spain. It is precisely for this reason that Surface Inspection has opened Customer Support Offices in these areas.

Table 6.1   2002 NAICS codes relevant to ceramic tile manufacturing

Segment	NAICS codes	Category
Sector	31–33	Manufacturing
Subsector	327	Non-metallic mineral product manufacturing
Industry group	3271	Clay product and refractory manufacturing
Industry	32712	Clay building material and refractories manufacturing
US industry	327122	Ceramic wall and floor tile manufacturing

Source: www.census.gov/epcd/naics02.

While a high degree of prospective customer concentration in a location would seem favourable, that really depends upon the nature of the industry. Companies providing goods or services that are easily transportable, such as maintenance services or specialist advice or design services, are little hampered by geographical distances from customers. Increasingly many services can even be delivered electronically (for example, translation services or software). For companies in resource-heavy industries (like many manufacturing companies creating bulky products in a few specific locations) there are problems associated with the transportation and delivery of their products over long distances. So, for example, a company like Surface Inspection has to trade off the wish to maintain manufacturing close to its suppliers in the UK with the costs of transporting end products. For customers in Europe the trade-off favours the maintenance of the whole manufacturing process in the UK. The decision is much more marginal when the transportation involves sea freighting by intermediaries, to the US, for instance (particularly when the carriage has led to damage to machines). The decision may swing further away from sole UK manufacture towards a degree of local assembly when the number of business leads start to increase in the US.

Customer size

The size of customer companies may be a sensible basis for distinguishing one from another. The basis for measuring size differs, depending upon what is being purchased. For a manufacturing company providing blow-moulded plastic bottles, larger companies will typically require greater volumes of product. For a company providing process equipment for inspection of tiles (such as Surface Inspection), larger tile manufacturers will have both the resources to afford enhanced tile inspection as well as the scale of production that will see the greatest value in use of the equipment. Thus, size often matters because of its relationship with the scale of the customer organizations' needs and therefore their demands for volume or inclination to buy and their ability to justify specific products or services. Marketers can make decisions about those companies that it is sensible to supply. For example, Surface Inspection typically only targets larger tile manufacturers on the grounds that they are more likely to invest in automatic tile inspection. On the other hand, the company making blow-moulded plastic bottles may decide not to target the largest customers on the grounds that it does not have the capacity to meet their volume needs. It may prefer to supply mid-sized customers that will match its capacity better, so that it manufactures efficiently but without danger of over-stretching and disappointing.

Operating variables

The next set of segmentation criteria move from the coarser-grained and most easily observed firmographic variables to those that are more precise descriptions of what customer companies can or could do. They are still relatively easily observed without having to put specific questions to customer representatives because they are visible beyond the firm. They are, however, the first manifestations of how customer companies behave rather than merely the general characteristics of the firms. As with the previous set of criteria, these variables can be applied singly or in combination.

Company technology

As indicated above when discussing customer size, Surface Inspection typically targets large tile firms with its automatic inspection equipment. As well as being a function of size, there is an element of technological readiness involved as well. The bigger tile makers have tended to make the greatest investments in process technology to control the manufacturing process. The technology is also likely to be the most up to date. For Surface Inspection, integrating its inspection machines within such processes is more feasible. Thus, an analysis of the technology of companies may be valuable in segmentation and aiding targeting decisions because it gives a strong indication of a company's buying needs as well as the ease with which the supplying company can meet those needs.

Product and brand-use status

Given that companies segment in order to establish targets for their products, it is only sensible that they would use the behaviour of customers with respect to products or brands to aid their segmentation. Customer reactions to products in terms of readiness to use (for those who are not yet customers) and usage rate (light, medium or heavy), for those who already purchase, are valuable means of distinguishing one from another. Existing customers bring additional knowledge benefits to a supplier: the nature of the need is more clearly understood, as is how they purchase. These customers also know something about the supplier's products and how the supplier has behaved towards them. Retaining heavy users may seem the most obvious use of segmentation on this basis. However, as Chapter 9 on relationship portfolio management shows, a balanced customer portfolio may come from investing in the growth of lighter users – the heavy users of the future.

While much less may be known about companies that are not yet customers, they may also share similar characteristics in their use of products. A company like 3663 in the UK, which provides food and cleaning products to away-from-home organizations (restaurants, bars, hotels, hospitals, care homes and universities) will recognize that all restaurants need washing-up detergent, or that all hotels need housekeeping cleaning products. They will even have a reasonable knowledge, on the basis of room capacity, of what the likely demand for housekeeping products would be by a hotel.

Customer capabilities

As we saw in Chapter 3, exchange involves matching the abilities and uncertainties of buyers and sellers. Given this situation, a supplier might genuinely want to establish what customers are capable of doing with either its product or the processes. In the garment industry, a clothes manufacturer that has adopted a modular scheme of production where work-in-progress is notionally only ever one garment (because the process is geared to working with the pieces of each garment from start to finish within the same work cell) would be interested in the extent to which customers could use that system. For the scheme to work at its most efficient, and not require further work, inputs from the customer are needed (such as sales stock tags and fabric care labels). Establishing the extent to which the customer would use the value of the modular scheme is important, not least because meeting the needs of customers who cannot operate in this way will require substantial warehousing for almost-completed garments. While Pilkington, the UK glass maker, will happily sell float glass to anyone who wants it, it has substantial interest in how the industry changes over time. Merely sticking glass in extruded UPVC for the domestic double-glazing market is not adding any extra value to the glass as a product, though it does constitute volume that may be valuable in itself. For this reason, it has a particular interest in any company that works with the glass itself, tempering it, for example, for use in a variety of safety applications. In recognition of customers that add extra value to the glass it has a Key Processor scheme that provides additional services to those customers it recognizes as members.

Customer strategic type

Verhallen et al. (1998) demonstrated that the nature of a firm's strategic type is a strong indicator of its industrial buying behaviour for new products. Using Miles and Snow's (1978) four-part typology – prospector (innovative), defender (efficient), analyser (efficient and adaptive) and reactor (no consistent strategy) – they found that it predicted buying behaviour better than firmographic variables like industry type and firm size. Within the nested approach to segmentation one would certainly expect variables that are more nested than others to be more predictive and Verhallen et al.'s study supports this for the purchase of new products.

Of course, the determination of the strategic type of a company is more difficult to ascertain than its size. It relies for measurement on either self-indication by customer representatives (which is subject to problems of socially acceptable responding), observation (very difficult for outsiders to undertake), or content analysis of company marketing plans (also rarely possible). It is more likely that a strategic type analysis would be further down the segmentation funnel to obtain finer distinctions between customers. It may add greatest value when applied to small numbers of customers, about which there is sufficient knowledge. This may involve input from multiple sources within the marketing company who all have contact with the customer firm (as a means of introducing a degree of triangulation to the evaluation). Such knowledge will not exist for completely new companies and it thus has greatest application for re-buy tasks for customers; it will also have limited value for establishing customer responses to new product launches.

Purchasing approach

It may be stating the obvious to say that the ways that companies choose to buy undoubtedly affect their buying behaviour. But the recognition that this is so has implications for marketing companies. How buying companies are organized to buy and the manifestations of these influences in terms of policies and buying criteria may constitute valuable intelligence to a marketer, as it may enable them to produce an offering that is most valuable to a target segment that is defined in terms of its purchasing approach.

Purchasing function organization

Buying companies differ in how they organize themselves for procurement. In smaller firms there may not be necessarily an identifiable group or department with purchasing responsibility, and there may be attendant uncertainties as to contact points. Where there is an identifiable purchasing function a big issue for the marketer is whether procurement is handled centrally (within a multi-divisional buying company) or whether responsibility is delegated to each division. Indeed, in some companies there may be central purchasing as well as a distributed structure. This was the case at Dalgety, which until recently traded in compacted animal feeds in the UK. It organized its purchasing so that each mill had its own purchasing group. However, in addition there was a corporate purchasing group that also bought grain on the international market. Sometimes local purchasers would have to accept some volumes that had been agreed centrally, even if the local purchasers did not necessarily require those volumes. However, the prices agreed centrally for the volumes purchased made economic sense to the company at large. Understanding how a customer's buying function is organized is invaluable in knowing who to approach, as well as understanding the levels and types of purchasing they control.

Power structures

Following from the previous point about organization, but extending beyond the purchasing role itself, the relative influence of different departments within the firm may well have an impact upon the nature of the buying process or the criteria that are applied. Ascertaining the priorities of the buying company based on the influence of particular departments will mean that a marketer will have to alter the communication of the strength of its offering to make it most meaningful to this department. For instance, it may be most appropriate to emphasize the technical performance in a situation where the production department strongly affects purchases.

Buyer–seller relationships

As this book emphasizes throughout, the relationship between the buyer and seller will affect how they interact. In respect of segmentation when the purpose is to identify prospects that are not yet customers, some prospective customers might favour the kind of business relationship that the supplier prefers. For instance, customers that have a particular reputation might be preferred, such as those that share similar environmental outlooks. As the earlier example about Pilkington indicates, they have a strong interest in forging relationships with companies that do more than merely cut float glass.

Freytag and Clarke (2001) point to the value in using customers' intentions towards collaboration with the supplier as a basis for segmentation. If the intention of a firm is to establish longer-term relationships with its customers then that attitudinal intention becomes important. Jackson (1985) distinguished between customers on the basis of their tendency to behave transactionally or relationally, demonstrating the different needs each has and thus the different supplier behaviour required. Those customers styled 'always-a-share' do not want relationships. They would rather focus on the current sale and are inclined to switch suppliers on the basis of price. For a supplier, they can always catch these fish; it only requires better bait in the form of better prices to reel them in and take them away from the competition. And how do you spot these sorts of customers? In a similar vein to Jackson's typology for 'always-a-share', Sako (1992) points to the 'arm's length' contracting style adopted by some buying organizations and typified in the auto industry by US/Western purchasing practices. They likewise are only focused on the current sale and their behaviour is directed by price-based market pressures, with no constraint on opportunistic exchange behaviour.

'Lost-for-good' customers are different. They want a relationship. They see value in working longer term with suppliers. This may be due to a more complex exchange situation: a product that is non-standard or customized in some way, or with delivery or fulfilment requirements that require very close working, or where there is a need for flexibility or innovation in supply over time. Whatever the reason for wanting such relationships, 'lost-for-good' customers are prepared to make the commitment to a relationship and expect likewise from suppliers. If a supplier is not prepared to behave that way or behaves opportunistically in the relationship then the customer will act to take their business elsewhere. And better prices will not bring them back; they will be 'lost-for-good'. These customers can also be spotted on the basis of their procurement behaviour. The buying activity will be characterized by greater interest in total costs of ownership, less focus on the initial sale price, and greater concern about service and maintenance activities, and greater willingness to work interactively with suppliers to resolve details of the need and how it can be met.

There is an element, in Sako's (1992) terms, of 'obligational contracting', where on the basis of ties that bind companies feel an obligation to behave in ways that are relational. After a period of competitive purchasing of architectural services in the UK, IKEA moved to forging stronger relationships with just two architect practices with which they work very closely (mirroring the sorts of relationships they forge on the product supply side). However, despite being a sought-after client by any practice in the country, large and small, IKEA chose to work with two medium-sized practices (with 30–40 employees) on the grounds that they wanted the suppliers to see them as a big client, commanding the attention that such a client deserves. They considered that small practices would not perhaps have been able to cope with the volume of work required, while large practices would be less responsive.

General purchasing policies

As the last paragraph indicated, the organizational structures and influences and the sorts of relationships preferred ultimately impact on and are typically embodied in specific buying policies (and criteria, see below). These will determine the particular practices of the company when purchasing from suppliers. Amongst other things, this will affect the forms of vendor rating used and forms of accreditation expected, the sorts of pricing and bidding methods used and the expectations of disclosure of costs. Marketers can use knowledge of policies to determine whether they want or would be able to meet the policy needs of a buyer.

Purchasing criteria

A whole range of purchasing criteria could be applied by a buying company. They may be financial, such as purchase price or total life cost, or they may concern more technical performance characteristics of the specified product (for example, weight, speed, power consumption, durability, quality consistency or reliability). Additionally, the quality of the service more generally might be important, including continuity of supply, delivery performance, amount and quality of technical assistance pre- and post-sale and standards of customer service. Knowing the specific criteria would enable segmentation to be undertaken more precisely. However, buying companies generally do not (and probably cannot) express completely the criteria to be applied or their relative importance. They are more likely to use a set of criteria across the board that suppliers are implicitly expected to meet.

This lack of comprehensive knowledge of exactly what the criteria are and their relative importance poses problems for marketers in segmentation terms. They will want to target those segments where they have the greatest potential and thus will have to make a judgement call as to whether the criteria to be applied are likely to match with their own capabilities. This may mean that a marketer whose products are technically strong, but that are slightly less price competitive, might choose to target those buyers who consistently want that level of product performance, ignoring the price preferences until such time as it becomes clear that price is the order-winning criterion.

Situational factors

Rather than the characteristics of buying companies themselves, how they ordinarily operate and the usual buying behaviour that they manifest, situations arise where companies are instead guided temporarily by the prevailing factors in the business environment. So, rather than defining all companies requiring a product as equivalent and thus putting them in the same segment, it may often be possible to define a segment in terms of the prevailing need. This need may be for urgent order fulfilment, so by considering that such a need may exist, a supplier can arrange to maintain stocks and provide a replenishment service, generally at a price premium. The important point here is that while the marketer may be providing the same product in each case, there are two separate segments based upon the urgency with which each requires the product.

As well as urgency affecting how companies buy, how they plan to use a product may mean that they will purchase the same product differently at different times. Likewise, companies may change their purchase behaviour depending on the size of the order they are making. There may be some companies that they consider able to supply in volume while there may be others that they would turn to for smaller order sizes. For the supplier, these constitute opportunities to decide which of these situations they would fit best. As the O_2 case in Chapter 9 indicates, smaller purchasers may well be referred to alternative sources of supply, such as distributors.

Personal characteristics of buyers

Ultimately, buying companies are only human. While organizational structures, policies and processes create the framework within which decisions are made, it is the buying staff, perhaps alongside others in a DMU (see

Chapter 2), who actually conduct the process. Consequently, marketers can segment in terms of the characteristics of the people themselves, such as what drives their buying behaviour, the extent to which it is believed that they share similar views to the marketer, how fastidious they are in searching for and evaluating suppliers, and their approaches to managing risk.

For a company to use such personal characteristics, clearly it must have some degree of contact with the buying company. The closer the contact, the better the calibre of information obtained and its usefulness for targeting purposes. But, of course, this sort of research and reporting process can get expensive very quickly when there are large numbers of prospective customers in the marketplace. For this reason, the volume of data gathered is likely to be restricted to those prospects that merit it because of sales potential. Information is best obtained by sales personnel from contacts they have had in prospective customers. Sales representatives from a marketing company can often report on how well they get along with the buyer, and how closely the buyer's views seem to favour the marketing company. The addition of such reports from the customer contact points to the company marketing information system as a matter of course enables the identification of positively disposed prospects.

Where to Stop? Successful Segmentation

Given its role in defining market segments about which companies can take clear decisions in respect of targeting, the fundamental issues in segmentation revolve around clarity of the definitions of segments and knowing where to stop. Marketers can apply a variety of segmentation bases, using finer-grained bases in combination with coarser-grained bases to derive ever more specific segment definitions. The greater the number of segmentation steps undertaken, and thus the number of differentiating criteria that are applied, the smaller and more fragmented are the segments produced. This fragmentation is, of course, the reason for wanting to segment in the first place. However, when the fragmentation begins to reach the point where further separation does not really lead to meaningful differences with respect to customer purchase behaviour then it is likely that the process should be curtailed. As indicated earlier in the chapter, by this point there are likely to be a range of different segments of differing sizes. A small number may be segments of one, each equating to a strategically important customer that requires individual and unique treatment. There may be a collection of segments containing reasonable numbers of potential customers in each (of the order of tens rather than hundreds), with each segment perhaps representing different product categories or applications for the company's products.

There may also be a group of segments containing large numbers (thousands) of individual customers. The number of small businesses, many of which are sole proprietorships, means that for some companies there may be segments comprising millions of customers. This is the case for RS Components, an operating company of Electrocomponents plc, distributor of a wide range of components and equipment including electrical, electronic, industrial, health and safety, and IT (with headquarters in the UK). It supplies products to 1.5 million engineers across the globe, with an order being placed every 10 seconds. In recognition of the many small businesses that could use its products, the company has invested since 1995 in e-commerce technology. Its award-winning Internet Trading Channel (E-Business Strategy of the Year, UK National Business Awards, 2003) brings over 300,000 products, which historically would only have been available through a 5,000 page catalogue, to these myriads of customers. This enables it to meet the needs of a range of segments directly, with the UK company alone processing 20,000 orders a day and delivering 25,000 parcels.

Whatever bases are applied there are a series of tests that business marketers can apply to establish the quality of the segmentation process and the usefulness of the segments that are proposed.

- *Measurable/distinctive:* In order to be used successfully, criteria for segmentation must be clearly measurable. For instance, if they are to be used, it must be possible to establish the size of the firm, its capabilities, its purchasing policies and selection criteria, the size of orders it is likely to seek and its attitude to risk. Without strong measurability it is not possible to define clearly distinctive market segments. Where it is not possible to apply a segmentation variable in a way that is clearly measurable, it is best to avoid its use since the consequences are segments that are insufficiently distinguished. With such segments there is the risk of offerings that are not adequately tailored and the possibility of being outdone by competitors with more precise segmentation, better targeting and more adequately matching offerings.
- *Accessible:* For a segment to be targeted usefully it needs to be accessible. If it is not possible to reach customers in the segment then the definition adds little value. 'Reach' includes the physical ease of getting offerings to the customers in the segment, as well as the ability to communicate with them. While technology makes it possible increasingly to communicate directly with prospects around the world, an issue for some companies remains the ability to get goods to far-flung customers, involving as it does logistical and/or channel management issues.
- *Substantial/profitable:* The size and potential profitability of segments are also important qualities. The segment needs to be big enough, or customers must be prepared to pay enough, to justify the costs of serving the segment. Where this is not the case then it is likely that the segmentation process has been taken too far and that the segments are more

fragmented than they need to be. The potential for profitability will certainly influence decisions about which segments to target.

- *Actionable:* It does not matter how big or accessible a segment is if a company cannot actually bring offerings to bear that will meet the needs of the segment. For this reason another test for a segment is the extent to which the company can put together effective marketing programmes for it. As Hlavacek and Ames (1986: 47) point out: '... one should know what capabilities the company has or needs to develop or acquire to serve the segment profitably'.

Gross et al. (1993) also point to *compatibility* between buyer and seller as important, on the grounds that similar approaches to risk taking, service standards and corporate style will be preferred. However, this compatibility is not really a measure of the quality of the definition of a segment itself, but of the characteristics of the purchasing approach of customers. In this respect, it is encompassed in the variables presented previously relating to the purchasing function and has strong implications for the ability to forge enduring collaborative relationships between buyer and seller.

Targeting

A key reason for engaging in segmentation activity is to establish how the marketplace is organized in respect of groups with homogeneous buying behaviour, as a prelude to making choices about the marketing response. Segmentation is of little value if it is not then used to make the best-informed choices about particular markets to serve and in what respects. This is targeting.

Target selection

While the criteria for successful segmentation will establish credible segments, a company will need to consider its possible competitive position in relation to each segment in order to determine whether it merits the company's provision of an offering to that segment. Abratt (1993) found that a company's competitive position within a market and their ability to reach the buyers were most often used in practice. The size of the market was also used more often than not. Marketers also cited the extent to which they estimated that the segment was compatible with their own objectives or resources, the extent to which they considered it was profitable and whether they expected to see growth within that segment. The criteria listed by Abratt correspond to those found in other studies (e.g., Doyle and Saunders, 1985). In observing how companies actually target market segments, it is often argued that there are three strategic approaches: undifferentiated targeting, differentiated targeting and niche targeting.

Targeting strategy

Companies that engage in an *undifferentiated* targeting strategy make essentially the same offer to all segments. While for the most part this strategy is likely to be followed by those companies that do not engage in any segmentation anyway, it is still possible that a company that has engaged in a segmentation of the market might decide to pursue such an approach anyway (on the grounds that its offering will appeal to the market at the level of its entirety because the relationship between the two is such that the market is homogeneous). A standard offering to the whole marketplace has many advantages in respect of operating efficiency and is particularly appealing when large volumes can also produce economies of scale. However, companies operating in this way risk exactly the sort of over-generalized offerings that, as we indicated earlier, expose the company to attack from competitors that might produce a less generalized offering that would meet the needs of one or more segments more effectively. That is not to say that such a strategy has no merit. In new marketplaces (or where there has been a major innovation) a company, recognizing its first-mover advantage, may seek to make as much return as possible before the inevitable arrival of competitors. Philips, the electronics giant with headquarters in Holland, has often been thought of in these terms.

Differentiated target market selection involves choosing a variety of different segments and providing offerings that are focused on meeting the needs of those targets more specifically. Such an approach is less subject to the challenges of an over-generalized offering because it should more precisely fit the needs of customers. And there are infinite possibilities to customize what might otherwise be a standard offering. Such customization is possible with respect to all elements of the marketing mix. As Chapter 10 indicates, just considering the offering itself, there are possibilities for customizing its physical form as well as the service elements that go along with it.

In competitive markets it is inevitable that some form of differentiated offering will be required. The big difficulty for a marketing company is knowing whether to produce a different offering for each different segment. This puts the segment selection task into much greater relief. There will always be opinions expressed about new segments that could be targeted and it is always tempting to chase additional sales. However, a company that is acting strategically will temper all the requests with proper analysis of the costs and benefits associated with meeting the needs of a segment, aiming to ensure that over the long haul the benefits outweigh the costs.

Companies can, of course, apply much more *concentrated* targeting strategies. This takes the customer focus to an additional level in respect of one or a small number of segments. This is often the result of a realization that the company has a particular capability in an area that is desired by the marketplace. Success in five-year partnership programmes with water utility companies led MJ Gleeson, the UK civil and construction engineering company, to take the view that its interests in terms of targeting were best served in managing programmes of this sort rather than bidding for piecemeal engineering projects on a competitive tendering basis in other service sectors. A more concentrated approach is more likely to be necessary anyway for smaller companies that lack the resources to meet the needs of a larger number of segments. Niche marketers can often defend those markets very successfully because they know and meet customer needs so well, and because the resources required by larger competitors to overcome that goodness of fit renders such segments relatively less economic for them.

Business-to-Business Positioning

Regardless of the segmentation that has been undertaken, the targeting strategy adopted and the specific target markets that have been selected, when it comes to each individual segment there is a need to consider the position that the marketer occupies in the mind of the buying company. Primarily, the reasons for this are two-fold. First, the offering from a marketer occupies a space in the mind of the buyer. This may be captured in just a few dimensions. For example, Dell has managed to cultivate a position for itself in relation to PCs in the minds of buyers (corporate and individual) as highly customizable but low priced, even though the product itself is quite complex. The position becomes a shorthand that evokes the supplier and establishes the supplier in an idealized position that most closely represents the customer need.

Second, in a competitive context, the relative position becomes the basis by which the supplier is compared to others as well as the ideal. It becomes necessary to ensure that the relative position occupied in the buyer's mind is most favourable. It may even be sensible to position against a particular competitor – Ries and Trout (2001) recount how Avis established itself deliberately as the 'No. 2 car rental' company, recognizing that its major competition came from a range of companies other than Hertz, the market leader. By associating themselves implicitly with the market leader rather than trying to compete directly with Hertz, Avis managed to make the No. 2 positioning statement a market reality, catapulting itself well ahead of its primary competition.

In establishing a relative position, the firm has to be clear where its strengths lie. The positioning it adopts also has to be both clear and clearly communicated to buyers. Perhaps the biggest mistake companies make is trying to appear to be all things to all customers. By establishing a clear positioning in target segments on the basis of sound segmentation analysis, the business-to-business marketer is best placed to achieve strong marketing outcomes.

Chapter Summary

- This chapter has introduced important processes for the business marketing company that enable it to make strategically important decisions about where it stands in relation to the market in general.

- Segmentation provides the marketer with the basis to achieve efficient as well as effective solutions to customer problems by establishing degrees of homogeneity in what would otherwise be a heterogeneous marketplace.

- The homogeneous groups that result from a process of segmentation enable the marketer to decide what parts of the market to target with its solutions, in the expectation that it can solve customer problems more effectively and profitably than competitors.

- Segmentation enables the best match between the problem-solving abilities and uncertainties of both buyer and seller so that sustainable relationships can be created.

- In deciding what segments of the market to target, the marketer can establish more clearly their particular competence with these segments and how they can position themselves most effectively against competitors. .

Questions for discussion

1. What are the benefits of segmentation? What are the drawbacks?
2. List four macro-segmentation variables and explain their value in business markets.
3. List four micro-segmentation variables and explain their value in business markets.
4. How might a company making and distributing kitchen equipment segment the marketplace? Compare this with a company making kilns for the manufacturing process in the ceramics industry.
5. What criteria are used to select target markets?

Case study: Segmenting the market for Wavin Plastics

Wavin Plastics is part of Wavin UK, a wholly owned subsidiary of Wavin BV in Holland. The wider Wavin group is one of the biggest manufacturers of plastic pipe systems and other industrial plastics products in the world. It was founded in 1955 in Zwolle in Holland, where it still has its headquarters, and has 40 manufacturing and distribution sites in 27 countries in Europe and South East Asia. It also has a network of over 90 agents and licensed partners. It had a turnover exceeding €1 billion in 2004, net profits of €47 million, and just over 5000 employees. A perusal of the corporate website (www.wavin.com) shows that it has a separate presence for each country in which it operates, in some cases operating under separate company names within the Wavin Group (for example, RCS in Austria, EKOPLASTIK in the Czech Republic, and Labko in Finland).

The UK website (www.wavin.co.uk) reveals that it has 17,500 products with over 550 patents. The company clearly sees the need to continue to innovate. There have been recent initiatives in environmental solutions within the company, including storm water management, and in rainwater and grey water reuse. The outcomes of initiatives like these are expected to be welcome at a time of particular concern with respect to the effects of climate change.

Its products are designed and produced for a wide range of applications including gas, water, sewer systems, building, land drainage and irrigation, cable ducting and irrigation. These products are organized into two product groupings: Building and Installation ranges, and Civils and Infrastructure ranges. In the UK it is the market leader for above- and below-ground drainage products through OSMA branded products. It provides complete solutions for customers, backed by a dedicated sales force with full marketing, technical, sales and operational infrastructure. It holds BS EN 9001 Registered Firm Status and BS EN ISO 14001, the new British Standard for environmental management.

There is a whole range of different end users for OSMA products, including:

- the jobbing builder replacing a set of gutters, fitting a new kitchen, building a new bathroom or repairing cracked drains below ground;
- the small building contractor refurbishing a whole house or building from scratch;
- large building contractors engaged in a whole residential housing development;
- engineering companies engaged in pipe lining repairs or laying public access cable networks; and
- large civil and mechanical engineering companies building whole water treatment plants.

However, no end user can purchase OSMA direct – it is always bought through builders' merchants. This makes relationships with the distributors very important for the company. Of course, that does not mean that the company has no contact with many of these types of end user. For example, Wavin's strength in specification appeals to national housebuilders. At the same time, while the company is interested in demand for its products in the round, with its sales team it recognizes that it may need to talk to clients and their designers about a whole solution, involving a whole range of products configured in the most appropriate way to solve a customer problem.

As well as contractors and distributors (and others such as clients, developers, trade jobbers and utility providers) in the marketplace, there are specifier markets that affect whether or not Wavin products are used. Professionals like architects and structural and mechanical engineers have substantial reference power. Furthermore, high-profile reference projects have substantial value in showcasing Wavin product solutions – the more publicly known and impressive the better. The installation of a new soil and waste plumbing system for the Scala Opera House in Milan that was efficient and reliable was only the starting point. Demonstrating that they were best able to meet the requirements for range completeness and performance in terms of low noise levels swung it for Wavin. Wavin has also provided the bespoke underfloor heating for 'The Core' Education Centre at the Eden Project in Cornwall, sitting alongside the large Biomes featured at the attraction. As well as these high-visibility projects, the company has been involved in reference projects for residential development companies like Persimmon in upmarket housing at Newcastle Great Park, where the customer was looking for ease of installation, flexibility and cost effectiveness when choosing the plumbing system for the development. It has also been involved in demonstrating that its products can be used in environmentally sustaining ways through the Welsh House of the Future project commissioned by the National Museums and Galleries of Wales.

The company segmentation strategy continues to develop in order to adapt to the changes in the marketplace. Unsurprisingly then, the company engages in category management activities with important customers. After all, when you're one of the biggest manufacturers in the world of industrial plastic pipe systems and other industrial plastics products then you undoubtedly know much more than many of your customers.

Case study questions

1. Identify some of the bases that Wavin can use to segment the market.
2. How would you characterize Wavin's overall targeting strategy?
3. Compare Wavin's possible market positioning in the Civils and Infrastructure segment with the Building and Installation segment and describe how it might target each segment.
4. Using Wavin's website (www.wavin.co.uk) to help provide greater knowledge of its product and technologies, identify additional segments for it, stating the segmentation bases that you use. Use the criteria for successful segmentation to evaluate the usefulness of these proposed segments.

Sources: www.wavin.com; www.wavin.co.uk.

We gratefully acknowledge the help of Denise O'Leary (Wavin Plastics) in the production of this case study.

References

Abratt, R. (1993) 'Market segmentation practices of industrial marketers', *Industrial Marketing Management*, 22 (2): 79–84.

Beane, T. and Ennis, D. (1987) 'Market segmentation: a review', *European Journal of Marketing*, 21 (5): 20–42.

Choffray, J.M. and Lilien, G. (1978) 'A new approach to industrial market segmentation', *Sloan Management Review*, 19 (3): 17–29.

Doyle, P. and Saunders, J. (1985) 'Market segmentation and positioning in specialized industrial markets', *Journal of Marketing*, 49 (2): 24–32.

Frederick, J. (1934) *Industrial Marketing*. New York: Prentice-Hall.

Freytag, P. and Clarke, A. (2001) 'Business to business market segmentation', *Industrial Marketing Management*, 30 (6): 473–86.

Griffith, R. and Pol, L. (1994) 'Segmenting industrial markets', *Industrial Marketing Management*, 23 (1): 39–46.

Gross, A.C., Banting, P.M., Meredith, L.N. and Ford, I.D. (1993) *Business Marketing*. New York: Houghton Mifflin.

Hlavacek, J.D. and Ames, B.C. (1986) 'Segmenting industrial and high-tech markets', *Journal of Business stretegy*, 7(2): 39–50.

Hopkins, D. (2005) 'Colliding worlds: B-to-B vs. B-to-C marketing', DMA News Stand, online resorce: www.the-dma.org/cgi/dispnewsstand?article=3607, accessed 16 May 2005.

Jackson, B.B. (1985) 'Build customer relationships that last', *Harvard Business Review*, 63 (6): 120–8.

Miles, R.E. and Snow, C.C. (1978) *Organizational Strategy, Structure and Process*. New York: McGraw–Hill.

Ries, A. and Trout, J. (2001) *Positioning: The Battle for Your Mind*. New York: McGraw-Hill.

Sako, M. (1992) *Prices, Quality and Trust – Inter-Firm relations in Britain and Japan*. Cambridge: Cambridge University Press.

Shapiro, B. and Bonoma, T. (1984) 'How to segment industrial markets', *Harvard Business Review*, 62 (3): 104–10.

Smith, W.R. (1956) 'Product differentiation and market segmentation as alternative marketing strategies', *Journal of Marketing*, 21 (1): 3–8.

Verhallen, T., Frambach, R. and Prabhu, J. (1998) 'Strategy-segmentation of industrial markets', *Industrial Marketing Management*, 27 (4): 305–13.

Yankelovich, D. (1964) 'New criteria for market segmentation', *Harvard Business Review*, 42 (2): 83–90.

7 Market Communication

Learning outcomes

After reading this chapter you will:

- be able to explain the meaning and importance of integrated marketing communications;
- understand the factors affecting the composition of the communications mix in business markets;
- be able to explain the budgeting methods used for communications programmes;
- be able to explain the role of advertising, sales promotion and public relations in the business communications mix; and
- understand the strategic and tactical decisions made by managers in relation to advertising and trade fairs/exhibitions.

Introduction

Organizations interact with other parties; they send signals, communicate messages and engage in dialogue. The business marketer is concerned with formulating a communication strategy, that sends a consistent message to target audiences, one that is of interest to and also engages those audiences so that the organization is able to achieve whatever objectives were set for its communication activities.

This chapter and the next are concerned with marketing communications in business-to-business markets. In this chapter we introduce what can be classed as generic aspects of communication because whatever the context (whether business or consumer market) these issues are essentially the same. They include the components and nature of integrated communications strategy, the formulation of the communications mix and budgeting for communications activities. We then focus on what we call 'market' communication, discussing in more detail the use and design of communications tools such as advertising, sales promotion and trade shows. These tools are used to engage whole markets (albeit specific segments and target audiences) rather than specific individuals, are essentially impersonal, and provide little scope for dialogue and interaction. The next chapter centres on 'relationship' communication, where the tools that are used involve some form of direct contact (whether tactical/transactional or strategic/ongoing) with known representatives in specific customer companies. 'Market' communication and 'relationship' communication are sometimes referred to, respectively, as 'impersonal' and 'personal' communication. However, we prefer the terms market and relationship communication since they emphasize the *scope* of the communication (broadly to a market or narrowly to a known individual) without in any way constraining the *communications medium* that may be used.

Integrated Communication Strategy

Communications strategy involves planning, implementing and controlling an organization's communication with target audiences, the purpose being to achieve specified objectives with each audience. Companies use a variety of tools to do this, namely advertising, sales promotion, public relations, personal selling and direct marketing. These are combined into a communications programme to enable a company to engage buyers, but equally other stakeholders, that can influence or have an interest in an organization's activities. Responsibility for the management of the various communications tools may be split between departments. Strategies for advertising, sales promotion, direct marketing and public relations are normally separated from personal selling. This can sometimes result in poor integration amongst tools and today the integration of marketing communications is a critical issue for organizations. Information technology makes it much easier to expose customers to material from a variety of sources so that the chances of target audiences encountering inconsistent messages are increased. Academics and organizations alike have argued that communications strategy must be integrated, that the planning, implementation and control of the various tools used by a business must be such that the message presented to target audiences is consistent. See Box 7.1 for an example of one company's efforts to do just this.

Box 7.1 *Rethinking global communication*

In 2003 Pitney Bowes overhauled its marketing and communications strategy worldwide. The company created 'centres of excellence', with each being responsible for a different communications activity, namely advertising, customer communication materials, public relations, trade shows and events and

---

the Web. Previously individual business units conducted their own communications activities; now each centre is responsible for handling all work specific to its particular communications activity across the organization's various business units. Clearly coordination is vital between the six centres to ensure a consistent message and Pitney Bowes have adopted a solutions-oriented approach as a key theme in presenting the company to customers, influencers and to its own employees. The reorganization of communications activities and the rethinking of corporate and brand image have had a number of positive effects. For example:

- The company has increased its trade show presence from 93 to 150 and trade show response rates have increased, yet expenditure has remained the same.
- In 2003 only 11 per cent of the company's sales force used available communications materials as part of their selling aids. Working with the salespeople to help them understand Pitney Bowes' brand proposition has resulted in 55 per cent of them reporting that they used the company's brand proposition and marketing materials to open doors in 2004.

Source: Krol, 2004.

So it is important that companies formulate communications strategies that are integrative to ensure consistent messages are conveyed. However, members of a target audience will aggregate a marketer's communication material whether the organization does this or not – integration occurs at the audience level rather than organizational level. Members of that audience will assimilate the information encountered in some way and it may be that they:

- arrange the messages as the marketer intended;
- ignore the messages and materials; or
- put them together in a way that the marketer never even considered, which could even be harmful to the organization or the brand (Schulz, 1996).

Companies cannot control this assimilation process, the best a marketer can do is to 'try to understand the integration process and to modify their own approaches to maximise the return on the integration which occurs naturally' (Schulz, 1996: 140). Whether an organization concentrates its efforts on presenting an integrative message or tries to understand and accommodate a target audience's assimilation of promotional material, the business marketer has to put together a communications strategy. The formulation of this strategy requires a number of decisions to be made, including:

- setting communications objectives;
- deciding on the role of each component to be used in the communications mix;
- determining the communications budget; and
- selecting specific strategies for each component of the communications mix.

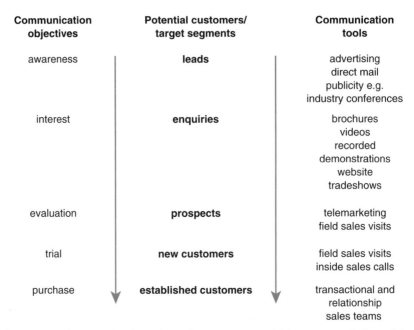

Communication objectives	Potential customers/ target segments	Communication tools
awareness	**leads**	advertising direct mail publicity e.g. industry conferences
interest	**enquiries**	brochures videos recorded demonstrations website tradeshows
evaluation	**prospects**	telemarketing field sales visits
trial	**new customers**	field sales visits inside sales calls
purchase	**established customers**	transactional and relationship sales teams

Figure 7.1   Communication mix and customer acquisition process (adapted from Anderson and Narus, 2004)

These are inevitably guided by an organization's choice of target market and positioning strategy, the latter determining the role that communication will play relative to the product, distribution and pricing in a firm's overall marketing strategy.

Communications objectives

Communications objectives help with deciding how the various communications tools will be used in a marketing programme. Essentially, the objectives can be related to what a firm wants its target audience to do with the information transmitted via its communication tools and, with this in mind, many objectives are associated with 'buyer readiness states' or the hierarchy of effects model. This model describes the stages through which a buyer progresses when engaging with communications material. The stages in the model can be linked to the process enacted by a company for acquiring and retaining customers and to the communications tools that might be used at the various stages of these processes. Figure 7.1 illustrates this progression.

Awareness is developed when potential customers become familiar with a product or brand. At this stage a company is trying to generate *leads* by aiming its communications campaign at all potential customers within a particular target market segment. To ensure exposure to what might be a large number of possible customers a company is likely to use impersonal, mass communications tools such as advertising and public relations. A firm might also use direct mail at this stage, drawing from mailing lists to distribute specifically designed mail shots to its target audience.

Interest is the next step, reflecting a potential buyer's desire to learn more about what (for example, product, brand, company) is being presented. Essentially, a company is trying to trigger a response from a target audience to generate enquiries and to encourage members of that audience to seek out more information, although not all potential buyers in a target market will do this. Where interest is generated, a company will use communication tools so that enquiries from potential buyers can be handled. A firm might issue brochures and catalogues in response to requests for further information, and increasingly this material is provided electronically. Recorded seminars, product demonstrations and presentations can either be emailed to interested parties or placed on company websites (Karpinski, 2005). The websites are a good medium in which a potential customer can search for detailed company and product information and learn more about an organization's product offerings.

Desire is the recognition by the buyer that when a supply need arises, a particular product or brand is the preferred option. To reach this point target customers will *evaluate* the product, brand and company information available from alternative suppliers. The number of *prospective* customers within a particular target for whom a company becomes a potential supplier falls, as those interested customers evaluate and eliminate some companies as potential sources of supply. Websites might continue to be one of the communication tools and information sources used by the business marketer and buyer respectively, although trade shows and field sales calls assume more importance at this stage.

To progress from the evaluation stage, the business marketer uses communication tools to elicit specific courses of *action*, which might be the placing of *trial* orders by its target audience. Prospects who place trial orders and who become *new customers* will obviously need to enter into dialogue with the supplier so at this stage personal selling (this could include field sales representatives and inside sales teams) becomes the critical communications tool.

These various stages of the state of buyer readiness represent a linear progression that is assumed to be essentially rational and over which the marketer has control (Schultz, 1996). In principle, the marketer sends messages via communications tools to affect the attitudes and behaviour of target audiences and is able to isolate the use and impact of each selected tool on members of those audiences. In reality this is not necessarily feasible. Customers (prospective and actual) are not passive recipients of messages; rather they can play an active part in the communications process, accessing and requesting information as needed, sending messages to marketing organizations. This has always been the case in business markets but this

Table 7.1 Buyer-ranked importance of communications tools by product type

	Product type				
Promotional tool	Major capital equipment	Minor capital equipment	Materials	Component parts	Supplies
Trade advertising	4	3	4	4	3
Technical literature	2	2	2	2	2
Direct mail	6	6	6	6	5
Sales promotion	5	5	3	3	3
Trade shows	3	4	5	5	6
Personal selling	1	1	1	1	1

Source: Adapted from Jackson et al., 1987: 30.

interaction is expanding as the use of IT and the web allows customers to engage with supply markets much more easily. The key for suppliers is to understand the type of information and messages preferred by customers and the format in which these are required. This does not negate the use of communications tools by the business marketer; rather there has to be a balance between the interests of supplier and customer companies in the communications process.

Communications mix

The promotional tools at the business marketer's disposal are not interchangeable and their effects at the different stages of the purchase process are not the same. So a company has to select the tools and their relative importance in the communications mix to reflect marketing communications objectives and the way in which information is used by its target audience. A customer's use of communications tools for purchasing decisions should inform the design of a business marketer's promotional mix – the design of this mix will vary depending on the product category, as illustrated in Table 7.1.

In the last 20 years or so the design of the promotional mix and value attributed by the business marketer to the various components have not changed dramatically – personal selling, advertising in trade magazines and tradeshow participation continue to be the most important tools. One significant difference is the importance now attached to web-based advertising. For example, in high-tech firms it outweighs sales promotion, technical seminars and direct mail and is almost as valuable to a firm as trade magazine advertising and trade show participation (Traynor and Traynor, 2004). Clearly, the importance attached to the various communications tools will be reflected in the business marketer's allocation of funds to support the use of those components.

Budgeting
A number of factors contribute to a company's sales performance. Some of these are determined by the organization itself, such as the design of the various elements of its marketing mix programme (including, of course, promotional activities) whilst others, such as competitor behaviour, government policy decisions or economic conditions, are beyond a firm's control. This means that setting a communications budget in relation to sales targets is difficult, with companies typically specifying improvements in the effectiveness of promotional activities and using practical methods to set budgets. These approaches include:

Objective and task
In using this approach, managers decide on the communication objectives, the tasks to be performed by the various promotional tools and the associated costs involved in achieving these objectives. Adopting this method allows managers to set the communications mix that is most appropriate for the tasks that are to be performed. This is by no means easy since estimating the level of effort (and therefore cost) to achieve certain tasks is particularly difficult.

Percentage of sales
This is more widely used and involves managers calculating the communications budget by multiplying a company's past sales by a standard percentage (for example, if last year's sales turnover was £1.5 million and the company aims to spend 4 per cent of turnover on communications, the budget will be £60,000). The calculation can be adjusted to take account of planned sales growth or decline, it reflects what an organization normally spends on communication activities, and may also take account of average spending levels in the industry. The problem with this approach is that it ignores that fact that sales are a consequence of promotional activities rather than the other way round. During a buoyant sales period, promotional expenditure may be wasted unnecessarily. By the same token, declining sales could trigger a downward spiral for a firm, where, rather than investing more to try and boost revenue, the communications budget as a percentage of those poor sales figures is reduced accordingly.

Competitive parity
Companies that use this method base their budget decisions on the amount invested by competitors and try to match it. Obviously it pays to have some idea of competitor expenditure levels (and many companies will engage in competitive tracking) but a firm cannot make budgeting decisions based solely on this approach. Competing organizations are likely to have different marketing strategies and so the communications strategies to help achieve these will also differ. The funds needed to support promotional activities should therefore be expected to differ also.

All that can be afforded

This approach bases expenditure on what a business can afford, with senior management determining how much can be spent on promotional activities. Budget limits are a fact of life in most organizations so the majority of decisions, whatever overall method is taken, will often include an element of affordability. Problems can occur when affordability is the only means for setting the budget, as it ignores a firm's marketing strategy and opportunities that might be open to a company to build sales and profitability via suitable investment in promotion.

These various approaches might typically be used to determine investment levels for advertising, sales promotion and public relations. Planned expenditure on advertising and sales promotion may be combined into one budget allocation, with firms having further budgets for public relations activities and personal selling respectively. Even if a firm does have separate accounts for these, at some point an overview of the various activities and associated resource needs/costs has to be taken to avoid fragmentation of an organization's promotion strategy.

Advertising

Leaving aside sales force costs, advertising represents the largest share of the communications budget for a lot of business marketers. It can serve a variety of purposes and its principal strength is that it allows a firm to communicate with large audiences at a far lower average cost per customer than with personal selling. Advertising is used to try to engage representatives of target customer organizations and it is equally useful in communicating with and trying to influence the behaviour of other stakeholders such as government bodies, financial markets, local communities and pressure groups. As far as the hierarchy of effects model is concerned, advertising supports the business marketer's investment in its principal communications tool, personal selling, and is typically used to create awareness amongst target customers, provide information and identify potential leads for sales personnel. Advertising can make a positive contribution to a firm's sales *effectiveness*, because when customers have been exposed to supplier advertisements it has been shown that sales revenue per salesperson call is frequently higher and sales personnel are rated more highly on product knowledge, service and enthusiasm (Morrill, 1970).

In addition to the above, advertising can also make selling more *efficient*. If a supplier needs to remind potential buyers of its problem-solving ability or to make customers aware of its new products, then a well-placed and suitably designed advert has the capacity to reach a far greater number of individuals than a sales representative ever could and at much lower cost.

Advertising strategy

A firm must make a number of decisions that result in the articulation of its advertising strategy, consisting principally of:

- setting advertising objectives;
- formulating the creative plan;
- media selection; and
- evaluation of advertising effectiveness.

Throughout the process of strategy development and implementation what must be borne in mind is that advertising is only one component of a firm's overall communications mix and must be integrated with other elements in order to realize strategic marketing goals.

Setting advertising objectives

Advertising objectives normally consist of *performance goals* (what should it accomplish?) and also the *target audience* (who does the organization wish to engage?). Clear articulation of objectives is crucial as they give direction to those involved in the formulation and implementation of an advertising programme. The goals are the principal means by which campaigns are evaluated and as such should reflect the functions that advertising can realistically perform and take account of the fact that immediate changes in sales that may result from campaigns are difficult to observe. So the objectives must be unambiguous but also realistic and expressed in such a way that the effect of an advertising programme can be measured. Where objectives are underpinned by the hierarchy of effects model, they are normally expressed in terms of communication goals such as brand awareness, recognition and buyer attitudes.

One of the principal purposes of advertising is to engage members of a customer organization who influence that company's purchasing activities – clearly these will not necessarily be restricted to employees with purchasing responsibilities, rather they could include managers from a variety of functions. As we have already noted in previous chapters, managers' choice criteria and interest in product attributes and the relative importance attached to them are in part determined by their functional responsibilities. Advertising objectives for a particular target audience must also reflect the choice criteria that are important to members of that audience.

Formulating the creative plan

The creative plan builds on the objectives set for an advertising campaign and essentially centres on the *development of a message* that will engage the specified target audience. The advertiser uses language, format and style in a campaign in order to present this message, which is informed partly by the advertiser's understanding of the target audience's choice criteria and also by the creative philosophy of the advertiser. As we have already explained, the hierarchy of effects model assumes a linear and rational progression in buyer readiness states. This is reflected in the creative strategy for advertising with arguments, problem-solving or unique selling propositions (USP) being central to the messages presented (West and Ford, 2001).

While in consumer markets it is often believed that messages that appeal to the emotions (notably humour) are particularly effective, in business markets messages tend to have a more rational appeal based on objective product characteristics and claims. Alternative views on buyer behaviour emphasize impulsive and irrational facets of purchasing. Where this is the case, emotion forms the basis of the creative strategy with brand image, identity, resonance or anomaly (West and Ford, 2001) driving message creation and presentation.

These approaches have been used successfully in consumer markets but is there room for emotion in business-to-business advertising? This may seem unlikely given the nature of the purchase process, the fact that buyers are accountable for purchases made, that products are not for personal consumption and are bought using non-personal funds. However, this ignores the contribution that emotion can have in shaping brand attitudes in business markets (Gilliland and Johnston, 1997) and the fact that emotional headlines are indeed prevalent in advertising copy (Cutler and Javalgi, 1994). At a strategic level a business brand might be presented using a rational approach but the tactical execution could, nevertheless, include emotion (West and Ford, 2001). For example the electrical engineering company Siemens worked with the agency Schubert Communications (www. Schubert.com) to present its distributed control system capability in the US. The adverts used headlines that indicated the unique selling proposition of the system and the copy provided detailed explanation in relation to the USP. The adverts contained two photos. One dominated the advert and was used to underline the basic idea of the USP but was completely unrelated to the product itself – for example, two people skydiving before their parachutes have opened – (this was used to underline the reduced risk in using Siemens systems solutions). A much smaller, offset photo of the product itself linked the copy with the eye-catching image. The execution of the advert mirrored the findings of Lohtia et al. (1995) relating to effective business-to-business print ads, namely that:

- a rational approach should be used in the creative strategy;
- information on performance and product quality should be included and
- be presented in a logical manner; and
- symbolism and metaphors can be useful in delineating the selling proposition. (Lohtia et al., 1995)

The adverts designed for Siemens underscore the fact that the creativity of an advertising message is equally significant in business markets, something to which high-tech firms now attach greater importance (Traynor and Traynor, 2004).

Media selection

Getting the message right is obviously crucial to gaining the target audience's attention and to ensuring that the signals conveyed in it are interpreted in the way intended by the advertiser. But for this to happen the audience has to be exposed to the advertisement in the first place, so media have to be chosen that will ensure that the audience is reached. Decisions about media selection are determined by the capacity of the selected medium to adequately convey the advertising message, the degree to which the medium can provide access to the target audience, and cost.

Broadcast and electronic media   Forms of *broadcast* media that a business marketer may choose from include television and radio. Although these feature to a lesser extent in business-to-business than in business-to-consumer markets, TV advertising may be used to raise the profile of an organization, contribute to corporate identity or positioning. The benefit of using TV for advertising lies in its combined audio and visual effect, offering the business marketer significant scope to attract audience attention. However, when using television an advertiser has to contend with the fact that a large number of those exposed to an advertisement will not be part of the target audience. So there can be considerable waste when TV advertising is used in business markets.

Company websites represent an *electronic* form of advertising that can be used by business marketers. Compared to other channels it is *interactive* in that a potential buyer is more likely to actively search out suppliers and has to make a conscious decision to enter a firm's website. Depending on site design, information communicated to a 'participant' can be tailored to individual requirements as a participant is guided through a series of web pages provided by the business marketer (Karayanni and Baltas, 2003). Obviously this interaction is quicker than other media, since requests for further information or specific queries can be issued by prospects via email and handled by the supplier electronically. However to determine whether members of a desired target audience are being reached (as opposed to, for example, competitors who may visit a company's site) and the level/nature of the interest amongst website visitors, the business marketer must measure:

- click-through rates;
- the duration of browsing time;
- the depth/number of assessed pages; and
- the number of repeated visits. (Hoffman and Novak, 1996)

Printed media   Trade publications that are specific to particular trades, professions or industries and the business press (such as *Business Week* and the *Economist*) are some of the principal forms of printed media used by advertisers in business markets. The business marketer will select publications based on their capacity to reach the specified target audience. This selection process is informed by the breadth and depth of a publication as well its circulation.

Horizontal publications focus on certain functions, technologies or tasks irrespective of industry, whereas *vertical* publications are more specific to a particular industry and may be read by managers from a variety of functions within an organization. For example *Marketing News* and *Logistics and Transport Focus* are horizontal publications and managers with marketing communications and logistics responsibilities respectively may subscribe to such journals, irrespective of the nature of the business or industry in which they are involved. Vertical publications such as *The Grocer, Hotel and Motel Management* and *Chemical Week* are more likely to be read by those involved in the food retailing, hospitality and chemicals industries respectively.

As well as considering periodicals to which members of a target audience may subscribe, an advertiser can make use of publications with *controlled circulation*. The magazines are industry- or profession-specific and individuals do not subscribe to them, rather they are issued free of charge to qualified readers. In order to receive the free publication a recipient must hold a position of influence in their organization's buying activities and provide the publisher with professional details such as title, function and responsibilities in relation to their organization's purchasing activities. Such information allows the advertiser to determine whether a particular publication can be used to access its target audience.

Sales Promotion

The use of sales promotion in business markets can be classified according to whether it is designed to trigger a response from members of a company's sales force, channel partners or organizational customers (see Figure 7.2 for a list of tools that may be used). For sales personel promotional tools are used principally to motivate staff or to support them in their selling roles. Where a company is trying to hit short-term targets staff are offered incentives such as prizes and cash rewards or may be awarded 'salesperson of the month' status in an organization's recognition programme. Such tools work well in one-off, transactional selling situations. However they can have a detrimental effect when a company is trying to build long-term relationships with key clients because such incentives encourage sales personnel to pursue short-term results.

To perform their various tasks sales staff may draw heavily from informational material provided by an organization. This material includes brochures, catalogues, and selling aids such as presentation kits which might be used to explain the features and benefits of new or existing products. As illustrated in the case of Pitney Bowes, for sales personnel to use presentation kits requires that they have confidence in and an understanding of the contribution of the materials to their sales efforts. Developments in technology have significantly improved the provision of information to customers, with salespeople now able to use portable multimedia presentations that can be interactive, to give

	Target		
Activity	Buyers	Intermediaries	Salespeople
Incentives			
Contests			
Trips			
Bonuses			
Prizes			
Advertising support			
Free items			
Recognition			
Promotional pricing			
Allowances			
Rebates			
Information			
Demonstrations			
Selling aids			
trade shows			

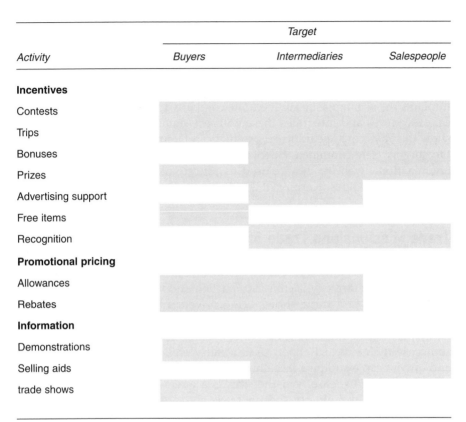

Figure 7.2 Sales promotion activities by target group (adapted from Cravens and Piercy, 2003: 633)

access to a complete product information system and to allow for the customization of proposals to clients (Widmier et al., 2002).

Sales promotion is also an important tool for organizations that rely on intermediaries in order to reach customers. Financial mechanisms (incentives and promotional pricing) are typically used as part of a company's push strategy (that is, trying to 'push' sales through distribution channels) and might be used to gain acceptance of new products by middlemen or to hit short-term sales targets. Given the fact that intermediaries assume a selling function on behalf of principles then the provision of informational material to support a distributor's sales efforts can also be important.

Incentives can be used to target business customers although they are less prominent than promotional pricing, which can be of more value in trying to cement a relationship with a customer or win a contract. Companies will also provide customers with informational material such as catalogues, brochures, application guides and speciality items (calendars, pens, and so on) to support sales activities. As we mentioned at the start of this chapter, organizations might also make use of IT and the Internet to provide more dynamic versions of informational material and to make this more readily available to potential or existing customers. Coapt Systems (www.coaptsystems. com), for example, develops, manufactures and markets bioabsorbable implants for use in plastic surgery. The company makes videotapes of surgical procedures and integrates these with presentations that are designed to show the physical appearance of products and demonstrate their use in real-life surgery. The combined videotapes and presentations are stored on the organization's website and are used to educate plastic surgeons about new surgical technologies (Karpinski, 2005).

Trade Missions and Trade Shows/Exhibitions

A key tool that is aimed at customers and which assists an organization's personal selling strategy is company participation in trade missions/shows. Trade missions and trade shows bring buyers and sellers together in one physical location. Organizations operating in business markets will normally participate in these promotional events because marketers are able to showcase their product expertise to a fairly well-qualified target audience and buyers can examine a large number of existing and potential new suppliers with relative ease. Whether this is a government-sponsored promotional event or an industry-specific trade show, the basic idea remains the same. This is that the events take place in specific locations and consist of multiple booths where suppliers display their products for anything from two days to two weeks. In many industries where firms are involved in or wish to develop overseas markets, trade missions and trade shows represent a key component of a firm's international communications activities.

Trade missions

A trade mission is a government-sponsored promotional activity. The purpose of a trade mission is to facilitate the economic growth of a particular region or country, typically via international trade in overseas markets. To achieve this trade missions can involve:

- the representation of particular regions or countries at major international trade fairs;
- major export drives where a government designates an overseas market as a priority for business development and then arranges, leads and partly funds promotional events in that target country; and/or
- major drives where a host government tries to encourage overseas companies to invest in its country. This type of activity is important for the

economic development of countries and is a key method for those countries to acquire skills, technology and know-how.

In Britain, the government body UK Trade and Investment (www.uktradeinvest.gov.uk) provides financial support to allow companies to participate in selected industry exhibitions, for example as with the Paris Airshow in France; the Asian Oil, Gas and Petroleum Exhibition in Kuala Lumpur, Malaysia; and the USA Bio 2005, in Pennsylvania. The support is designed to help firms gain initial exposure in new markets.

Trade missions can be particularly useful where firms are trying to develop export markets, especially if a company has limited international marketing experience in general, or with a specific country. Trade missions enable participants to acquire information fairly quickly about overseas markets as well as knowledge about the process of exporting to those countries. Exporters are able to learn about:

- the way in which business is conducted overseas;
- the services and products that are available in overseas markets;
- the level of interest amongst potential buyers in sourcing from foreign suppliers;
- the level of commitment and resources needed to compete in the overseas market; and
- the features of a particular overseas market and the process of exporting to them (Seringhaus and Rosson, 1998).

Trade shows and exhibitions

Trade shows are a bit like temporary versions of the shopping centres or retail parks that are such a prominent feature in consumer markets. Potential buyers visit prospective sellers, with most of the visitors having specific plans to buy a product or to influence the eventual purchase decision for a particular product (Gopalakrishna and Lilien, 1995). Key differences include *representation* and *'permanence'*. In consumer markets, intermediaries such as retailers are the principal means through which producers are able to present their products to target customers. In business markets, distributors will represent producers at some industrial trade shows (typically at regional or smaller national exhibitions) but in many instances suppliers will participate directly in shows that are key events within their industry.

Shopping centres and the retailers found within them are permanent, unless of course a retailer closes down its store. The location sites of most industrial trade shows are also fixed and can be quite substantial in terms of size. See Table 7.2 for details of the largest exhibition sites in various countries.

Table 7.2   Key Exhibition and convention centres around the world

Location	Capacity (metres²)
Hanover, Germany	495,265
Milan (New Exh. Center), Italy	345,000
Frankfurt/Main, Germany	324,277
Cologne, Germany	286,000
Düsseldorf, Germany	252,214
Valencia, Spain	230,837
Paris expo, France	227,380
Chicago, USA	204,461
Birmingham NEC, UK	200,000
Orlando (Orange Country), USA	195,167

Source: AUMA, 2005.

Table 7.3   The largest trade fairs worldwide (based on exhibitor numbers for 2004/5)

	Exhibitor numbers	Visitor numbers
Buchmesse, Frankfurt/Main 2005	7,225	284,838
ITB, Berlin 2005	6,723	139,024
CeBIT, Hanover 2005	6,246	474,082
HANNOVER MESSE, Hannover 2005	6,133	208,234
Anuga, Köln 2005	5,930	158,817
Ambiente, Frankfurt/Main 2005	4,665	141,344
MEDICA, Düsseldorf 2005	4,492	137,944
Automechanika, Frankfurt/Main 2004	4,464	163,337
ACHEMA, Frankfurt/Main 2003	3,819	192,161
Tendence, Frankfurt/Main 2005	3,419	85,002

Source: AUMA, 2005.

The events that take place within them however are not permanent; rather, they are temporary. Throughout any given year, a site will play host to numerous trade shows from a variety of industries. For example Hanover, the largest convention site in the world, also plays host to some of the largest trade fairs. See Table 7.3 for details of the world's largest fairs.

The idea behind trade shows is that they provide a close match between supply markets and target audiences, between buyer needs and seller offerings, with the following characteristics:

- Trade shows can be regional exhibitions within a particular country, designed to support companies in that area. Even so, the events might attract participants and visitors beyond the geographic boundaries of a particular region or country. See Box 7.2 for an example of how one region in Italy attracts members of the textile industry to its bi-annual exhibition in Florence.

- Trade shows might be used to showcase a country's expertise in a specific industrial sector. The Farnborough International Air Show is a key event for companies involved in the aerospace industry in the UK, attracting more than 900 exhibitors each year from the UK and abroad. In addition to the latest military and commercial aircraft being on display, companies supplying that industry also feature heavily in the show.
- Trade shows often represent one of the major international exhibitions in a particular industry. For example, companies involved in the rail industry would probably participate in Innotrans (www.innotrans.de) in Berlin, the industry's largest event.

Box 7.2 *Stretching a yarn*

For many years, spinners in the Tuscan region of Italy were renowned as world leaders in the production of yarn for high-quality fashion clothing, with their expertise being displayed at the semi-annual trade fair in Florence, Pitti Filati. By the mid-1990s however, the spinners' dominance was being undermined by competitors from developing countries who were able to imitate the Tuscan products at far lower cost.

To defend their position the Tuscan spinners worked with university researchers and leading designers to come up with new fabric and clothing styles, and the scope of Pitti Filati was broadened so that it became a platform for innovation in fabric and clothing design, rather than just yarn. The exhibits at the show sparked considerable interest, attendance at Pitti Filati doubled and the excitement has attracted industry visitors beyond the usual fabric producers.

The fabric and clothing designs that are displayed are free for anyone to copy – by presenting them, the Tuscan yarn producers are trying to demonstrate that their competence in the fashion industry spans the whole production chain and, as a consequence, their image has improved significantly.

Source: Adapted from Golfetto and Mazursky, 2004.

Functions performed by trade shows

Trade shows perform selling and non-selling tasks. We know that communication tools can be used to perform a variety of functions, with the design and use of selected tools complementing one another and contributing to a company's overall communications strategy. Tasks that can be performed by

New customer/ prospect buying phase	Key seller: communications objective and tasks		Relative communication effectiveness	
	Communications objectives	Task	Low	High
Need recognition	Generate awareness	Prospecting		
Developing product specifications	Feature comprehension	Opening relationship Qualifying prospect		
Search and qualification of suppliers	Lead generation	Qualifying prospect		
Evaluation	Performance comprehension	Presenting sales message		
Supplier selection	Negotiation of terms/ offer customization	Closing sale		
Purchase feedback	Reassurance	Account service	Advertising Trade Personal shows selling	

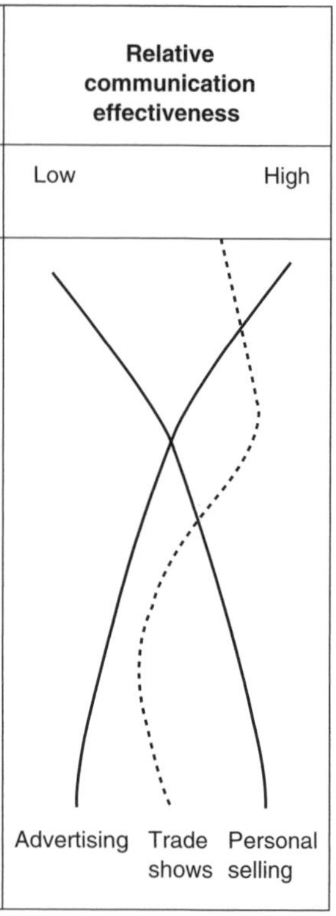

Figure 7.3   Relative effectiveness of business communication tools (Gopalakrishna and Lilien, 1995)

trade show participation are typically divided between those which are sales related and others that are not linked to the selling process.

Non-selling functions include: building or maintaining company image; gathering competitor information; product testing/evaluation; and maintaining company morale (Bonoma, 1983).

Non-sales tasks are cited by companies as reasons for participating in trade shows, but sales-related functions are nevertheless the principal motivation for investment in these promotional events (Blythe, 1997). The key sales-related functions that can be performed by trade show participation include: the identification of prospects; gaining access to key decision/ makers in current and potential customer companies; disseminating facts about vendor products, services and personnel; actually selling products/ winning orders; and servicing current accounts' problems via contacts made (Bonoma, 1983).

Given that the importance of trade shows is frequently compared to advertising and personal selling, and a company's exhibition strategy should complement other communications tools, then it is worth considering the extent to which these three communications tools can be combined in light of organizational buying and selling processes respectively. As can be seen from Figure 7.3, trade shows are useful in the early stages of the purchase decision process and in identifying and qualifying prospective new customers. However, as customers progress to evaluating potential suppliers and reaching final purchase decisions, and the sales process moves to presenting the sales message, closing a sale and even servicing an established account, then the trade show is less valuable compared to personal selling.

Money well spent?   As a communications tool, trade shows are important to companies operating in business markets not only in terms of the potential to contribute to a firm's communication activities but because of the money invested in these events. Leaving personal selling aside, trade shows are one of the most significant expenditure items for many firms, accounting for anything between 5 and 35 per cent of advertising spend and between 5 and 20 per cent of total marketing budgets (Bonoma, 1983). And that is without taking account of the time taken up by involving sales teams and senior management in the events. There has been growing scrutiny in recent years of the return on monies invested in trade shows yet this promotional tool continues to play a major role in communications activities, and perhaps with good reason. Even if funds allocated to trade shows and exhibitions are considerable, it has long been argued that compared to personal selling these promotional events offer significant savings. For example:

- it can cost up to 60 per cent less to make an initial contact at a trade show compared to the expense incurred by a salesperson visiting a prospective new customer in person;
- a salesperson might be able to make up to six sales calls per day, yet trade show participation can generate 40–50 leads per day; and
- when initiated by the salesperson, the entire sales cycle can cost four times more than if the transaction was triggered by a supplier's participation in a trade show (Browning and Adams, 1988; Hart, 1988).

So trade shows can have a positive impact on sales effectiveness and efficiency. However some companies can be discouraged by the costs of participating in trade shows in general, and in large exhibitions in particular, the result being that organizations might be more selective in the number of shows at which they exhibit in any one year and the size of the individual shows. For example, in 2003 MasterCard International participated in just two shows compared to between 10 and 12 in previous years, while others are opting for smaller, regional shows or are organizing invitation-only breakfasts and seminars as a way to target selected customers and prospects (Krol, 2003).

Audience attention and quality   Beyond using their effect on sales performance as a justification for investing a large proportion of the firm's advertising budget into trade shows, these events appeal to business marketers for a variety of other reasons. Although trade shows were initially seen as a means for boosting staff morale, the principal appeal for a company participating in these events relates to their contribution to a firm's communications activities (Gopalakrishna et al., 1995). If one of the reasons for communication is to engage a target audience and one of the challenges lies in attracting that audience's attention, then trade show participation can certainly facilitate this. Visitors to trade shows will select the events that they choose to attend purposefully, will go with specific objectives in mind and are likely to be aware of some of the participating suppliers whose stands they wish to visit. So the audience visiting a trade show will be on the lookout to:

- see new products and developments;
- try new products and go to demonstrations;
- obtain technical or product information;
- see new companies;
- discuss specific problems and talk with experts;
- compare products and services;
- make business contacts; and
- meet a specific company (Blythe, 2002).

Trade shows therefore provide the business marketer with a means of influencing purchase behaviour. Not only that, but a supplier can access members of the DMU that their sales personnel may have previously not succeeded in reaching. This is because audience quality at trade shows is much broader than simply consisting of managers with specific purchasing roles, who might be the business marketer's usual point of contact. Indeed, a large number of visitors have no role in purchasing and are instead involved in the areas of sales and marketing, general administration, design, engineering, and research and development (Blythe, 2002).

Managers with these functional responsibilities can influence different stages of the decision-making process, such as initial problem/need recognition or evaluation of different suppliers, and it is known that these stages can be affected by information obtained at trade shows (Moriarty and Spekman, 1984). See Table 7.4 for an indication of the motivations of managers from different functions in visiting trade shows.

One of the problems with a trade show is that it lasts for only a short period of time, with the result that interested parties might not be able to

Table 7.4   Visitor reasons for trade show attendance by job role

Reasons	Sales and marketing	General administration	Design	Engineering	R&D
See new products/ developments	19.1	16.6	6.66	7.5	4.16
Obtain product/ technical information	0.83	4.16	3.33	7.5	5.0
Try new products/ demonstrations	2.5	4.16	3.33	7.5	5.0
See new companies	2.5	4.16	1.66	0.83	1.66
See a specific company/ product	3.33	0.83	0.0	0.0	0.83
Discuss specific problems	0.0	0.83	1.66	4.16	1.66
Compare products	0.83	1.66	0.83	0.0	3.33

Source: Blythe, 2002.

attend or might overlook some stands. While exhibitors might fail to reach key members of their target audience. One way that is increasingly being used to deal with this and to provide ongoing access to trade show information and exhibitors is the use of virtual trade shows (Axelson, 2001). For example INNOTRANS, one of the leading international shows for transport technology, takes place each year in Berlin. As well as the physical event, the organizers offer a virtual marketplace – which is an electronic variation of the way in which a trade show normally operates. See Box 7.3 for an outline of how it works.

Box 7.3   *Buying and selling 24/7*

INNOTRANS Virtual Market Place – More fair, 365 days a year
Although INNOTRANS only lasts for a few days, the organizers of this international show also operate a year-round Virtual Market Place. This is an information and communication platform providing those who exhibit and visit the show with a means of getting and giving information about companies once the final exhibition stand has been dismantled and the lights have been switched off.

For an exhibitor the Virtual Market Place provides:

- listing on a specific platform containing company and product information;
- a presentation of a company and its offers, 24 hours a day, 365 days a year;
- a presentation of product films, corporate videos and 360-degree panoramas;
- links to company home webpages;

- a support service offering advice and help on how to update company data;
- the ability to update a company's virtual stand;
- an extra advertising and sales channel; and
- promotion of the platform by Messe Berlin GmbH.

Companies that visit the Virtual Market Place:

- can get a rapid overview of current transport technology by sector, any day of the year;
- can access precise information about exhibitors and their products at any time of the day;
- have access to a marketplace, making it easy to contact exhibitors and to send them enquiries, whatever their location in the world might be; and
- can make use of online facilities to prepare for a visit to INNOTRANS and to process results afterwards.

Source: www.messe-berlin.de

Planning trade shows

Although a trade show event lasts for a relatively short period of time, planning for it can take much longer, particularly when preparation prior to and evaluation after an event are taken into account. The planning process normally includes the following stages:

Setting trade show objectives   As we discussed previously, trade show participation can serve a variety of selling and non-selling purposes. A company might select any number of these as its principal reasons for investing in a particular trade show, focusing on short-term objectives such as performing product and sales presentations (selling functions), gathering competitor intelligence information or making new contacts (non-selling functions). Longer-term objectives could include launching new products, generating new leads (selling functions), and building customer relationships or company image (non-selling functions) (Shipley and Wong, 1993). However, to have any meaning, objectives have to go beyond the functions that can be served by trade show participation and, as with any objectives, must be articulated in such a way that they are measurable, can be achieved (given a firm's resources) and are realistic. For example, by performing product presentations what exactly is a firm hoping to achieve, what types of leads is a firm trying to generate and how many would it expect to accumulate over the exhibition period, and what systems will be used to monitor the number and types of leads generated?

Trade show selection   From setting objectives, a key decision for a company is to decide on the shows in which it should participate. Criteria that can be used in choosing between different events include:

- the type of products typically featured;
- the costs of exhibiting;
- the availability of suitable space at the show location;
- the timing of the event;
- the reputation of the show;
- the number and types of visitors that would normally attend the show; and
- the geographic scope of an event (is the emphasis regional, national or international?).

Large, prestigious international shows will attract massive visitor numbers and will therefore have an obvious appeal to a company when it selects events. However, this does not guarantee that the larger the show, the more people will visit a company's stand. In fact, the reverse can be the case: the larger the event, the more there is to choose from and therefore the greater the likelihood that a company's booth will not be visited. It is not only the size of events and multitude of competing participants that can make it difficult to attract visitor attention. Most visitors do not attend for the full duration of a show, rather they are likely to be present for a few days at the most and therefore the number of booths at which a visitor can spend a significant amount of time is quite small, no matter how big the event itself. This means that trade show tactics can be critical in ensuring that a company's involvement in a show is known and that visitors are motivated to seek out and/or stop at the firm's stand.

Tactics   Crucial to the success of trade show participation are the tactics surrounding involvement in a specific event. Decisions that can affect a company's degree of success include:

- *Promotional activities to support participation:* If a company is going to take part in a trade show, then prospective visitors to the event need to know about it! Pre-show promotion can include direct mail and advertising as well as invitations from sales personnel. Direct mail can be used to inform potential visitors of the company's participation in an exhibition and to invite them to call in on its stand. Listings can be developed using a show organizer's advance registration list as well as the firm's own customer/prospects database.
- *The design and location of a firm's stand:* This can be a key factor in determining the number of visitors to a company's stand. Given that a large number of exhibition visitors want to see or try new products or obtain technical or product information, the stand needs to be sufficiently eye-catching to make someone want to enter a company's display area rather than just pass by. Sample products, models, demonstrations and printed material must to be readily visible and the message conveyed by these display items clearly articulated. A company might have the most dynamic

and attractive booth at a trade show, but if it is hidden away in a corner, far from the hubbub of the main event, then it is of no use. Firms must also therefore decide on the site for their booth. The obvious choice would be to select high-traffic locations such as those near to market leaders, refreshments areas or even booths on corner sites (Shipley and Wong, 1993). Such locations are normally more expensive so a company has to balance the extra cost with the likely visitor numbers that could be realized.

- *The selection and behaviour of staff on the stand:* The composition and behaviour of stand personnel can be critical to successful trade show involvement. Sales personnel are the obvious choice, but the objectives of participation in a specific event should be borne in mind, as should the fact that a large proportion of trade show audiences do not have purchasing responsibilities and will typically use events for information-gathering purposes. So for example, if a company is trying to raise awareness of its organization and its latest products, then it could use less technically qualified and commercially experienced staff to deal with general queries and to provide visitors with selected promotional material. Only a limited number of sales personnel might be needed provided that those who do staff the stand can deal with more explicit product, and research and development queries.

  Where an organization is trying to generate leads then sales as well as technical staff should be more prominent throughout the duration of an exhibition event. This would enable more specific enquiries to be dealt with and the quality of potential leads to be determined. Leaflets and brochures should still be available, although these might only be released in exchange for visitors providing company and contact details. This information allows the firm to follow up leads after the show.

  If a company is using an event to build or sustain particular relationships and invites representatives from target organizations, then it goes without saying that managers responsible for handling the relationships need to be present when the invited customers are scheduled to visit! Arrangements would also need to be made to enable discussions to take place in a designated meeting area on the exhibition stand itself, or alternatively, at a venue away from the trade show location.

- *Post-exhibition follow-up:* To make best use of opportunities that arise during a trade show a firm must pursue leads quickly after the event before interest from those contacts starts to decline. The nature of the leads will vary so the urgency and the business marketer's response and responsibility for pursuing them should also vary. For example, details of the various leads that have been logged can be handled according to three characteristics:

1. Are visitors mainly interested in company rather than product information? In such instances communications material can simply be posted and any particular queries handled in an accompanying

letter. Processing of such leads can be handled by a company's internal sales team.

2. Are visitors interested in the company's products and likely to make a purchase decision at some point in the future? Again, a firm's internal sales team can deal with the contact, but rather than relying on written communication could use telemarketing in order to qualify the prospect and handle the contact's queries.

3. Is a purchase decision imminent? These leads should be forwarded to sales representatives (even transmitting them during the trade show) so that the potential customer can be contacted on their return from the trade show.

- *Post-show evaluation:* Assessment of the effectiveness of trade show participation requires, as already discussed, objectives that are measurable and realistic. In addition to this, there has to be a means of recording activities in relation to these specific objectives during the show, and conducting research once the event is over might also be necessary.

Public Relations

Public relations (PR) is used to manage the image of an organization with its stakeholders and to close the gap between a company's desired image and the way in which it is perceived by its various publics. PR has gained greater prominence in recent years as companies recognize the importance of managing relationships with key stakeholder groups and the contribution that these relationships can have on corporate image and reputation. In comparison to other communications tools PR has a broader scope, although its use can make a business's marketing activities easier. In dealing with external publics it can be used to:

- attract and keep good employees;
- handle issues and overcome misconceptions relating to an organization;
- build goodwill amongst publics such as governments, local communities, suppliers, distributors and customers;
- build an organization's prestige and reputation; and
- promote products.

PR activities include the use of lobbying and charitable donations, press releases, corporate advertising, seminars and publications. All of these uses and activities are relevant to organizations operating in business markets, but the running of or contribution to seminars and publications can be particularly valuable in enhancing a company's reputation and its products or problem-solving abilities. See Box 7.4 for an example of this.

Box 7.4 *Spreading the word*

Gartner is an international organization that provides research and analysis about the global information technology industry. Key elements of this company's business activities are its

- engagement in consultancy work, where it guides major enterprises in their formulation and implementation technology based strategies, and
- organization of events around the world, including its Technology Summits and IT/Expos.

The Technology Summits are organized around the world, including at locations in North and South America, Europe, Japan and Australia. These conferences focus on particular topics such as security, wireless technology and outsourcing, and are made up of presentations by Gartner analysts as well as contributions from leading experts in the IT industry. As these are fee-paying events Gartner have to convince their target audience of their expertise and ensure that Gartner is automatically associated with selected IT topics by its audience. The events that it organizes itself may go some way to achieving this, but equally important is the regular appearance of the views, expertise and work of its analysts in readily accessible publications. Its analysts will frequently comment on industry trends in IT-related publications and feature in professional and management publications. See for example the November/December 2005 issue of the *Business Integration Journal* that features the work of a number of Gartner's researchers (www.bijonline.com).

Chapter Summary

- Communication is central to positioning strategy and as such companies must ensure that communication is integrated to ensure that consistent messages are conveyed to target audiences.

- By understanding and accommodating customer information needs and ways in which information contained in the various communications tools is processed, there is a greater likelihood that the audience's assimilation of the marketer's messages will be unified.

- The communications tools available to an organization can serve a number of purposes and their importance (in terms of the resources allocated to fund them) will vary, reflecting the objectives for the overall communications programme as well as each of the communications tools, and accounting for market conditions and customer information needs.

- To engage whole markets (albeit specific target segments and audiences) a company can make use of advertising, sales promotion, trade shows and public relations – of these, advertising and trade shows are the most important.

- Leaving personal selling aside, advertising represents the largest share of an organization's communication budget and is typically used to generate awareness, develop leads and generate inquiries. The formulation of an advertising strategy requires decisions on the role of advertising in the overall communications mix, objectives, creative strategy and the media to be used.

- Trade shows are a key element in the business marketer's communications mix, second only to advertising (that is, if we ignore personal selling) in terms of the resource invested, performing a variety of selling and non-selling functions. Trade show participation requires the business marketer to determine objectives, to choose specific shows at which to exhibit and to make tactical decisions in relation to pre-show promotion, stand design and location, staff involvement and behaviour, and post-exhibition follow up and evaluation.

- Sales promotion can be used to trigger a response from members of an organization's sales force, channel partners or customers. Financial incentives are used to motivate staff and channel partners, and with customers they can help to cement a relationship or win a contract. Informational tools, such as catalogues, brochures and presentation packs are used by sales staff and intermediaries to present an organization, its problem-solving abilities and products to interested parties.

- PR is used to manage the image of an organization with its key stakeholders and has grown in prominence in recent years as companies recognize the effect of relationships with these stakeholders on company performance.

Questions for discussion

1. To what extent is the business marketer able to present an integrated communications message to target audiences?
2. Is TV advertising of any value to companies operating in business markets?
3. Emotion has no part to play in advertising messages aimed at the business customer. Discuss.
4. Trade shows can be prohibitively expensive for some companies to participate in, as well as being time-consuming for visitors. What alternative ways can participants and visitors access the benefits normally associated with being physically present at a trade show?

Case study:	The serious business of football in China

China has a total population of 1.3 billion people, is emerging from a period of remarkable change and is progressing rapidly to becoming one of the most influential economies worldwide. Its GDP has been increasing year on year by more than 7 per cent and it is now the largest mobile phone market in the world and one of the biggest consumers of energy. In effect, it is becoming an economic goliath. So any firm that has global aspirations, that wants to operate internationally, cannot afford to leave China out of its strategic calculations. Those companies that are clear about wanting to capture some of the opportunities in the Chinese market and those who act quickly could be very successful. The biggest challenge, however, is knowing how to get started.

One way that companies can make inroads into establishing themselves in overseas markets is to make use of government-sponsored international trade missions. For example, the British and Chinese governments operate joint programmes to encourage investment in China by UK organizations. Quite separate from these trade missions, is the work that the UK soccer team Stockport County Football Club (Stockport FC) is doing to help British companies find new business contacts in the burgeoning Chinese economy – a novel role for a soccer club!

The club's role as a facilitator of international business development started as a consequence of a chance meeting in a Chinese restaurant in Manchester between the club's commercial manager and a Chinese businessman. The two men started talking about the developing sports market in the East. Twelve months later club representatives visited China and the visit resulted in the club bringing Chinese teenagers over to the UK for football training and education. One of the youngsters was signed for the club, became its youth team captain and went on to be chosen for the Chinese Olympic squad. The Chinese were impressed with Stockport FC's commitment – it may not be the biggest football club in the UK, but its representatives were sincere and interested in China for the long term.

Over a four-year period the club's commercial manager and county officials continued to visit China, targeting cities and provinces not often visited by Westerners. Stockport scored first by becoming joint owners of a Chinese football club. Stockport FC started doing football tours and again took the decision to go to provinces where other clubs had not previously gone. By chance, the Chinese and British government had launched a campaign trying to encourage investment in China, which resulted in the club being greeted in places that were being visited by senior officials at the same time (vice mayors/mayors/heads of bureaus). The club maintained these contacts and those people have since been promoted to more senior positions – so now Stockport FC has good links with government officials, which helps to smooth the business development path.

The club went on a summer tour of China, but the tour was not just about the 'beautiful game'. Now it was more about companies developing business in China on the back of football. A British football club is still a bit of a novelty in China, but more unusual is that the team is accompanied by British businesses keen to trade with the booming Chinese economy. Stockport FC is seen as a gateway to China and it makes money by charging fees to companies participating in trips or taking commission on benefits earned. The club is selling its knowledge of and connections in some of the Chinese regions that are normally left out of trade mission visits. It is able to bring British companies into a city that has the right fit in terms of sector and gives the organizations governmental contacts. In turn, the government representatives provide the businesses with industrial and commercial contacts. In every city visited by the club the delegation is given trade packs, selling the virtues of doing business in their town and detailing lists of projects on offer and contacts for those seeking business partners. The delegation is greeted by top government officials and treated like VIPs – both sides have one common aim: to do business in China. And all of this with the fun of football alongside it! At the matches, there is a VIP section in the spectator stand for government officials, Communist Party members and the Stockport delegation.

In a country where commercial law is still developing, close personal and business ties are one of the best ways of ensuring success. After each game there is a banquet, giving delegation members the opportunity to make contacts. For example:

- At one of the soccer games, a British company did a circuit of the pitch with pre-match promotional material. The company joined Stockport FC's tour because it was looking to do business with established companies that might be interested in its design, marketing and brand management expertise, with the build-up to the 2008 Olympic Games in Beijing being an obvious focus. At the post-match banquet the British company was introduced to representatives from the region's trade and economic department and then to managers from a local company that made high-quality clothing. This company's main concern was to try and develop its brand worldwide and to improve its design. By the following day, the British manager has visited the factory and met the owner and the two were talking about the possibility of joint brand development.
- At another post-match banquet, the textile table included a British company that was hoping to strike a deal to promote a sportswear brand. The region that hosted the banquet had over 3000 textile factories and was famous for clothing and football. Less than 24 hours after leaving the UK, the British manager had met government people and representatives from other provinces.

- Another business involved in the motor racing world was proposing a $300 million project to set up a high-tech centre of excellence for automotive engineering, effectively creating an automotive and motor sport village. Using Stockport FC to try and set up the venture enabled the consortium to leapfrog bureaucracy and to deal with government officials who had decision-making authority. The consortium met with the town's deputy mayor on the afternoon of the football match, during the banquet four representatives from the mayor's office asked further questions and the following day a meeting was set up with the mayor himself. At this meeting, the mayor identified the official in the town planning department responsible for allocating land for business development opportunities, contacted the official on behalf of the consortium and personally endorsed the consortium's project.

The soccer games act as a hook for the business and Stockport FC's commercial innovation has been spotted by the British government's trade and export arm, UKTI, which now helps to sponsor the tour and uses the club as one of its case studies for doing business in China.

Case study questions

1. The case study shows how sporting and cultural activities can be used to help to bridge wide inter-cultural gaps and facilitate B2B trade links. Using Internet research, identify one or more other examples where sporting or cultural activities have been used to facilitate B2B trade.
2. Refer back to the material on trade missions earlier in the chapter. What are the benefits to the B2B marketing organizations that take part in the Stockport FC missions to China?

Source: BBC Radio 4, November 2004.

References

Anderson, J.C. and Narus, J.A (2004) 'Gaining new customers', in *Business Market Management* (2nd edn) New Jersey: Prentice Hall. pp. 315–60.

AUMA (2005) Association of the German Trade Fair Industry.

Axelson, B. (2001) 'Virtual trade shows await their turn', *B to B*, 86 (5): 23.

Blythe, J.W.D. (1997) 'Does size matter? Objectives and measures at UK trade exhibitions', *Journal of Marketing Communications*, 3 (1): 51–9.

Blythe, J.W.D. (2002) 'Using trade fairs in key account management', *Industrial Marketing Management*, 31: 627–35.

Bonoma, T.V. (1983) 'Get more out of your trade shows', *Harvard Business Review*, January–February: 75–83.

Browning, J.M. and Adams, R.J. (1988) 'Trade shows: an effective promotional tool for the small industrial firm', *Journal of Small Business Management*, October: 31–6.

Cravens, D.W. and Piercy, N. (2003) 'Promotion, advertising and sales promotion strategies', in *Strategic Marketing* (7th edn). Maidenhead: McGraw-Hill. pp. 399–423

Cutler, B.D. and Javalgi, R.G. (1994) 'Comparison of business to business advertising: the United States and the United Kingdom', *Industrial Marketing Management*, 23: 117–24.

Gilliland, D.I. and Johnston, W.J. (1997) 'Toward a model of business-to-business marketing communications effects', *Industrial Marketing Management*, 26: 15–29.

Golfetto, F. and Mazursky, D. (2004) 'Competence-based marketing', *Harvard Business Review*, 82 (12): 26.

Gopalakrishna, S. and Lilien, G. (1995) 'A three-stage model of industrial trade show performance', *Marketing Science*, 14 (1): 22–42.

Gopalakrishna, S., Lilien, G., Williams, J. and Sequiera, I. (1995) 'Do trade shows pay off?', *Journal of Marketing*, 59 (July): 75–84.

Hart, N. (1988) *Practical Advertising and Publicity*. Maidenhead: McGraw-Hill.

Hoffman, D. and Novak, T. (1996) 'Marketing in hypermedia computer mediated environment: conceptual foundations', *Journal of Marketing*, 60(3): 50–68.

Jackson, D.W., Keith, J.E. and Burdick, R.K. (1987) 'The relative importance of various promotional elements in different industrial situations', *Journal of Advertising*, 16 (4): 25–33.

Karayanni, D.A. and Baltas, G.A. (2003) 'Website characteristics and business performance: some evidence from international business-to-business organizations', *Marketing Intelligence and Planning*, 21 (2): 105–14.

Karpinski, R. (2005) 'On-demand events better at converting registrants to qualified sales leads', *B to B*, 90 (5): 28.

Krol, C. (2003) 'Economy size', *B to B*, 88 (9): 17.

Krol, C. (2004) 'Pitney "centres" centralise marketing across business units', *B to B*, 89 (12): 16.

Lohtia, R., Johnston, W.J. and Aab, L. (1995) 'Business-to-business advertising: What are the dimensions of an effective print ad?', *Industrial Marketing Management*, 24: 369–78.

Moriarty, R.T. and Spekman, R.E. (1984) 'An empirical investigation of the sources of information used during the industrial buying process', *Journal of Marketing Research*, 21 (May): 137–47.

Morrill, J.E. (1970) 'Industrial advertising pays off', *Harvard Business Review*, 48 (March/April): 4–14.

Schulz, D.E. (1996) 'The inevitability of integrated communications', *Journal of Business Research*, 37: 139–46.

Seringhaus, F.H.R. and Rosson, P.J. (1998) 'Management and performance of international trade fair exhibitors: government stands vs. independent stands', *International Marketing Review*, 15 (5): 398–412.

Shipley, D. and Wong, K.S. (1993) 'Exhibiting strategy and implementation', *International Journal of Advertising*, 12: 117–30.

Traynor, K. and Traynor, S. (2004) 'A comparison of marketing approaches used by high-tech firms: 1985 versus 2001', *Industrial Marketing Management*, 33: 457–61.

West, D. and Ford, J. (2001) 'Advertising agency philosophies and employee risk taking', *Journal of Advertising*, XXX (1): 78–91.

Widmier, S.M., Jackson, D.W. and McCabe, D.B. (2002) 'Infusing technology into personal selling', *Journal of Personal Selling and Sales Management*, 22 (3): 189–99.

8 Relationship Communication

Learning outcomes

After reading this chapter, you will:

- understand the nature and role of direct marketing and personal selling in relationship communication;
- be able to describe how direct marketing and personal selling can be used to acquire new customers and win orders;
- be able to describe the customer and order acquisition process;
- understand the issues and decisions that a firm must address to enable the coordination of relationship communication between firms and within the vendor company; and
- be able describe the control systems that a firm can use to direct the behaviour of employees that communicate with customers.

Introduction

In the previous chapter we considered the overall process of communications, the components and nature of integrated communications strategy, the formulation of the communications mix and budgeting for communications activities. We also distinguished between communication tools that are impersonal, allowing little scope for dialogue, and others that involve some form of direct contact and interaction between the business marketer and known individuals in customer companies. The former, which we classified as market communication and discussed in the previous chapter, includes advertising, sales promotion and public relations. The latter, which we term relationship communication and consider in this chapter, consists of direct marketing and personal selling. To start with we look at general features of these two communication tools before going on to discuss how they are used in the processes of gaining new customers and building relationships. We then consider the coordination of relationship communication activities, both between supplier and customer companies as well as within the vendor organization itself.

Direct Marketing

Direct marketing involves *interaction between individual customers and the vendor organization, with customer responses to communication from and transactions with the vendor being recorded and the data used to guide the formulation, execution and control of relationship management programmes with those customers* (adapted from Institute of Direct Marketing, 2002). Key features of direct marketing are:

- the *absence of face-to-face* contact;
- the use of media such as *direct mail, telemarketing and electronic media* (such as, the Internet and email) for communication and transactions;
- the *facility to measure responses* to communications (which can be difficult for advertising campaigns and personal selling activities); and
- the use of a *database* from which targets for communications activities are drawn and to which responses and transactions are added.

Clearly the database is central to the operation of all direct marketing activities. IT systems provide a company with the means to store and access a variety of information relating to areas such as:

- *customers and prospects* (name, contact details, company size, activities, purchase process, key decision-makers and influencers, choice criteria);
- *transactions* (frequency, timescale, amount, product categories);
- *promotions* (campaigns to which a customer is exposed and results such as leads generated, contacts made and sales obtained);
- *products* (where promotion campaigns are used and to which customers respond); and
- *industry, market or geographic regions* (that may impact on opportunities and customer behaviour).

Direct marketing campaigns

As with any communications activity, the *target audience* for direct marketing activities needs to be identified and might consist of enquirers, prospects and lapsed or existing customers. Based on the audience for the campaign the vendor compiles a *list* of individuals who will be targeted, with the list either being drawn from the firm's own database or purchased from external brokers. Direct marketing *objectives* can have a financial emphasis (such as to achieve specific sales or profitability targets) or might be expressed in terms of generating awareness or interest, acquiring a percentage of new customers from those organizations targeted or retaining a specific level of previously acquired customers. In order to reach its target audience, the vendor has to choose the most suitable *media*.

Direct mail

Direct mail consists of material sent through the postal service and can be particularly effective in delivering a personalized message to a specific target recipient at a precise point in time. This medium is more expensive than print advertising and email but cost per contact is typically lower than telemarketing and personal selling. Printed material might be used to develop familiarity with and interest in a vendor or a particular product. Alternatively a company might use direct mail to encourage recipients to visit its trade show exhibit or members of its dealer network. As mentioned in Chapter 7, dynamic product explanations and demonstrations can be contained in the direct mailing by including electronic presentations or video recordings in the communication.

A key contributor to the success of direct mail campaigns is the quality of the mailing list. For example, a company supplying materials or equipment for the production of plastic packaging in the food and beverage industry could try to target potential customers by purchasing mailing lists from directory producers such as Kompass (www.kompass.com) or Dun & Bradstreet (see Chapter 5 for more information on the services that this company provides). It could also obtain subscription lists to trade magazines such as *Plastics News International* (www.plasticnews.net) and attendance lists for the food processing trade fair, Anugafoodtec, which is held every 3 years in Cologne, Germany (www.anugafoodtec.com). Such sources can be helpful in identifying new targets, although the most useful lists may frequently be those compiled by the marketing organization using its own database.

Telemarketing

Telemarketing consists of a marketing communication system where marketing and sales activities are performed by trained specialists using telecommunications and information technologies. Inbound telemarketing is where contact is initiated by a potential or existing customer and outbound is where contact is made by the vendor. Irrespective of who initiates the contact, where the vendor already has data on a customer this information should be readily accessible via the organization's IT system to facilitate dialogue between the telemarketer and client. Compared to direct mail, telemarketing is more versatile and it can be an important tool because of the various roles that it is able to perform. These roles include the following.

- *Account management:* When sales to a customer are insufficient to warrant field sales calls, telemarketing can be used to service accounts. A customer might simply call to enquire about or place a repeat order, requiring little technical expertise on the part of the vendor's employee. However, this medium can also be used to handle more complex situations provided employees are technically skilled and have ready access to the vendor's database of product information and customer account records. Indeed, when used in conjunction with faxing and the Internet, it can provide a more efficient means of handling accounts than would be possible with a field sales force.
- *Field support:* In some cases customers might require personal visits from field sales representatives, yet handling all aspects of an account can be beyond the capacity of a single salesperson. So an account manager will make personal visits to a customer's premises but will be supported by telemarketing representatives. Telemarketers can act as a communications link between the customer and account manager, handle enquiries and problems as well as process orders placed by the customer.
- *Prospecting:* Telemarketing can be used to screen leads generated by direct mail (or direct response advertising) and, depending on the potential, telemarketing representatives will make appointments for field sales representatives to visit prospective customers (see later section on acquiring new customers and winning orders).

In spite of its versatility, telemarketing does have its disadvantages. For example, it is not suitable for dealing with complexity. The nature of the customer's requirements might be such that they cannot be clarified without face-to-face communication, and the vendor's proposals may need to be seen so that various managers involved in the purchase decision understand them. As a standalone medium telemarketing may be inadequate, but it can be a useful tool when used in conjunction with other communications activities.

Electronic media

Electronic media such as the Internet and email enable a degree of interaction that is not possible using direct mail and is more difficult to achieve via telemarketing. 'The interaction' associated with direct mail is limited to customers responding to a vendor's campaigns. Email can be used as an alternative medium for direct mail campaigns but a customer has the scope to communicate more than the information or response sought in a vendor's campaign, can initiate dialogue and engage in on ongoing communication process with the supplier. Likewise, telemarketing facilities allow a customer to initiate and participate in ongoing dialogue and to trigger responses from a supplier. However, it lacks the capacity to share complex or large volumes of data and websites and extranets can fill this gap. Tools such as the Internet and extranets can facilitate transactions and communications between firms. In using such web-enabled technology companies do have to deal with their effect on company activities, such as:

- *The challenge of 24/7:* Website trading does not stop for restocking, corrections to programming errors or repairs to broken links with other business systems.
- *Marketing in real-time:* Customers might expect instant query resolution or an immediate response to requests because websites deal with customers in real time.
- *Customization:* Website customization can make use of a variety of data sources (such as clickstream, company data and previous purchases).
- *Data volumes and integration:* Websites can collect more and varied data than other contact points, but this does pose challenges in terms of system integration and information overload.
- *Global reach:* Internet communication eliminates spatial distance.
- *Maintaining contact:* Email allows firms to keep in touch with customers more easily.
- *Low transaction costs:* The fact that the cost of handling online orders and information requests is much lower can offer scope for lower margin transactions (Institute of Direct Marketing, 2002).

Personal Selling

Personal selling involves a supplier's employees communicating directly with managers from a customer company. This direct exchange allows:

- the customer to communicate and the business marketer to determine precise supply requirements;
- the negotiation of adjustments to the supplier's product offer or the formulation of a bespoke offering to match the customer's needs; and
- interaction between representatives from both organizations, which underpins the initiation, development and ongoing handling of supplier–customer relationships.

Our discussion about this form of relationship communication introduces some of the responsibilities associated with the sales function and the types of salespeople that a supplier might employ. We then move on to consider the communication process, from acquiring new customers and winning orders to building relationships with customers. In doing so it should become clear that it is not just those managers with sales or relationship management responsibilities that contribute to a customer's experience of dealing with a supplier. In fact, any employee who interacts directly with managers from a customer company adds to that customer's experience of the supplier. The challenge for the marketing organization lies in coordinating activities to ensure consistency in the behaviour of its representatives and the experience of its customers.

Sales responsibilities and people

One of the principal functions of employees with sales responsibilities is to identify and secure revenue-generating opportunities, to *win business* from targeted customers. Getting to this point involves the salesperson in a variety of related activities. The supplier's representative has to *match* the marketing organization's product offering with a customer's supply needs. The salesperson might be expected to *augment* the supplier's product, using technical expertise and industry experience to recommend optimum solutions to customer sourcing problems or to advise, for example, on how a customer might achieve cost reductions or productivity improvements. A salesperson also assumes an important *representation* role. Clearly, they represent the *supplier* in exchanges with customers, but they also act on behalf of customers inside their own organization; that is, they represent *customer* interests and articulate their requirements when dealing internally with other functions.

Sales representatives also perform an important role in *maintaining customer files* and *feeding back information* (resulting from exchanges with customers) into the supplier company. Accurate information that is readily accessible to supplier employees is important in ensuring consistency in the supplier's handling of a customer. As the principal point of contact with customer companies, sales representatives might be expected to oversee the *handling of complaints* received from customers. Complaints that lie within the expertise and authority of the sales function can be resolved by the sales personnel themselves. Others, which are technically and commercially more complex, will require the involvement of other functions and levels of management authority. The salesperson might then assume responsibility for overseeing the supplier's response to the customer complaint.

The sales function can take a variety of forms within a marketing organization such that a company makes use of three different characteristic types:

1. *Missionary salespeople.* In such cases supplier representatives do not actually try to secure orders, rather they direct efforts at creating business by influencing individuals or companies who have the authority to specify particular suppliers when orders are issued. See Box 8.1 for an example of how one company uses its sales personnel to ensure consideration and eventual specification of its products.
2. *Frontline salespeople.* The principal responsibility of such representatives is to win orders from existing customers or to target new ones. In many

relationships, companies might agree contracts to cover a specific time period. Whilst elements such as the product specification might be fixed for the duration of a contract, other conditions such as volume, price and payment terms can require regular renegotiation. In such instances one of the salesperson's tasks is regularly to review customer requirements and renegotiate selected conditions in order to secure orders within the constraints of a broader supply agreement.

3. *Internal salespeople.* These staff are mainly responsible for administering the order process, from initial receipt to the eventual delivery of an order. They normally coordinate activities with other functions in the supplier company to ensure accurate and timely delivery of specified orders. They are likely to be in regular contact with a customer so that contracts and individual orders are administered according to customer requirements. Whilst they may not have responsibility for creating new business or closing deals with customers, they play an important role in ensuring that the supplier fulfils client needs.

Box 8.1 *Missionary selling in the ship industry*

Shipbuilding involves multi-million dollar investment projects and a variety of companies, including:

- future owners that commission the construction of new vessels;
- builders that succeed in winning contracts for construction projects such as Hellenic Shipyards SA in Europe (owned by Thyssen Krupp), Samsung Heavy Industries in Korea and Shandong Shipbuilding Industry Corp in China (owned by Samsung);
- power suppliers such as the Finnish company Wartsila, who design and supply marine propulsion systems for newly commissioned vessels; and
- companies such as the power transmission components supplier Renold, who vie with competitors to ensure that their components are specified in the propulsion systems for newly commissioned vessels.

Wartsila's propulsion systems are used to power a variety of ships, including bulk carriers, cargo and container vessels, defence ships, cruiseliners, fishing vessels and ferries. Since it is estimated that one third of all ships are powered by Wartsila systems, the component manufacturer Renold has identified Wartsila as a key target customer. The propulsion systems supplied by Wartsila are significant, in terms of contribution to vessel performance, technical complexity and financial value. Renold components might seem to be a small cog in an entire marine propulsion system. However, Renold's salespeople invest considerable time and effort in maintaining contact with Wartsila's project managers and systems designers. This contact means that the supplier stands a good chance of learning about the future commissioning of vessels in advance of the specification for the propulsion system being agreed. The sales representative can also work with Wartsila's managers to show how Renold's components can contribute to optimum solutions for marine propulsion systems.

Being part of the specification for a system to be contained in a new vessel has significant value for Renold. New vessels have to go through a certification process – once a specification (including the components from various named suppliers) has been agreed and a vessel has been approved by certification bodies such as DNV (Det Noske Veritas), then business for Renolds is guaranteed. This includes the supply of original components for inclusion in the marine propulsion system and the servicing of those components once a new vessel is in use.

(To find out more about some of the organizations featured in this case study, visit the following websites: www.dnv.com; www.hellenic-shipyards.gr; www.renold.com; www.wartsila.com.)

The Relationship Communication Process

Having considered general aspects of direct marketing and personal selling we can now go on to look at how they are used to acquire new customers and build relationships. See Figure 8.1 for the stages involved in acquiring new customers and orders.

Acquiring new customers and winning orders

Handling leads and prospective customers
In the previous chapter we discussed the means by which an organization might progress from a market of potential customers to developing business with those that best match the problem-solving abilities of the company. We know that communication tools such as advertising, direct mail and trade shows can be used to generate *leads* by marketing organizations and that a company might use sales promotion tools such as brochures, websites, electronic demonstrations and catalogues in response to *enquiries* received from potential customers. From these leads and enquiries a company has to determine which of these might be *prospective* future clients. The marketing organization can use a simple qualification process in which potential customers are asked a series of questions, such as:

- whether the company is using a similar product or is considering purchasing that offered by the marketing organization;
- the timescale and value/volume for likely purchases;
- who the ultimate decision-maker is (if it is not the person with whom the company has contact); and
- whether funding for purchase has been approved. (Griggs and Rabinowicz, 1997)

The questions might be included in direct mail or advertisements containing response cards, they can also feature on a company's website, or an organization might conduct this qualification process via fax or email. For

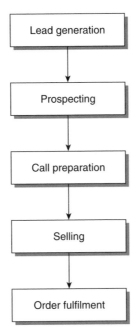

Figure 8.1 New customer and order acquisition

leads and enquiries that appear to offer significant potential (for example, prospects that are known to be major clients in the company's target market) then qualification could be conducted via telephone by a telemarketing or even a sales representative (Griggs and Rabinowicz, 1997). The same questions would be asked but phone contact allows additional information to be obtained.

The ongoing qualification of leads and enquiries provides information that can be added to an organization's databases. It can help to refine future communication activities by making available a broader range of 'qualified' potential customers that the firm is able to target. In terms of following the customer and order acquisition process in response to specific leads and enquiries, the data obtained has to be analyzed. The purpose of this analysis is to assign priority to prospects and in doing so to determine the urgency of and responsibility for making follow-up contact with prospective clients (Griggs and Rabinowicz, 1997). Clearly, criteria have to be used to prioritize prospects, which would include the information obtained via the qualification process and what might already be known about the prospects. Lowest priority prospects might be those that a firm is able to serve indirectly by using intermediaries, catalogues (or electronic hubs) and direct mail. Others might be contacted for follow up by a company's internal sales/telemarketing team, whereas an organization would make greater use of its external/field sales team to pursue highest priority prospects.

See Box 8.2 for an example of how one company has used its lead management system to win business.

Box 8.2 *Follow my leader!*

Edge Telecom buys, refurbishes and resells used enterprise phone systems dealing with wholesalers and business end-users. One of the challenges faced by the firm is what to do with contact information when representatives do not succeed in securing a sale. Even if a customer has no immediate requirement for Edge Telecom's product offering, salespeople need some means by which a relationship with a buyer can be maintained so that the time and effort in making customer calls do not seem wasted.

Edge Telecom invested in a database system that includes lead follow-up provision that allows salespeople to make use of prospect data collected. The provision includes an automated lead follow-up facility and organizes data on customers and prospects according to specified criteria. This enables Edge Telecom's salespeople to send highly focused, relevant and personalized sales pitches to targets, and quickly – this is critical in allowing the company to grab short-term business opportunities. For example, one salesperson found that over 600 phones had become available. The sales agent conducted a quick search on the contact management system and emailed wholesalers that normally bought the type of phone that had become available. Within 30 minutes the rep had an offer for all of the phones and closed the biggest deal of his career. As well as improving response to business opportunities, the introduction of the lead management system has contributed to the doubling of an individual rep's annual sales and company growth of 15–18 per cent in one year.

Source: Lager, 2005.

Call preparation

Before any contact is made with prospective customers, sales representatives must plan communication activities. *Objectives* have to be set for sales calls or a customer visit. These could be, for example:

- making the customer aware of the company as a viable alternative source of supply;
- establishing customer difficulties with their existing product supply; encouraging the customer to reveal information on future sourcing strategies; and/or
- presenting supplier solutions to previously discussed sourcing requirements; and/or
- negotiating supply contracts with and getting definite purchase decisions from customers.

Clarity of objectives is important as it will certainly determine the content and scope of communication with a customer, who might be involved and the subsequent evaluation of a planned sales call and the representative's performance.

It goes without saying that a representative must have adequate *product knowledge*, knowing the features contained in the supplier's products and, more importantly, what these represent to a customer in terms of benefits. This is particularly important as it is easy to become enthralled with the supplier's own product expertise rather than thinking about how this can be used to satisfy a customer's supply needs. In addition to familiarity with their own product, representatives should also have adequate knowledge of competitor offerings, allowing them to make comparisons and also deal with any objections or inaccuracies that feature in exchanges with customers. Beyond product familiarity, the supplier representative should also give some thought to the behavioural features of the target customer such as key members of the DMU, the nature of the purchase situation and the likely complexity of the solution sought. These elements (product and customer knowledge) should also contribute to the content and scope of a salesperson's anticipated communication with a customer.

Selling

Low priority prospects/transactional customers   Whether contact is made via the internal or the external field sales team, the basic idea behind this initial contact is to determine the nature and scope of a long-term relationship with a potential customer. We might assume that where a prospect has been assigned lower priority and discussions with the potential customer are handled principally by the internal sales team, then some initial judgement may have been made with regards to the nature of any potential relationship and sales mode, namely that it is likely to be *transactional* in nature. In these instances the customer makes straightforward purchases that would equate to straight or modified re-buys, as outlined in Chapter 2. Such purchase situations for customers that a company does not normally supply might be triggered by unforeseen supply needs or problems with an existing vendor. For these types of purchases the customer is clear about the specification and application of the product required and consequently needs little technical explanation or probing from the supplier. In these instances, the business marketer might adopt two alternative sales approaches, namely script based or needs–satisfaction selling (Marchetti, 2000). *Script-based selling* involves the use of a standard presentation or dialogue to engage the customer and can be effective when there is little difference in the way in which prospective customers use a supplier's product and where the product itself is relatively easy to understand.

Whilst an individual client might be quite clear about their own specific needs, there can be differences between customers within the same broad product group and, rather than following a scripted presentation or dialogue, supplier representatives will adopt a *needs–satisfaction* approach to selling (Marchetti, 2000). Here the sales representative engages a customer in a series of questions and answers to determine the customer's actual product needs. This allows the salesperson to match customer requirements with specific products available in the supplier's portfolio.

Irrespective of whether the business marketer uses a scripted or needs–satisfaction sales approach, there is only limited interaction between company representatives, with priority for the supplier lying in closing a sale and negotiating the terms and conditions of a contract.

High priority customers   Where a prospect has been assigned a higher priority and initial assessment suggests scope to develop a potential relationship and a supply need that has some degree of uncertainty, then the business marketer is more likely to adopt a *consultative sales approach* (Marchetti, 2000) and make more use of its external sales team to do this. The purchase situation can be classified as either a *modified re-buy* or *new task* and, as we discussed in Chapter 2, normally involves high-risk purchases (bottlenecks or critical products) for which the prospective customer is unable to articulate precise requirements and is unclear as to how its supply needs might be met. As we know from Chapter 2, these purchase situations are frequently handled by buying teams, with members of the DMU requiring a variety of information from potential suppliers during what is often an extended decision-making process.

One of the first tasks for the business marketer in such instances is to identify the gatekeeper in the buying organization, as this person controls access to and information flow from and to other members of the customer's buying team. A key function of an initial meeting with the gatekeeper is to develop some understanding of the customer company's purchase problem and requirements. The precise nature of these are unlikely to be clarified with just one meeting involving the gatekeeper only. Rather, the business marketer would typically expect to conduct numerous meetings with various members of the decision-making team and might also need to include managers beyond the sales team in these discussions. In doing this, the business marketer is able to gradually progress from generalities to the specific requirements that the customer's managers expect to satisfy.

Rather than using sales pitches, supplier representatives must rely on questioning members of the buying team in order to uncover requirements and to determine how the supplier might use its problem-solving abilities to configure an offering that will match these needs. The salesperson draws from their own product expertise to establish supply needs and rather than presenting the customer with a range of existing products from which to choose will typically formulate a bespoke offering for a customer. Presentation of the offering to the buying team might include the actual features of the proposal, the functions that these features will perform and the benefits to the customer – not only in meeting the requirements of a particular supply need but also the value to the customer of the product offer.

Consultative selling might be an option for some business marketers, but for companies that provide highly bespoke services such as corporate finance and tax advice, market research and advertising it can be the only way of securing business with a customer. In 2005, for example, the advertising agency Leo Burnett won the contract to handle the £1 million advertising, account of Spanish wine producer Freixenet (Marketing Week, 2005). To win contracts like this an agency has to have a detailed understanding of the industry and market sector in which its client operates, understanding of brand values for the product in question and of the objectives assigned by the client in issuing the contract. Only then could the agency enter into dialogue with the client on advertising strategy proposals to raise awareness of the Freixenet brand and boost appeal among young drinkers (Marketing Week, 2005).

A supplier might identify some customers not as high priority but as companies with whom it might or would like to develop strategic partnerships. This recognition would not emerge from a supplier's procedure for qualifying prospective new customers; rather, it is more likely a result of the company's strategy development process and previous experience of having already dealt with particular customers for some time. In these instances a supplier would more likely adopt *strategic partner selling*. This approach is less about how to close a deal with a customer and more about supplier and customer companies combining resources and expertise to pursue opportunities that benefit both parties, and it typically involves managers from a variety of functions from each company (that is, not just buyers and sales representatives) (Marchetti, 2000).

Dealing with objections and closing sales   During exchanges, sales representatives will normally have to handle queries or negative statements from customers. Whilst these might seem to present barriers to securing a sale they can actually provide the business marketer with additional information about the customer's requirements or competitor offerings and, assuming the sales representative is able to handle objections effectively, they will not necessarily hinder the sales process. Objections can be addressed as follows:

- Focus on the *substantive* elements. So, for example, if a customer believes that the product specification being proposed is incorrect then the supplier's representative should pose further questions to seek clarification. The representative then has to incorporate this information into the product offer, convincing the buying organization of the supplier's problem-solving ability, the representative's own expertise and the match between the solution sought by the customer and that being proposed.

- *Listen* to what the customer says and *avoid interruption*. By doing this the sales representative is indicating that the problem raised by the customer is being taken seriously and allows the supplier to get a better understanding of the problem from the customer's perspective.
- *Agree and counter*. The salesperson acknowledges the customer's point of view but then tries to counter this with an alternative. So, for example, if a customer says that the supplier's product is more expensive than a competitor's offering, the sales representative might acknowledge that whilst the initial purchase price is higher, the total cost of ownership is in fact lower.

In transactional selling, a company might get an order from a customer after only one sales call. However, in other instances, particularly when the sales process involves more than one exchange, rather than trying to secure an order the supplier simply tries to conclude discussions with the customer signalling increasing commitment to doing business with the supplier. This might be by getting the customer to agree to further exchanges with the supplier, allowing the sales representative to make contact with other managers in the customer company or agreeing to use the supplier's product on a trial basis, for example.

Order fulfilment

Sales activity does not end with the winning of an order; rather, key to the development of business with a customer is the effective delivery of the product offering. It goes without saying that the sales manager must ensure that the agreed product offering is within the technical and operational capabilities of the marketing organization. The manager must also negotiate and agree with the customer the contract details (for example, technical specification, availability, delivery location and date, price, payment terms, supporting documentation and post-sales service) and transmit these details inside his/her own company.

A variety of functions are normally involved in the order handling process from initial receipt to final delivery. This means that coordination and communication are essential to ensure that necessary tasks are completed, duplication of effort is kept to a minimum and that the product is supplied as agreed with the customer. Internal sales teams are likely to handle this on a daily basis with the sales manager overseeing the process. Discrepancies in any element of the contracted order will undermine the credibility of the sales representative and his/her organization, and will consequently hamper any scope for the further development of business between the two companies.

Figure 8.2 gives an indication of the role of various business functions in the order management cycle. In some senses the cycle presented in this diagram is generic and quite conventional. The applicability of this process to the

Customer participation	Steps in order management cycle	Sales	Marketing	Customer service	Engineering	Purchasing	Finance	Operations	Logistics	Top management participation
Plans to buy	1. Order planning	◯	☼	◯	◯	◯	◯	☼	◯	coordinates
Get sales pitch	2. Order generation	☼	◯	◯	—	—	—	—	—	some
Negotiates	3. Cost estimation and pricing	◯	☼	◯	◯	◯	◯	◯	◯	some
Orders	4. Order receipt and entry	◯	◯	☼	◯	—	—	◯	◯	none
Waits	5. Order selection and prioritization	◯	☼	◯	◯	—	◯	◯	◯	some
Waits	6. Scheduling	◯	◯	◯	◯	◯	—	☼	◯	none
Accepts delivery	7. Fulfilment	◯	◯	◯	◯	◯	—	☼	◯	none
Pays	8. Billing	◯	◯	◯	—	—	☼	—	◯	none
Negotiates	9. Returns and claims	☼	—	◯	◯	—	◯	◯	◯	some
Complains	10. Post-sales service	◯	—	☼	◯	—	—	◯	◯	none

☼ leading role   ◯ supporting role   — no role

Figure 8.2 Functional contributions to order management cycle (Shapiro et al., 2004: 164)

handling of service business can be problematic, and even where a company is dealing with tangible goods, the distinction between supplier and customer involvement in the management cycle is becoming increasingly blurred due to closer coordination between firms and shifts in responsibilities for performing various tasks. For instance, in some exchange relationships a supplier will take on responsibility for the order and supply process. The summary case study in Chapter 11 notes how toy manufacturers handle supply administration previously dealt with by intermediaries. Wilson (2000) describes the growing contribution of supplier employees located in customer premises in coordinating product supply and logistics on behalf of customers.

Relationship building

Provided that new clients represent viable long-term prospects for a supplier, the emphasis for the business marketer switches to building an on-going relationship with and winning repeat business from that customer. Whether the sales representative is dealing with a relatively new customer or one which the marketing organization has been trading with for some time, the principal tasks for the representative centre around;

- overseeing the handling of ongoing contracts;
- obtaining and acting on feedback from the customer regarding the supplier's performance;
- determining the scope for and negotiating the expansion of the supplier's share of the customer's existing product requirements;
- responding to and seeking to resolve new sourcing problems communicated by the customer;
- monitoring developments within the client organization and identifying new product opportunities for the business marketer; and
- negotiating new contracts.

The extent to which a sales representative deals with all of the above areas is determined in part by the nature of the product supplied by the marketing organization and the type of relationship sought by both the supplier and customer companies. See Box 8.3 for an example of the activities of a 3M representative in handling a relationship with an IT customer.

Box 8.3 *Persistence rewarded*

3M is an internationally diversified chemicals processing and materials company. Part of its business is involved in the supply of label technologies for identification, instructional and safety purposes in the electrical and electronic industries. For IT users the labels that are used on products are insignificant and if you were to inspect the computer hardware that you use yourself, you would come across labels that identify the hardware company (and also contain producer information stored in bar codes) as well as the software and microprocessor brands that support the functioning of the hardware product. If you dismantled your computer, you would also find additional labelling contained within the hardware items themselves. In spite of the low levels of recognition for its products, 3M works hard to ensure that their labelling technology is one of those specified by IT customers. Technical sales engineers call periodically on IT companies and during discussions:

- help hardware designers select the most suitable adhesives and label designs for particular applications (after all, you would not expect a product designer to know about this sort of thing); and
- try to identify (via discussions with designers) development projects that might present 3M with product opportunities.

Persistence in maintaining contact with designers and the recognition of the company's problem-solving abilities has paid off for 3M. One of its customers in Germany approached the company for help in improving the recyclability of its hardware products. The customer was faced with increased material recycling costs because of the difficulties in removing labels and adhesives from plastic components retrieved from returned IT equipment. 3M drew on the expertise of its technical sales engineers, environmental experts and product development managers and involved these managers in meetings with the customer and with a plastics supplier. This multi-company and multi-manager team worked together to understand the problem, explore various ways in which it might be resolved, identify and finally agree on a viable solution. The collaboration resulted in 3M developing a labelling and identification system for its German customer which was compatible with plastic components (so did not need to be removed prior to recycling). The development of this product presented new sales opportunities with the IT customer and provided 3M with a means of gaining access to other divisions that were part of the same customer organization.

Source: Canning, 1999.

Coordinating Relationship Communication

Relationship (and for that matter, market) communication is not just about finding the next customer or winning the next order; rather, for many organizations operating in business markets it is about managing relationships with customers, it is about handling ongoing exchanges between supplier and customer companies. These day-to-day activities can involve managers from a variety of functions as well as those with sales-related responsibilities. Our discussions in this section cover:

- The organization of functions with customer-facing responsibilities. This can centre solely on a sales department or alternatively can include other functions that also deal with customers.

- The role of communication within the vendor organization in coordinating customer relationship management.
- The contribution of relationship promoters to the processes of inter- and intra-firm communication and coordination.

Inter-firm

A variety of ways exist in which a company might organize its sales force and this is in part determined by the nature of the product and market in which a company is involved, the marketing organization's strategy for dealing with customers in its target market and the type of communication necessary to enable satisfactory exchanges between both parties. The ways in which those dealing with customers can be organized fall under three broad categories:

1. *A geographically based sales force.* This is arguably the most basic structure, in which a field salesperson is given the responsibility of selling all of the company's products to and dealing with all of the customers within a specified geographic area. It gives the sales representative a simple and unambiguous definition of his or her area of responsibility. The territory that can be covered by an individual manager does have to be realistic and would normally be determined by the workload involved in dealing with customers in the allocated area and the potential that they might offer. This type of design is effective when a business marketer's products are relatively simple and customers have broadly common requirements in using these products.

2. *A product-based sales force.* If a company has a diverse range of products that are based on different technologies then a supplier is more likely to use product specialists to deal with customers. Where representatives from different product divisions are dealing with the same customer, a company has to try to coordinate activities and share information to help manage the overall relationship with that client and avoid duplication of effort and/or confusion.

3. *A customer-based sales force.* In some markets, suppliers might offer the same basic product technology but the application of that technology to solve customer supply needs in different sectors can vary significantly. This means that sales representatives will need to have considerable understanding of a particular sector and to possess sufficient expertise to enable the product technology to be configured so that it matches the needs of customers in that sector. In such cases the business marketer will organize their sales teams according to the customer industries served. For example, Bayer MaterialScience AG produces polymers and high-performance plastics for use in automotive, construction, electrical and electronic, household sports and leisure sectors. The differences in the way in which products are used in these sectors and the requirements of

the customers that Bayer deals with means that its sales teams are organized such that they each deal with a different segment. Bayer's IT team consists of an international marketing manager who is responsible for and oversees sales of plastics to the IT industry worldwide, and technical sales managers that are assigned to particular customers in this sector. (To find out more about the BayerMaterial Science division visit www.bayer.com.)

Many companies extend this customer/market-based sales force and set up structures that enable them to deal more specifically with some customers who represent key accounts for their organizations. Selling companies can typically identify a handful of customers who are strategically important to them (Millman and Wilson, 1995). This might be because those customers:

- are technologically demanding, requiring leading-edge solutions that stretch the vendor's problem-solving abilities (the learning from which the firm can subsequently transfer to dealings with other customers);
- provide the vendor with access to critical resources; or
- account for a significant proportion of the firm's turnover.

The organization of the vendor's dealings with customers through account management teams is motivated not only by the strategic importance of those customers but is also in response to changes in the purchasing environment, namely:

- consolidation in many industries resulting in increased purchasing power amongst those customers that remain;
- the drive to make more efficient the sourcing of bought-in goods and services that can account for 50–70 per cent of a customer's operating costs;
- the use of buying teams and centralization of procurement activities; and
- the preference for suppliers who have international supply capabilities, provide customers with access to a global supply base and are able to offer systems solutions (McGinnis and McCarty, 1998).

Industry consolidation and the centralization of procurement activities means that a single customer can provide a vendor with a major source of revenue and equally can make a big hole in that company's sales if the account were to be lost. Centralization of procurement activities (which can include sourcing requirements for various locations around the world) necessitates that a vendor is able to coordinate responses to supply needs such that there is consistency in handling a client, irrespective of the location at which the marketing organization might be dealing with that customer at any given time. As we learnt in Chapter 2, customer desire to make sourcing more efficient and to use suppliers for systems solutions means that a vendor might typically help to reduce the costs of operational and administrative systems

Table 8.1   Characteristics of solutions by category of customer 'problem'

Problem category	Characteristics
Product	Design, technical and performance specification, quality, technical and service support, availability
Process	Operational process issues, application of process knowledge, special attention relating to cost reduction and logistics
Facilitation	Value creation, strategic alignment, compatibility and integration of systems, integration of personnel, handling of customer peripheral activities

Source: Wilson and Croom-Morgan, 1993

between the companies, use their core competencies to contribute to the customer's product development activities and take on the responsibility of managing some of the customer's supply chain by becoming a first-tier supplier.

If a company is dealing with or wishes to build business with such customers then the way in which it handles exchanges with them and organizes its 'sales efforts' can determine the effectiveness of relationship-handling and business-building endeavours. The nature of the involvement that a vendor might have with a customer and the tasks that it performs for and in conjunction with that client will depend on the relationship between the firms. Indeed, Wilson and Croom-Morgan (1993) argue that inter-firm interaction will change as the relationship develops, from focusing on product-related issues in fairly new/distant relationships to issues of facilitation and integration in much closer relationships. See Table 8.1 for an indication of the three 'problem' categories – clearly, developing solutions to these will require various skills and contributions from those involved in handling customer requirements.

Given the scope of involvement that a vendor might have with a key customer, the company has to draw on the expertise of managers beyond the personal selling function both in its direct dealings with the customer and in the tasks that are performed internally for that customer. For this reason, many companies have set up key account teams in which team members' principal responsibilities centre on the performance of tasks for that customer. An account manager typically oversees all dealings with and the successful development of a key customer relationship and will lead a team of individuals from the supplier's various functions. These individuals are also likely to deal directly with the customer and normally coordinate efforts within their own functional area such that objectives for that key account are realized. So, as well as having an account manager the team could consist of:

- field sales representatives responsible for winning new orders, and internal sales managers who administrator contracts awarded by the customer;

- product specialists who are able to advise on the configuration of product offerings for and contribute to new product development activities with the key customer;
- commercial managers responsible for handling client credit and invoicing; and
- operations, logistics, quality and service managers.

As we have discussed in previous chapters, a vendor is likely to adopt differing strategies to reflect the importance of a customer to the firm and this variation in strategy will be reflected in the way that the business marketer organizes sales activities. This means that whilst a firm might have account teams for a small number of key clients, a vendor would have other structures in place for customers who are not as strategically important to the company. For example, Motorola's semiconductor business has an internal sales team as well as three different external sales structures.

1. The *inside sales team* makes outgoing telemarketing calls and takes incoming orders from transactional customers via phone and fax.
2. The *distributor sales force* works with intermediaries, persuading them to stock and sell Motorola products, training distributor sales staff in merchandising techniques and helping the intermediaries to sustain relationships with the producer's smallest customers.
3. Representatives in the *geographic sales force* work independently, calling on the vast number of customers that purchase Motorola products and performing personal selling tasks such as giving presentations, solving customer problems and taking orders.
4. The *strategic market sales force* includes technical sales, applications and quality engineers and service personnel, working with strategic accounts and providing the technical and manufacturing expertise needed to make these partnerships function successfully (Anderson and Narus, 2004).

Whatever structures a firm puts in place for organizing its dealings with customers, membership of those structures and contribution to the activities performed by them is not necessarily fixed. In organizing its interface with customers, a firm must decide what functions should have permanent involvement in the formulation of relationship strategies and the execution of tasks to satisfy both the vendor's and the customer's relationship requirements, and what other functions the vendor will need to call upon to achieve relationship objectives but for which the involvement in dealings with and the performance of tasks for customers is temporary.

Intra-firm (vendor perspective)

Being able to access and present the necessary expertise in dealings with customers is certainly important. Whichever way a vendor organizes those with customer-facing responsibilities, relationship objectives will be difficult to achieve unless mechanisms are in place internally that allow transactions, coordination and communication between the different functions inside the supplier company. Transactions can include:

- The release of *resources* to support marketing programmes. For example, the finance department can directly impact the allocation of funding needed to support investment in a key account.
- The allocation of 'productive' (or *work*) capacity to allow tasks to be performed. For example, without the work performed by staff in research departments the development of a new product for a customer can be hampered.
- The provision of *assistance* to support managers with customer-facing responsibilities. For example, an account manager might seek the advice of product specialists in formulating offerings for a customer, or help from IT experts to resolve problems of systems integration with a particular customer. (Ruekert and Walker, 1987)

These transactions between different functions have to be synchronized. *Coordination* is needed so that the supplier's activities operate efficiently and the firm is able to meet the needs of its various customers. Coordination includes formal rules and procedures that managers must follow to access resources, work or assistance (Ruekert and Walker, 1987). So, for example, before 3M was able to offer the plastic-compatible labelling system to its IT customer in Germany, managers had to seek internal authorization to initiate exploratory research; obtain agreement from the firm's European business centre to escalate the exploratory research to a formally approved product development project; and gain approval from the US corporate headquarters for inclusion of the newly developed product in the company's portfolio (Canning and Brennan, 2004). Although formal systems might be in place, managers will not always rely on official lines of authority but will use informal means to influence decisions and coordinate activities.

Obviously *communication* is necessary between functions and between managers in the different departments (Ruekert and Walker, 1987). The volume (frequency) will vary depending on the contribution and complexity of transactions between departments to realizing customer-specific objectives and the need to coordinate these. Communication is not always straightforward. Dispersed geographic locations and the fact that managers from different functions do not necessarily share the same 'world view' means that getting the message across (both in terms if it reaching the target and its meaning being correctly understood) can be particularly challenging (Hutt, 1995). See the case study at the end of this chapter for an example of how companies supplying complex control and automation systems to customers in the Finnish paper, pulp and energy industries interact internally and with customers.

Chapter 4 clearly identified the contribution of relationships to the formulation and implementation of business and marketing strategies, and Chapter 9 discusses the strategic importance of managing portfolios of customer relationships for organizations that operate in business markets. At its core, customer relationship management (CRM) has a strategic focus and is concerned with identifying and investing in valued customer relationships, matching problem-solving abilities to customer requirements and making relationship decisions based the vendor's performance with those customers. At an operational level, CRM presents the business marketer with numerous concerns and this includes ensuring that employees are aware of the company's strategy for a particular customer and the actions taken or planned to support the relationship with that customer. From our discussions in Chapters 7 and 8 it is clear that, first, vendors engage customers with multiple forms of communication over extended time periods, and second, that a variety of employees can come into contact with customers and might be responsible for internally disseminating information, performing tasks, allocating resources or authorizing programmes of action in relation to a particular customer.

It follows that a vendor's employees must be familiar with its communication activities with a customer and have the means to share as well as access information in relation to that customer. This is where IT, which has been associated with much CRM activity (Rigby and Ledingham, 2004; Rigby et al., 2002) can help an organization. IT systems can provide employees with access to customer-specific information such as that relating to products (for example, new products, order quantities' scheduling or delivery), the account itself (for example, share of business, profitability data or credit performance) as well as all communication with the customer (for example, field and/or telemarketing representative reports). Given the range of employees who may deal with a customer, prior knowledge of recent interaction can avoid duplication, confusion and possibly inconsistency in discussions between managers from supplier and customer companies. Challenges for the vendor, however, lie in ensuring that common systems (both in terms of technology and the methods of reporting information) are used by different departments and that there is a shared understanding of how available information should be analyzed and interpreted (Campbell, 2003).

Relationship promoters

Internal marketing features heavily in services marketing literature and is based on the acknowledgement that customer satisfaction requires coordinated action/effort amongst customer contact and service support personnel inside the supplier company. A key component of internal marketing is the investment by the service organization in training and motivating employees to ensure a customer orientation throughout the company (Rafiq and Ahmed, 2000). This is quite a narrow view of the marketing that goes on inside a company, because in some senses managers continuously use processes of negotiation and persuasion and offer incentives to motivate other employees, managers and functions to align themselves to particular objectives or courses of action. For example, internal marketing is an important skill for employees in the product management groups in the hi-tech firms featured in the case study at the end of this chapter. These groups are responsible for bringing new product technology to the marketplace. Getting access to those markets, to the organizations' customers, means that the product groups have to nurture the support and interest of the sales and service team, particularly account managers who act as gatekeepers to target clients (Möller and Rajala, 1999).

Marketing activities and the associated interaction that takes place between supplier and customer companies and inside the vendor organization cannot be readily separated. We know that employees with various functional responsibilities (such as sales, customer service and key account management) interact with customers in order to satisfy those customers' needs and to develop relationships with them. We also know that customer satisfaction and relationship management entail the performance of tasks inside the vendor organization. Those employees that interact with customers play key *boundary-spanning* roles; they operate as relationship promoters (Walter and Gemünden, 2000), linking the customer with the supplier company and working to coordinate activities inside the supplier organization to support the development of relationships with selected customers. The principal objective of relationship promoters is to influence the attitudes, behaviour and decisions of managers so that the customer relationship can be developed and maintained. Personal attributes that relationship promoters should possess include:

- *Social competence:* They must be skilled in communication, conflict management and coordination, and must be flexible and empathetic in group processes involving managers from different functions and organizations.
- *Knowledge:* They must be familiar with the resources, needs and strategies of both the supplier and customer organizations.
- *Portfolio of relationships:* They need to be well connected and have good personal relationships with managers in partner organizations who control resources that contribute to the development of the supplier–customer relationship (Walter and Gemünden, 2000).

Using these attributes helps:

- information sharing and communication between members of relationship teams, as well as with others who are in powerful positions and whose support can impact the relationship;

- to find the right managers who can and are willing to perform tasks as part of supplier–customer collaboration;
- facilitate relationships between managers in both companies;
- to coordinate activities between companies; and
- negotiation and conflict resolution (Walter and Gemünden, 2000).

Controlling Relationship Communication

As well as trying to synchronize inter- and intra-firm communication a company must also direct the actions of those that deal with customers, such that the endeavours of its employees contribute to relationship-specific, marketing and overall company objectives. Directing employee behaviour requires some type of control system, a 'set of procedures for monitoring, directing, evaluating and compensating its employees' (Anderson and Oliver, 1987: 76). The two principal systems associated with controlling sales force behaviour are incentive pay systems and monitoring (Menguc and Barker, 2003).

Incentive pay systems reward employees for achieving specific performance targets and in using this type of control, priority is placed on an employee realizing targeted outcomes rather than the way in which these are achieved. So, for example, a salesperson might discuss and agree with their manager targets for sales revenue, market-share or specific customer share gains, new product sales and the profitability of business won by the sales representative. Where an outcome-based control system is used a significant proportion of a salesperson's remuneration is accounted for by performance-based commission and bonus payments. Clearly in using this type of system account has to be taken of the relative ease/difficulty, for example, in selling a particular product line or generating business with a given customer at the point when targets and resulting rewards are agreed (Oliver and Anderson, 1995). An employee might have little room for negotiation in terms of the measures against which their performance is assessed and for which they are rewarded but they typically have considerable discretion in how they go about realizing agreed targets.

Whereas incentive pay systems direct the actions of employees by providing financial compensation for the achievement of measurable, financial sales-related targets, a monitoring-based system controls employee actions by directing, evaluating and rewarding sales-related activities. The idea behind this is that effective performance in sales activities will subsequently lead to company financial objectives being realized. So, for instance, a salesperson might be evaluated and rewarded according to their technical knowledge, use of adaptive selling, teamwork, sales presentations, sales planning and sales support (Grant and Cravens, 1996). This type of control system lacks measures that can be readily observed, which affects employee remuneration (only a small proportion of employee salaries would normally be linked to individual commission and bonuses) and requires closer monitoring of employee behaviour in order to evaluate performance. If behaviour is to be monitored in this way then a company has to prescribe how various sales activities should be performed. There is an inherent tension in such prescription, in that the definition of behaviours (instructions, procedures and standards) necessary to perform specified sales-related tasks can stifle the flexibility and discretion that a salesperson would expect to have in dealing with different types of customers and purchase situations.

The two control systems that we have discussed should not be viewed as being mutually exclusive; indeed, some companies are known to use a mixture of the two, or to at least use control systems that reflect the strategies adopted for different customers and the communication activity necessary to support these strategies. So outcome measures might be used for transactional customers, for example, where emphasis lies in closing sales and winning orders, and would typically be based on individual employee performance. For high-priority customers that involve complex purchase situations and require the contribution of various functions within the supplier company then a behaviour-based control system is arguably more appropriate, with team rather than individual employee performance being rewarded.

Chapter Summary

- Relationship communication is about the exchange of 'messages' between a vendor and *specific* prospective or actual customers.

- The principal tools used in relationship communication are direct marketing (via print, telephone or electronic media) and personal selling.

- Direct marketing and personal selling can be combined in order to acquire new customers and build/manage relationships with existing ones, but in doing so the vendor must take account of the ways in which personal selling and the various direct marketing media differ.

- The main parameters differentiating direct marketing and personal selling are:

  - the scale of communication activity for which they can be used;
  - the breadth and depth of information that can be exchanged;
  - the scope for tailoring communication to suit specific situations and individual client needs;
  - the capacity for interaction between supplier and customer companies.

- In addition to thinking about how to acquire new customers or manage relationships with existing ones, a vendor must also decide how to coordinate relationship communication activities. The organization of the firm's interface with external markets and customers might centre on those with selling responsibilities, or may involve managers from a variety of functions that deal directly with customers.

- Whatever structure a company uses to organize inter-firm communication, internal coordination and communication are also important. IT systems can help to ensure the dissemination of and access to customer-specific information, and relationship promoters can be used as a link between firms as a means of coordinating activities to support specific customer relationships within the vendor organization.

Questions for discussion

1. Describe the different direct marketing tools and how they can be used for relationship communication.
2. Describe the customer/order acquisition process. What stages do you think are the most critical?
3. Why might a business marketer use different types of salespeople and sales approaches?
4. What effect has key account management had on personal selling?
5. What challenges does the business marketer face in trying to coordinate relationship communication activities internally? How might these be addressed?

Case study: Coordination in high-tech companies

Process control and automation technology involves the supply of complex systems used in process industries such as chemical and life sciences, food and beverage production, metal and mineral processing, oil and gas/refining, paper and pulp production, and power generation, among others. The systems represent major investments for clients and are a key contributor to the functioning of those clients' operations. Suppliers such as ABB, Honeywell and Siemens have to draw from highly differentiated professional skills and capabilities in order to develop the product technology and to adapt and sell

Case study

systems that match customer needs in these diverse industries. Whatever the industry, the design, installation and ongoing maintenance of control systems necessitates intense personal interaction and information exchange between supplier and customer representatives, and cooperation between groups of functional experts within the supplier and customer organizations (as well as between them).

The description that follows outlines how some companies that supply these systems have organized their product management, sales and marketing activities to facilitate intra-firm coordination and ensure consistency in a customer's experience of dealing with an automation and control system supplier.

The product management group focuses its attention on two main areas of activity. One is the development of the basic technology used for product platforms such as quality control systems and production management and information systems. The other is applications development, where advances in the basic technology are modified according to the needs of customers in different sectors such as pulp, paper, energy and graphics. Work on product platform and applications development is carried out in conjunction with centralized research centres, which are frequently organized around customer sectors. Efficient information exchange is essential between the platform and application groups and the research centres for effective product development. Applications developments also need the cooperation of specific pilot customers.

The sales and service group consists of account managers, sales personnel, project managers, and service and maintenance personnel. The principal task for service and maintenance personnel obviously centres on the maintenance/servicing of installed systems but they are often the principal conduit for feedback information (in terms of customer satisfaction, needs and competitor behaviour, for example). Not only that, they can also contribute to pre-sales activity by informing other parts of the organization about market opportunities (such as customer plans for systems upgrades or purchases). The service and maintenance personnel therefore have close contact with other managers in the sales and service team but also interact frequently with the product management group. Sales managers initiate new relationships and negotiate new projects with customers, and are supported by the product management group. Project managers have responsibility for carrying out projects once sales personnel have negotiated contracts with customers. This includes coordinating the work of those people needed to install or start up a project such as technical personnel, customer's employees (who need to be trained) and also IT personnel. The supply of high-technology systems is characterized by a project-based sales approach in which the correct and timely involvement of various managers from the sales and service group is essential. The key account manager is responsible for coordinating this contact with customers and

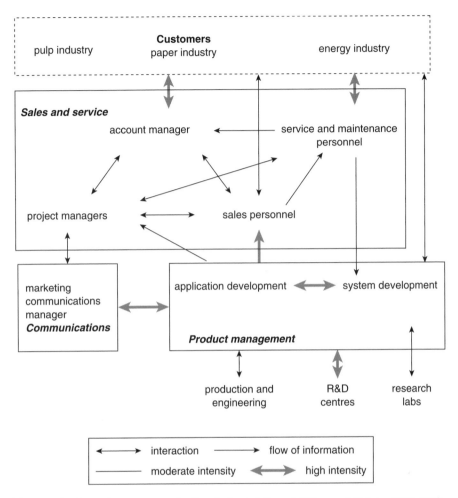

Figure 8.3 Intra-firm communication (adapted from Möller and Rajala, 1999: 530)

for making interaction with the systems supplier as easy as possible for the client.

The product management and sales and service groups are quite distinct, yet coordination between them is important to ensure the dissemination of marketing information such as that in relation to product lines and market areas. The marketing communication group assumes partial responsibility for this internal marketing activity. In addition to this the marketing communications group works with the product groups on new product releases (which might include running seminars or participating in major trade fairs) as well as performing normal marketing communication tasks, such as managing general publicity and advertising and producing sales support material for the sales and service group.

Case study questions

1. Using Figure 8.3, itemize the interactions and flows of information involving sales personnel.
2. How can we distinguish between the roles of the account managers and of sales personnel in this industry? Is there any scope for conflict here?

Source: Adapted from Möller and Rajala, 1999.

References

Anderson, J.C. and Narus, J.A. (2004) 'Sustaining customer relationships', in *Business Market Management*, (2nd edn). London and New York: Prentice Hall. pp. 394–439.

Anderson, E. and Oliver, R.L. (1987) 'Perspectives on behaviour–based versus outcome-based sales force control systems', *Journal of Marketing*, 51 (4): 76–88.

Campbell, A.J. (2003) 'Creating customer knowledge competence: managing customer relationship management programmes strategically', *Industrial Marketing Management*, 32: 375–83.

Canning, L.E. and Brennan, R. (2004) 'Strategy as the management of adaptation', 20th Industrial Marketing and Purchasing (IMP) Conference, Copenhagen Business School, Denmark, 2–4 Septemper

Canning, L.E. (1999) 'The introduction of environmental issues in supplier–customer relationships. An investigation of inter-firm processes in Britain and Germany', unpublished PhD thesis, Bristol: UWE.

Grant, K. and Cravens, D.W. (1996) 'Examining sales force performance in organizations that use behaviour-based sales management processes', *Industrial Marketing Management*, 25: 361–71.

Griggs, R. and Rabinowicz, V. (1997) 'Give us leads', *Sales and Marketing Management*, 149 (7): 66–72.

Hutt, M.D. (1995) 'Cross-functional working relationships in marketing', *Journal of the Academy of Marketing Science*, 23 (4): 351–7.

Institute of Direct Marketing (2002) The IDM guide to e-marketing expertise. IDM Certificate in e-marketing, September.

Lager, M. (2005) 'Back from the dead lead management', *Customer Relationship Management*, August: 43.

McGinnis, F. and McCarty, L. (1998) 'Strategic account management in the new procurement environment', *Supply Chain Management*, 3 (1): 12–16.

Marchetti, M. (2000) 'Cost per call survey', *Sales and Marketing Management*, September: 81.

Marketing Week (2005) 'Leo Burnett triumphs in wine tussle', *Marketing Week* 14 April: 12.

Menguc, B. and Barker, A.T. (2003) 'The performance effects of outcome-based incentive pay plans on sales organizations: a contextual analysis', *Journal of Personal Selling and Sales Management*, XXIII (4): 341–58.

Millman, T. and Wilson, K. (1995) 'From key account selling to key account management', *Journal of Marketing Practice*, 1 (1): 8–21.

Möller, K. and Rajala, A. (1999) 'Organising marketing in industrial high-tech firms: The role of internal marketing relationships', *Industrial Marketing Management*, 28: 328–37.

Oliver, R.L. and Anderson, E. (1995) 'Behaviour- and outcome-based sales control systems: evidence and consequences of pure-form and hybrid governance', *Journal of Personal Selling and Sales Management*, XV (4): 1–15.

Rafiq M. and Ahmed, P.K. (2000) 'Advances in the internal marketing concept', *Journal of Services Marketing*, 14 (6): 449–62.

Rigby, D.K. and Ledingham, D. (2004) 'CRM done right', *Harvard Business Review*, 82 (11): 118–29.

Rigby, D.K., Reichheld, F.K. and Schefter, P. (2002) 'Avoid the four perils of CRM', *Harvard Business Review*, 80 (2): 101–09.

Ruekert, R.W. and Walker, O.C. (1987) 'Marketing's interaction with other functional units: a conceptual framework and empirical evidence', *Journal of Marketing*, 51 (January): 1–19.

Shapiro, B.P., Rangan, V.K. and Sviokla, J.J. (2004) 'Staple yourself to an order', *Harvard Business Review*, 7 (8): 162–71.

Walter, A. and Gemünden, H.G. (2000) 'Bridging the gap between suppliers and customers through relationship promoters: theoretical considerations and empirical results', *Journal of Business and Industrial Marketing*, 15 (2/4): 86–105.

Wilson, D.T. (2000) 'Deep relationships: the case of the vanishing salesperson', *Journal of Personal Selling and Sales Management*, XX (1): 53–61.

Wilson, K.J. and Croom-Morgan, S.R. (1993) 'A problem-centred approach to buyer–seller interaction', 9th Industrial Marketing and Purchasing (IMP) Conference, University of Bath, Bath, September.

9 Relationship Portfolio Management

Learning outcomes

After reading this chapter you will:

- understand the principles of portfolio management and how they can apply to the management of customer relationships;
- be able to apply the processes of relationship portfolio analysis and management;
- know a range of variables, including life cycle concepts, that enable the marketer to classify customer relationships for portfolio management decisions; and
- recognize the need for a balanced relationship portfolio and know a set of rules for establishing balance.

Introduction

As we saw in Chapter 3, business-to-business marketing often involves the management of customer relationships and so necessitates a focus at the level of the relationship rather than the product. Of course, typically a company has a collection of customers, each differing from the others in specific ways. A substantial task for the business marketer then is to recognize the differences between customers and to manage the collection of relationships in ways that add value to the business. Drawing from the concept of portfolio management, this chapter presents the means by which business marketers can do just that: manage the collection of relationships with which they are faced.

Ostensibly, this portfolio management is at a level that is separate from the decisions marketers face within the firm in respect of any specific customer – for example, which product or process technology to pursue in that relationship, or how to communicate the value the company can bring to that customer. It can also generally be seen as a precursor to these decisions since the results of the relationship portfolio analysis will enable day-to-day marketing decisions of the firm to be taken more intelligently. For example, there is little value in committing substantial resource to new product variants with a customer that is clearly unreceptive and, in reality, of much lower strategic value than other customers (where such initiatives would be well-received and would add further value to the relationship). This is particularly true if to commit greater resource to the former would mean foregoing commitment to the latter, which may be the case given finite resources. Of course, the link between the customer relationship portfolio management and day-to-day marketing management is more complex than that. For instance, one of the bases for analysing the collection of customer relationships may arise from internal characteristics of the firm (such as the extent to which a customer makes use of a new product technology from the firm).

In the chapter we will outline the principles of portfolio management and indicate how they have resonance in business-to-business marketing. Then we will consider a selection of commonly used criteria for undertaking the portfolio analysis, including the use of relationship life cycle concepts that may aid the analysis. Finally, we will establish some guidelines for achieving a balanced relationship portfolio as a precursor to the sorts of product management decisions that are considered in greater detail in Chapter 10.

Principles of Portfolio Management

For a business marketer the relationships they forge and maintain with their customers constitute the basis for creating value for the firm. As Peter Drucker (1955: 35) pointed out a half a century ago:

> There is only one valid definition of business purpose: to create a customer ... It is the customer who determines what a business is. For it is the customer, and he alone, who through being willing to pay for a good or for a service, converts economic resources into wealth, things into goods ... The customer is the foundation of a business and keeps it in existence.

Of course, businesses do not generally have just one customer. They typically rely upon a range of customers, each bringing their own type of value. In some cases, this may be straightforward monetary value in terms of level of sales. In others, it may be in terms of the profit contribution the customer makes aside from sales volume. In yet others, it may have little to do with current monetary value and more to do with future value. It may even involve negative current value in the expectation of future revenue or profit streams, essentially up-front investments in the future of the business with the concomitant risks that accompany such investment.

When one sees the variety of types of relationships, the sources of value they bring, and the time horizon over which the value may accrue, then inevitably one is drawn towards financial investment notions and how financial managers have traditionally managed sources of risk and return. As we will see in the next chapter, marketers have long borrowed terminology from the financial management sphere to help deal with the difficulties of managing a range of different products. Just as financial managers like a balance of investments that begin and mature at different times, producing a steady stream of returns over the longer term, so marketers have seen the usefulness of such concepts for the management of products and strategic business units. Portfolio planning tools allow for the sorts of analyses that enable clear decisions to be made in order to obtain a well-balanced portfolio. A well-balanced portfolio is one that ensures that the business earns value over the long term by selectively harvesting excess current returns and ploughing them into future products. The notions of portfolio management have equal applicability to customer relationships:

- they constitute sources of risk and return;
- they are varied in the type of risk they constitute;
- they vary in the level of return they bring; and
- they also vary in the time horizon over which they provide that return.

When seen in these terms, it is clearly appropriate to consider relationships in portfolio management terms. Indeed, we agree with Ford et al. (2002: 99) who consider that the integrated management of the whole portfolio of relationships is a key task for the business marketer:

> *The business marketer must manage his portfolio of relationships as a totality, according to the respective contributions, of each one to its corporate success, the risks that each involves, the demands that each makes on his resources and the effects that each has on his other relationships.* (italics in original)

Successful portfolio management requires that the marketer make the best decisions possible with the portfolio of relationships he or she has. The strategic options for specific relationships or relationship groups are typically those in Table 9.1. However, chosen options for each relationship or relationship cluster should be taken in an integrated way, rather than separately and as though they were unrelated to each other.

In order to reach the right decision the business marketer needs to be well informed about the possible risks and returns from the relationships in the portfolio. Establishing the relative standing of each relationship necessitates undertaking a series of analyses that essentially divides the relationships into different categories of customer. The number of categories depends upon how fine-grained the firm wants to be in identifying different customer relationship groups. Ultimately, it is possible to apply sufficient classification

Table 9.1 Typical strategic options for a relationship

Option	Actions
Build	Build a relationship further for growth, investing where necessary to achieve this growth.
Maintain	Maintain the current levels of management effort in a relationship in order to reap the benefits from the relationship now through large volumes, high profits or a greater share of the customer's purchases.
Harvest	Harvest the value in the relationship by taking the current monetary value it brings while at the same time beginning to reduce the cost of servicing the relationship over time.
Reduce	Reduce in the immediate future the level of management commitment to a relationship because the returns are diminishing with little prospect of reversal.

criteria to create sets of one for every single customer. However, as Chapter 6 on segmentation established, it is generally not sensible for a firm to treat every customer as wholly unique – though there may well be some customers, by dint of their relative importance strategically, who deserve individual consideration. Rather, there are likely to be collections or clusters of customer relationships that, to all intents and purposes, require similar treatment in terms of management commitment and in terms of the level of return that they provide to the firm. Thus, as with segmentation, successful portfolio analysis requires an iterative process of breaking down the customer base into a smaller number of substantially different clusters, with the members of each cluster sharing similar characteristics.

A variety of classificatory criteria can be applied during the iterative deepening process in order to achieve a level of clustering that produces a meaningful set of groups in the portfolio. 'Meaningful' in this context needs to be defined by the firm itself on the basis of its own business context and the peculiarities of its customer base, and may be refined over time. However, it is likely that the number of groups for most companies will number between 8 and 14. Also, while there may be singleton relationships that are distinct, for the most part each group will contain more than one customer. While all groups will comprise customer relationships that have a degree of commonality within the group, there is also likely to be at least one set that contains a substantial number of customers where the unifying commonality has more to do with their lack of individual importance to the company (what Ford et al. (2002) call 'minor relationships'). Once a meaningful set of groups in the portfolio has been established, decisions can be taken with respect to each element in the portfolio in order to achieve balance overall.

The Relationship Classification Process

An early pioneer of differential customer management, Barbara Bund Jackson (1985) advocated a binary split of the customer base into those customers where a supplier can always get a share of the business and those that want stability in their supply dealings so that they prefer to form closer relationships with suppliers. The former, *always-a-share*, customers are driven by price for the current business and thus make decisions about supply on the basis of the best deals in the market at the time. In this respect they are highly opportunistic, happy to switch supply for a financial saving on the current deal. If you have been supplying a customer like this and they have just switched then the one consolation is that it is always possible to win the business back; when the next sale comes through it is merely a matter of providing a better price-based deal than the competition.

Customers who want greater stability will often subordinate price-based issues to other considerations, such as continuity of supply, levels of product quality or a shared market view with their suppliers. For example, Sun Microsystems, for whom the quality of its supply base is crucial given that the greatest set of costs it has to manage are purchasing costs, has reduced its supply base and consolidated 80 per cent of its spend with just 40 suppliers (Harrington, 2004). The investments that companies looking for stability make in their suppliers to achieve these sorts of advantages are neither arbitrary nor transient. Cost reductions for Sun Microsystems do not come from merely negotiating lower prices with suppliers but from involving the suppliers in ways that reduce costs for both themselves and the suppliers. Because of the investment companies make in their supply base they are reluctant to switch suppliers, sometimes even preferring to work with failing suppliers to improve the situation. However, they have a breaking point in their preparedness to accept ongoing poor performance or opportunistic behaviour on the part of suppliers. While they want a close relationship with their favoured suppliers, if a supplier lets them down badly then that will be the end of the relationship. In this respect, when lost, they are *lost-for-good* (Bund Jackson, 1985).

Sako (1992) witnessed behaviour in the auto industry that led her to make a similar dichotomous distinction between types of relationship. Her analyses of the behaviour of the car assemblers indicated a cultural predisposition amongst US and European assemblers to use formal and controlling mechanisms in their relationships; the relationships manifested a basic mistrust and tendency to conflict. She called this the *arm's length contracting* approach. This approach she contrasts with a tendency in relationship management amongst Japanese assemblers to manifest greater amounts of trust in partners. She attributes this to a cultural tendency towards acknowledging the responsibilities that go with a relationship. The parties to a relationship understand that they are working together and that the relationship obliges them to work in particular ways that are more about mutual respect, since it is only through such attitudes and cooperative behaviour that the relationship objectives can be met. Sako (1992) calls this approach *obligational contracting*.

The sort of binary splits to which Bund Jackson and Sako refer are clearly useful in distinguishing the two ends of a relationship continuum. In both cases, as the description above indicates, a whole series of indicators are at play in distinguishing both ends of the spectrum. As a first foray into splitting up the customer base into relationship types, it has merit. It is particularly useful for reducing the size of the analysis space because it is possible to discount from further analysis all those customers who are clearly not interested in a closer relationship. That is not to say that these customers are to be ignored, merely that the basis of trading with them is best focused on negotiating the best deal at any point in time.

Of course, from a managerial perspective it is not clear exactly how the split is established and the specific variables that should be applied in combination in order to achieve the split. It is also the case that many relationships fall into the space between the two extremes. There is not likely to be just two sets of behaviour manifested in the customer base but a whole collection, and neither are there just two ways in which a firm should manage its relationships. Consequently, the use of a broad-brush approach like the binary split can only be a start. For this reason it is managerially more useful to undertake a process of sequential application of classificatory variables in order to split the customer relationship base into more than just two clusters.

There is a range of variables that can be used to make qualitative distinctions between relationships. Some criteria are easily available and easily applied; some involve undertaking specific additional analyses in order to derive the benefit from them. We will start with the more easily undertaken analyses, which typically use the sorts of financial information that companies generate as a matter of course. As these are typically accounting based there is a sound reason for starting here anyway: a balanced portfolio needs to be financially stable. A portfolio of relationships with great potential but little current profit that require substantial investment will merely bankrupt the company, ensuring that the potential will never be achieved anyway. By the same token, a portfolio of relationships that produce current cash or profits but that will dry up in two or three years is not the basis for longevity for the firm.

Classification Criteria: More Easily Observed

As a starting point for a portfolio analysis of the customer relationship base, it is most sensible to undertake analyses that draw from existing, easily obtained information sources. The accounting system constitutes the most readily

Table 9.2 Simulated sales and cost to serve figures for SpareParts Ltd, 2003/2004 and 2004/2005

	2004/2005				2003/2004			
Customer	Sales (£m)	Cost to serve (CTS) (£m)	Sales minus CTS (£m)	% sales	Sales (9£m)	Cost to serve (CTS) (£m)	Sales minus CTS (£m)	% sales
Acme Corp.	6.442	5.995	0.447	50	5.250	3.010	2.240	40
Loser Ltd	2.653	3.000	−0.347	20	4.345	3.000	1.345	33
Hodge Podge Ltd	2.351	2.110	0.241	18	2.460	1.970	0.490	19
Bits & Bobs plc	1.555	0.675	0.880	12	1.355	0.685	0.670	10
Totals	13.001	11.780	1.221		13.410	8.665	4.745	

available central source of information on relationships, containing, as it does, a record of the sales made to specific customers as well as company cost information. By making use of this source and undertaking some basic analyses, it is possible to start distinguishing relationships from each other without having to make deeper judgement calls about every customer. The application of criteria that require deeper personal insight is best left until there is a need for such insight with a smaller number of relationship cases. Consequently, they are best used to further refine cluster definitions created by the application of a collection of the set of criteria in this subsection.

Sales

The *amount of sales* can be used directly as a means of ranking customers. In some companies it may be better to consider the *number of units sold*. It is, of course, in either case more illuminating to talk about a customer relationship in terms of *proportion of total sales*. The sales figures for the imaginary company in Table 9.2 clearly show that Acme Corp. is the biggest customer by sales. However, the sales figure percentage shows just how important a customer it is. Of course, sales alone do not say anything about the level of profitability of an account.

Profits

Sales alone do not make a relationship attractive. It may be more sensible to focus on notions of profitability. Shapiro et al. (1987) used both *net price achieved* (that is, price after all forms of discounting have been applied) and *cost to serve* as means of establishing relative profitability. As Figure 9.1 indicates, customers below the break-even point (customer Y) are unprofitable, while those above it are profitable (customer X). Using the simulated figures

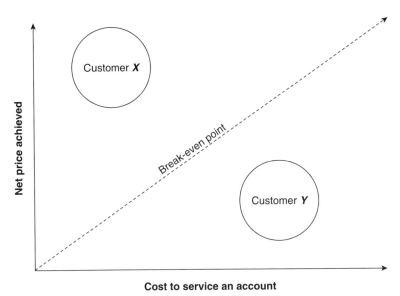

Figure 9.1 Depicting customers in terms of the prices achieved and the cost to service their accounts (adapted from Shapiro et al., 1987)

for SpareParts Ltd in trading year 2004/2005 (Table 9.2), it becomes clear that while Acme Corp. is the biggest customer in terms of sales, it is also a highly demanding customer.

While still profitable, it is not as profitable, from a lower sales base, as Bits & Bobs plc, which generates £880,000 of profit compared to the £447,000 produced by Acme. Incidentally, Loser Ltd is ranked second in terms of sales but is unprofitable. To be a reliable depiction of the state of the customer base, net price and cost-to-serve figures need to be calculated over a fixed time span with respect to all transactions. Typically this would be the last trading year, but may be longer in some contexts if the cost accounting system can facilitate it. The cost accounting system also needs to enable strong tracking of the costs required to support a customer: all the sales calls, all the technical support or time taken to resolve difficulties, specific costs associated with a customer in terms of production set-ups or tooling, training or installation costs, and so on. All these need to figure if one is to establish a clear cost to serve. Furthermore, it is possible to extend Figure 9.1 so that the relative proportion of sales is also captured, as in Figure 9.2.

From a portfolio management perspective, Shapiro et al. (1987) use just the two financial criteria of net price achieved and cost to serve in order to derive four different types of customer (based on ratings of high or low for the two criteria in a two-by-two matrix).

Bargain basement customers (low net price and low cost to serve) are those who are very price sensitive, but they are insensitive to levels of quality or service. They are thus much cheaper to manage than their opposites, *carriage*

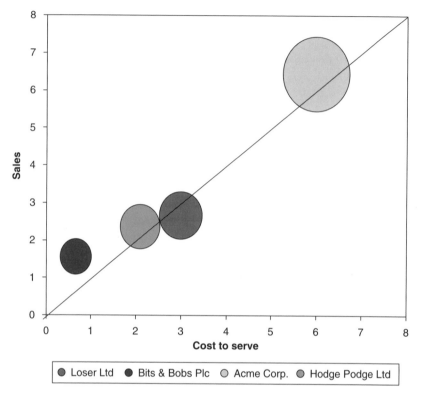

Figure 9.2 Relative sales versus cost to serve for four customers of SpareParts Ltd (adapted from Shapiro et al., 1987)

trade customers (high net price and high cost to serve). These customers may be prepared to pay premium prices but they want the levels of service and quality that go with that, so they cost more to serve.

Both of the above are balanced in terms of the demands they make for the prices they pay. With some customers there is an imbalance in respect of what they pay and what they expect for it. *Passive* customers are prepared to pay higher prices despite commanding equivalent levels of service or quality from their suppliers. Where there is a product dependence, or the nature of the product does not warrant great attention by the buyer, or there is buyer inertia, then the buyer may just pay the price demanded. These customers are at the opposite end of the spectrum from *aggressive* customers. Aggressive customers want it all, the highest levels of service and product quality at low prices. What makes them aggressive rather than carriage trade is that they generally get it; because of the relative power they have in a relationship they can command top quality at low prices. Their power may come from such characteristics as their superior access to end markets, the volumes they purchase or their relative importance to the counterpart.

Shapiro et al. (1987) demonstrate how quickly it becomes possible to split a customer base into different clusters of customers, each with a separate management agenda.

Cost savings

Sticking with financial criteria, it may be the case that relationships can be distinguished on the basis of their potential to reduce costs for the company over time. Krapfel et al. (1991) argue that cost savings are important in generating relationship value. So, for example, a customer creates a degree of slack and therefore a cost saving for the supplier if it is prepared to carry more stock, pay its bills earlier, provide earlier and more accurate demand forecasts, or engage in forms of automated order processing. The preparedness and potential of customers to provide such cost savings can be used as the basis for distinguishing them.

Rather than being directly available from the accounting system, analysts will have to use the cost information that exists and establish in addition the potential cost savings for specific relationships. In this respect, the use of cost savings as a means of distinguishing between relationships relies upon a judgement call about the future on the basis of the historical information that already exists.

Relationship age

It is often relevant to use the age of relationships as a means of distinguishing them from each other, since the concept of 'relationship' has a temporal dimension. As Table 9.3 indicates, there can be a wide range of relationship ages in a supply base. In both the examples depicted the degree of importance of the counterparts and the complexity of the exchange show a tendency to longer-lasting relationships. While not all relationships will be as important or as complex as this, age certainly enables them to be distinguished.

It is also possible to combine an element of the passing of time with the sort of financial analysis depicted in Figure 9.2. The diagram in Figure 9.3, using data from Table 9.2, shows how with financial data over as little as a two-year-period it is possible to depict the changing position. Figure 9.3 shows the trends in respect of all three of the dimensions of percentage of sales, cost to serve and level of sales at the same time. The appropriate time span will, of course, depend on the specific sector and what passes for normal relationship lengths in the sector. As Anderson and Narus (1991) indicate, there are natural industry bandwidths in respect of the propensity for relationships to be more collaborative or more transactional.

The concept of time has an additional relevance for relationship portfolio management. The point of arriving at some clustered breakdown of the relationship base is to make relationship decisions in respect of the resulting

Table 9.3 Indication of the diversity of ages in a relationship base

For companies engaged in technical development with suppliers		Relationship age of top 17 suppliers to vehicle manufacturer (≈33% of purchase costs)	
Duration	*# Relationships*	*Duration*	*# Suppliers*
0–4 years	28%	1–4 years	2
5–14 years	41%	5–14 years	5
> 15 years	29%	15–24 years	4
		25+ years	6
(Håkansson, 1982)		*(Ford et al., 2002: 81)*	

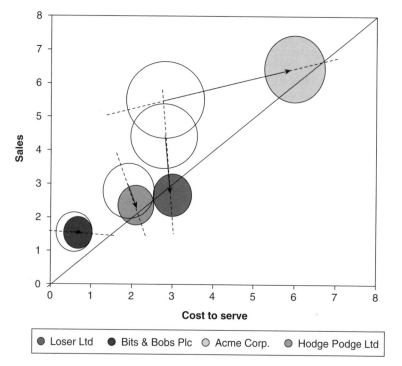

● Loser Ltd ● Bits & Bobs Plc ○ Acme Corp. ● Hodge Podge Ltd

Figure 9.3 Extension of sales versus cost to serve for SpareParts Ltd to include trend indicators over time

clusters. Relationship life cycle notions (Ford, 1980; Dwyer et al., 1987; Barnes, 2004) tell us that relationships change over time and thus the correspondingly appropriate behaviour with respect to them from either party should change over time. Having an idea of the age of a relationship and using it to cluster enables resulting relationship strategies to embody the appropriate behaviour so that the relationship participants clearly do act their age.

Classification Criteria: Less Easily Observed

The criteria in the previous section are generally easily obtained for companies as they typically emerge from the financial information systems that companies use as a matter of course. However, there are other criteria that may be useful in further refining any portfolio clusters created through the application of the criteria in the previous subsection. Some of those financially defined clusters (or numerically, if relationship age is used) may need further subdivision. The way to do that division is through the application of other relevant distinguishing criteria to the customers. In this section we present some variables that can be used to achieve the division. They rely on non-standard evaluations, typically conducted specifically for the purposes of a relationship portfolio analysis. This makes them more difficult to conduct, relying on judgement calls from the analyst in the absence of other more objective sources of data such as accounting reports. They are thus better undertaken by someone who has sufficient strategic knowledge of the firm and its direction as well as good knowledge of the individual customer accounts.

Replaceability of a customer

The strategic importance of a customer is often defined in terms of the volume of business conducted with it. In this respect, sales figures are useful. However, in distinguishing between two customers that are of roughly equivalent sales value companies will typically consider other characteristics.

One important consideration is the extent to which a customer is replaceable (Krapfel et al., 1991). The loss of some customers may be highly damaging to the company because there are few alternatives to replace them. With other customers, on the other hand, though the loss is regrettable, it may be offset by finding alternative customers from a large set of those available. As well as the direct loss of sales, there may also be investments already made with respect to strategically important customers in terms of dedicated plant or people or procedures that need to be considered when assessing their degree of replaceability. This assessment should also trade-off any additional costs of acquiring alternative customers (even if there is a stock of substitutes available). These costs could concern potential process or material changes, higher quality standards or changes to distribution levels.

Companies will certainly want to think carefully before losing an irreplaceable customer and thus may consider the use of this variable in distinguishing between relationships.

Use of critically important products or processes

Some products or services are more critical to the customer's business than others. For example, the braking system of a car is more critical than the floor covering. All other things being equal, a supplier would prefer to supply more rather than less critical products and services. The concept of criticality is used by Krapfel et al. (1991). Critical products and services typically demonstrate the supplier's specific technical and/or market competences and thus establish the relative strategic competitive position of the supplier in the marketplace.

Criticality can be used to distinguish between customer relationships. Of course, the dynamic nature of customer markets, developments in supply markets and decisions about changing competences within the firm mean that the critical products or processes may change over time. Companies need to be aware of future as well as current users of these strategically important sources of differential advantage.

Shared vision of the future

Companies have their own view of how their industry or sector is developing – for example, where the next big developments are going to be and where they see themselves with respect to these changes. It is always easier to work with customers who share similar views. For that reason a portfolio analyst may use the extent to which there is a shared vision with customers as the basis for distinguishing between relationships. This is similar to what Krapfel et al. (1991) call *interest commonality*, where a supplier and a customer have compatible economic goals.

For example, Pilkington in the UK in the mid-1990s saw that development in the glass industry involved more than merely cutting float glass and wrapping it in extruded UPVC. There had been growth of double-glazing companies, all pretty much substitutable, all merely buying glass for these purposes. In an effort to move the sector forward Pilkington was itself investing in product developments to provide for greater thermal efficiency performance of its glass – investments that led to its 'K' glass. At the same time, it introduced a downstream Key Processor initiative as the means of identifying and treating differently those customers that did more than just cut and wrap glass. These customers, it considered, shared the same vision of where the sector was going and in that respect these were relationships that Pilkington wanted to encourage.

By considering interest commonality (low or high) against a measure of relationship value (low or high), Krapfel et al. (1991) identified four different relationship types, each of which requires a different relationship management approach.

Acquaintance (low value, low commonality)

Customers like this should only be offered standard products and services. The low value means that there should be no customization or anything that incurs extra costs. It doesn't mean that such relationships should be discouraged. Apart from anything else a number of such relationships constitute the means of reducing vulnerability by being overly tied to a smaller number of relationships.

Rival (high value, low commonality)

While there is great value in the relationship currently, and relationships with such customers should be maintained for their economic value, the level of strategic interest commonality is low. Such customers are just not going in the same direction as the marketer and there is strong potential for opportunism (such as the customer trying to extract substantial price reductions at a time of excess capacity). A business marketer might want to ensure that it is protected from opportunistic action from these customers and may strive to achieve this by looking for new customers. It would certainly not be advisable to engage in additional specific investments for such customers.

Friend (low value, high commonality)

Friends show that they are clearly interested in the same things as the supplier. They might have similar views about the direction that technology is going in the market. They might even use the supplier's products in ways that are new and thus be a source of innovation in the sector. However, the value of the relationship itself is relatively low overall. This may be because the relationship is embryonic and yet to establish the volumes needed to be more valuable in revenue terms or operating efficiency. If such relationships are indeed embryonic then they may require the sort of attention that will lead to greater volumes and will thus incur expense in the short term. However, despite the level of interest commonality, if the investment does not lead to greater relationship value then over time this sort of customer is merely destined to become an occasional acquaintance rather than a strategic partner.

Partner (high value, high commonality)

Partners, on the other hand, are important for the economic value they represent and the alignment with the strategic interest of the seller. The volumes, criticality of the products they use, their relative irreplaceability, or the cost savings they bring, allied to the common direction they are taking, mean that specific investments in these are recommended. Calls for adaptations (to products or processes) may originate from customer but may also be welcome to the supplier; they signal the shared interest of the two parties. While in a politically balanced relationship the extra value created by adaptations might naturally be shared equitably between the parties, in a relationship where the customer has the balance of power the marketer will need to be careful that it is not just funding value creation for the customer alone. This involves careful negotiation and a mutual understanding that the long-term strength of the business relationship depends on equitable distribution of value.

A source of learning for the company

Some customers may be considered important purely because the demands they make are valuable in increasing the problem-solving abilities of the seller. That is, these customers set the bar for requirements technically or commercially so that by reaching the threshold the seller's abilities across the board with its customer base are enhanced. They may not even be profitable relationships financially, requiring as they do such high levels of investment in product or process improvements. However, the learning opportunities they provide compensate for the direct financial loss. For example, many automotive component suppliers have benefited greatly from working with Japanese car manufacturers such as Toyota and Nissan. By meeting the very high technical and quality standards of these companies, the supplier develops engineering skills and management processes that serve it well with other customers and in other markets.

The supplier's share of customers' purchases

The notion of share of a customer's overall purchases makes this criterion sound like it should belong amongst those variables that use hard data in the previous section. However this is a judgement that the analyst makes, typically in the absence of the ability to confirm the exact relative proportions. It can be a very subjective measure and analysts should be encouraged to justify the estimates that they use. They are also best advised to make conservative estimates. The quality of the estimates can, of course, be enhanced by attempts to triangulate. The most obvious way of doing this is to solicit estimates from several sources, along with evidence from each source of the validity of their estimate. These can be used to derive an average of the weighted estimates reported, based on an index of the credibility of the supporting evidence. Ford et al. (2002) show how the share of supply of the customer requirements can be combined with a measure of change in sales volume over time to help distinguish customer relationships (see Figure 9.4)

Short-term advantage-taking

As Ford et al. (2002) point out, business-to-business relationships aren't always about being nice and aren't always about mutual benefit. Where the potential to take advantage exists with companies for which the supplier has no longer-term plans, companies in a position to do so may well take the opportunities that exist. Of course, irreplaceable customers (see above) who bring special benefits to the seller make them less likely to be targets of advantage-taking. However, others amongst the customer base that are the source of short-term sales volume/profits/technical or commercial knowledge

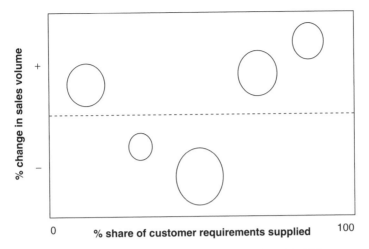

Figure 9.4 Customer portfolio change matrix (Ford et al., 2002: 226)

to the firm, but who offer little in the way of long-term benefit, are prime targets for relatively poor treatment at a particular point in time (for example, inflated price rises at a time of particular customer need just because it is possible). Ford et al. (2002) call these customers the 'fall guys' because of this. While such behaviour from a supplier may not be seen as wholesome, it is certainly possible for companies to use their potential to take advantage as the basis for distinguishing some relationships from others.

Combining Classification Variables to Produce Varied Clusters

The ultimate aim in undertaking a relationship portfolio analysis is to generate a series of different, but internally consistent, clusters of customer relationship types. Throughout the description of specific variables above there have been examples of the sorts of clusters that can be produced, typically by combining the use of classification variables (the four Shapiro et al. (1987) clusters of carriage trade, aggressive, passive and bargain basement customers; the four Krapfel et al. (1991) relationship types of rival, partner, friend and acquaintance). In this section, we present other examples of how variables can be combined and the resulting clusters produced.

Campbell and Cunningham (1983) combine five different variables (see Table 9.4) to derive four categories of customer that were appropriate for a packaging company. They also indicate how companies can establish the appropriateness of their resource commitment to these clusters. In this case, where the company pursues an innovation strategy, it is appropriate to focus

Table 9.4 Four-cluster portfolio analysis of the customer base (N=222) of a packaging company and the management checks undertaken to establish appropriate resource commitments

	Yesterday's customers	Today's regular customers	Today's special customers	Tomorrow's customers
(a) Classification criteria:				
Sales volume	Low	Average	High	Low
Profitability of customer to supplier	Low	Average	High	Low
Relationship age	Old	Average	Old	New
Use of strategic resources	Low	Average	High	High
Supplier's share of customer's purchases	Low	Average	High	Low
(b) Management checks:				
Cluster size	175	38	2	7
% of sales	12	44	43	1
% of technical development expenditure	–	23	38	39

Source: Adapted from Campbell and Cunningham, 1983.

on the proportion of technical development expenditure that each cluster consumes. It is also appropriate that the greatest proportion of sales should come from today's customers. The company would not want to see any technical development resource being consumed by yesterday's customers and would certainly not like to see them constitute a sizeable proportion of sales.

The Campbell and Cunningham (1983) clustering shows a useful combination of the more easily derived financial measures alongside those that require a more subjective judgement call from the analyst. Turnbull and Zolkiewski (1995) advocate just such an approach, applying the hard measures (profitability of customers) before moving on to the more judgemental measures in a two-stage process. They propose the use of a three-dimensional (2 × 2 × 2: net price × cost to serve × relationship value) matrix with eight different categories.

Ford et al. (2002) take the notion of portfolio analysis further than most when they depict a series of relationship types that have proved useful (see Table 9.5).

Relationship Life Cycles

The life cycle concept has long been used by marketers to derive an understanding of the appropriate marketing strategies to be used to support a

Table 9.5   Indicative application of a progressive series of portfolio analysis variables and the resulting clusters, as named by Ford et al. (2002: 100 ff.)

	Criterion applied	*Resulting Ford et al. (2002) clusters*	*Description of cluster*
Degree of subjective judgement being applied	Sales	'Cash cows'	Those customers currently generating the greatest proportion of sales income, typically because of higher volume demands.
		'Minor relationships'	Small customers in terms of individual sales demands and relative importance to the firm. This doesn't mean they are unprofitable, just not individually significant. There may be quite a lot of them and as a group they may account for a sizable income.
	Profits	'Today's profits'	The most profitable customers currently.
		'Yesterday's profits'	Those customers whose profitability trends indicate that they are on the wane.
		'The "Old Men"'	Customer relationships that are past their heyday. There may be some residual personal interests in maintaining these relationships but generally they absorb resources that could be more profitably used.
		'Tomorrow's profits'	Relationships that may currently be unprofitable and require ongoing investment but which hold the promise of substantial profits in the medium to long term.
	Source of learning opportunities	New technical requirements	Relationships that, because of the demands they make technically in product or process terms, force the firm to improve its game, leading to innovations that prove valuable in the business at large.
		New commercial requirements	Similar to the category above but where the innovation comes from its commercial rather than technical operations.
	Source of advantage-taking	'The fall-guys'	Customers that are not of any long-term strategic import and where the scope for taking advantage exists. In essence, it does not matter how badly you treat them because they are just not important to you.

market offering. The best-known life cycle concept is probably the Product Life Cycle. While the life cycle concept has been criticized in general terms for being overly idealized and of little practical help at the micro-management level, it is a concept that makes intuitive sense to most managers. We see birth, growth, maturity and decline in the living world all the time and thus suppose that human constructions like products have a life and death that corresponds to the natural world in general terms. The extension of the life cycle concept to relationships is of arguably greater use. Relationships are constructs that actually do involve people in more direct ways than a product does and thus the living elements are very real, rather than abstractions. Unlike artifices like products, the social constructions that are relationships are also clearly organic; they have a life of their own as a result of the range of different people involved and the cultures and affiliations of these people. This is what can make relationships highly flexible. However, it also is what makes relationships very difficult to control. In recognition of the fluid nature of relationships, researchers have set out to establish how they develop over time. Ford (1980) examined the relationship life cycle in terms of several variables:

- the experience of dealing with each other;
- the uncertainty associated with working with each other;
- the distance between the parties, incorporating social, geographical, time, cultural and technological manifestations;
- the commitment the parties make to each other; and
- the specific adaptations they make to what they do and how they do it that brings them closer to the counterpart (what Williamson (1979) refers to as 'transaction-specific investments').

Ford established that relationships that became close and enduring manifest reductions in uncertainty and distance over time. At the same time they exhibit increases in the experience of working together, in commitments to each other and in the number of adaptations that the parties make in their normal operations to avail themselves of the relationship with the other. These are depicted diagrammatically in Figure 9.5.

Relationship stages

The *pre-relationship stage* is that transient time between when there is nothing resembling a relationship at all and the point at which there could just be a relationship. It is sparked by a need for change that has a customer searching for new suppliers, whether as a result of company policy or a change in the relationship with the current supplier. In this respect the customer is in the driving seat, evaluating possible suitors against the performance of the incumbent or responding to changing marketplace information. As a largely analytical stage there is no commitment; it is only when a decision is taken on the strength of the analysis that a relationship can be said to have come into being.

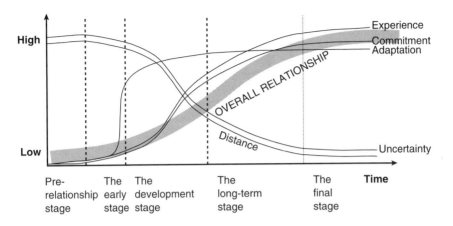

Figure 9.5   Ford's (1980) relationship life cycle stages

The *early stage* is characterized by the need to deal with substantial unknowns. The parties have no experience of working together and thus have great uncertainty about how the relationship will unfold and the value it may bring. As the parties do not know each other well, social distance is likely to be great. There may also be great technological distance because the parties have not yet had the opportunity to see how their respective product and process technologies can work together. A contract manufacturer of office chairs to a large multinational went through nearly two years of product concept proofing with the customer before any chairs were even accepted into the customer's catalogue. Where the relationship extends across frontiers there may also be geographical and cultural distances to be reduced.

Reducing the uncertainty and the distance and increasing the experience they have of each other requires substantial commitment of management time to understand each other. In the early stages there is unlikely to be much more than time committed; neither party is likely to make capital commitments until sure of the other. The commitment of time is likely to lead to reductions in the distance between the parties.

It is only during the *development stage* that the commitment of time leads to manifest reductions in uncertainty and distance between the parties. As a result of informal adaptations to what they do for each other their mutual experience of each other grows. More formal adaptations embed the practice of relationship and both parties start to see the benefits financially of adapting to each other more closely. When their levels of experience of each other reach their peak, during the *long-term stage*, there is little distance between them socially, technologically and culturally. There is then little more commitment that either can demonstrate, with extensive adaptation largely having taken place. At this point, the way in which the parties interact with each other starts to settle into forms of institutionalized working; established operations and working practices have become routine, without need to constantly re-appraise them.

When these forms of institutionalization become the way things are done more generally in the sector, embodied in forms of industry practice, then the relationship has essentially gone full circle. From something that starts for both parties on the basis of what is common practice and then proceeds into a way of working that is singular and unique, the relationship has now become common practice again because this way of working has become the norm. This is the *final stage*, only manifest in stable markets over the long term.

Dwyer et al. (1987) also argued that there is a closing of the gap between the two parties to a relationship over time. Their model of relationship development features four phases during which the relative dependence of buyer and seller upon each other increases.

Awareness corresponds roughly to Ford's (1980) pre-relationship stage. Here the parties are looking around for potential partners but have not yet engaged in what could be construed as an interactive relationship. That is, they are essentially independently eyeing and evaluating each other. The seller is communicating its strengths to the market more generally through advertisements or directly through targeted media. At the same time, the buyer may be gathering information about sources of supply, or new product specifications.

Exploration corresponds roughly to Ford's (1980) early stage of relationship development. At this point some interaction between the parties takes place such that they start to learn about each other. There is still relatively little investment in the relationship and either party can walk away easily. However, already at this stage what Dwyer et al. (1987) call the five enabling processes that underpin deepening relationship dependence are in action:

1. There is clear *attraction* in that both parties start to see the value to them of the relationship with the counterpart.
2. There is an increasing amount and breadth of *communication* and negotiation about how the relationship should unfold. This *bargaining* further deepens the communication at the same time as clarifying how the value in the relationship is to be shared.
3. The exploration of relative *power* dependence and the consequences of that for the relationship can start to be seen. The exercise of power by the stronger party can be just or unjust in the eyes of the counterpart, so the extent to which *justice* may prevail in the relationship is already being witnessed. For the relationship to achieve greater deepening, power must be seen to be exercised justly.
4. As a consequence of the behaviours manifest through communication, bargaining, and power and its exercise, it becomes possible to see *norm development* – a set of behaviours that constitute the norm in the relationship.

5. All of the above give rise to *development of expectations*. These are the pre-
    dictions of future behaviours in the relationship on the basis of what has
    gone before and up to the present. They are, of course, affected by the
    expectations companies bring into a relationship in the first place, but they
    also develop on the basis of how the parties see the relationship unfolding.

Expansion corresponds to what Ford (1980) calls the development stage.
Here the rate and extent of dependence increases, with the parties doing
more with each other and adapting what they do to enable themselves to
work more closely and obtain greater benefits of the partnership. The underlying processes see more attraction, greater and wider communication, just
exercise of power and the development of norms that meet expectations and
give rise to confidence in future expectations.

Commitment marks the point when the parties do not want an alternative
partner and will happily commit resources to the continuance of a relationship,
even to the point of withstanding problems that may arise in the relationship. They are prepared to make such commitments because there is a
shared belief in the value of the relationship to them.

Value of the relationship life cycle concept

The value of the relationship life cycle notion is the information that it can
give to relationship managers over time. Relationship marketers can assess
the levels of relationship indicators over time in order to establish the extent
to which the relationship has developed and to obtain some guidance on
appropriate relationship interventions. For example, they can assess the
amount and nature of the communication taking place in a relationship or
gauge the level of commitment, the amount of distance, or the degree and
nature of adaptations. These indicators provide sufficient intelligence that
relationship marketers can make sensible relationship decisions. For instance, where an assessment indicates levels of cultural distance that are presenting a barrier to relationship development across frontiers, alongside
clear adaptations by a customer and thus a willingness for greater commitment, then the marketer can work with the customer to reduce the levels of
cultural distance. Among other things in an international marketing context,
this could be achieved through language study, social and cultural
exchanges and workshops focused on hot topics that have specifically been
seen to be sources of difficulties in mutual understanding.

Of course, there are managerial limitations to the life cycle concept. While
it describes the processes that close relationships have traversed over time,
there are two major difficulties for relationship managers. First, they can
never be sure the current relationship was ever destined to be a close relationship. Some relationships may develop in ways that look like they will
endure only to falter because the wider marketing environment has changed
(for example, new potential partners have arrived, or competitive changes in

the network more generally have rendered the relationship less significant). Some may start out in ways that show little inclination to closeness in the longer term but change through adaptations that make the relationship more significant given the over-arching marketing environment. Business is all about making judgement calls and relationship managers are faced with just the same. They need to make the best call they can based upon the intelligence with which they are faced and their own relationship objectives. Second, even where a relationship has been destined for greater closeness over time, as an idealized concept it is never clear exactly where a relationship is or should be on the life cycle at any particular time. The measures of progress themselves are also not precise. They typically involve qualitative judgements (of level of commitment, for example, or degree of distance) rather than more objective measures.

Not knowing exactly how you are doing on a cycle, where it is not clear where you are or even should be, may seem to make the concept of dubious managerial value. However, the value of the concept does not come from the ability to use it prescriptively. Its value is in the potential it has to inform strategic decision-making. On the basis of assessments of the relationship life cycle position over time it becomes possible to know whether a relationship is heading towards a close and enduring future or whether it has reached its maximum potential already and so has a less close future. Knowing this enables relationship managers to make more informed relationship judgement calls. The request for capital investment to meet the demands of a customer that has manifested decreasing commitment over time can be evaluated from a more informed position. Equally, the opportunity (perhaps unsolicited by the customer) to improve a product formulation, delivery arrangement or payment terms for a customer that has shown a deepening commitment and preparedness to adapt to produce further value for both parties can also be more clearly evaluated.

Chapter Summary

- This chapter has introduced an important task in strategic business-to-business marketing management, that of relationship portfolio analysis.

- The management of customer relationships as strategic assets requires an analysis of the differential value of each relationship in the customer base as a precursor to formulating differential strategies for the management of the relationships.

- This does not mean that all relationships are treated completely differently. Rather, a sensible collection of relationship types can be derived that are the basis of differential treatment.

- Differential treatment of customer relationships is not merely 'better' or 'worse'. By identifying the different types of relationships it becomes possible to specify a whole range of relationship strategies: some involving reducing distance while others may involve adding to it; some involving investments in new processes, products or other technology; some involving merely demonstrating commitment through words, others through actions. The overall objective is to arrive at a notion of balance in the relationship portfolio, recognizing that it is not possible for all relationships to be close and the subject of substantial investment.

- To aid the analysis process a series of criteria were introduced that can help differentiate customer accounts from each other, from broad binary splits to the application, singly or in combination, of a series of variables. The variables range from those that are relatively easy to apply because they are financial in nature and use accounting data as their basis, to those that require judgement calls from the portfolio analysts on the basis of the wider knowledge they have of the future company strategy, relationship histories and the potential of those relationships.

- The dynamic nature of relationships and the continuing need for strategic realignment means that portfolio analysis is not done on a once-and-for-all basis. Rather, it needs to be conducted on a regular basis, typically yearly, and needs to accommodate the changing needs of the company and the changes in relationships over time. For that reason, relationship life cycles have an impact on this process. In the chapter we describe the stages of relationship development and what these mean for relationship variables over time. Further, we indicate the value that the relationship life cycle concept can bring in informing relationship decisions.

Questions for discussion

1. Explain the process of portfolio management and its value.

2. Compare and contrast the use of financially derived criteria for portfolio analysis with those relying on the judgement of the analyst.

3. For a company that you know well, describe four criteria that you would use for analysing its portfolio of relationships.

4. Discuss the merits of binary splits when analysing a relationship portfolio.

5. Using a relationship with which you are familiar, discuss the extent to which the life cycle concept provides you with clear indications of how to proceed.

6. For a relationship where you have strong knowledge of its history over time, identify the stages in its life cycle development, highlighting key moments that have affected its development.

Case study: Reseller relationship portfolio management at O₂

O_2 is one of the biggest mobile phone service providers in the UK (number two in subscriber terms as of March 2006). Originally a spin-off joint venture between BT and Cellnet in the UK, the company now has 100-per-cent-owned-businesses in the UK, Ireland and Germany. It has an estimated 25.7 million customers and approximately 15,000 employees. It reported revenues for the financial year ending 31 March 2005 of £6,683 million (with interim revenues for the 6 months ending 30 September 2005 of £3,615 million). Its recent acquisition by Telefonica of Spain brings O_2 into a much larger group that has a very strong presence in Spain, Africa and Latin America. Telefonica boasts 147.7 million customers (according to Telefonica's website http://www.telefonica.com/home-eng.shtml) and a workforce of over 200,000. It reported revenues for 2004 of €30,321.9 million.

In a competitive marketplace like the UK, where there is an increasing number of mobile phone providers (those who sign customers up to a service rather than the company who owns the network) and where market growth has started to slow from the heady days of the early 1990s, acquiring customers becomes more difficult for providers. Churn rates that were sources of inconvenience to the providers in the 1990s have become much more pressing. This is doubly so when one calculates the costs of providing increasingly feature-laden phones (with integral cameras, larger coloured screens, downloadable tones, MP3 devices, web data connectivity, 3G streaming video capability, and so on) and yet cannot guarantee that customers will stay beyond the contract tie-in period. Like the other operators, O_2 has put greater efforts into managing its relationships with end customers in order to improve this situation (what it has called its 'Customer Experience' strategy). The intention has been to ensure that the relationship with the end customer is embedded as early as possible and managed so that the customer feels no compulsion (or even motivation) to leave. It has introduced a customer relationship management programme underpinning its commitment in this respect that attempts to integrate all the contacts that customers have with the service provider.

Of course, like its competitors, O_2 does not always get to deal directly with its individual or corporate end customers. In fact, its own direct retail channel accounts for little more than 50 per cent of its connections. The rest are recruited through independent sales channels and, while customers sign up to contracts with O_2, they often have strong personal relationships with the independent intermediary who recruited them. This strength of relationship may not seem so obvious when one considers only the big national retailers of mobile services in the UK (such as Carphone Warehouse or Phones4u): they are highly visible to individual end customers and while they may be natural sources for the general public to pick up a handset and a contract, the relationship may not be that strong. However, up until about four years ago O_2 had about 30 direct independent sales intermediaries working for it, all with the rights of distributors, particularly in the corporate sales market. Some were large with wide geographic spread (for example, 20:20 Logistics from the Caudwell Group in the business-to-business market), with others being small and local, providing phones and connections for business and private customers.

This variety made it difficult to ensure the consistent high-quality customer experience that was then starting to drive O_2 strategy. O_2 may have had little visibility to some end customers because there may in fact have been two or more intermediaries in the channel between it and the end customer. The strong relationship with an intermediary may also have meant that the account with the end user was more fragile; if an intermediary decided to switch to another service provider then O_2 would often lose the individual or corporate end customers with them.

Unsurprisingly, the relationship thinking O_2 had been doing with its end customers had also extended to its management of its channels to market. A major issue for O_2 marketers has always been the relative efficacy of the different routes to market, and key to this is the management of the relationships it builds with channel members. The first efforts at managing its portfolio of channel customers were aimed at creating a channel that was more responsive to O_2's 'Customer Experience' strategy, and were initiated about four years ago. Up to that point, O_2 had been happy to have any company undertake channel sales as long as they were financially sound and could get 250 connections per month. Delivering a new connection always got the intermediary an upfront connection bonus plus a flat 5 per cent share of the customer's bills. Of course, the connections could have been obtained by a company further down the channel, so involving little effort by the direct independent, and for some independents the upfront fee itself was often the only value they were interested in obtaining. It mattered little to them that a customer left at the earliest opportunity; they could always get signing-on fees from new customers.

O_2 were keen to create greater stability in the channel and to provide incentives for their independents to obtain their own connections, particularly connections that would endure. They took the view that if the independents were getting paid for acquiring phone customers then they should actually demonstrate the commitment to doing just that. So they changed the five different contract types they had with the 30 or so direct independents (often with up to 300 pages) to one standard contract. They recognized that the previous 30-day contracts could perhaps have bred some of the instability so they changed the contracts to rolling 30-day contracts with a 12-month minimum duration. The requirement was now also for a minimum of 50 connections a month. This may seem small compared to 250 but was still considered challenging for some (and it removed the impetus to obtain connections through onward sales via second-or third-level intermediaries). Those who were able to could, of course, go beyond 50 per month. They also moved from a flat 5 per cent fee to a tiered mechanism: there was no commission at all for the first 6 months, at which time the 5 per cent rate applied, rising to 10 per cent for contracts lasting over 24 months. The intention was to obtain lower churn rates and higher ARPU (average revenue per user). All the existing customers were moved over to the new contract terms. Those who wanted to and could achieve the target of 250 connections per month had the opportunity to become proper 'distributors' with a different set of terms and conditions. Full distributors had to demonstrate that they had their own field sales team and clear channel management objectives.

With the established new arrangements for the direct independent channel, a new phase of channel development could then occur. Over the next couple of years the number of direct independents grew from 30 to 150 and the business grew accordingly, at the same time reducing the degree of exposure to any individual account. In portfolio management terms, this brought its own set of problems. All were classed as 'direct independents' and were all subject to the same standard commercial contracts, all getting paid the same regardless of how much effort they were putting in and regardless of how much better they could perform. O_2 recognized that there were opportunities to support different independents differently, depending on their relationship value. A series of analyses (including financial measures, total connection numbers, churn rates, ARPU and lifetime customer value) were undertaken. This revealed substantial diversity amongst the direct independents. Some were delivering 1500 connections per quarter, while others were only delivering 100 per quarter – yet their treatment was essentially the same. There had always been some marketing funds that O_2 had used to help some customers with communications activities (for example, mailshots) and those delivering the most connections typically tendered for and obtained these, but this was about the limit of the differential treatment.

A new O_2 Advance programme aimed to deal differently with those that performed demonstrably better. For those who could provide lower churn rates and higher ARPU, O_2 were prepared to share customer data, guarantee a share of marketing funds and provide a dedicated contact (rather than the usual helpline), with increased access to these extras over time. For some, additional resources for further business development could also be available.

Membership of the scheme required that the independent continued to meet targets (though one lapse over a two-quarter period is allowed). The terms of the contracts were also changing to become more relational.

Additionally, O_2 has been very active in discussing difficulties in meeting targets for the accounts. It has been envisaged that the group of direct independents can be further split into a relatively small number of big accounts (though still doing less business than the full distributors), with a greater proportion of smaller accounts. For the smallest accounts the level of O_2 support will increasingly be provided by technology, through automated telephone systems. Some might even be encouraged to move their accounts to the distributors rather than dealing directly with O_2.

When it comes to making decisions about where to invest efforts, account managers at O_2 are now having those discussions with their sales directors armed with greater in-depth knowledge of particular accounts because they have been involved in investigating what has been happening with the customers. The account managers will know the history and will have been finding out from the customer what exactly has been happening in their business, and will know when it can grow further and what it requires as input from O_2. By the same token they will also know more intimately when further investment in an account will not generate greater returns and will thus be able to make better resource allocation decisions. Overall, they will have the right level of knowledge of a variety of different accounts so that they can achieve the balance of connection and revenue targets that are best for O_2.

Case study questions

1. What variables would you use to analyze O_2's independent sales channels?
2. What relationship clusters would you identify and how would you manage each to achieve a balanced portfolio for O_2?
3. How could the life cycle concept be used effectively by O_2 in its portfolio management?

The assistance of Brian Latham at O_2 in the preparation of this case study is gratefully acknowledged. See also www.telefonica.com and www.02.com.

References

Anderson, J. and Narus, J. (1991) 'Partnering as a focused market strategy', *California Management Review*, 33 (3): 95–113.

Barnes, B.R. (2004) 'Is the seven year hitch premature in industrial markets?', *European Journal of Marketing*, 39 (5/6): 560–84.

Bund Jackson, B. (1985) 'Build customer relationships that last', *Harvard Business Review*, 63 (6): 120–8.

Campbell, N. and Cunningham, M. (1983) 'Customer analysis for strategy development in industrial markets', *Strategic Management Journal*, 4: 369–80.

Drucker, P. (1955) *The Practice of Management*. London: Heinemann Professional Publishing.

Dwyer, F.R., Schurr, P.H. and Oh, S. (1987) 'Developing buyer–seller relationships', *Journal of Marketing*, 51 (April), 11–27.

Ford, D. (1980) 'The development of buyer–seller relationships in industrial markets', *European Journal of Marketing*, 14(5/6), 339–54.

Ford. D., Berthon, P., Brown, S., Gadde, L.E., Håkansson, H., Naude, P., Ritter, T. and Snehota, I. (2002) *The Business Marketing Course*. Chichester: Wiley.

Håkansson, H. (ed.) (1982) *International Marketing and Purchasing of Industrial Goods*. Chichester: John Wiley.

Harrington, L. (2004) 'Building the sense and respond company', online source: www.inboundlogistics.com/articles/features/0904_feature03.shtml, accessed September 2004.

Krapfel, R., Salmond, D. and Spekman, R. (1991) 'A strategic approach to managing buyer–seller relationships', *European Journal of Marketing*, 25 (9): 22–32.

Sako, M. (1992) *Prices, Quality and Trust – Inter-Firm Relations in Britain and Japan*. Cambridge: Cambridge University Press.

Shapiro, B., Rangan, V., Moriarty, R. and Ross, E. (1987) 'Manage customers for profits (not just sales)', *Harvard Business Review*, 65 (5): 101–08

Turnbull, P. and Zolkiewski, J. (1995) 'Profitability in customer portfolio planning', paper presented at the 11th Annual IMP International Conference, UMIST, Manchester 7–9 September.

Williamson, O. (1979) 'Transaction-Cost Economics: The Governance of Contractual relations', *Journal of Law and Economics*, 22 (October) 233–61.

10 Managing Product Offerings

Learning outcomes

After reading this chapter you will:

- know what the concept of a product offering means;
- be able to apply portfolio planning techniques to decisions about offering investment, development or divestment of products;
- be able similarly to apply life cycle and portfolio approaches to the management of product offerings;
- be familiar with the process and activities associated with the development of new offerings.

Introduction

The success of a company's marketing only materializes at the point where a customer is prepared to buy its products and services. As Chapter 2 indicated, it is the problem-solving abilities of the marketer that constitute a source of value to customers. Therefore, the problem-solving abilities of the supplier are very important. It does not really matter how well the marketer has undertaken all the tasks up to this point; if the firm cannot create an offering that satisfactorily meets customer needs then everything else is pointless.

If the marketer wants to continue to meet customer needs then the offering must adapt to changing needs. Clearly, this is a dynamic process. It implies that there is a development cycle for product offerings, from conception through to deletion, and that they are not just made once and for all but need constant reappraisal. It implies a need to adjust to changes in market circumstances, such as competitive action, over and above changing customer needs. This chapter considers just what needs to be done throughout this dynamic process. We start by examining the offering concept, its nature and extent. We then look at the offering management tasks that face the business marketer: making the right interventions throughout the life of an individual offering and managing each individual offering as part of a balanced portfolio. Subsequently we focus on the process by which offerings can be conceived and brought to market in the first place. The long-term health of the firm depends on how successful it is at bringing new products to market and managing them throughout their life.

Business-to-Business Product Offerings

It may seem pedantic, but it is always more precise to use the term 'product offering' rather than the more generic word 'product'. It is for this reason that this chapter talks of 'managing product offerings' rather than the more usual 'product management'. This is because the word 'product' is more often considered as something relatively physical, that you can point to and/or handle. Consequently, the word 'product' may only capture a part of an overall offering, namely its *physical attributes* (see Figure 10.1). In many cases there is certainly a physical aspect to the offering that is transferred to a customer. That is the case, for instance, when the customer is buying MRO supplies, raw materials or components. It is, after all, these physical goods that are used, consumed or transformed by the customer's own value-adding activities. It is also very easy to talk about these products in terms of their physicality. They have a size, shape, material composition and other particular physical properties, including performance levels (for example, tensile strength). In cases like this the *physical attributes* are of the utmost importance in creating the *core benefit* that all offerings have to provide to be of value. Without the ability to deliver the fundamental customer benefit, the offering will never be considered as a viable choice. This core benefit may or may not arise largely out of its physical attributes.

It is sometimes argued that industrial marketers prefer to talk in terms of the physicality of offerings because they are engineers at heart. That may have some truth. However, even for product categories such as raw materials, there are often less physical, ancillary elements that are fundamental to the offering. Components do not add value for a customer until they are delivered and are ready at the point when they can be integrated as part of a larger assembly. Thus, for a customer, the value it gets from an offering is often more than its physical properties. It may be the level of support that is provided for the physical product through services such as training and responses to problems in use, or the ability to guarantee delivery schedules within a 30-minute tolerance that is really valuable. For situations where *service elements* have a role in creating the value of the offering, these elements also need to be considered from the offering's inception.

Many developed economies generate most of their wealth not from tangible product manufacturing but from intangibles services, which are increasingly

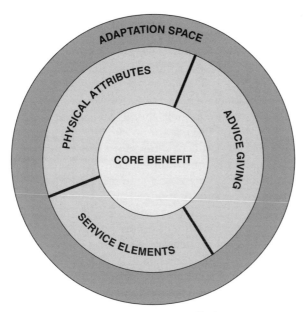

Figure 10.1   Elements of a business-to-business offering

information intensive (see Chapter 1 for a discussion of the structure of developed economies). In a service and information economy, much of the value of the offering may be highly intangible even though the results of the delivery of the offering are tangible. For example, the UK water companies that make use of the engineering skills of a company like MJ Gleeson will obtain a design document and drawings for an asset such as a waste-water pumping station, and ultimately the station itself. However, the service that they want most is the design abilities of the engineers, including their speed of design and their ability to respond flexibly to customer requirements. It is this service performance that leads to the physical artefacts; but separating out the tangible and the intangible aspects of the offering is often difficult.

For some offerings where the physical product itself is highly substitutable, because all competitors can achieve much the same standard, the sole basis for differential advantage may be the additional elements of the service. A construction material like float glass is largely a commodity and is readily available from a range of global suppliers (for example, Asahi of Japan, Pilkington of the UK, St Gobain of France, and Guardian of the USA). While price will undoubtedly play a strong role for highly substitutable products, Pilkington works hard to differentiate itself by providing a range of services to customers over and above the glass itself, including applications advice and market forecasts. A regional sales representative may even pass on possible sales leads to customers. This sort of *advice-giving* constitutes another relevant element of the design of offerings (Ford et al., 2002). Those companies that recognize the nature of the uncertainties that a customer faces (see Chapter 3) and are able to help to provide solutions to those uncertainties put themselves in a stronger position competitively, and these solutions can draw from any or all of the elements of the offering.

Product offering management is not a once-and-for-all activity. Both customers and marketers improve their abilities over time, even with respect to individual offerings. A supplier may be able to introduce materials changes in a component that has economic benefits to itself without compromising performance for the customer, for example. Changes in downstream customer needs may mean that a customer is happy to reduce the performance demands made of a supplier and obtain economic benefits in doing so. Further, if the parties work together they may be able to simplify production processes or product formulations that provide additional economic value to both. These examples typically concern reductions in offering complexity and hence cost reductions. It is equally possible to engage in changes that add extra cost but that are seen as economically valuable to either or both parties over the longer haul because of improved performance. Consequently, it is possible to talk about an *adaptation space* that surrounds an offering, and the sorts of changes just described are facilitated within that space.

In conceiving of new offerings, a marketer may have some understanding of what is possible with the offering. However, the full extent of what is really possible can only become known through interaction with the customer. Indeed, lots of potential adaptations may become evident. The degree to which the marketer or customer is prepared to engage in any adaptive behaviour with respect to the offering will be a function of how they feel about the relationship with the counterpart. Ford et al. (2002) argue that an adaptation in relationship terms is really only worth the name when it involves doing something in a relationship that isn't intended to be replicated for all customers. The example cited in Chapter 3 of the plastic blow-mould bottling company that introduced an additional line to cater for all sizes of bottles required by its major customer can clearly be seen in these terms; it involved a capital investment on the company's part to add the extra line. We concur with this view in terms of the consequences of adaptation for relationships between buyer and seller. However, from an offering management perspective, it serves to demonstrate the value of considering what is sometimes called the 'potential product offering', even from inception.

The lesson in semantics around the use of the term 'product offering' rather than just 'product' is not meant to be merely academic. A business marketer must be clear about the range of uncertainties facing customers and must respond by putting together clear solutions to those problems. The solutions may arise from the problem-solving or transfer abilities of the marketer or a combination of both. The success of an offering will be measured by the extent to which it provides a complete solution to the customer's problem. It is only then that the core benefit of an offering is completely delivered.

Strategic Tools for Managing Product Offerings

Two of the most useful strategic management tools that can aid the business marketer when making decisions about market offerings have been introduced in Chapter 9 in our coverage of Relationship Management. These are the life cycle tool and portfolio analysis. In the following discussion we will consider their application to offering management in more detail. They can be applied at different levels of abstraction when it comes to offering management. A company may have several product ranges, each with a range of individual products, and several different technologies or technology platforms may be manifested in the product mix – see Box 10.1 for an illustration.

Box 10.1   *Multiple technologies and multiple products*

National Gummi AB of Sweden produces a range of extruded, moulded and punched rubber and plastic products for use as seals and dampeners in the automotive industry and for washing machines. It can make these different products using solid rubber, cellular rubber, cellular plastics with open cells, or cellular plastics with closed cells. All these technologies have different properties in terms of the hardness of the product that is produced, its tensile strength, its weight and the working temperature at which it should be used. Decisions about the range of technologies it needs to offer, the production capacity it makes available to them, and the range of products making use of the materials technology are constant considerations for the firm, and these decisions are helped by analyses such as life cycle analysis and portfolio analysis. The firm originally dealt only with solid rubber materials technology. Environmental preferences are now such that the company needs to work in forms of plastic, and elastomers, rather than just solid rubber. As well as life cycle and portfolio trends at the level of the technology, there is also a need to observe such trends in respect of specific product lines and even specific products. Indeed, National Gummi's ability to provide strategic insight at all levels (technology, product line, and product offering) means that these analyses are invaluable to the business marketer.

Managing product offerings using the life cycle concept

The principle that different strategies are appropriate at different life cycle stages was introduced in the last chapter when discussing relationships. The use of the concept, however, originates in the management of product offerings, where it has been most often described. The classic idealized model of a product life cycle (Figure 10.2) depicts a series of stages through which products notionally proceed during their life. Recognition of the life cycle stages and the different management needs at those various stages prepares managers to act in ways that are most appropriate for the product at any point in time. As Figure 10.2 shows, a life cycle is typically described as four major stages, with those stages occurring once a product is released to the market.

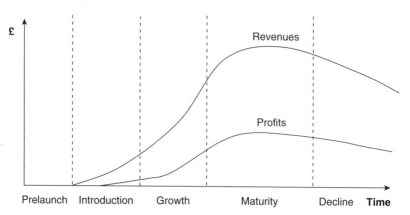

Figure 10.2 Stages in the life cycle of an offering

From a managerial perspective, of course, there is substantial activity before launch in development and preparation for launch (the *prelaunch* stage), which we have chosen to include in our diagram. In business markets, the time from product concept to market launch may be substantial, even when working directly with a customer that has a particular product need in mind. In one example, a UK manufacturing company was commissioned to make an office chair for a large office furniture maker. After several iterations of product concept testing and then value engineering activities to ensure it could be made at an acceptable price point, almost two years had elapsed before the chair was even ready to enter the customer's catalogue. Two years, of course, seems a short time when one considers the amount of time required for the design and manufacture of a new aircraft such as the Airbus A380. The research and development costs of the offering itself along with those incurred in bringing an offering to market such as production costs (possibly involving new processes and equipment or additional tooling) are met prior to launch, of course, with the intention that they will be recouped by the product after its introduction. While making a commitment in principle to the A380, Airbus needed the assurance of advance orders for the aircraft to confirm that it was worth the investment. It set a viability threshold of 50 aircraft and had 149 confirmed orders by the time of the Reveal Ceremony in Toulouse on 18 January 2005, well on the way to the estimated 250 aircraft needed to break even. It remains to be seen just how many aircraft the market will buy.

Introduction stage

No value is made from a product offering until it is brought to market. It is only at this point that any contribution to the development costs can be made. However, during the introductory phase it may still be costing more money than it is bringing in, since there is a series of marketing tasks to be carried out. Up to and beyond the launch of the new offering, customers need to be made aware of it so there will be a series of communications activities: public demonstrations, exhibitions or trade shows or other publicity. If this is a completely new concept to the market there may be a need to generate primary demand for this type of offering. There may be trial offers with existing key customers, particularly if they are important reference customers. In addition, field sales time is likely to be invested in communicating its value (advice-giving), and the sales force must be trained in the product and shown how to demonstrate its benefits to customers. Where indirect channels are being used, distribution channels must be secured. These activities are likely to continue until sales start to rise, indicating a degree of market acceptance. By this time early problems with the offering can also be identified and resolved, and even more specific examples of the product in use will have been obtained that can enhance sales training.

Growth stage

As the offering is increasingly accepted by the market (assuming it is), and sales and profits begin to increase more rapidly than before, the nature of the demands on the business marketer change. Competition is likely to increase, with consequent pressure on prices, and this pressure creates greater demand and thus fuels further growth. For particularly innovative market offerings competition is most likely to be from copycat products, tapping into the same primary demand but from a lower cost base (without the costs of development in creating the primary demand in the first place). Defending market share through attempts to differentiate may be successful in achieving secondary demand. This may involve incurring additional costs in expanding production, increasing the product line, adding product extensions or securing additional distribution. It may involve adding some additional service elements or working with some specific key customers to consider how adaptations to the product might benefit both parties. In all cases the business marketer will want to ride the growth wave as long as possible achieving the best margins possible.

Maturity stage

Ultimately, the rate of sales growth slows. Profits may continue to rise in the aftermath of the growth phase. To maintain the profit trend requires cost reductions. They can be achieved by cutting the amount of sales force time spent on pioneering activities such as determining new applications for the product. A shift from more personal forms of marketing to forms of telemarketing may also reduce costs. This may be combined usefully with a promotion focus on trade customers rather than end customers, with the aim of maintaining availability levels, and could accompany price-based promotional activities aimed at increasing the loyalty of heavy users. Where the offering needs maintenance and repair it is important to have sufficient capacity for this, and if spare parts are needed then there should be good availability. Reductions in other cost sources may also be worthy of consideration, such as logistics/transportation.

Decline stage

The efforts at maintaining price levels and reducing the cost base that have been initiated in a mature market will work for a limited time (unless a product can find a completely new primary demand source). Profit margins will decline and the business marketer must look for ways to extract further value. The example of the Peugeot 206 in 2006 makes the point well. At a time in its life cycle where aggregate demand for the model had probably reached a plateau and competition was intense, it was understandable that Peugeot-Citroën considered a contraction in production capacity for the model. It made sense to the Peugeot management to cut capacity at Ryton in the UK where model costs were reportedly over €400 greater than at other Peugeot 206 facilities in Europe because most of the components are imported from France. Of course, this decision about a single product is conflated with wider production investment decisions in respect of the new 207 model, where lower cost facilities in Slovakia seem to be preferred (Griffiths, 2006).

Even where the degree of competition has declined so that there is less direct price competition, the drop in the level of demand means that sustaining levels of profitability typically requires cost reductions. Marketing expenses should be at a minimum. In terms of relationship portfolio management (see Chapter 9) the business marketer should drop unprofitable customers and channels. There should be no further development of the offering. Where specific profitable customers continue to use the offering and where strategic value exists for the marketer then there may be a case for adaptations with this customer. These may be in respect of the product attributes or the service elements. Such adaptation comes at a cost, though, and the customer needs to bear it, unless the adaptation opens up new market or technology possibilities for the marketer so that new offerings or markets become obtainable.

Criticisms of the life cycle approach

The life cycle concept is not without criticism. As an idealized pattern for the development of an offering, it is certainly possible that an offering may not necessarily correspond to the life cycle shape depicted in Figure 10.2. In fact, through the latter stages much marketing endeavour is committed to ensuring that the profile does not follow the idealized shape. In an ideal world the marketer would see demand for an offering just grow and grow and there would be no real need for defensive strategies. Such cases are truly exceptional and thus marketers must have a strong view about what marketing actions are appropriate at any point in the life cycle. However, the life cycle concept is criticized in respect of this latter point as well. The life cycle alone does not provide a day-by-day prescription for how to manage an offering. It can be difficult for a marketer to be clear about exactly where the offering is in its life cycle. However, this is perhaps to misunderstand the purpose and value of the life cycle concept. It is at its most valuable when it is seen as a conceptual tool for strategic management rather than as a tactical or operational prescription.

Managing offerings using portfolio analysis

In Chapter 9 the principles and practice of portfolio management were introduced, specifically in the context of managing a portfolio of customer relationships. It was indicated there that marketers have long seen value in the use of portfolio management techniques for strategic marketing purposes. Just as the portfolio approach was seen to be useful for analysing a set of customer relationships, so it can be useful for analysing a set of market offerings. There is an enduring need to consider all sources of potential value in order to determine which specific marketing responses are required. At a given time some product offerings will require money to be invested in them to help unlock further value. At the same time, some may be generating good returns as they stand and may require little additional marketing intervention. Meanwhile, some may not be producing good returns and may show little potential for future profitability; the firm will want to consider cutting back investment in these offerings and perhaps deleting some.

Two well-established frameworks for analysing product portfolios are the Boston Consulting Group (BCG) market share/growth matrix and the General Electric (GE) market attractiveness/strength matrix. The former, also known as the Boston Box, uses two measurement scales to position offerings on a 2 × 2 matrix. These are *relative market share* and *relative market growth* respectively (Figure 10.3). The GE framework, often used to position strategic business units within a multidivisional business, acknowledges that market share and market growth on their own are not necessarily sufficient to give a clear indication of relative performance. Consequently, two composite dimensions are used:

- *Market attractiveness:* This includes variables such as size of the market, its growth rate, competitive structure, market diversity and the impact of market environmental factors (sociocultural, political, legal, technological) and gives a firm indication of the relative possibilities in the various market segments where its offerings may be present.
- *Business strength:* This includes variables such as the firm's relative share of the market and its growth rate, along with profitability and the quality of the specific resources it can bring to the market such as company image, human and technological resources, and it provides a clear idea of how well the firm is doing in the market.

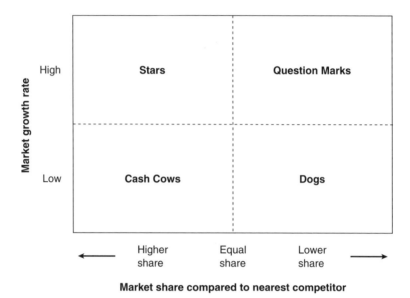

Figure 10.3   Boston Consulting Group market share/market growth matrix

The Boston Box is clearly easier to use and for many product offerings is sufficient to provide the firm with good intelligence from which to undertake marketing decision-making. The decisions taken are a function of the relative position of offerings within the framework. Relative market share is calculated as a proportion of the market share held by the market leader and is often presented on a logarithmic scale. Market growth is expressed as an annual percentage rate.

Those offerings that have a relatively low share in a fast-growing market, labelled *Question Marks* in the BCG nomenclature (see Figure 10.3), pose particular difficulties for the marketer. New offerings typically start in this position (a new and growing market presenting a strong marketing opportunity in the first place) and so inevitably take time to establish themselves and to achieve profitability (as the life cycle concept indicated). Supporting these offerings in the early stages of the life cycle is necessary and this would be seen as a reasonable investment. However, if the development of an offering positioned in this quadrant of the matrix fails to head to the left (increased relative share) and preferably upwards (higher growth) over time then it may be that the offering is not as successful as was expected at launch. At this point decisions need to be taken about whether to continue with the offering at all, or whether to reposition it.

A product offering that has followed a path downwards and to the right will invariably end up in the bottom right quadrant of the Boston Box. Such products are termed *Dogs* in BCG parlance and are clearly not achieving much in their own right. They may have been successful products at one time, or may just have been Question Marks that quite quickly failed to achieve their potential. Either way, there is little point in committing additional resources to Dogs; they are candidates for deletion, unless a value-creating strategy can be devised.

When an offering has captured the largest share of the market, it has clearly arrived in the left-hand side of the Box (see Figure 10.3). An offering that has managed to become market leader in a growing market is clearly successful and will generate positive cash flows. However, these *Stars* also need money invested in them to maintain or enhance their position. They are likely to be at the growth stage of the life cycle and, while awareness amongst customers may already be strong, there may also be new market segments to develop.

When growth in a market starts to slow, the market is getting to its most competitive stage; there are few new customers to reach. Companies competing in a market of this kind are typically competing against each other for a share of relatively static customer demand. This demand may be quite stable and so a firm with high market share, achieving economies of scale and with no further product development requirement, is likely to be generating substantial positive cash flows. This can be used to sustain the development of new offerings, or Question Marks that have recently just been brought to market. At the same time, these *Cash Cows* will make the greatest contribution to company profits. Of course, as the growth slows even more and the market starts to contract, profit margins will decline. This requires vigilance, since market leaders are the natural target for competitive action and losing share in a contracting market will diminish the cash generation from cash cows.

While efforts need to be made to protect share, and these are likely to be price based, the choice of price reductions or additional costs needs to be taken with a clear view as to their impact on specific customer relationships within the wider customer portfolio. As Chapter 9 indicates, it may be necessary to accept margin erosion with some customers on the basis of their relative value within the portfolio of relationships, but the same principle may not apply to all. Even in a contracting market some customization of the offering may be possible for some customers, perhaps through service elements or advice giving, or through forms of adaptation, that reduce the level of price competitiveness by creating relationships where the level of substitutability is reduced. Apart from anything else, this may create avenues for further innovation in the offering. The increases in customization do not guarantee that customers will become less price sensitive, merely that they will recognize the value that comes from this offering. For the marketer, while it may not be possible to obtain price premiums for the offering, it may at least be possible to obtain greater levels of share from these customers.

While Chapter 9 indicated that portfolio management at the level of the relationship is necessary to ensure that the business marketer is making best use of the relationships it already has, the discussion above has shown that portfolio management at the level of the offering is also necessary to ensure that the firm is obtaining the best value from the set of offerings it makes. The greatest value for the firm ultimately comes from having the best set of offerings available to the best set of customers and being able to do this time after time after time.

New Product Offering Development

While the previous section considered the management of offerings once they get to market, the firm also needs to develop successful new offerings. As we established in Chapter 9, portfolio management is intended specifically to ensure that a balance of investments exists over the longer term. New offerings need to be added to the portfolio as existing offerings go into decline. These new offerings will begin the cycle once more as Question Marks but the firm will hope they in turn will become the Stars and Cash Cows of the future.

New product offerings: an unavoidable risk

This takes us directly to new product offering development, generally considered to be a risky undertaking. Research indicates that most new product offerings fail. Clancy and Krieg (2003) estimate that no more than 10 per cent of all new products or services are trading profitably three years after launch. Berggren and Nacher (2001) indicate that the failure rate could be as high as 95 per cent. These may seem rather pessimistic estimates. Schilling and Hill (1998) present a much broader band of between 33 per cent and 60 per cent of products not generating an economic return; this is a little more optimistic but still shows the difficulty for new offerings. Even an optimistic estimate of failure rates for new industrial products only puts it as high as 30 per cent (Armstrong and Kotler, 2005).

Given the inauspicious omens, one could understand if companies did not want to get involved in new offering development. However, they are in an invidious position because ultimately they have no choice. Failure to engage in forms of new offering development leads inexorably to a portfolio that over time will come under greater pressure and ultimately produce less value for the firm. Even the mightiest of firms recognize this need. Intel, despite its dominant position in computer chip manufacture, recognizes the threat that loss of share to AMD brings to its business and realizes that the way to reverse the situation is to bring forward new offerings that create the new basis for competition. It plans to launch the new *vPro* brand of chips in the second half of 2006 (WARC, 2006). These are designed to enable businesses to automate the management of whole groups of PCs by enabling remote repair, thus reducing costs and increasing productivity.

Often, the proportion of sales revenue spent on R&D is a good indicator of the level of new product activity. Bowonder and Yadav (1999) have shown

Table 10.1 Average R&D spending as a proportion of sales for a range of business sectors in 1997

Industry sector	Average R&D spend as % of sales
Software	13.68
Pharmaceuticals and health care	12.04
Medical instruments	9.68
Scientific, photo, control equipment	6.40
Electronics	6.30
Computer	5.96
Miscellaneous	4.85
Chemicals	4.76
Aerospace	4.56
Automobiles	4.19
Telecommunications	3.63
Soap	3.56
Rubber and plastic products	3.56
Heavy industrial and farm equipment	2.48
Building material and glass	2.04
Food	1.34
Publishing and printing	1.25
Metal and metal products	1.17
Gas and electricity	1.00
Forest and paper products	0.90
Tobacco	0.96
Engineering and construction	0.73
Petroleum	0.66

Source: Adapted from Bowonder and Yadav, 1999: 46–9.

that US firms have dominated spending in the major categories of industry, with particular dominance in sectors such as software. As Table 10.1 shows, the range of investment in R&D ranged from over 13 per cent for pharmaceutical companies down to just above 0.5 per cent for petroleum companies, with several other sectors showing spends of less than 1 per cent. Individual companies within each of these sectors can see the extent to which their own spend exceeds or fails to meet the sector standards.

The risk in offering development is compounded by the costs of development that often accompany it in the first place. The large development costs in some sectors for completely new product offerings make this point very clearly. The cost of developing the Airbus A380 is estimated to exceed $11 billion. It is understandable that Airbus would want upfront options to buy from its customers before committing to the huge expense of the development.

When it comes to drug developments, DiMasi et al. (2003) estimate the cost to be $802 million for each successful new product. Adams & Brantner (2004) put the figure at between $839 million and $868 million. Of course, the cost depends upon the disease or condition being treated; for instance, a treatment for HIV/Aids is estimated to be $479 million, while a drug for treating rheumatoid arthritis is estimated at $936 million (Adams and Brantner, 2004).

These examples are obviously at the extreme end of the scale of development costs. Many smaller business-to-business companies will not face such high costs, though in comparison to their size the commitment may seem just as great, because typically they will face a capital investment cost. For example, the concept of a new offering may well need changes in production processes and material or distribution arrangements to make it a reality. Clares Merchandise Handling Equipment Ltd (see the case study at the end of this chapter) can come up with lots of shapes, sizes and configurations of shopping trolley. However, to produce a new shape, size and configuration requires that a series of production processes change, including the creation of new jigs. To justify the commitment of costs for a new offering the company will want to be sure that there will be sufficient demand to obtain a return that easily covers the development cost and makes an acceptable contribution to profits.

Given these costs and risks it is inevitable that many companies choose to develop incrementally, in the sense that they just add new variants to existing product lines, or add sufficient changes to create a wider range of product lines. This seems to be a lower-risk approach because there is at least a clear indication that the marketplace already accepts the product concept. It may also deliver incremental sales. However, the risk is that the portfolio of offerings becomes ever more complex and difficult to manage. The potential for economies of scale may diminish. For companies producing manufactured goods it also increases the number of setups required (with associated retooling and swapping of product jigs) and thus reduces operating efficiencies; less time is spent adding value in production compared with getting ready to add value. Such a situation would perhaps be acceptable if individual customers were prepared to pay the large premiums required to make this situation economically valuable (if not efficient). In practice, few are.

New product offering development process

Because of the inherent risk, much research has been conducted into the new offering development process and over the years substantial efforts have been made to enhance the process in order to reduce this risk. Typically, efforts have gone into establishing a clear development process whereby consideration can be given to the issues that are important at each stage of the process. By managing the process well and taking appropriate decisions at each stage, the risk becomes manageable.

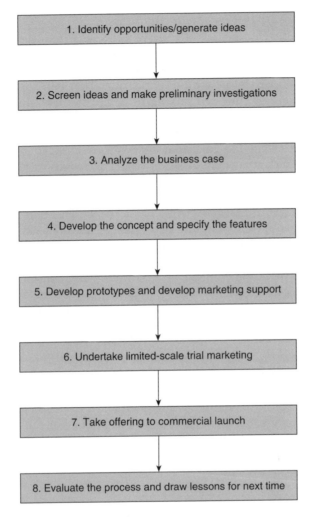

Figure 10.4   The new offering development process

There are a variety of different stage models of the new offering development process. For example, Crawford and DiBenedetto (2003) proposed five
phases: opportunity identification, concept generation, concept evaluation,
development and launch. Gross et al. (1993) proposed seven steps to the
process: idea generation, screening, business analysis, concept development,
prototype development, test marketing, and commercialization. Dwyer and
Tanner (2002) likewise proposed a seven-stage process, albeit slightly different
to Gross et al. (1993): idea generation, screening and preliminary investigation,
specifying features, product development, beta-testing, launch and evaluation. While similar to other stage models, we propose that the business marketer consider eight different elements of the process (see Figure 10.4).

Identifying opportunities/generating ideas

New offering development is a creative process. It requires the seeds of creation and these seeds are ideas, the more of them the better. The more ideas that can be generated the greater the prospect of finding one or more that will lead to a successful new product offering. They can come from many sources; for example, through talking to end customers, distributors and suppliers, by examining what competitors are doing, and by allowing staff to make suggestions. They can come out of the blue or they can be solicited. They might be solicited in particular areas (for example, identifying opportunities that a particular target market would welcome, or ideas for extensions to an existing product line).

Regardless of where they come from there is a need to establish a repository of ideas and to establish someone as the keeper. That person might readily be charged with promoting the generation of new ideas in the firm more generally. They could do this in a variety of ways. For example, they could actually organize workshops that bring people together to brainstorm ideas. The workshop participants might be lead users within customer companies feeding ideas of 'what I'd really like is … '. Or they might be cross-departmental staff groupings providing ideas on how elements of an offering could change or how its production could change and reduce costs.

Screening ideas and making preliminary investigations

Having a strong stream of ideas is a good starting point. The more ideas that can be generated the lower the cost per idea produced. Beyond this, the effectiveness of a company in spotting good and bad ideas comes into play. The earlier it can discard ideas that have no real potential, the better. For this reason there is value in having a screening process for each idea that establishes it very quickly as good or bad. There are some criteria that are fundamental and that can be applied first:

- company ability to make the offering;
- fit with company production capabilities or technical expertise;
- fit with company objectives and image;
- market sales and profit potential; and
- fit with current offerings and distribution channels.

By getting managers' assessments of these, using rating systems such as five-point scales (with scores ranging from –2 to +2, with 0 as the mid-point) it becomes possible to arrive at aggregate scores and a ranking for each idea.

This initial screening will remove the weakest ideas from further scrutiny in the most efficient way. The remaining ideas can then be subjected to further screening. This incorporates preliminary investigations of how customers will react to the offering and how competitors will respond. As far as customer reactions are concerned the focus will be on which particular segments will be interested and what it is about the offering concept that will be attractive to them. Again, on the basis of rating managers' evaluations it becomes possible to discard further ideas.

Analysing the business case

Analyzing the business case takes the screening process further. However, rather than looking specifically for the fastest route to discard the weakest ideas, which was the previous focus, the emphasis shifts to trying to establish which ideas have the greatest business potential. The business analysis needs to involve careful financial estimates of the market size, growth rate and potential for each product offering idea. This data may be available from secondary data sources. As well as trying to determine market potential, the business case needs to establish what the development costs are likely to be for each new idea offering before it can be brought to market. These costs may include the nature of the capital investment needed, the staff costs, and the break-even level and payback period, along with the rate of return on the investment. When each new offering proposal can be seen in these financial terms it becomes possible to compare them as prospective projects.

Developing the concept and specifying the features

During the preliminary investigations the offering concept starts to become better developed. The closer identification of the likely targets and their reactions to the offering starts to allow for the features to be specified. This knowledge can be used with the small number of proposed offerings that have emerged with a sound business case in order to start specifying them. It then becomes possible to state what the concept is and the benefits it brings to customers, as well as how the offering will be used. A likely price can be estimated. Concept boards or drawings may be used to communicate all this information and may also be employed to solicit the continuing support of management on the one hand as well as to convey the concept to suppliers where there are specific implications for the sourcing of materials or components for the offering.

Developing prototypes and developing marketing support for the offering

Having arrived at a clear concept statement for the new offering and having received a positive response, the offering can be prototyped. A prototype is a facsimile of the final offering that enables evaluation of form, design, performance and material composition. The intention is to develop a series of working prototypes that can be successively fine-tuned towards the final offering. The fine-tuning may involve slight performance enhancements or layout changes that progressively improve the offering. At the same time that the prototyping is moving towards the final offering, the marketing support activities for the offering need to commence. These activities are likely to revolve around packaging and labelling designs, pricing and distribution strategy, and the promotional plans that will see the offering up to and beyond commercial launch.

Undertaking limited-scale trial marketing

At some point the successive refinements of the offering will lead to fewer and fewer changes; it is at this point that the offering is ready to be used by customers. It is only through use by customers that the value in use of the offering can really be established (see Box 10.2). However, it is generally best to identify any remaining adjustments and the cost of production that might entail before full-scale launch.

Where feasible, test marketing in a small market area will also be beneficial in obtaining feedback on the whole offering, including the marketing activities that accompany it (such as communications materials, marketing approach and prices). Of course, this kind of approach makes less sense where the size of the market segment for the offering is estimated to be small.

Box 10.2 *Customer involvement in product offering development*

Surface Inspection Ltd (see the case study in Chapter 3) recognizes that the performance of its machines in a full-scale tile production line may differ from test setups in the factory. It has been lucky that through the relationship it has with a UK tile manufacturer it has had access to a tile production line where the full extent of the impact of the operating environment (dust and heat) can be seen on machine performance. The use of key customers for this kind of trial is one way of obtaining good feedback on a new offering in use. In the software industry companies will often look for beta-test sites for their software. These customer sites will naturally be obtaining the earliest release of the software, often discounted accordingly, recognizing what that entails in terms of software bugs and the feedback required to the software originator in order to iron out the bugs.

Taking the offering to commercial launch

On the basis of a successful trial, final changes can be made to the offering and the strategy for bringing it to market. The launch itself could be planned as a big bang. However, depending on the size of the company, the nature of the offering and its innovativeness and the readiness of the market itself, it may be more sensible to roll the offering out sequentially, often on a geographical basis. Smaller companies are likely to need to do this anyway because of the resources required for a big launch. If the product is novel then customer education may be needed concerning the offering's function, the benefits it brings and how it can be used. If there is an ongoing service need associated with the product then the support personnel need to be trained.

Evaluating the offering development process

While not strictly an element of the offering development process itself, it is good practice each time an offering is launched to reflect upon the process, the soundness of decisions and the effectiveness of implementation. The intention is to learn lessons that can be used for subsequent products. What matters is to establish if the next offerings need to proceed through all the stages of the process in the same way. The criteria that determine when the offering is ready to be moved on through the stages can be fine-tuned. In some cases steps in the process might be missed out for future development processes. For example, for extensions to earlier offerings where the market is familiar with the technology and the use of the product offering, it may be that trial marketing is unnecessary.

By following a strong new product offering development process, the prospect of a good series of new offerings adding value to the offering portfolio is increased. By managing each of these in ways that are appropriate to their stage in development and in respect of the value they bring to the portfolio overall, the firm is in the strongest position to solve customer problems as effectively as it can and thus to grow and bring value to its shareholders.

Chapter Summary

- This chapter has focused upon the activities that business marketers need to undertake in the management of offerings to business customers. It has described the elements of the product offering, arguing that it is often more than just a physical good.

- We saw that the product offering incorporates service and advice components that often enable an otherwise standardized product to become a more customized offering.

- We then turned our attention to the major product offering management tasks that face business marketers: ensuring that the right marketing interventions are made with offerings throughout their life cycle so that they add the greatest value they can to the firm, and ensuring that the portfolio of product investments that the firm has made are managed to ensure balance and thus greater value over the longer term.

- Finally, we focused on one of the riskiest activities for business marketers, the task of bringing the next generation of product offerings to market so that they too can add to the portfolio over time. During consideration of new offering development we described a well-established process for ensuring that the inevitable risk involved in the task of bring offerings to market is as low as possible.

Questions for discussion

1. What are the elements of a product offering and why do we need to identify them?
2. Describe the product offering life cycle stages for an industrial offering with which you are familiar and indicate how you would have managed the offering through the stages.
3. Choosing a mature business offering, indicate how you propose to manage it to avoid decline.
4. What is the value of a portfolio analysis approach such as the Boston Box?
5. Working in small groups, decide on a business marketing firm that you will all represent and, on the basis of your knowledge of what the company does, initiate a new offering development process.

Case study: **Trolley's up for Clares MHE**

Clares Merchandise Handling Equipment Ltd is one of those many companies that most people have never heard of, despite the fact that they are the largest suppliers of wire trolleys, dollies and baskets to the UK retail trade. Though you might not recognize the name, you have seen their customer trolleys if you have shopped in any of the big UK stores (including Tesco, Sainsbury, Marks and Spencer, Boots, Halfords and Homebase). You will probably also have seen their roll cages used in stores to carry stock for replenishment. As well as the UK market, Clares has sold trolleys to the French retail giant Carrefour. And if you have been through any of the big airports in the UK (Heathrow, Gatwick or Stansted) you will also have seen the range of airport trolleys that the company designs and builds.

Part of the wider Clares Retail Services Ltd, whose retail interests extend beyond trolleys into retail shelving and displays, cash desks and checkouts, kiosks and even consulting rooms within pharmacies, Clares MHE specializes in the technology for moving merchandise around. And that means making over 250,000 trolleys a year. Trolleys may seem quite simple but they are important in the retail experience; try carrying more than six items in your arms and you see the need. The facilitating role can be particularly acute at an airport; after the car park the trolley may be the first real contact that a traveller has with the airport and it is certainly what brings them from the outside world right into the heart of the airport experience. The facilitating role at its most functional, of course, is embodied in those work-horses of retail replenishment, the roll cage. The alternative to transporting upwards of half a tonne of merchandise is many trips to and from the stock room; not a recipe for retail efficiency.

Clares MHE has a range of different products serving several different segment needs:

- shopping trolleys with different sizes, shapes, capacities, castors, child seating configurations, stacking space requirements;
- garden and DIY trolleys, with different shapes, basket or tray configurations and load capacities;
- shopping baskets with different materials, sizes, weights and capacities;
- roll cages with different finishes, chassis bases, number of sides and stacking space requirements;
- airport luggage trolleys with different sizes, shapes, weights, stacking space requirements and customer purpose.

A perennial issue for Clares MHE is where to take its merchandise handling technology next. When you're selling to all the big names in retail, where do you go if you are interested in growing the business further – particularly if the technology itself is well established?

Of course, it is always possible to look for additional markets – for example secure material handling for governmental organizations, or residential uses such as recycling. It is also possible to do more for existing customers, including offering a full 'cradle to the grave' solution for all trolley needs, with a full servicing package, and even by bundling the complete offering differently (such as selling use by the hour or leasing by the day).

The demands of the customers affect the offerings that need to be provided. Increasingly, airports are adopting a systems approach to purchasing trolleys – just selling trolleys to them is not enough. As a consequence, trolley companies need to ensure they have the supply partners and alliances with the right systems technology firms to create a total offering that satisfies their airport customers' requirements completely.

While this is a mature technology it is possible to find additional innovations to the existing technology itself that will meet the needs of business-to-business customers, delivering even greater value from trolleys, as well as providing a functionality that continues to meet the needs of end customers. There are specific areas where there is particular scope for innovation. Greater security possibilities exist with caster technology, as does the potential for better matching to the physical demands of locations. Anti-bacterial applications have further potential as well. One major driver for innovation is advertising and combined with the converging potential through airwave and displays technology, the possibilities for income from renting advertising space is becoming very attractive to retailers – the equivalent of the Formula 1 trolley!

As far as roll cages are concerned, the design has changed little in 20 years. Often companies will also buy exactly the same trolley for all logistics needs. However, a company like Tesco has five different types of store, each with slightly different needs for the product. Recognizing the different segment needs and meeting the more diverse needs more precisely also presents opportunities.

Developments to integrate the checkout and trolley are fully underway in pilot stores around the globe. Using intelligent shelving and trolleys, the idea is to eliminate the need for checkouts and queuing completely. As you take the product from the shelf into the trolley it self-scans and upon exit automatically charges the goods to your credit card.

The potential for all these adaptations raises the question of the limit to standardization and the extent to which it is sensible to do different things for special customers. Establishing those customers that warrant special attention may become the cornerstone of offering management for Clares MHE. Of course, the payback for such investment may not necessarily be cash right now. Rather, some customers may be sources of adaptations to offerings that could ultimately lead to changes in the technology that spawn a whole new generation of market-leading offerings.

Case study questions

1. Describe how the life cycle concept might apply to shopping trolleys and discuss the extent to which the life cycle for roll cages is the same as for shopping trolleys.
2. On the basis of your view of the life cycle stage of (a) airport trolleys and (b) roll cages, describe the marketing activities you would undertake, assuming strong market share in both product markets.
3. Generate some ideas for new product development that extend the existing technology platform for trolleys (you could refer to www.clares.com to help broaden your knowledge of this technology).
4. Generate some ideas for novel new product developments that might appeal to end customers and retailers (again, you could refer to www. clares.com to broaden your knowledge of this technology).
5. On the basis of screening in a group, take one of the ideas generated in (3) and (4) and develop it further, establishing end-customer acceptance for the concept.

We gratefully acknowledge the support of Richard Smith, Managing Director, Clares Retail Services Ltd and Alan Bromley, Plant Manager, Clares MHE Ltd in the production of this case study.

References

Adams, C. and Brantner, V. (2006) Million 'MARKET WATCH: Estimating the costs of new drug development: is it really $802 Million?', *Health Affairs*, 25(2): 420–28.

Adams, C. and Brantner, V. (2005) 'Spending on new drug development'. Available at *SSRN*, online source: www. ssrn.com/abstract=869765. Accessed 12 December 2005.

Armstrong, G. and Kotler, P. (2005) *Marketing: An Introduction* (7th international edn). Upper Saddle River, NJ:Pearson Education.

Berggren, E. and Nacher, T. (2001) 'Introducing new products can be hazardous to your company: use the right new-solutions delivery tools', *Academy of Management Executive*, 15 (3): 92–101.

Bowonder, B. and Yadav, S. (1999) 'R&D spending patterns of global firms', *Research Technology Management*, 42(6): 44–55.

Clancy, K. and Krieg, P. (2003) 'Surviving innovation', *Marketing Management*, March/April: 14–20.

Crawford, C. and DiBenedetto, A. (2003) *New Products Management* (7th edn). Boston, MA: McGraw-Hill.

DiMasi, J., Hansen, R. and Grabowski, H. (2003) 'The price of innovation: new estimates of drug development costs', *Journal of Health Economics*, 22: 151–85.

Dwyer, F. and Tanner, J. (2002) *Business Marketing* (2nd edn). Boston, MA: McGraw-Hill.

Ford. D., Berthon, P., Brown, S., Gadde, L.E., Håkansson, H., Naude, P., Ritter, T. and Snehota, I. (2002) *The Business Marketing Course*. Chichester: Wiley.

Griffiths, J. (2006) 'End of the road for Peugeot's Ryton plant was not unexpected', *Financial Times*, 19 April.

Gross, A., Banting, P., Meredith, L. and Ford, D. (1993) *Business Marketing*. Boston, MA: Houghton Mifflin.

Schilling, M. and Hill, C. (1998) 'Managing the new product development process: strategic imperatives', *Academy of Management Executive*, 12 (3): 67–81.

WARC (2006) 'Intel launches new business brand', *News@WARC.com*, 26 April. http://www.warc.com/Search/WordSearch/Results.asp?txtWordSearched=Intel &LimitTo=News&radSortBy=REL&selNarrowByDate=selNarrowBySource=&txt SearchWithin=vpro

11 Routes to Market

Learning outcomes

After reading this chapter you will:

- understand the tasks performed by intermediaries in reconciling the interests of supplier and customer companies;
- know about the different types of intermediaries and kinds of exchanges that they handle;
- be able to explain conditions under which companies will choose to use the different types of intermediaries;
- be able to describe the various channel structures and reasons for the use of multiple routes to market;
- know about the effect of market and company factors on the role of intermediaries and on channel structures;
- be able to explain the impact of IT on routes to market; and
- be able to describe the challenges involved in managing relationships and coordinating activities between the parties involved in a marketing channel.

Introduction

This chapter looks at the means by which a business marketer might try to reach target markets and gain maximum market coverage for their problem-solving abilities. For many organizations the only way that they can maximize market coverage is by making use of third parties, that is, intermediaries. Intermediaries such as agents and distributors help companies achieve marketing objectives by handling some of the exchanges involved in business transactions and by connecting suppliers with customers. As companies outsource non-value-adding activities and make increasing use of IT to ease coordination between the various parties involved in reaching and satisfying end customers, so the role of the intermediary and the way in which a company might work with an agent or distributor can change.)

In this chapter we revisit the types of exchanges conducted between supplier and customer companies, considering the contribution that intermediaries might make in handling some of these exchanges. We introduce the routes that can be used to bring suppliers and customers together and take account of the complexity and flexibility that can feature in channel structures. Effective channel performance requires that companies minimize the transaction costs associated with coordinating activities between the various channel members. We consider the contribution of relationship management and means of controlling behaviour to channel coordination.

One More Time: Exchanges in Business Markets

By now it should be clear that organizations operating in a business-to-business context have to deal with a variety of inter-firm exchanges in order to match a supplier's problem-solving abilities with the solutions sought by a customer and to make those solutions available to target markets. If we briefly recap the nature of those exchanges then clearly the supplier's product offering in return for the customer's financial compensation represent the essential exchange in a relationship. If we were talking about the supply of tangible goods then agreement would be reached on the precise product specification, volume requirements and delivery schedule (including locations and estimated call-off periods). For the duration of a contract a customer's confirmation of the actual product needed would trigger:

- the release of items for delivery;
- the arrangements for and the actual physical transportation to specified locations; and
- the issue of documentation to accompany deliveries (invoices and possibly accompanying certificates from the supplier; bills of lading from the logistics company/freight forwarder).

A customer's receipt of the products and accompanying invoices would in return trigger payments to the supplier according to agreed credit terms.

For a product that is intangible that is, a service, then agreement also has to be reached in terms of the service specification, amount ('capacity'), timing and location of where the service will be required by a customer. Services cannot be transported physically, so a supplier would need to determine whether the service should be made available to the customer from a distance or whether physical proximity would be needed to enable a customer to use the service. The issuing and payment of invoices might be on completion of the service contract, or at fixed points where a contract is set to last for an extended time period.

From our discussions in previous chapters we know that the products might be standard items that are necessary to enable a company to go about its business but are of limited strategic importance. This could range from the MRO items used by a manufacturing company to the collection and disposal of waste generated by an organization. Impersonal marketing communications would be used to raise awareness and trigger demand and some personal selling might be required to close a deal as well as to negotiate terms and conditions of supply. Ongoing information exchange would be needed in order to coordinate supply and payment for the duration of a contract.

At the other extreme a product supplied might be of critical importance to a customer's own activities and might also be formulated specifically for that customer's use. This might include items that are integrated into a customer's own finished product, or equipment or systems used in the customer's operational process, or the handling of a company's marketing communications activities or its IT requirements. Again, impersonal communication might be used to raise awareness. However, personal communication is of critical importance as a supplier becomes involved in the process of consultation with a client to determine the nature of the problem faced and to formulate/present an optimum solution to the customer and to negotiate the details of an eventual supply contract. Direct involvement of members of a supplier's 'sales/service team' with a customer would continue for the duration of a contract, to administer ongoing supply, perform agreed installation, service and maintenance activities, handle supply problems that might arise, and conduct periodic performance reviews with the customer. Communication and information exchange would also be needed between supplier and customer companies to coordinate product supply and use.

From the above discussion we can see a number of exchanges/flows that occur between companies to support transactions, namely communication, information exchange, product/service delivery and payment.

Reaching and Satisfying Customers: Third-Party Involvement

Wherever it might be in a supply chain, amongst an organization's objectives will be the intention of using its core competencies and capabilities to deliver superior customer value and to gain maximum market coverage for its problem-solving abilities. Maximum market coverage could mean targeting a broad range of customer groups, having as extensive a geographic scope as possible (involving regions, countries and continents) or indeed both. Herein lies the problem: few organizations have the resources simultaneously and independently to deliver superior value to all customers in all locations. So at some point a company has to decide whether to involve third parties in helping to reach and satisfy customers, the form that this 'intermediary' role might take, and how to allocate responsibility for handling the flow of communication, information exchange, product/service delivery and payment.

Traditionally the composition of routes to market has been approached from a linear/hierarchical perspective, with the principal company (the organization with the product capability) deciding on the type of intermediaries to use and the channel structure to enable product to reach target customers. To start with, let us adopt this approach in order to introduce variations in intermediary types, activities and channel design but taking into account the product technology being used and the control sought by the marketing organization.

Bespoke/complex offerings

Where the risk/uncertainty associated with a customer's supply needs is high and it involves a complex product offering, the marketing organization may choose to deal directly with customers. This could be used for goods and services alike, allowing the principal company to have complete control of exchanges with customers. A concentrated customer base and the high-value contracts typically associated with such complex offerings can normally support the investment of the supplier's own resource to trigger interest and formulate product offerings, as well as negotiate and administer contracts, even when customers are geographically dispersed. The technical expertise used to devise an optimum solution and 'assemble' the finished product is normally contained within the marketing company. The high value of tangible forms of these products can also sustain necessary physical transportation of the finished item from the supplier's to the customer's premises, whatever the distance might be.

The challenge for an organization arises when it wants to enter new markets (product or geographic) with which it is unfamiliar. In such instances a company might rely in part on a *sales agent*. In Chapter 8 we described how the company Renold uses its own sales team to maintain contact with target customers involved in the design and supply of marine propulsion systems. The company cannot use its sales force in this way around the world so, for example, in South Korea it uses appointed agents to maintain its profile with potential customers such as the marine engine builder Hyundai Machinery. Agents essentially operate as independent sales representatives for a company, using their product, customer and market knowledge to generate business for a supplier. These representatives act as a link between the supplier and end users, make contact with customers, introducing the supplier's capabilities to potential customers and acting as a mediator in the formulation and presentation of product offerings to customers and the negotiation and handling of contracts.

Common to the use of independent sales representatives is payment by commission for orders actually won by a supplier. What can differ however, are the activities performed by independent representatives. See Box 11.1 for a description of how Lucent Technologies uses representatives to promote business on its behalf.

Box 11.1 *Connecting with customers*

Lucent Technologies designs and delivers systems, services and software for the operation of communication networks. As well as having its own sales force, the company uses agents to identify potential sales opportunities and position Lucent product and service solutions to end customers such as independent phone companies, municipalities and utility companies. To do this, the company employs sales referral and manufacturer's representatives. The *sales referral representatives* focus on identifying, qualifying and developing sales opportunities and they also feed customer information back to Lucent. The *manufacturer's representatives* also identify and develop opportunities but a more important task involves managing the sales cycle from initial opportunity to closure. These representatives operate as an extension of Lucent's sales force and are responsible for ongoing customer relationship management of allocated accounts. To enable them to effectively position the company's solutions to prospective customers, the referral and manufacturer's representatives have access to Lucent marketing information, sales tools and technical resources.

Source: Based on information provided on company website www.lucent.com.

Uniform product offerings

Where the risk/uncertainty associated with the solution sought by a customer is somewhat lower and involves a rather more standard product offering, the marketing organization will be less inclined to want to control all exchanges with all customers. The customer base is likely to be more fragmented as well as being geographically dispersed and contract value will vary significantly. The marketing organization's expertise centres on the design and efficient production of products that match end customer needs. To make these available to customers, a company that produces tangible goods would use distributors. Distributors can act as a key link between a company and its end customers and will normally handle related products from a range of suppliers, generating volume sales from a large number of customers. A distributor's income is derived from the difference between the price at which products are sourced from the original supplier and the price at which those same products are then sold on to the end customer. This margin has to allow for some net profit once the distributor's operating costs have been deducted. These costs are incurred as a result of the distributor taking title to the original supplier's products and assuming principal responsibility for initiating and handling all exchanges with end customers in a specified geographic territory. Activities associated with these exchanges include:

- *Communication:* handling all communications activities with targeted customers in allocated territory. This could include the use of impersonal tools such as advertising and sales promotion as well as the more obvious use of sales teams responsible for initiating and handling contact with and orders from customers.
- *Modification and assembly:* standard products might be supplied unchanged to customers. In other instances a distributor might adapt a supplier's product or assemble elements from a variety of sources to meet a customer's individual product specification.
- *Product supply:* ensuring local product availability (by carrying necessary stock) and facilitating transactions. This facilitation could include advice on product specification and selection as well as necessary commercial and logistical support such as the provision of credit/finance terms, order processing and product delivery.
- *Service and repair:* distance from and the geographic dispersion of end customers can mean that distributors play an important role in maintaining the supplier's products at customer locations.

Whilst this might work for products that can be physically transported and stored, distributors are of no use to companies that supply service-based products that require the physical presence of the service operation in close proximity to customers to ensure ready availability of the service. Where the product is essentially a standard offering, the marketing organization can opt to enter into franchise arrangements. Franchising is essentially a form of licensing whereby the principal (the franchiser) allows another organization (the franchisee) the right to conduct business in a specified manner. The right might include selling the principal's product and using its name, operational or marketing methods. As with licensing, the franchisee pays royalties for this right and in return is able to use the principal's trademark and may also benefit from training programmes as well as the franchiser's experience, credit facilities and marketing communications programmes. Franchising is an important means of extending market coverage (without major capital investment) for organizations involved in service sectors where a physical presence is necessary to enable customers to access a company's service. See Box 11.2 for a description of Rolls-Royce's use of franchising.

Box 11.2   *Staying airborne*

Rolls-Royce manufactures turboprop, turbofan and industrial gas turbine engines for sale in the defence and civilian aerospace and industrial markets. In addition to original equipment sales the company also provides aftermarket support to customers for some engine models. It does this via a mixture of its own service centres as well as independent third-party authorized maintenance centres (AMCs). For example, AMCs play a particularly important role in the company's helicopter business, enabling Rolls-Royce to provide its 4500 commercial customers around the world with services to keep their fleets airborne. AMCs can be found under contract with Rolls-Royce in North America, England, Spain, Malta, South Africa, Australia, Japan, South Korea and Singapore, offering customers:

- repair and maintenance services;
- overhaul capabilities;
- power-by-the-hour programmes;
- unit exchange of engines, components and accessories; and
- warranty administration.

Source: Based on information provided in company website www.rolls-royce.com).

At a very basic level it can be argued that in order to exploit its own operational efficiency, a supplier's principal interest is to have as narrow a product range as possible and to maximize the sales of those products. By contrast, customers do not necessarily have high-volume requirements and would want to choose from as broad a range of alternative products as possible. So intermediaries can reconcile the needs of suppliers and end customers by sourcing relatively high volumes of products from a number of suppliers and offering customers a broader product choice and order levels that suit their specific requirements.

If we think about the variety and number of exchanges that can occur between a supplier and customer to get to the point of agreeing a contract and those associated with the subsequent fulfilment of that contract, it is clear that many companies cannot realistically deal directly with all of their customers (or for that matter, customers their suppliers) and operate efficiently in their marketplaces. By using different types of intermediaries, a supplier's dealings are directed towards a reduced number of contacts, to their chosen third parties who then handle some or all exchanges and transactions with end customers (depending on whether they are sales agents, distributors or franchisees). This allows the supplier to concentrate on its areas of expertise and simplifies the means by which supplier and customer companies gain access to their output and input markets respectively.

From single to multiple routes to market

Figure 11.1 shows the various permutations that we have discussed so far. Whilst some firms may start out by relying on one principal route to market, the reality is that most organizations are likely to operate a number of alternative channels. This might be because market conditions have

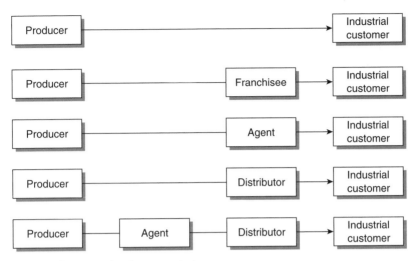

Figure 11.1   Routes to business markets

changed, forcing a company to rethink its channel strategy, or because a company is trying to serve a variety of target customers, who can each require different levels of servicing to which the organization might be more or less willing to commit its own resources.

For example, companies operating in the IT industry sold their equipment for many years via direct sales channels, that is, using their own sales force. However as market conditions and the range of customers changed, so the reliance on company sales representatives became less sustainable. Demand for IT products switched from large mainframe systems to those that were designed around the mini-computer and with applications software for different user groups. These systems were being used by an increasingly diverse customer base rather than the large multinational corporations that the major IT companies were accustomed to dealing with (Cespedes and Corey, 1990; Gandolfo and Padelletti, 1999). For some, the specialist applications required by emerging customer groups were beyond the expertise of the IT companies and the volume sales of these new segments were not sufficient to warrant the investment of the companies' sales force. So the IT companies developed multiple routes to market in order to harness the opportunities presented by the changing market conditions. Manufacturer representatives (agents) and value-added resellers became important intermediaries in the IT industry. A value-added reseller (VAR) is a type of distributor. VARs are common in the IT industry where, for example, computer components might be purchased to produce a fully operational piece of hardware or a software application might be added to existing hardware equipment. The reseller adds value by integrating, customizing, consulting, training and installing products.

Whether the use of multiple routes to market (also known as hybrid marketing systems) is a deliberate adjustment to a company's channel strategy or simply an ad hoc response to changing market conditions, to work effectively clarity is needed regarding the responsibilities of the various channel members as well as the coordination of activities and communication between the different parties. According to Cespedes and Corey (1990) there are two principle structures for organizing multiple routes to market, which are evident across a variety of industries.

A pluralistic multi-channel system

In this system (see Figure 11.2), a company uses multiple routes to market but they are organized so that each channel has responsibility for a separate group of products and in doing so targets quite distinct market segments (a pluralistic system). Ingersoll-Rand is involved in the capital equipment market, with its stationary air compressor division supplying compressed air to a variety of industries. As well as targeting a wide range of segments, Ingersoll-Rand's route to market had to accommodate variation in the product itself in terms of size (power) and the core technology used (reciprocating, rotary screw or centrifugal). To handle these differences it set up the following system:

1. Because of the level of necessary technical expertise, all centrifugal compressors used in industrial, military and government sectors as well as large reciprocator and rotary screw compressors (above 250 and 450 horsepower (hp) respectively) were only available directly from the company and it used its own service unit to handle after-sales service and the supply of spare parts for this large equipment.
2. Distributors and Ingersoll-Rand air centres supplied smaller reciprocator and rotary screw compressors (below 250 and 450 hp respectively) to industrial customers and also handled service and spare part requirements for these customers.
3. Agents were used to sell compressors below 25hp to retail customers such as hardware stores.

To avoid conflicts of interest and to take account of distributor development of service capability and its investment in Ingersoll-Rand machinery and spare parts, air centres and independent distributors were allocated distinct geographic territories. Cooperation between the channels was also encouraged: for example, commission could be earned where members of one channel referred a customer to another (and it resulted in a sale) or if they actively assisted that other channel in winning an order (Cespedes and Corey, 1990).

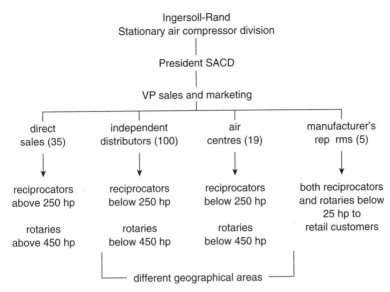

Figure 11.2 A pluralistic multi-channel system (Cespedes and Corey, 1990: 72)

A monolothic multi-channel system

(In this system a company uses one structure, consisting of direct and indirect channels to reach customers, with each channel member adjusting the functions that it performs according to the segment that it is dealing with (see Figure 11.3). Beckton Dickinson supplies a wide variety of blood collection tubes and needles for different applications to hospitals, commercial laboratories, general practitioners and a vast number of health care organizations. Its network of over 400 distributors carries the company's entire product range, with the various channel functions being divided between Beckton Dickinson's own sales team and distributors themselves. The idea behind the structure is to create greater flexibility and integration between channel members by adjusting the functions carried out by those parties according to customer groups. For larger hospitals, laboratories and buying groups the company's direct sales representatives generate sales and the distributors handle inventory, delivery and after sales service. For smaller customers the distributors perform most channel functions, namely sales generation (with help from Beckton Dickinson's sales team), inventory, credit, delivery and after-sales service (Cespedes and Corey, 1990).

The route used can affect the business marketer's operations. See Table 11.1. for an indication of some of the effects of hybrid marketing systems.

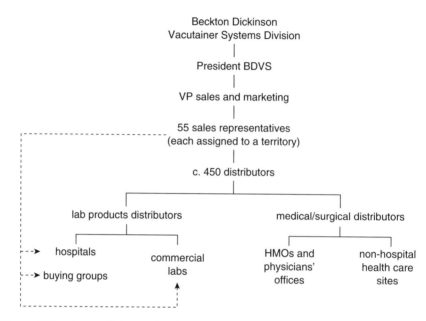

Figure 11.3   A monolithic multi-channel system (Cespedes and Corey, 1990: 73)

Improving Channel Performance

So far we have given a relatively straightforward account of the types of intermediaries that operate in business markets and the alternative means by which a company might make its problem-solving abilities available to target customers. The reality for many organizations is much more complex as they seek to marry firm-specific objectives and resources with the opportunities and constraints of the markets in which they operate. In this section we take a more detailed look at how external and internal factors can determine the structure of routes to market, the types of parties involved and the contributions that they make.)

Customer expectations

In many industries customers have increasingly higher expectations of the value that they seek to derive from products purchased and the sources used to obtain them. For the products themselves, standard items are no longer guaranteed to meet customer needs, principally because customers have become used to being able to purchase products that have been customized according to their own individual specification. In addition to the tailoring of products to individual needs, customers are also more demanding of services offered to support purchases, including ready availability and rapid

Table 11.1   Effect of hybrid marketing systems

	Pluralistic	*Monolithic*
Marketing overhead costs	Higher	Lower
Producer/reseller field coordination	Higher	Lower
Ability to differentiate technical services	Higher	Lower
Flexibility in customer buying patters: multi-channel structure preference	Lower	Higher
Development of selling expertise: customer's vs reseller channels	Higher	Lower

Source: Cespedes and Corey, 1990: 74.

order fulfilment via their preferred channel (Anderson et al., 1997). Clearly such product and service expectations place particularly exacting demands on supply/distribution chains as companies seek to simultaneously meet market demands and remain cost competitive.

The rethinking of value/distribution chain activities

In response to customers' increasingly exigent demands (but also in an effort to eliminate activities that do not contribute to delivering superior value), many companies have rethought their internal operations and transferred activities to other points in the value chain where organizations are able to perform those activities better (Anderson et al., 1997). Hewlett-Packard, for example, has successfully used production postponement (delaying the differentiation of a product for an individual customer until the latest point possible in the value chain) to deal with market demands for mass customization (Feitzinger and Lee., 1997). For this to work the company had to rethink product design and the supply network. The design of products changed so that they consisted of independent modules that could be easily and inexpensively assembled into different product formats. The supply network changed in terms of the positioning of stock and the location, number and structure of production and distribution facilities. The network had to be designed so that the basic product was readily available at locations performing the customization and the network had to have sufficient flexibility and responsiveness to receive, process and subsequently deliver orders for customized products quickly. In fact, while the basic products are produced centrally, these are subsequently shipped to HP's local distribution centres. The centres customize the products and purchase the items that are used for differentiation (such as power supplies, packaging and manuals) (Feitzinger and Lee 1997).

As well as rethinking activities to enable a firm to accommodate market demand for mass customization, we know that many organizations out-source non-value-adding activities. So in the automotive industry, for example, a company such as Honda uses its expertise in engine and power train design to compete. It completes final assembly of the automotive prod-uct and invests considerable effort in handling relationships with its dealer-ship network. In addition to this it relies on a tiered supply chain of companies for sub-assemblies and components that make up the finished product, and logistics companies to manage the movement of cars between its manufacturing plants and dealers. Like many other companies, Honda buys in activities to which it is unable to add value. So the organization has to handle a number of relationships up and down the value chain in order to reach and satisfy target customers.

Outsourcing has had a significant effect on the role of the parties that con-tribute to the value chain that delivers product to the end customer, and this includes intermediaries. Outsourcing is not restricted to items that might be contained in a company's own finished product, rather it can also include the management of supplies for items such as MRO products. The average expenditure on MRO items by the various budget-holders in a company can be as little as £500 (Croom, 2001). Given the transaction costs involved in sourcing what are typically low-value/low-importance items, some compa-nies have opted to transfer the management of their MRO supply needs to distributors (Anderson and Narus, 1996). Although this can present distrib-utors with significant opportunities for building business, it can stretch their resources as customers typically expect a broader product offering than that normally supplied by an MRO distributor. To deal with this challenge, W.W. Grainger set up Grainger Integrated Supply Operations. This organi-zation consists of the company's own distribution business, a series of best-in-class suppliers for a variety of products and an internal sourcing group. When the company receives an order from a customer it can either supply directly from its own distribution business, or if it cannot fulfil the order it will look to the best-in-class suppliers or its sourcing group (Anderson et al., 1997). So the distributor is effectively covering some of the transactions costs associated with searching for and securing supplies that would previously have been incurred by the customer.

What should be clear from our discussion of postponement and out-sourcing is that it is difficult to think of routes to market as simply being associated with a firm's decision about whether to use an intermediary, what type to use and what activities the selected intermediary might perform. Instead, supply/distribution chains frequently consist of a network of orga-nizations, of 'a confederation of specialists that are flexible and specialised, and pool complementary resources and skills to achieve shared goals' (Anderson et al., 1997: 61).

Coordination: the contribution of IT

Prices charged for products consist of three elements: product costs, coordination costs and profit margin. A key challenge for any supply/distribution chain, or for any group of organizations involved in activities that contribute to addressing end customer needs, lies in trying to minimize the costs of coordination between the various parties in that chain (Croom, 2001). At each point in the chain costs are incurred as a result of having to identify appropriate partners, allocate tasks between partners and specify contracts, exchange information to ensure timely and accurate task performance, and administer financial settlements in line with contract specifications (Malone et al., 1987).

(Entering into long-term relationships with channel partners is one way in which to reduce transaction costs) The repeated exchanges associated with such relationships result in structures, and processes and norms that link firms becoming institutionalized. This means that patterns of behaviour between firms in a distribution channel become routine and the various parties in that channel do not have to invest time and effort in repeatedly searching for and learning about/accommodating new exchange partners. Indeed the routinization of tasks performed by channel members and the sharing of information between them to support these activities can be automated through the use of IT such as continuous replenishment programmes (CRP) and just-in-time (JIT) delivery systems. CRP operates on the basis that the need to replenish stock is only triggered when a sale is made to the end consumer. The use of scanners and point-of-sale equipment at retail outlets and the integration of channel members' information systems means that individual stores, warehousing and distribution centres can control the movement of goods and stock levels through the supply chain to ensure that end-user demand is met and channel costs are kept to a minimum (Buzzell and Ortmeyer, 1995). Although used in a business-to-business context, the principle behind the JIT delivery system is pretty much the same, whereby suppliers align their delivery schedules according to a customer's production programme and the planned/actual use of their products (Mukhopadhyay et al., 1995). In this way stock levels are kept to a minimum, although delivery frequency does typically increase.

The use of IT to facilitate the coordination of distribution channels raises some interesting and apparently contradictory issues. The integration of the IT systems of the various parties in a supply chain and the closer coordination of activities and the information sharing it seeks to realize require significant commitment in the form of resource investment by channel members. In using such systems it can shift the balance of power in channel relationships and even challenge the role of channel members. For some this is in favour of intermediaries that deal with end customers who are able to use transaction processing systems to capture sales data (Anderson et al., 1997; Weitz and Jap, 1995). Others, however, argue that the role of the intermediary in some markets can be diminished as IT systems enable producers to perform some of the functions for which they usually relied on distributors. For example, one of the principal functions of a distributor has been to carry inventory in order to reconcile the delay between a producer's ability to supply a product and the customer's demand for that product. However, systems such as JIT delivery enable a manufacturer to produce items according to customer needs rather than simply producing to stock (Kudpi and Pati, 1996). This responsiveness can also be extended to after-sales service activities that may be provided by distributors. See Box 11.3 for an example of how one company has used IT to improve its service in dealing directly with its customers

---

Box 11.3   *Keeping people on the move*

Otis is in the business of moving people and it produces, installs, modernizes and maintains elevators, escalators, moving walkways and shuttles. For those with the responsibility of the management of building facilities that require the movement of large numbers of people between different levels or locations, then the continuous operation of installations such as elevators, escalators and moving walkways is critical. The company recognized that facilities managers preferred to deal direct with Otis rather than via an intermediary so consequently set-up OTISLINE, which allows elevator customers to contact the company's service centre any time of the day or night. In addition to 24–hour direct access to customer service representatives, OTISLINE provides customers with remote elevator monitoring (REM). This continuously monitors the performance of installed escalators, can detect servicing needs and initiate service requests to OTISLINE's REM centre. The system has improved Otis' management of customer calls and the company's diagnostic capabilities. This has consequently improved customer satisfaction levels.

Source: Armistead and Clark, 1992; www.otis.com.

Whilst intermediaries are unlikely to be removed entirely from a company's channel system, some authors have argued that routes to market in many industries are being compressed, with fewer channel members and those that do remain operating highly integrated networks of distribution (Anderson et al., 1997; Croom, 2001). In some senses this seems to contradict the point made earlier that companies outsource non-value-adding activities – the result being that a network of various organizations can contribute to a finished product reaching the end customer, rather than simply the manufacturer and intermediary (Abecassis et al., 2000). Indeed, IT systems facilitate this by improving the accuracy and timeliness of information needed to coordinate the activities of the different network organizations.

Web-enabled technology

Whatever the number and functions of organizations involved in a route to market, the fact is that to realize the degree of flexibility and responsiveness expected by customers and the tightness of coordination of activities required between firms to minimize transactions costs, the integration of IT systems in the form of EDI and, more recently, extranets, is necessary. The migration to web-enabled IT systems perpetuates the ties between firms and can create hierarchical networks of relationships in a supply/distribution chain (Croom, 2001) – this seemingly goes against the expectation that the facility to conduct business via a 'highly open and ubiquitous public data network infrastructure' such as the World Wide Web would create an electronic marketplace in which buyers and sellers could transact with whoever they wished (Croom, 2001).

Coordination: handling channel partners

Whatever the structure and functioning of the routes to market used by an organization, a number of factors have to be taken into account to ensure the effective management of channel operations and the relationships with other parties in the channel system. These factors include:

- selection of channel members;
- support provided to channel partners;
- means of controlling channel behaviour; and
- dealing with channel conflict.

Selection of chanel members 'Given the obvious contribution that intermediaries can play in a company's ability to reach and satisfy target customers, then identifying and selecting suitable channel partners are important activities for the business marketer.' This process can be time-consuming, yet it is important to get it right, bearing in mind that an ineffective (foreign) distributor can set you back in years; it is almost better to have no distributor than to have a bad one in a major market. For some companies, it is not necessarily a question of going through a search-and-selection process in appointing intermediaries; rather more often it is one in which they try to persuade key channel players to represent them and to carry their products.' However, for the purposes of the ensuing discussion, we will assume that the principal company has some scope for selecting specific intermediaries.

Before a company can make a selection decision, it has to be able to find potential intermediaries. Sources used for identifying possible channel members include trade sources and the intermediaries themselves. Government bodies, can, for example, conduct preliminary searches and provide lists of possible agents or distributors in overseas markets that a company may wish to develop. A particularly useful means of finding potential intermediaries is via trade fairs and exhibitions. Companies participating in trade fairs might be approached by agents/distributors looking to build their supplier/product base and likewise a supplier might visit an event specifically to identify likely channel partners who themselves could be exhibiting.

(However a company locates possible intermediaries, the criteria used to select eventual channel partners have to be clear.)Selection will normally depend on a(partner's resources, product and marketing capabilities, and commitment.)If a company is going to enter into agreement with an intermediary, then it needs to be certain that the channel partner has the necessary *resources* to support its marketing plans. For example, if a company wanted to pursue an aggressive growth strategy, it would need representatives that had sufficient financial resources to expand with the business, a sales team that was big enough to support target growth rates and the capacity to formulate marketing plans that reflect both the intermediary's objectives as well as the principal's sales targets. A company also needs to ensure that an intermediary's *product* range complements its own, that it has the necessary physical facilities to handle stock and (where production postponement or customization is part of the supplier's strategy) perform some light manufacturing or assembly. In the case of technically complex products then the quality of an intermediary's sales and service personnel would be particularly important for a supplier. In addition to product capability, a supplier would be interested in a channel partner's *marketing* capability, in its market coverage (customer and geographic) and its aggressiveness in developing market demand, its expertise in market and relationship communication and the level of after-sales support provided to customers. A potential intermediary might score favourably in these areas, but a company also has to be certain of a channel partner's *commitment* to building business with the supplier. A company might determine this based on an intermediary's willingness to keep minimum stock levels, invest in equipment, advertising and personnel training specifically to support the development of sales of the supplier's products, and to provide market, customer and competitor information where it is representing the company (Tamer-Cavusgil et al., 1995).

(Figure 11.4 lists these various criteria – clearly the suitability of these would differ depending on whether a company is looking to recruit an agent or a distributor.)Partner selection is not one-sided; intermediaries also consider conditions under which they would agree to enter into partnership with a supplier. Criteria that inform an intermediary's selection decision can be grouped according to whether they contribute to the economic conditions needed to satisfy end customer need, channel partnership or intermediary support (Shipley and Prinja, 1988). These criteria are listed and ranked in order of importance according to research by Shipley and Prinja (1988) in Table 11.2.

Channel support (In addition to recruiting intermediaries, a company has to develop programmes of activity to support channel members, including methods of motivating and training intermediaries as well as reviewing performance.)Incentives and behaviour that can be used to encourage an

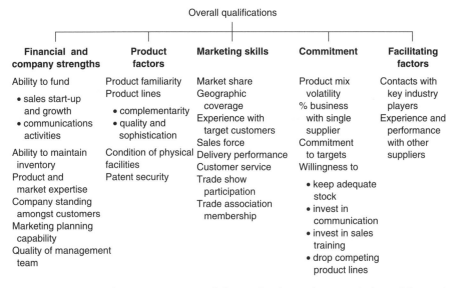

Figure 11.4 Considerations in a monolithic multi-channel system (adapted from Tamer-Cavusgil et al., 1995: 300)

intermediary to devote necessary resources and commitment to a particular company's products include:

- financial incentives (in the form of attractive commission rates or margins; bonuses for realizing or exceeding target sales or winning business with specific customers);
- territorial exclusivity;
- provision of supplier resource (such as sales team involvement in dealings with selected customers; sharing of market research information; market communication support; training of intermediary staff);
- the working relationship approach to intermediary dealings (such as joint planning of strategies for regions, customers or products handled by an intermediary; demonstrable understanding and appreciation of intermediary efforts to handle supplier products; regular communication including information exchange and interpersonal contact; and signalling of supplier long-term commitment by, for example, having a sales team responsible for handling dealer relationships). (Adapted from Shipley et al., 1989)

While the above represent a variety of ways in which a supplier might try to motivate channel members, those actually used would depend on the requirements of the intermediaries themselves. The use of training to support channel activities will depend on intermediary expertise but also the

Table 11.2 Influences on industrial distributor's choice of supplier

Influence	Ranking
Economic	
Product quality	1
Service delivery quality	2
Product range	3
Product superiority compared to competitors	5
Product replacement service	13
Prices, discounts, commission	14
Channel partnership	
Receptive to complaints and advice	4
Quality of working relationship	6
Regular communication	8
Long-term business commitment	11
Regular personal contact	15
Intermediary support	
Image	7
Product information service	9
Quotation service	10
Well-known products	12

Source: Adapted from Shipley and Prinja, 1988: 183.

complexity of the product offering and rate of new product introduction. For example the North American telecommunications supplier Nortel uses intermediaries around the world to maximize its global sales of telecommunications equipment. In the UK, British Telecommunications Plc (BT) is known for its telecommunications operations, but it also acts as a distributor for Nortel, handling equipment that is used in business telecoms systems. Obviously BT has a wealth of telecommunications expertise, but the technical complexity of the operating systems developed by Nortel means that BT engineers have to undergo periodic training to enable them to install and maintain equipment that BT sells and distributes on Nortel's behalf in the UK.

Given the potential contribution of intermediaries to a supplier's position in target markets, the evaluation of channel member performance is important. Table 11.3 details criteria against which intermediary performance might be evaluated.

Evaluation should allow a company to spot weaker intermediaries, to identify gaps in necessary capabilities (offering training to help close these gaps) and where necessary to terminate contracts. Assuming that a supplier is using a working relationship approach as means to motivate intermediaries, then it might be expected that criteria and actual measures would be agreed by both parties. However, research conducted by Shipley et al. (1989) determined that sales volume and revenue were the only measures against

Table 11.3   Evaluating intermediary performance

Criterion	Factors to consider
Intermediary contribution	to supplier profitability, sales growth
Intermediary competence	experience, product knowledge, administrative and supervisory skills, strategic thinking of senior management
Loyalty	commitment and motivation towards supplier
Compliance	acceptance of supplier channel policies and programmes
Adaptability	innovation in handling supplier products
Customer satisfaction	measures in terms of level and quality of services

Source: Adapted from Kumar et al., 1992.

which mutually agreed targets were set. Setting targets and determining actual performance also presumes that the supplier is in such a position that intermediaries are willing to participate in performance reviews. This is not always the case, and indeed, powerful intermediaries may be unwilling to participate or may at best contribute infrequently to supplier reviews of channel performance.

Channel 'control': power, contracts and trust   From our discussions in this chapter it should be clear that channel activities can provide companies with a means to create strategic advantage and end customers with an important source of value-added benefit (Weitz and Jap, 1995). The mechanisms by which activities between various channel partners are coordinated are therefore key concerns, and interest has been devoted to determining the contribution of *power-*, *contractual-* and *trust*-based means of controlling inter-firm behaviour (Weitz and Jap, 1995).

Of these three means of organizing routes to market, the one which has attracted considerable attention in channels research (Gaski, 1984) is the means and effect of a single organization using its position of *power* to control the activities of other channel members. The ability to do this occurs as a result of the more powerful organization having more resources that are valued by the less powerful channel member. So, for example, a supplier that has a strong brand or product that is highly valued by target customers could use incentives to encourage dealers to invest more effort in supporting its products. The supplier could rate dealers according to effort expended and link this to price discounts, marketing assistance and credit terms available to the dealer. Using such influence with channel members can result in a dealer eliminating products available from other companies and allows the favoured supplier to improve its position by restricting competitor access to markets by the same distribution channels (Mohr et al., 1999). Power lies not only with suppliers, however, since intermediaries can enjoy considerable positions of influence over producers, particularly where they have large volume requirements and provide suppliers with significant market coverage and access to a fragmented and dispersed customer base (Kumar, 1996). A dealer can use its power over producers to dictate terms and conditions of supply and might readily switch between alternative sources if companies are unwilling to accept dealer-specified conditions.

The use of power in channel relationships can be viewed negatively if one party is coerced into acceding to the demands of the more powerful party. It can also lead to conflict in relationships where coercion restricts the ability of the weaker organization to achieve objectives that it might seek from involvement in a channel relationship (Gaski, 1984). However, if the more powerful company uses its influence to improve channel coordination and then shares the benefits equitably with channel members, conflict will not necessarily arise and weaker organizations may be satisfied with the relationship outcomes (Weitz and Jap, 1995).

An alternative to one organization using its position of authority to coordinate activities in a channel relationship is for companies to use *contractual arrangements* as the principal means of control. In a channel setting this is typically associated with franchising and requires companies to agree on the activities to be performed by each party, the policies and procedures that both companies will follow, and the rewards for carrying out activities and complying with policies (Weitz and Jap, 1995).

Rather than using power or contracts to control actions, coordination might be *trust*-based, where companies develop norms – patterns of behaviour as a result of repeated interaction and ongoing dealings with channel partners. These 'rules' of behaviour guide each party's behaviour and expectations of the other in terms of trade-offs between long- and short-term profit opportunities, the extent to which the other party's interests are considered in reaching decisions, the nature and extent of the sharing of proprietary information, and the degree to which previously agreed arrangements can be altered (Weitz and Jap, 1995). One of the principal mechanisms for facilitating such relationship norms is through *collaborative communication* between channel members. This consists of:

- a high frequency of interaction across all communication mediums (face-to-face, telephone, e-mail, etc.);
- extensive two-way communication consisting of ongoing dialogue between supplier and intermediary;
- the use of formal policies guiding communication behaviour; and
- the use of influence tactics that place priority on common goals. (Mohr et al., 1996).

Using such collaborative communication can improve an organization's commitment, satisfaction and perceived coordination with a channel partner (Mohr et al., 1996, 1999) and is particularly effective where a manufacturer lacks power over a dealer and both parties are independent of each other (so there is no form of vertical integration or franchise agreement in operation) (Mohr et al., 1996, 1999).

Whilst collaborative communication reflects the apparent shift in many industries from competitive to collaborative relationships between suppliers and intermediaries, it is not necessarily suited for all market or relationship conditions. Indeed an organization is likely to draw from each of these coordination mechanisms to control activities with channel partners (Weitz and Jap, 1995).

Channel conflict   Whatever approach is used to coordinate activities, conflict between the channel parties is inevitable and can vary from being minor disagreements that are easily forgotten or significant disputes that can lead to acrimonious relationships between companies. For the business marketer, it is important to understand both the potential sources of conflict and the ways in which it might be handled.

The principal causes of conflict include the following:

- *Differences in objectives*. Disagreement can occur between channel partners because a supplier would typically prefer to offer intermediaries low margins and limited allowances, and expect a dealer to carry a large inventory and invest heavily in communication activities to support the supplier's products, whilst an intermediary is interested in improving its profit performance by being able to operate with high margins, carry a small inventory and keep expenses incurred in supporting a supplier to a minimum.
- *Differences in desired product lines*. One way in which an intermediary can achieve growth objectives is to expand the product lines that it handles. This can cause dissatisfaction amongst its original suppliers who may view the intermediary as disloyal and be concerned about any reduced support caused by the dealer's product expansion.
- *Multiple routes to market*. We know that the business marketer might use multiple channels to maximize market coverage. Intermediaries may become frustrated when they are restricted from targeting certain customers because the principal company wishes to deal with those customers directly. Difficulties can also occur when the various channels are competing for the same business – a dealer might spend time dealing with potential customers or building a case for a major contract with a customer, only to be rewarded by the customer opting to deal with or place the order with an alternative channel partner used by the supplier.
- *Inadequate performance*. Conflict is inevitable when, for example, an intermediary fails to hit agreed sales targets, does not carry necessary inventory or support services do not meet necessary performance

standards. Likewise, poor delivery performance or product quality and inadequate financial incentives or promotional support on the part of the supplier can trigger conflict in a channel relationship. (McGrath and Hardy, 1989)

What, then, can channel members do to avoid and manage conflict? We discussed previously the contribution of collaborative communication to channel relationships and that frequent interaction that results in shared understanding, mutually agreed objectives (to be achieved via the channel) and performance targets (for each party in achieving these objectives) can help avoid conflict occurring in the first place. Where an intermediary is not reaching set targets, a supplier can try to understand the underlying causes and in consultation with the intermediary determine and agree on ways to *improve performance. Training* in how to handle high-conflict situations can help mangers deal with difficult problems without resorting to emotional or blaming behaviour. Where companies are using multiple channels, conflict can be avoided by *partitioning markets* between the various intermediaries based on geographic area, industry, application, customer size or product group. For this to be effective channel members have to agree to the basis for the partition and operate according to their individual allocation. A supplier can also try to eliminate conflict by taking *control* of the channel relationship; this might be via forward integration or, as we have previously discussed, by using power or contractual arrangements such as franchising (McGrath and Hardy, 1989).

Chapter Summary

- Routes to market provide a necessary means of connecting multiple firms and handling the flow of products from producer to customer.

- Coordination between the various channel parties should be such that a customer gets the actual product that they want as well as support services, spatial convenience and time utility from an intermediary – benefits that a supplier could not ordinarily supply to all of its customers.

- Configuring routes to market requires a company to take account of customers' preferred means of accessing products and the tasks that different types of intermediary can perform.

- The use of multiple parties and channels provides customers with choice and allows a company to accommodate the capabilities of various types of third party. It also presents challenges in terms of added complexity and transaction costs as the number of parties and channels that contribute to reaching and satisfying customer needs increases.

- IT and approaches to handling inter-firm relationships provide the means by which costs can be contained, behaviour managed and channel performance improved.

Questions for discussion

1. Under what conditions might a supplier choose to use (a) direct and (b) indirect channels of distribution?
2. Compare and contrast the tasks performed by distributors and agents.
3. Are franchise operations a suitable route to accessing business customers?
4. How are market and firm-specific factors affecting routes to market?
5. What impact has IT had on marketing channels?
6. How might a company go about recruiting intermediaries?
7. Describe the ways in which channel activities can be coordinated.
8. Does the growth in partnerships mean that channel conflict is a thing of the past?

Case study: Routes to market in the toys and games industry

Berchet is a French producer of traditional toys. Although the company still retains some production facilities in France, continued cost reduction programmes have resulted in Berchet relocating a significant proportion of its manufacturing operations to Hungary and China. Berchet's plant in Budapest supplies to order, with items being shipped direct to retailer locations throughout Europe. Production at its facility in China relies on the company's own forecasting. To ensure on-time supply to intermediaries production planners build in a delivery delay of ten weeks and determine optimum space usage for the 40-foot containers that come from China every month.

The supply and distribution structure in the European toy industry varies by country. Even though a small number of international producers feature in most geographic markets, the majority of countries tend to consist of mainly regionally based toymakers. Likewise the distribution infrastructure varies by country. For example, in France hypermarkets account for 70 per cent of all toy sales and in the UK supermarkets are responsible for 12 per cent of all toy sales. In France, the UK and Germany there are 1600, 450 and 2800 independent toy retailers respectively. Whilst the major retailers in France and the UK will deal directly with toy producers, because of the number of independent retailers in Germany, product supply is handled by buying groups.

Berchet deals with retailers in different countries through its sales offices in Belgium, France, Germany, Holland, Hungary, Italy, Poland, Spain and the UK. Many of the larger intermediaries (or buying groups in Germany) use buying teams to handle supplies of different products. The structure of buying teams varies depending on the retailer, but typically includes a number of buyers (supported by assistant buyers) responsible for various product categories such as girls' and boys' toys respectively, as well as pre-school, media (TV games, etc.), electronic games and board games. Within any product category, the buying team is faced with a significant task, having to process up to 300 quotes from suppliers for one product item. Given the scale of this, retailers are keen to reduce the number of vendor accounts in any one category.

Retailer purchasing and order cycle

An intermediary's purchasing cycle is essentially driven by seasonality, with the decision-making process being initiated as much as 18 months before a product is made available in stores. So in preparing for Christmas 2006, for example, buying teams will have spent summer/early autumn 2005 visiting trade fairs around the world in search of ideas, trends and new toy products that might have sales potential in national European markets. As well as attending trade fairs, buying teams will review products offered by existing suppliers. So, in the case of Berchet, for example:

- Buying teams from the principal intermediaries in various European countries visit the company's head office in France in autumn 2005 to view Berchet's new product proposals for Christmas 2006. Discussions also include a review of existing products and which of those will be carried forward to the next season, as well as others that the retailer is likely to delete and reasons for their removal.
- Based on the business meeting held at the company's head office, 'photo-quotations' are sent to the retailer for every item viewed by the buying team and for which the retailer signalled interest and desire to evaluate the product further.
- For each item, the supplier sends a one-sheet quotation electronically to the retailer. Information sent includes: cost price, a photograph, size (disassembled and assembled), size of packaging, size of outer packaging, weight of product, country of origin, battery needs and accessories that

can accompany the product. Amongst other things, such detail enables the retailer to calculate handling and storage costs.

- Evaluations using the photo-quotations lead to sample requests for some of those items by early December. Samples are used by larger retailers in their 'dummy stores', allowing in-store planograms to be used for further product evaluation.
- The combined photo-quotations and presentation of the samples in the retailer's 'dummy stores' contributes to the retailer's internal approval process. Buying teams evaluate competing products and present this evaluation, along with recommended product selections, to merchandise managers/directors for approval.
- During this internal evaluation process, discussions between buyers and the supplier are ongoing. Areas might include scope for price reductions, changes to the product specification or own-label options.
- If successful, Berchet's receives confirmation of final product selection by March 2006. This then leads to the onset of negotiations regarding price/product contribution and volumes for product delivery in July 2006, with in-store availability by autumn 2006.

Retailers select from the entire product range offered by a supplier. Companies such as Berchet have up to 300 product items, with a retailer typically choosing up to 10–15 different items. Criteria used for product selection include:

- profitability;
- communication campaigns planned by suppliers to drive customer demand;
- dealer support provided by a supplier, such as tag advertising, pricing promotion and funding of in-store displays and catalogues; and
- 'exit plans' for product supplies (previously known as sale-or-return).

Berchet does not receive orders before shipping products; rather a retailer will confirm items that have been selected from the supplier's product range. Once an item has been selected Berchet provides product and packing details and requests a supplier order number. The dealer then advises order number and volume requirements, which allows Berchet to calculate the delivery schedule and results in it requesting appointments for delivery of products to retailer warehouses. Only after an item has been purchased by a consumer and its details have gone through the retailer's electronic point of sale (EPOS) system does Berchet actually receive order confirmation from the retailer.

Larger retailers expect toy producers to manage supply logistics on their behalf. For example, in the UK, Berchet uses Argos' extranet facility to key in product information, generate order numbers and invoices and trigger payment on the retailer's behalf for Berchet products that have been sold through Argos channels.

Relationship management

The principal points of contact between toy producers and retailers are the sales representatives and purchasing managers. However, other managers would regularly deal with each other (including the point of sales personnel, display managers, marketing communications staff, warehouse and quality control managers) to facilitate relationship administration. In addition to this, senior managers from both the supplier and retailers (such as sales and purchasing/merchandise directors) meet periodically to reinforce the relationship.

Face-to-face meetings normally occur every 2–3 months, principally to review ongoing contracts, negotiate future contracts and to present product ideas for future business. These meetings would normally involve the category buyer and possibly senior buyers/purchasing directors. As well as meeting with the purchasing team, the supplier would also make a point of seeing other managers in the retailer's business centre.

Toy producers who deal with retailers on a regular basis are subject to periodic reviews of their 'serviceability'. The review would typically feature as part of the supplier–retailer meetings and consists of:

- *Profit performance.* This assesses the extent to which a supplier is contributing to targets set by the buying team in terms of profit return per linear metre.
- *Delivery performance.* Contracts are agreed using an initial estimated figure that the retail business believes it can sell during a season. Once the product has gone to a store, sales are monitored and estimated volume requirements adjusted on a weekly basis. Supplier delivery performance is evaluated in terms of the accuracy of information provided on lead times (which is used by the retailer for forecasting and order fulfilment) and accuracy of completed deliveries (in terms of volume and timing).
- *Quality of contact.* In a broad sense the administration of a relationship is helped when both the supplier and dealer have a good understanding of each other's business, and this contributes to the dealer's evaluation of the quality of contact with a supplier. More specifically, the retailer will use comments/feedback from managers across the business to evaluate the supplier in terms of flexibility, responsiveness and problem-solving abilities.

Trends in the European toy industry

Traditional toys consist of dolls, sit-and-ride toys, tricycles, puzzles and games which are typically aimed at children between 18 months and eight years of age. The basic range of products offered does not tend to change, rather companies have to:

- search for new ideas regarding manufacturing processes and the use of materials;

- be innovative in terms of ways in which to make toys interesting (such as the inclusion of electronics); and
- keep abreast of trends in the children's entertainment industry and have good links with companies involved in forthcoming films as well as with brand/character licensing companies. For example, in 2004 Berchet won the right to produce toys based on characters from the children's 1960s TV programme, and more recently the film version, of 'The Magic Roundabout'. The success of such a film and the licence to produce toys associated with it can make a significant short-term contribution to revenue generation for Berchet.

Berchet's principal markets are France and the UK, and sales in both of these countries have been subject to significant price erosion due to retailer competitive strategies. In the UK Woolworth adopted an aggressive market penetration strategy from 2002 onwards, offering consumers major price reductions across its toy range. The company succeeded in increasing volume sales but actual revenue fell and has resulted in the company selling off some of its large retail sites.

In France hypermarkets such as Carrefour, Auchan and Leclerc account for the vast majority of toy sales at Christmas. The companies typically stock only the most popular toy products and these will be competitively priced (normally with no added margin) to ensure a good footfall. Toys'R'Us has retail operations in a number of European countries including France, where it has tried to counter the hypermarkets' short-term pricing strategies. This however has simply resulted in retaliation, with the hypermarkets extending their pricing strategy beyond the Christmas period.

Price wars between retailers inevitability affect the toy producers, with retail customers looking to suppliers for cost reductions. For small producers such as Berchet, the future is uncertain in a market where growth is stagnant (due in part to an ageing population in Europe), competition from low-cost producers is increasing and retailer strategies are, at best, squeezing producer profitability and, at worst, forcing some out of business.

Case study questions

1. What is your assessment of the balance of power between toy producers and toy retailers? What influence does this have on Berchet's marketing and distribution strategy?
2. Using the case study, and additional Internet research, identify the principal differences in the distribution structure of the toy industry in France and the UK. What are the key implications of these differences for toy producers wanting to sell their products in both markets?

Source: The majority of information presented in this description is based, with thanks, on discussions with M. Evans, Director, Berchet.

References

Abecassis, C., Caby, L. and Jaeger, C. (2000) 'IT and coordination modes: the case of the garment industry in France and US', *Journal of Marketing Management*, 16: 425–47.

Anderson, E., Day, G.S. and Rangan, V.K. (1997) 'Strategic channel design', *Sloan Management Review*, Summer: 59–69.

Anderson, J.A. and Narus, J.C. (1996) 'Rethinking distribution', *Harvard Business Review*, July–August: 112–20.

Armistead, C.G. and Clark, G. (1992) *Customer Service and Support*. London: Pitman.

Buzzell, R.D. and Ortmeyer, G. (1995) 'Channel partnerships streamline distribution', *Sloan Management Review*, Spring: 85–96.

Cespedes, F.V. and Corey, E.R. (1990) 'Managing multiple channels', *Business Horizons*, July–August: 67–77.

Croom, S. (2001) 'Restructuring supply chains through information channel innovation', *International Journal of Operations and Production Management*, 21 (4): 504–15.

Feitzinger, E. and Lee, H.L. (1997) 'Mass customisation at Hewlett Packard: the power of postponement', *Harvard Business Review*, January–February: 116–21.

Gandolfo, A. and Padelletti, F. (1999) 'From direct to hybrid marketing: a new IBM go-to-market model', *European Journal of Innovation Management*, 2 (3): 109–15.

Gaski, J. (1984) 'The theory of power and conflict in channels of distribution', *Journal of Marketing*, 48 (Summer): 9–28.

Kudpi, V.S. and Pati, N. (1996) 'How advanced manufacturing systems affect marketing channels', *Business Forum*, Winter/Spring: 16–20.

Kumar, N. (1996) 'The power of trust in manufacturer–retailer relationships', *Harvard Business Review*, November/December: 92–106.

Kumar, N., Stern, L.W. and Achrol, R.S. (1992) 'Assessing reseller performance from the perspective of the supplier', *Journal of Marketing Research*, XXIX (May): 238–53.

Malone, T., Yates, J. and Benjamin, R. (1987) 'Electronic markets and hierarchies', *Communications of the Association of Computing Machinery (CACM)*, 30 (6): 484–97.

McGrath, A.J. and Hardy, K.G. (1989) 'A strategic paradigm for predicting manufacturer–reseller conflict', *European Journal of Marketing*, 23 (2): 94–108.

Mohr, J.J., Fischer, R.J. and Nevin, J.R. (1996) 'Collaborative communication in interfirm relationships: moderating effects of integration and control', *Journal of Marketing Management*, 60 (July): 103–15.

Mohr, J.J., Fischer, R.J. and Nevin J.R. (1999) 'Communicating for better channel relationships', *Marketing Management*, Summer: 39–45.

Mukhopadhyay, T., Kekre, S. and Kalathur, S. (1995) 'Business value of information technology: a study of electronic data interchange', *MIS Quarterly*, 19 (2): 137–56.

Rolls-Royce (2005) 'Rolls-Royce announces Model 250 Authorised Maintenance Centre awards at Heli Expo 2005', Rolls-Royce Media Room, online source: www.rolls-royce.com/media/showPR.jsp?PR_ID=40172, accessed 8 December 2005.

Shipley, D., Cook, D. and Barnett, E. (1989) 'Recruitment, motivation and evaluation of overseas distributors', *European Journal of Marketing*, 23 (2): 79–93.

Shipley, D. and Prinja, S. (1988) 'The services and supplier choice influences of industrial distributors', *Service Industries Journal*, 8 (2): 176–87.

Tamer-Cavusgil, S., Yeoh, P.L. and Mitri, M. (1995) 'Selecting foreign distributors', *Industrial Marketing Management*, 24: 297–304.

Weitz, B.A. and Jap, S.D. (1995) 'Relationship marketing and distribution channels', *Journal of the Academy of Marketing Science*, Fall: 305–20.

12 Price-Setting in Business-to-Business Markets

Learning outcomes

After reading this chapter you will:

- understand how cost analysis, competitor analysis and customer analysis, are essential elements of well-informed price decisions in business markets;
- be able to apply sales break-even analysis (cost–volume–profit analysis) to business pricing decisions;
- understand the different price positioning strategies that can be used in business-to-business markets;
- know what types of inter-departmental conflict can arise in pricing decisions;
- understand how long-term buyer–supplier relationships affect pricing in business markets;
- understand why bidding processes are important in business-to-business markets;
- know what types of bid process may be encountered;
- be able to draw up a strategy for key decisions in the bidding process, including whether or not to bid for a given contract and the analytical procedures involved in deciding on a bid price;
- know how online auctions work and what influence they are likely to have on business markets; and
- appreciate that pricing decisions may have an ethical dimension.

Introduction

Paradoxically, pricing is both one of the most important and yet one of the most neglected aspects of business-to-business marketing. On average, a 5 per cent increase in price increases earnings before interest and taxes (EBIT) by 22 per cent, whereas a 5 per cent increase in sales turnover increases EBIT by 12 per cent and a 5 per cent reduction in the cost of goods sold increases EBIT by 10 per cent (Hinterhuber, 2004). Price has a direct and substantial effect on profitability. Despite this, there is evidence that relatively few companies do systematic research on pricing, and pricing has received comparatively little attention from marketing scholars – only 2 per cent of all articles published in major marketing journals concern pricing (Malhotra, 1996). According to Hinterhuber (2004) managers suffer from some pervasive misconceptions about pricing: that industrial buyers are highly price sensitive, that pricing is fundamentally a zero-sum game and that firms are generally price-takers who must follow the prices set in the market. Yet there is research evidence to show that industrial buyers often regard price as a comparatively unimportant decision criterion (Avila et al., 1993), suggesting that managers may have greater discretion than they think when setting price.

The business environment in which companies have to set their prices is growing ever more challenging. There are deflationary pressures in world markets, meaning that in many sectors prices are declining from one year to the next (Christopher and Gattorna, 2005). Some of this can be explained by normal cost-reduction processes such as the experience effect (unit costs tend to decline in a predictable way as accumulated experience rises), but other factors are also at work. These factors include the availability of new low-cost manufacturing capacity in emerging economies such as China, reductions in international trade barriers, the deregulation of many markets, and perhaps the impact of the Internet, which has made price comparisons so much easier. In addition, business-to-business customers are increasingly sharing pricing information, and as business buyers and purchasing managers become better trained and qualified, so they gain improved negotiation skills in dealing with their suppliers (Lancioni, 2004). These pressures have put a growing emphasis on business-to-business organizations to get their pricing strategy right.

In this chapter we begin with the classic three Cs of pricing – costs, customers and competitors – and then move on to consider strategic aspects of pricing, including price positioning, the pricing plan and the role of different departments in the pricing process. Two key aspects of business-to-business pricing are addressed in the middle sections of the chapter, dealing respectively with the impact of long-term buyer–supplier relationships on pricing and with the bidding process under competitive tendering conditions. As the chapter unfolds a number of ethical issues in pricing emerge, and the final section of the chapter directly addresses ethical issues in business-to-business pricing.

Costs, Customers and Competitors

Clearly it is the case that costs, customers and competitors – the three Cs of pricing – all have an important part to play in pricing decisions. However, it would be misleading to think that any one of these factors necessarily

To calculate the price of a manufactured component:

Variable costs of production	£
(e.g. materials, direct labour)	5.75
Allocated overhead costs	3.49
Full cost of production	9.24
Desired profit margin (10%)	0.92
Final selling price	10.16

Calculation of allocated overhead:

Total overhead cost for factory	£150,000
Expected sales volume	43,000
Overhead per unit	£3.49

Complicating factors:
How to allocate overhead between multiple products manufactured using the same facilities?
What happens if sales volume is above or below target?

Figure 12.1   Cost-plus pricing

determines price. To put it succinctly, the relevant costs associated with making a product or delivering a service determine the *price floor*, the benefits that the customer perceives the product or service to deliver determine the *price ceiling*, while the intensity of competition and the strategies of competitors affect the *feasible pricing region* that lies between the costs floor and the customer benefits ceiling.

Costs and break-even analysis

Cost-plus pricing is a common approach to pricing in business markets. The price is determined by calculating the average cost of production and then adding on a standard profit mark-up – a method illustrated in Figure 12.1.

This approach to pricing creates the illusion of security, since at first sight the firm will necessarily both cover its costs and make a respectable profit. However, cost-plus pricing completely ignores both competitors and customers, and so must therefore be flawed. In fact, cost-plus pricing contains a fundamental logical flaw at its very heart:

- in order to set price one must know average costs of production;
- one cannot know the average cost of production without knowing production and sales volume;
- sales volume is expected to vary with price; and
- therefore, in order to set price one must first know ... price!

In order to calculate the full average cost of production the fixed overheads of the business have to be allocated, and this allocation is based on a sales volume estimate. If sales volume is overestimated then the fixed costs per unit of production will be higher than expected, and the firm will make less than its target profit margin. If sales volume is underestimated then fixed costs per unit will be lower than expected, and the profit margin will be above target. A particular danger of cost-plus pricing arises where sales fall below forecast so that profits are lower than expected, which encourages the firm (using cost-plus logic) to increase price in an attempt to capture the desired profit margin. Elementary economic theory suggests that raising price in these circumstances is likely to reduce sales further, leaving the firm even further away from its target profit goal.

There are two key questions that managers will invariably be interested in concerning pricing decisions, and for which an understanding of costs is essential. They are:

1. If we cut price, then by how much must sales volume increase so that we increase our profit?
2. If we raise price, then by how much can sales decline before we incur a loss?

These question can be answered with the help of break-even sales analysis (cost–volume–profit analysis), which is illustrated in Box 12.1.

Box 12.1   *Break-even sales analysis – Bricolage Manufacturing*

Table 12.1 and Figure 12.2 show the level of costs, revenues and profits for a small firm, Bricolage Manufacturing, for a typical month. Fixed costs amount to £7500 per month, while variable costs are £2.50 per unit manufactured. These two amounts combine to give the total cost per month at different volume levels. Two revenue lines are shown in Figure 12.2, one for each of two price levels of £10.00 per unit and £12.00 per unit. Table 12.1 shows the complete data for the month, while the graph in Figure 12.2 shows a classic graphical linear break–even analysis.

Notice that the gradient of the revenue curve depends on the price (technically, revenue equals price multiplied by volume $[R = PV]$, the gradient of the revenue curve is the first differential of revenue with respect to volume, and for a linear function the first differential is a constant $[d/dV(PV) = P]$). From the graph we can see that the break-even point for Revenue 1 is around 1000 units and the break-even point for Revenue 2 is around 800 units. A simple calculation can be used to find the precise break-even volume for each revenue curve; the break–even volume equals fixed costs divided by the difference between price and variable costs.

Table 12.1 Break-even sales analysis

Volume	Variable cost	Fixed cost	Total cost	Revenue 1	Revenue 2	Profit 1	Profit 2
0	£0.00	£7,500.00	£7,500.00	£0.00	£0.00	-£7,500.00	-£7,500.00
100	£250.00	£7,500.00	£7,750.00	£1,000.00	£1,200.00	-£6,750.00	-£6,550.00
200	£500.00	£7,500.00	£8,000.00	£2,000.00	£2,400.00	-£6,000.00	-£5,600.00
300	£750.00	£7,500.00	£8,250.00	£3,000.00	£3,600.00	-£5,250.00	-£4,650.00
400	£1,000.00	£7,500.00	£8,500.00	£4,000.00	£4,800.00	-£4,500.00	-£3,700.00
500	£1,250.00	£7,500.00	£8,750.00	£5,000.00	£6,000.00	-£3,750.00	-£2,750.00
600	£1,500.00	£7,500.00	£9,000.00	£6,000.00	£7,200.00	-£3,000.00	-£1,800.00
700	£1,750.00	£7,500.00	£9,250.00	£7,000.00	£8,400.00	-£2,250.00	-£850.00
800	£2,000.00	£7,500.00	£9,500.00	£8,000.00	£9,600.00	-£1,500.00	£100.00
900	£2,250.00	£7,500.00	£9,750.00	£9,000.00	£10,800.00	-£750.00	£1,050.00
1000	£2,500.00	£7,500.00	£10,000.00	£10,000.00	£12,000.00	£0.00	£2,000.00
1100	£2,750.00	£7,500.00	£10,250.00	£11,000.00	£13,200.00	£750.00	£2,950.00
1200	£3,000.00	£7,500.00	£10,500.00	£12,000.00	£14,400.00	£1,500.00	£3,900.00
1300	£3,250.00	£7,500.00	£10,750.00	£13,000.00	£15,600.00	£2,250.00	£4,850.00
1400	£3,500.00	£7,500.00	£11,000.00	£14,000.00	£16,800.00	£3,000.00	£5,800.00
1500	£3,750.00	£7,500.00	£11,250.00	£15,000.00	£18,000.00	£3,750.00	£6,750.00

1. Variable cost per unit = £2.50
2. Price 1 = £10.00
3. Price 2 = £12.00

$$BEV = \frac{FC}{(P - VC)}$$

Hence for Revenue 1, the break-even point is [7500/(10.00 − 2.50)], which is exactly 1000 units, and for Revenue 2 the break-even point is [7500/(12.00 − 2.50)], which is 789 units.

Suppose that the price is currently £10.00 per unit and the sales volume is 1400 units, so that the current profit level is £3000.00. If Bricolage were to raise the price to £12.00 per unit, by how much could volume decline before profits were reduced? An approximate answer can be derived from Table 12.1. At a price of £12.00 Bricolage makes £2950 profit on a sales volume of 1100 units, so if sales volume declines by less than 300 units (21.4 per cent) then profits will increase as a result of the 20 per cent price increase.

Suppose that the price is currently £12.00 per unit and the sales volume is 1200 units, so that the current profit level is £3900. If Bricolage were to reduce the price to £10.00 per unit, by how much would sales volume have to increase if profits were not to decline? Again, an approximate answer can be found from Table 12.1 − at price £10.00 and volume 1500 Bricolage makes profits of £3750, which is reasonably close to £3900. This means that if sales volume increases by over 300 units (25 per cent) then profits will increase as a result of the 16.7 per cent price cut. This indicates that the price cut will only increase profits if sales are reasonably elastic with respect to price; strictly, Bricolage are looking for an own-price demand elasticity value of in excess of 1.5 to make the price cut profitable (price elasticity of demand is discussed further in the next section).

As with the break-even sales volume, it is quite straightforward to calculate exact break-even sales changes associated with specific price changes when one has the data shown in Table 12.1. The percentage break-even sales change can be calculated from the price change and the change in contribution margin (CM) (Nagle and Holden, 2002):

$$\% \text{ Break-even sales change} = \frac{- \text{ Price change}}{CM + \text{Price change}}$$

For the price increase from £10.00 to £12.00 this equation gives

$$\% \text{ Break-even sales change} = \frac{-2.00}{7.50 + 2.00} = -21.05\%$$

For the price cut from £12.00 to £10.00 this equation gives

$$\% \text{ Break-even sales change} = \frac{-(-2.00)}{9.50 + (-2.00)} = 26.7\%$$

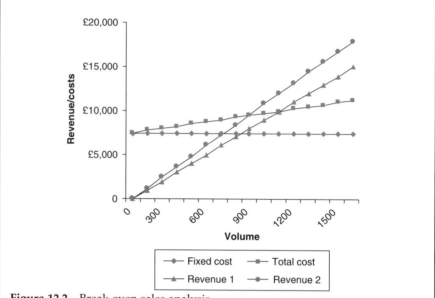

Figure 12.2 Break-even sales analysis

In summary, on grounds of profitability (and neglecting other issues that may affect the pricing decision) Bricolage should consider increasing the price from £10.00 to £12.00 if research tells them that their sales volume will fall by less than 21.05 per cent. If their price was already at £12.00, then they should consider cutting the price to £10.00 only if their sales volume will increase by more than 26.7 per cent.

Customers and demand analysis

It is clear from the preceding analysis that the responsiveness of demand to price changes is a critical issue in pricing decisions. One of the elementary flaws in cost-plus pricing is that this factor is completely ignored. In making pricing decisions managers are forced to make assumptions about demand responsiveness, which is most conveniently measured using the elasticity of demand with respect to price – this is usually simply referred to as *demand elasticity*. Demand elasticity can be readily understood graphically by considering the shape of a firm's demand curve.

Figure 12.3 illustrates three forms of the demand curve. Curves A and B fall under the general heading of 'normal' demand, meaning that the quantity demanded declines continuously as the price rises. Curve C is an example of perverse demand – above a certain price the demand curve is 'normal' and demand declines as price decreases, but below that price demand declines as the price decreases. The lower section of this curve (the 'perverse demand' section) indicates that firms wish to buy more of the product as the price rises. This may be because price is seen as a clear indicator of quality, so that

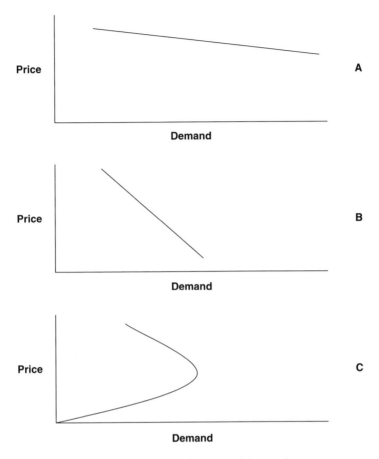

Figure 12.3   The demand curve and price elasticity of demand

buyers steer clear of very cheap products on the basis that they cannot be of high quality (Shipley and Jobber (2001) suggest that nobody would want to buy the services of a very cheap management consultant, and that industrial buyers would be deeply suspicious of truck tyres that were offered at a price far below the prevailing market price).

Most of the time and in most market segments business marketers are dealing with conditions of normal demand – the conditions implied by demand curves such as A and B. Curves A and B have been constructed to illustrate quite different circumstances however. The market segment illustrated in curve A exhibits *elastic demand*, meaning that a 1 per cent change in price causes a change in demand of more than 1 per cent. In general terms demand elasticity can be calculated as the percentage change in demand caused by a 1 per cent change in price. An examination of the demand curve for segment B will show that a substantial change in price is needed to cause much change at all in demand – a 1 per cent change in price will cause far less than a 1 per cent change in demand. Market segment B shows *inelastic demand*. The following conditions relate demand elasticity to the firm's revenue:

- where demand is *elastic*, a price increase will reduce revenue and a price cut will increase revenue; and
- where demand is *inelastic*, a price increase will increase revenue and a price cut will reduce revenue.

According to Shipley and Jobber (2001: 305), demand will tend to be inelastic for industrial brands that:

- customers need urgently;
- are strongly differentiated;
- compete against few alternative customer solutions;
- are complex and difficult to compare;
- are complementary to other highly priced products;
- involve high switching costs;
- customers see as the price being a quality indicator;
- customers buy for ostentatious motives;
- account for a small proportion of the buyer's total expenditure; and
- where the price can be shared by multiple buyers.

In addition, it is generally the case that the elasticity of demand for the products of a single company is lower (more inelastic) than the elasticity of demand for the products of the industry as a whole. The reason for this is that demand will be more inelastic where more close substitute products are available – within an industry, the products of competing suppliers are normally regarded as fairly close substitutes for each other.

Competitor analysis

Shipley and Jobber (2001) make the point that most business-to-business firms operate in oligopolistic markets, while Nagle and Holden (2002) make the important and related point that in terms of game theory, pricing should generally be considered a zero-sum game (although notice that Hinterhuber (2004) argues that managers should avoid thinking of pricing as necessarily a zero-sum game). In the hypothetical perfectly competitive market (this entails some very unrealistic assumptions such as zero entry and exit barriers and perfect information) all firms are price-takers, which means that they can either sell their product at the market price or not sell it at all. In a pure monopoly (which is, of course, very uncommon but not as unrealistic as perfect competition) the firm has a great deal of discretion over price.

In practice, virtually all markets lie nowhere near the extremes of perfect competition or monopoly, and most are dominated by 'a few' substantial competitors, each with a substantial market share (a point that we also made in Chapter 1, when discussing market concentration in business markets).

These are the conditions of oligopoly. The key feature of oligopoly is that the decisions of each competitor directly affect its rivals (interdependence), which means that in terms of economic theory there is no determinate solution to the strategic problems of oligopoly, and oligopoly can be conveniently analyzed as a formal game (hence 'game theory'). Under oligopoly pricing is generally a zero-sum game because the gains of one 'player' are the losses of another. If one firm cuts its price and increases its market share, then that market share (and associated revenue and profits) must have been lost by one or more rival firms. Under conditions of oligopoly there is always a danger of a price war that will see prices spiralling downwards as the rival firms try to grab market share from each other, with profits for individual firms and for the industry as a whole declining as a result.

Two types of legal price behaviour, characteristic of oligopoly, are designed to avoid the risk of a price war. First, there is price leadership, where the acknowledged leader in the industry (probably the firm with the highest market share) is closely watched by rivals who follow its lead on pricing decisions. When demand is slack and there is over-capacity, the price leader is the first to cut prices, which provides rival firms with a signal about the appropriate magnitude of price reductions. When the industry is operating near to capacity, the price leader will be the first to raise price, with rival firms following shortly after. The price leadership mechanism introduces discipline into the market and reduces the risk of a destructive price war. The second mechanism is price stability. Where there is no acknowledged price leader, prices can become very 'sticky', and the firms in the industry adjust their production volume rather than their price to adapt to changing market conditions. If one of the competitors cuts its price, then the other firms can be expected to follow, but there is no similar guarantee that rival firms will follow when one of their number raises price. The result will tend to be lengthy periods of price stability interspersed with brief periods of price cutting by all firms in the industry.

While the circumstances described in the previous paragraph are the common legal methods of handling price-setting under oligopoly, this type of market structure lends itself to illegal and unethical practices of price fixing and collusion. These issues will be discussed further in the final section of this chapter on ethical issues in pricing.

Pricing: Strategy and Organization

Shipley and Jobber (2001) have argued that it is essential to adopt a systematic and well-organized approach to pricing. They proposed a comprehensive, multi-stage pricing process that takes account of all of the relevant factors affecting pricing effectiveness – a process that they called the 'pricing wheel'. The pricing wheel is illustrated in Figure 12.4.

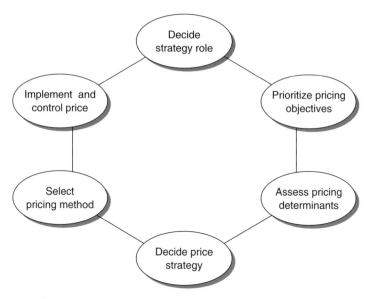

Figure 12.4 The pricing wheel (Shipley and Jobber, 2001: 303)

The point of the pricing wheel is to emphasize that pricing is not a decision that is taken once and then forgotten about. Rather, pricing is a more or less continuous process, in which pricing decisions must be constantly updated to take account of factors within the control of the firm, such as new product features, and factors outside of the control of the firm, such as new competitor pricing strategies. The first decision to be made is how great a role pricing is to play in the overall marketing strategy. In industries with highly customized products that are designed specifically to meet the needs of each individual customer, price is a comparatively unimportant component of marketing strategy. Naturally, there are other industries, such as the office-cleaning sector for example, where price is a much more important factor. Even within a single industry sector, there is scope for a firm to put more or less emphasis on price as a component of its marketing strategy – if the firm positions itself as a differentiator offering enhanced customer value, then it will de-emphasize price as a factor in its marketing strategy.

Although business-to-business organizations may pursue a very wide range of price objectives, research has shown that the most common objectives are concerned with profits, survival, sales volume, sales revenue, market share, image creation, competitive parity or advantage, barriers to entry and perceived fairness. Of these, profit targets are the most common. Survival pricing usually only arises in industries with chronic over-capacity, where firms are desperate to make as much use as possible of their fixed assets. Pricing to maximize sales or market share will generally imply lower prices than profit-driven pricing, and may indicate a longer-term orientation (with the strategic aim of building a dominating position in the market) or a belief that higher market share will inevitably bring about higher profits. It is well known that there is a correlation between profitability and market share (Buzzell and Gale, 1987), but there is no obvious reason to suppose that this shows that higher market share *causes* higher profitability – it is equally likely that firms that pursue effective competitive strategies achieve both higher profitability and higher market share (Nagle and Holden, 2002). Image-based pricing associates the price with the desired value position of the product in the mind of the business buyer; a premium price will be associated with above-average customer value, which may be delivered through product characteristics such as enhanced quality or additional customer service. Competitor pricing may be aimed at achieving price parity, at aggressively under-cutting competitor prices, or at deterring new market entrants by keeping price sufficiently low that the prospects of profitable market entry are minimized. Whatever pricing objective is adopted, fairness will often be an additional consideration. For example, a shortage of a particular type of computer memory chip might encourage suppliers to raise their prices sharply (a practice known as 'price gouging') in the knowledge that personal computer OEMs have no ready substitute and must pay the higher prices if they are to maintain production. Such a pricing strategy would very likely be seen as unfair by the OEMs, would encourage them to seek alternative products or alternative manufacturers of similar products, and would reduce the loyalty of the OEMs to their suppliers once supplies of the memory chip became more plentiful.

Price positioning

Price-positioning strategy takes account of three elements: the price itself, the customer benefits derived from using the product or service, and competitor positioning. Figure 12.5 illustrates an approach to price-positioning strategy recommended by Shipley and Jobber (2001). In a particular market segment, nine possible price positions are defined in terms of relative customer value. Remember that we have defined customer value as the trade-off between customer-perceived benefits and customer perceived sacrifices (see Chapter 4).

In Figure 12.5 we are using price as a proxy to represent customer-perceived sacrifices. The strongest price–benefits trade-off is offered by the *market ruler* position. This position is difficult to achieve, since delivering enhanced benefits to the customer generally involves additional costs, making it difficult to offer a low price while also achieving an acceptable profit margin. In any case, a firm trying to establish itself in the market ruler position would probably find it difficult to convince customers that the customer value offering was genuine – buyers would need to be convinced that this firm could deliver above-average benefits for below-average prices.

Perceived benefits of competing suppliers' offerings

	Low	Med	High
Low	Chancer	Thriver	Market ruler
Med	Bungler	Also-ran	Thriver
High	No-hoper	Bungler	Chancer

(Left axis label: **P R I C E**)

Figure 12.5   Alternative price–benefit positioning strategies (Shipley and Jobber, 2001: 308).

The market ruler makes sense when there is a long-term goal, such as becoming the established market leader and maximizing long-term market share, associated with forgoing potential short-term profits. If there is no such long-term goal then a firm that can genuinely offer above-average customer benefits is probably better off in the *thriver* (medium price/high benefits) position. The thriver (medium price/high benefits) position is more sustainable than the *thriver* (low price/medium benefits) position because rival firms generally find it easier to cut price and accept smaller margins than to deliver enhanced customer benefits.

The *chancer* positions become viable where the thriver and market ruler positions are unoccupied. Both chancer positions are vulnerable – the low price/low benefits chancer is particularly vulnerable to a rival offering higher customer benefits for a similar price, and the high price/high benefits chancer is vulnerable to a rival who offers equivalent customer benefits at a lower price. Of the remaining four positions in Figure 12.5 it is clear that the *bungler* and *no-hoper* positions offer poor customer value and are unlikely to be sustainable other than in the very short term and in unusual market conditions (for example, during an acute shortage of supply of a key industrial component). The *also-ran* position is also very vulnerable to attack, since rivals can attack it on price or customer benefits alone (the two thriver positions), or on both simultaneously (the market ruler position).

The pricing plan and the pricing committee

The pricing plan comprises seven components:

- Overall summary.
- Overview of the current marketing situation.
- Pricing SWOT analysis.
- Pricing strategy.
- Pricing objectives.
- Pricing programmes.
- Pricing control and review.

These seven components are characteristic of many types of planning process. In essence, they can be reduced to an analysis of the current situation (overview and SWOT analysis), strategy determination (strategy and objectives), and an implementation and control process (programmes, control and review).

According to Lancioni (2005: 177): 'Building value-added into a pricing program requires that a company develop a comprehensive pricing plan that integrates all of the components of the pricing process into a single document that details how the value-added strategy of the company will be implemented.' The two major hurdles to establishing a pricing plan are, first, the perception that pricing is too interdependent with other elements of the marketing mix and, second, difficulties in establishing a pricing organization in the firm (Cravens, 1997). Clearly, marketing strategy involves a wide range of elements such as target market selection, positioning, distribution strategy, product features and quality, many of which interact with price. While it is true that there are interactions between many of the elements of the marketing mix, the contention is that price in particular depends upon a very large number of other mix elements.

Similarly, just as price affects and is affected by so many other elements of the marketing mix, a wide range of different functions within the company have a legitimate interest in pricing decisions. For example, one could argue that in addition to senior management the sales, marketing, finance, operations and customer service functions all have a legitimate interest in pricing decisions. Pricing is inherently a cross-functional activity that involves people from several different departments. For this reason, many firms have a pricing committee which oversees the pricing process. The principal functions of the pricing committee are to administer pricing policy, to respond to competition and to develop the pricing strategy for the firm (Lancioni, 2004). Membership of the pricing committee is likely to include finance, accounting, marketing, sales, operations and senior management personnel. Each department brings its own perspective. For example, the concerns of the sales department tend to be the impact of price upon customers and the opportunities to use price as a tool to increase sales; the finance department tends to focus on the analysis of profit margins and return on investment.

Intra-organizational aspects of pricing

Obstacles to the development of effective pricing strategies can arise from internal organizational factors (Lancioni, 2005). Each department tends to have its own perspective on pricing decisions, and these perspectives may conflict. The finance department often seeks to control the whole of the pricing process and tends to have a short-term perspective on pricing. This leads the finance department to insist that all products must always make profits. This can cause conflict because the marketing department may wish to sell one or more products at a loss in the short term for a variety of reasons for example, to respond to a competitor's strategy, to build a customer relationship, or to increase demand for complementary products in the product line. The accounting department tends to emphasize traditional costing methods and, in particular, cost-plus pricing (that is, setting price equal to fully allocated costs plus a target profit margin). In general, the finance and accounting departments are far less inclined than the sales and marketing departments to respond quickly to competitor action and customer preferences.

Obstacles to price-setting arise out of these conflicts between departmental positions; it would be quite wrong to see one department or another as the 'problem' in the pricing process. The tendency within finance and accounting departments is to emphasize the importance of costs and short-term considerations in pricing – such considerations are important, but if considered paramount can lead to pricing inflexibility. The tendency within sales and marketing departments is to emphasize the importance of customer relationships and competitor actions in pricing and an inclination towards optimism regarding the responsiveness of demand to price (price elasticity of demand). Clearly, although a concern for customers and competitors is essential, it must be tempered by a realistic assessment of the impact of pricing decisions on short- and long-term profitability.

The role of the sales force in pricing

Chapter 8 addressed the principal functions of the sales force from the point of view of relationship communications. The sales force has a particularly important role to play in mediating between the company and its customers with respect to pricing decisions. Business-to-business sales executives can carry more or less responsibility for pricing, depending on how much authority is delegated to them from the company generally and from the sales manager specifically. The conventional view is that since sales people are the closest to the customer, it follows that they understand the customer's valuation of the company's product offerings better than anyone else and so they should have considerable delegated authority to make pricing decisions for individual customers. As long as the remuneration structure for the sales force is based on gross margin rather than simply on sales revenue – so that the salesperson is rewarded according to profits generated and not just on sales – one would expect the salesperson to make informed decisions about making profitable sales. However, in a study of 108 business-to-business marketing organizations, Stephenson et al. (1979) found that those firms that gave sales-people the least pricing authority generated the highest levels of gross margin. They suggested that five factors caused salespeople to make pricing decisions that resulted in sub-optimal profits:

- Salespeople may use price discounting to avoid the work or time involved in creative selling or customer problem solving. They may offer discounts rather than try to overcome customer objections during the selling process.
- Salespeople may not have sufficiently objective knowledge of the customer's response to price; they may overestimate customer price sensitivity because of their high motivation to make a sale.
- When salespeople are given greater price discretion this may alter competitive behaviour in the market. Competitors may feel compelled to give their salespeople more price discretion as well. The result may be an industry-wide decline in profit margins, rather than increased sales.
- Greater price discretion for salespeople may alter buyer behaviour – when they know that the salesperson has price discretion, buyers may adopt more aggressive price negotiation tactics.
- Using a sales incentive scheme based on gross profit margin may not be sufficient to ensure that salespeople make optimal price decisions for the company as a whole. First, salespeople may not completely understand the implications of such an incentive scheme, and may prefer to use sales revenue as a simpler measure of success. Second, on any one deal the loss of commission resulting from giving the customer an extra discount may appear insignificant, compared to the sense of satisfaction arising out of making the sale.

For these reasons Stephenson et al. recommend *against* giving the sales force substantial pricing authority. More recently Joseph (2001) developed a formal model of price delegation and suggested a contingency approach for sales managers. An important feature of Joseph's model is the inclusion of the difficulty of making a sale (the 'effort cost' of the sale) as well as the remuneration associated with the sale. Joseph (2001) concluded that salespeople should be given high pricing authority when the effort cost of making the sale is either relatively low or relatively high, but should be given limited pricing authority for intermediate levels of effort cost. This suggests that salespeople should have high pricing authority in market segments where sales are either fairly easy to achieve or are hard to achieve, but they should have limited pricing authority in market segments where the difficulty of making sales is intermediate. Where sales are easy to achieve the salesperson does not need to abuse the delegated pricing authority in order to make the sale; where sales are hard to achieve the salesperson needs to have extra pricing discretion as a tool in the armoury. However, in intermediate sales situations limited pricing authority removes the possibility that the salesperson will take the easy route to making the sale and simply offer a discount.

Relational Aspects of Business-to-Business Pricing

The pricing effects of long-term buyer–supplier relationships

We know that buying and selling in business-to-business markets often takes place within relatively stable inter-firm relationships, which can last for many years. The processes of developing and managing inter-firm buyer–seller relationships were discussed earlier in the book. The reader might reasonably wonder what the implications of long-term buyer–seller relationships are for pricing strategy. Clearly, in a business world where long-term relationships are a fact of life, one must take account of them when considering price. Research in business markets has suggested that there are both costs and benefits to suppliers from entering into long-term buyer–seller relationships with customers (Kalwani and Narayandas, 1995).

The advantages arise from increased sales and greater sales stability, from using loyal customers as a source of new product ideas, as a test-bed for new product development and as showcase accounts – long-term customers can be used to help attract new business. In addition, long-term customers may be locked-in to the relationship through the creation of switching costs that make it far more economical for the customer to do business with their long-term supplier than with a potential rival. On the other hand, there are costs associated with being tied into a long-term customer relationship. Customers that are willing to enter into such relationships may be particularly demanding and difficult to serve (Jackson, 1985); they may demand short-term price concessions from the supplier while continuing to expect a long-term orientation towards the relationship, so that it is not clear that the investment in the relationship pays an economic rate of return. Certainly, there is plenty of evidence that major manufacturing firms expect their long-term suppliers to deliver continuous price reductions. Of course, the justification for price reductions is that the greater volume and stability of business with a major customer generate long-term cost savings for the supplier (through the experience effect and economies of scale).

In a study carried out in the American manufacturing sector, Kalwani and Narayandas (1995) found that supplier firms involved in long-term customer relationships generally benefited from higher sales growth and reduced inventory costs when compared to comparable firms pursuing a transactional approach to marketing. However, they also had lower gross profit margins, indicating that their long-term customers had benefited most from the cost reductions achieved – the cost benefits had been passed on to the customers in the form of reduced prices. Nevertheless, the firms engaging in long-term customer relationships had performed better than comparable transactional marketing firms in terms of return on investment. In short, long-term customer relationships brought the benefits of lower costs to the suppliers, who, despite seeing their gross profit margins shrink, had also benefited in terms of return on investment. Long-term customer relationships commonly place suppliers under price pressure, but the benefits of being involved in such relationships mean that customer relationship building in business-to-business markets can be expected to pay off in terms of profitability.

Supply chain pricing

Changes in the environment of global business have encouraged companies to concentrate on their core competencies and to outsource an increasing number of business activities. This means that companies find themselves relying on suppliers for an increasing proportion of their business activities. Under these circumstances supply chain management becomes a critically important management process, and companies seek to build partnerships with preferred suppliers. When this becomes the case, the traditional role of price must change. Traditionally, pricing has been regarded as the way in which the value associated with a transaction is divided up between the buyer and the seller – thus, price has primarily a 'distributive' function. In this traditional view price is seen as the means of dividing up a fixed 'pie' of value that is created during a business transaction, and the predominant approach to pricing is win/lose or a zero-sum game, meaning that if one party is better off then the other party must be worse off.

In supply chain pricing the various companies involved at the different stages of the production process (companies located at different links in the chain of derived demand) are seen as collaborators in the production of an end product, rather than as rivals in a single transaction. Logically it is plainly the case that the value accruing to all of the companies in the supply chain can only be turned into cash when the end product is sold to a final customer. When this idea is applied to pricing, we have the concept of supply chain pricing. First, the participants in the supply chain should collaborate to ensure that the realized value from the sale of the end product is optimized, and then a second, and subsidiary, question is how that value is distributed between the members of the supply chain.

Under most circumstances the aggregate profits accruing to the members of the supply chain will be maximized when supply chain pricing is employed rather than any other pricing method (Voeth and Herbst, 2005). This means that a more collaborative approach to pricing by members of the supply chain will increase their overall profitability. Of course, the key dilemma associated with this idea is that the benefits of supply chain pricing must subsequently be distributed between the companies involved. Powerful members of the supply chain may use their position to appropriate more than a fair share of the overall profit; there is also an incentive for members of the supply chain to act deceitfully (for instance by exaggerating their costs) in order to claim a higher share of the profits. Supply chain pricing relies on open-book costing, meaning that all of the suppliers involved provide full, honest details of their costs to the final manufacturer (the company that will convert the end product into cash). Clearly there is a risk of dishonesty.

Bid Pricing

Types of bidding process: four basic auction mechanisms

The four basic auction mechanisms are the English, Dutch, first-price sealed-bid and second-price sealed bid auctions. The English auction is the most familiar auction format – an ascending-price auction in which the last remaining bidder receives the good and pays the amount of their bid. In a Dutch auction a public price starts at a very high level and the price falls until the first participant finds the price low enough to submit a bid. The first bidder is the winner and receives the good at the price prevailing when the clock was stopped. Both of these auction types are 'real-time' auctions. Sealed-bid auctions are not real-time auctions. Each bidder submits a single sealed bid and all of the bids are opened at a stipulated time. The bidder submitting the highest bid price is the winner. In a first-price sealed-bid auction the winner pays the price of their own bid. In a second-price sealed-bid auction the winner pays the amount of the second-highest bid.

That branch of economics concerned with auctions – auction theory – shows that where bidders are revenue neutral and their valuations of the good are independent of each other ('independent private values') then all four auction types yield the same expected revenue to the auctioneer. Under these conditions the English auction is *strategically equivalent* to the second-price sealed-bid auction, and the Dutch auction is strategically equivalent to the first-price sealed-bid auction. Strategic equivalence means that an identical bidder would follow the same bidding strategy in the two different auction types (Lucking-Reiley, 1999).

Internet auctions

Estimates of the scale of B2B e-commerce vary. It is clear that the business-to-business sector pioneered e-commerce, that e-commerce is of greater importance in the business sector than in the consumer sector, and that the value of B2B e-commerce transactions exceeds the value of B2C e-commerce transactions by a large amount. Although B2B e-commerce pre-dates the Internet, the Internet has brought the advantages of common standards, resulting in lower costs and ubiquitous adoption by business organizations (Timmers, 1999). As a result, e-commerce is available to small firms as well as large, and has become an important part of both marketing and procurement practices in firms of all sizes (Wilson and Abel, 2002).

The *Internet auction* is an important and fast-growing mechanism for facilitating B2B transactions. Major companies started to investigate the use of Internet auctions in the mid-1990s (Sashi and O'Leary, 2002). General Electric was a pioneer in developing its own in-house auction site, which has become one of the most successful Internet auction sites. An ex-employee of GE developed the pioneering independent B2B Internet auction site www.freemarkets.com. Subsequently, many other large firms have developed their own in-house auction sites, and other independent auction sites have sprung up to compete with www.freemarkets.com. Freemarkets. com itself merged with the software company Ariba in 2004. Box 12.2 uses www.auction4biz.net to illustrate the concept of a B2B Internet auction site.

Box 12.2   *Auction4Biz.net*

Are you getting your best price from your suppliers, are your suppliers holding you over a barrel, because they have convinced you that they are the only game in town, or do you just not know if you are receiving the 'best' prices available for the commodities, material or services that you purchase. **Auction4Biz** provides all type [*sic*] of auction and eprocurement capabilities and negotiation opportunities to the business community to help you make sure you are getting the best ROI. (www.auction4biz.net)

This is the sales pitch for the business-to-business auction planning, hosting and systems integration service Auction4Biz. Or, as they put it much more succinctly (and with the exuberant use of question marks): 'Isn't it time to regain control of your supply chain???'

Auction4Biz.Net is an online reverse auction platform that promises to achieve cost savings for customer organizations that use their service. They claim that 14 per cent cost savings against previously negotiated prices can typically be achieved. The service also puts customers in touch with additional, qualified global suppliers of which they might otherwise have been unaware. Auction4Biz facilitates the purchasing process in many ways. They will produce and host an auction on behalf of the client, and prepare and distribute RFQs to potential suppliers electronically. Auction4Biz also provides supplier training and support to suppliers throughout the bidding process. After the auction, the client receives an audited copy of the results in a spreadsheet to help with the decision-making process. Alternatively, Auction4Biz offers to host an auction site on behalf of the client organization, so that the client has unlimited online auction capability for a monthly fee. Auction4Biz claims that the costs associated with the auction process are far less than the typical savings that clients achieve – often amounting to less than 10 per cent of gross savings.

Source : www.auction4biz.net

Internet auctions can be conveniently categorized into the English (or ascending price) auction and the Dutch (or reverse) auction. In both cases the Internet acts as a medium to bring together buyers and sellers and to exchange information about product specifications, terms and conditions and, most importantly, price.

In an English auction, as mentioned previously, firms offer goods for sale and buyers offer to buy those goods. The seller starts the bidding at a reserve price and the buyers offer higher and higher prices until no one is willing to go any higher. The buyer with the highest bid wins the auction. This is a very suitable mechanism for companies to sell off excess stocks. The ubiquity of the Internet means that sellers can reach a much larger number of potential buyers than in the past.

A Dutch auction, as explained earlier, is a descending price auction. The original meaning of a Dutch auction arose where a seller offered a good for sale at a very high price, with that price then gradually declining until a willing buyer could be found and a bargain struck. In the case of B2B e-commerce the Dutch auction has come to refer to reverse auctions of contracts by buying organizations. The buying organization specifies exactly what it wants to buy, makes this information publicly available, and invites bids from qualified suppliers. The buyer posts an RFQ describing the detailed requirements at an auction website and sellers respond to the RFQ. The sellers provide details of how they propose to respond to the bid, including technical and commercial details as well as the price at which they are prepared to sell. As the auction proceeds the price that potential suppliers are prepared to accept to undertake the contract declines – hence the expression 'reverse auction'. The buyer will generally apply several criteria when choosing between the competing sellers, and will choose the bid that best matches those criteria. A particular problem that can arise with reverse auctions is the *winner's curse*. Reverse auctions often take place in conditions of uncertainty, where neither the buyer nor the seller can be sure of the true costs of fulfilling the contract. The purpose of the auction is to ensure that the buyer does not pay a much higher price than is justified. However, if price is used as the most important criterion to judge between the competing sellers, then it follows that the winning seller will be the one that has made the lowest estimate of the costs of fulfilling the contract *under conditions of uncertainty*. It is entirely possible that the winner has underestimated the costs, and therefore stands to make a loss on the contract – the *winner's curse*. For this reason, some authorities have suggested that further contract negotiation between the buyer and the seller should be allowed even after the auction has been completed (Daly and Nath, 2005).

Of course, auctions pre-date the Internet by many centuries! However, the Internet has created a particular set of conditions that are favourable to the auction approach. The costs involved in buying and selling (the 'transaction costs') are lower, geographical proximity is no longer an issue so that businesses have easy access to many more potential buyers and sellers, and

Responding to bids

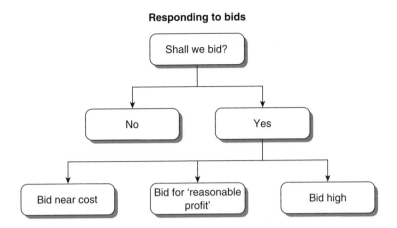

Figure 12.6   A simplified view of the bidding decision process

the timing of the auction can be more flexible – buyers and sellers can join at any point in the auction process. Internet auctions may have a rigidly specified closing time (a hard close) or may be allowed to continue as long as there is a substantial amount of continuing bidding activity (a soft close). If an auction has a hard close, then participants may use 'sniping' tactics – that is, they may try to win the auction by putting in a bid at the very last minute.

Bidding decisions

Figure 12.6 outlines in a simplified way the decisions that face a company which has the opportunity to bid for a contract through a competitive tendering process. First, there is the decision of whether to proceed with a bid or to refrain from bidding. If the decision is made to proceed with a bid, then a bidding strategy must be determined. In Figure 12.6 the bidding strategy decision has been simplified into three categories – to bid at or near cost, to bid for a normal level of profit for the industry, or to bid at a price that would yield a much higher level of profit than normal.

The very process of bidding for a contract can be time-consuming and costly. This applies particularly in the case of major industrial contracts but it also applies to business-to-business services such as marketing research. For example, when buying marketing research services a firm will typically prepare a brief and then invite between three and five qualified market research firms to submit proposals – that is, detailed specifications of the methods that will be used to gather and analyze the data to answer the specified research questions. In order to put together a competitive research proposal each market research firm has to conduct some preliminary secondary research and expend considerable managerial time. Clearly, there are costs associated with submitting a bid. These costs are much greater with a major industrial project such as the construction of a warehouse or factory. Because of the costs associated with bidding, business-to-business firms have to be selective concerning the bids to which they respond. Firms will be more inclined to bid where they believe they have a good chance of winning and where the contract is 'attractive'.

Clearly, expected profitability is an important criterion in deciding on how attractive a contract is. However, other factors are also relevant. In particular, there are relational aspects to the bidding decision. Where a supplier believes that it has a long-term partnership with a particular customer, then it is more likely to bid even though the individual contract may not appear lucrative. Equally, where a supplier wishes to try to establish a business relationship with an important buying organization – so that future contracts will flow out of the relationship – then it may be rational to enter into the bidding process even though the first contract looks relatively unattractive.

Having made the decision to submit a bid, the bidding strategy may be to bid low (near cost), to bid high, or to bid at a price that will yield a normal level of profit. All other things being equal a higher bid price will reduce the probability of winning the contract. It follows that making a bid at or near cost should maximize the probability of winning the contract. However, such a strategy also runs the risk of suffering the winner's curse, since in most cases it is not possible to calculate the costs of delivering a contract with complete accuracy, and when the price quoted is at or near cost then there is clearly a real chance that the costs involved in delivering on the contract will exceed the revenue generated. A low-price bidding strategy makes sense where the bidding firm has spare capacity, or where there is a good chance that by winning one contract with the customer there will be further, more lucrative contracts to follow from the same customer.

A high-price bidding strategy (bidding at a price that will yield a profit in excess of industry norms) may make sense where the bidder believes that they have certain special competences that make their bid more attractive to the customer on non-price grounds – for example, a management consultancy firm that believes that it employs the best legal experts on corporate mergers. That is to say that the bidder believes they can deliver enhanced customer benefits so that their value proposition will be attractive to the customer despite the relatively high bid price. Where there are no such enhanced benefits then a high-price bid may be used simply to signal that the bidding firm is working close to capacity and really does not need the extra business. For example, when an automotive components supplier is invited to bid for a contract by a major automobile OEM such as Ford, it may feel compelled to respond positively in order to demonstrate a desire to do business with an important player in the industry. Submitting a high-price bid may be considered a wiser response than simply not submitting a bid, since the latter response could be treated as evidence that the supplier is simply not interested in business with the OEM.

Under most normal business conditions a supplier responding to a competitive tender will aim to achieve a standard rate of profit on the contract. This still provides fairly wide scope for variations in the quoted bid price. If one makes the convenient simplifying assumption that the contract will always go to the lowest bidder, then the probability of winning a bid depends on how many other bidders there are and on how close to the estimated costs of delivering the contract one bids (Nagle and Holden, 2002). For example, suppose that experience within the industry has demonstrated that when you bid for an expected profit margin over costs of 10 per cent, there is a 50 per cent chance that your price will be lower than a single bidding rival, whereas when you bid for a 20 per cent profit margin there is only a 10 per cent chance that your price will be lower than a single rival. It follows that if you know that there will only be one bidding rival, then pricing for 10 per cent over costs will give you a 50 per cent chance of success, while pricing for 20 per cent over costs will give you only a 10 per cent chance of success. However, the chance of success falls sharply as the number of rivals increases. With two rivals, at a price of 10 per cent over cost your chance of success is now 25 per cent (50 per cent chance of beating rival A, 50 per cent chance of beating rival B, hence a 25 per cent chance of beating them both). With two rivals, at a price of 20 per cent over costs, your chance of success is now 1 per cent (10 per cent chance of beating rival A, 10 per cent chance of beating rival B, 1 per cent chance of beating them both). The method of calculating the probabilities against more than one rival is to express the probabilities as a decimal, and then multiply the probabilities together (hence, $0.25 = 0.5 \times 0.5$, while $0.01 = 0.1 \times 0.1$). The key message is that both the competitiveness of the proposed bid price *and* the expected number of rival bidders must be taken into account when evaluating the likelihood of success in a competitive tender.

Ethical Aspects of Business-to-Business Pricing

Pricing – common ethical concerns

Pricing is an aspect of the marketing mix within which ethical issues often arise. Stohs and Brannick (1999) carried out interviews with the managing directors of 348 Irish businesses to investigate their perceptions of the importance and frequency of various unethical practices. They found that 'unfair price' was perceived to be the second most common out of a list of ten unethical practices – 39.5 per cent of their respondents thought that it occurred 'very commonly'.

The principal ethical issues that arise concerning business-to-business pricing decisions are anti-competitive pricing, price fixing, price discrimination, and predatory pricing or dumping (Schlegelmilch, 1998; Smith and Quelch, 1993). Anti-competitive pricing arises where a group of producers collude to raise prices above the level that would apply in a freely operating market. Such behaviour is regarded as unfair and damaging to the free enterprise system and so is often prohibited by law; these are known as antitrust laws. Such laws apply, for example, in the USA (the Sherman Act), in the EU (Article 81 of the EC Treaty) and Japan (Act Concerning Prohibition of Private Monopoly and Maintenance of Fair Trade). Article 81 of the EC Treaty states that it is prohibited to 'directly or indirectly fix purchase or selling prices or any other trading conditions'.

Companies may be tempted to enter into explicit price-fixing arrangements because they believe that otherwise there is the risk of a price war leading to financial losses, and eventually to job losses and potential bankruptcy. However, price fixing is illegal in all of the major economies of the world. For example, price fixing was alleged in the American explosives market during the 1980s and 1990s. The allegation was that explosives manufacturers had artificially raised and fixed prices, allocated customers between themselves, and rigged commercial bids between 1988 and 1992. Following legal action instigated by the US Department of Justice under the Sherman Act, several companies were found guilty on price-fixing charges and were fined. In 1995, ICI Explosives USA Inc. received a $10 million criminal fine for conspiring to fix the prices of commercial explosives sold in western Kentucky, southern Indiana and southern Illinois. Dyno Nobel, the world's second largest commercial explosives manufacturer, was fined $15 million for similar offences (Schlegelmilch, 1998; US Department of Justice, 1996).

Unethical pricing practices arise particularly in industries where competitive tendering is in common use. Collusive tendering occurs where there is 'an exclusive agreement between [competitors] either not to tender, or to tender in such a manner as not to be competitive with one of the other tenderers' (Zarkada-Fraser, 2000: 270). It is sometimes found in the construction industry, the defence industry and in a wide range of government procurement arrangements (Zarkada-Fraser, 2000). The essence of collusion in tendering is that there is an agreement between the bidders to win the contract for one bidder, with the other parties receiving some other benefits – these may be direct financial benefits, or agreements that they will win future contracts. Collusion aims to undermine the rationale for competitive tendering by avoiding direct price competition between the bidders. In commercial contracts this means that the buyer is disadvantaged by paying more than they otherwise would, while in government contracts the ultimate loser is the taxpayer. Collusion is illegal in all of the world's major economies but nevertheless is by no means an uncommon practice (Zarkada-Fraser, 2000).

Dumping is 'the selling of exported goods in a foreign market below the price of the same goods in the home market', and claims of dumping have been made in a range of industrial markets including computer chips, nylon yarn, semiconductors, steel, transformers and vinyl (Delener, 1998: 1747). The General Agreement on Tariffs and Trade (GATT) of the World Trade Organization (WTO) permits countries to take measures against dumping – Box 12.3 contains the relevant text from article VI of GATT 1994.

Box 12.3 *Dumping*
Determination of Dumping

2.1 For the purpose of this Agreement, a product is to be considered as being dumped, i.e. introduced into the commerce of another country at less than its normal value, if the export price of the product exported from one country to another is less than the comparable price, in the ordinary course of trade, for the like product when destined for consumption in the exporting country.

2.2 When there are no sales of the like product in the ordinary course of trade in the domestic market of the exporting country or when, because of the particular market situation or the low volume of the sales in the domestic market of the exporting country, such sales do not permit a proper comparison, the margin of dumping shall be determined by comparison with a comparable price of the like product when exported to an appropriate third country, provided that this price is representative, or with the cost of production in the country of origin plus a reasonable amount for administrative, selling and general costs and for profits.

   2.2.1 Sales of the like product in the domestic market of the exporting country or sales to a third country at prices below per unit (fixed and variable) costs of production plus administrative, selling and general costs may be treated as not being in the ordinary course of trade by reason of price and may be disregarded in determining normal value only if the authorities determine that such sales are made within an extended period of time in substantial quantities and are at prices which do not provide for the recovery of all costs within a reasonable period of time. If prices which are below per unit costs at the time of sale are above weighted average per unit costs for the period of investigation, such prices shall be considered to provide for recovery of costs within a reasonable period of time.

Source: WTO, 1994.

Allegations of dumping are increasing, because the independent nation state remains the key building block of international politics while at the same time major corporations prefer to see the world as a single, global market. In ethical terms dumping is a troublesome concept. On the one hand, it can be seen as an aggressive action that will cause harm to a domestic industry and threaten the jobs of those who work in them; on the other hand, it is offering consumers lower-priced products. In many cases of dumping a consequentialist (for example, a utilitarian) approach to ethics (see Chapter 4) would suggest that dumping creates net *benefits* when the interests of all parties are taken fully into account. Indeed, Delener (1998: 1751) concludes as follows:

> There is little justification in theory or in practice to say that predatory pricing or dumping is wrong ... There are no persuasive economic, business or consumer welfare arguments for why dumping should be illegal ... Ethically, then, one could argue that a marketer involved in low or discount pricing in another country is not violating any moral law, breaking a promise or causing injury.

Responding to ethical issues in pricing

Nagle and Holden (2002) provide a spectrum of ethical behaviour concerning price that can provide a useful basis for understanding one's own ethical position in pricing matters. They arrange their five ethical levels from the least restrictive ethical principle, upon which virtually everyone would be agreed, to the most restrictive ethical principle, with which most people would disagree:

1. Pricing is ethical where the buyer *voluntarily* pays the agreed price.
2. Pricing is ethical where both parties have equal information.
3. Pricing is ethical where there is no exploitation of a buyer's 'essential needs'.
4. Pricing is ethical where it is justified by costs.
5. Pricing is ethical where everyone has equal access to goods and services regardless of ability to pay.

In capitalist economies there would be near-universal agreement with level 1 – coercing the buyer into paying a price they would not pay willingly is more consistent with criminal activity than with commerce. Level 2 is more restrictive, and requires that the seller should disclose all information that is relevant to the purchase (in their study of Irish managing directors, Stohs and Brannick (1999) found that 'mislead buyer' was considered to be the second worst unethical business practice, while 30.1% of the respondents believed that it occurred 'very commonly'). In business-to-business markets the development of long-term supplier–customer relationships (see Chapter 3) depends on this kind of information flow; a trusting relationship between the buyer and the seller cannot be established if important items of information are withheld. At level 3 the seller is urged *not* to exploit opportunities for 'price gouging' (price gouging is defined by Laczniak and Murphy (1993: 128) as 'taking advantage of those who must have your product and are willing to pay an inordinately high price for it'). Then level 4 generalizes from level 3 and asserts that prices must be justified by costs for *all* products and not just for essential products. Finally, level 5 moves well beyond the ethical considerations that are normally observed in capitalist economies and towards a communist perspective.

For most business-to-business exchanges in capitalist economies there would be near-universal agreement with ethical level 1 and near-universal disagreement with level 5. No doubt there would be substantial debate about the levels in between, which would depend upon the ethical preferences of the people concerned and the specific aspects of any particular exchange process. For example, some people might argue that it is fair to withhold key information from a powerful buying organization that has extensive resources and employs professionally trained buyers (whose job it is to uncover all relevant information) but unfair to withhold key information from a small business with limited resources and no trained buyers. Some people would argue that it is legitimate to make very high profits on, say, a critical electronic component when there is a shortage of supply – and, indeed, that this makes up for the lean times when the price is driven down to cost or below by the forces of supply and demand. Each individual manager has to make their own decisions, and these five ethical levels provide a useful framework within which to do so.

Chapter Summary

- A basic framework for approaching pricing decisions is the three Cs of costs, customers and competitors. Although cost-plus pricing is often used in business markets it is fundamentally flawed since it does not take account of customer price sensitivity. Sales break-even analysis (or cost–volume–profit analysis) is a useful technique for understanding how profitability is affected by pricing decisions, and for informing decisions about price changes. Customer price sensitivity is usually measured using the price elasticity of demand – the percentage change in demand for a 1 per cent change in price. Most business markets are oligopolies, so that there is an ever-present risk of a price war, leading to price stickiness, price leadership and also providing an incentive for firms to engage in such illegal practices as price fixing and price collusion.

- Pricing is a continuous process rather than a once-off decision; prices need to be constantly rethought in the light of factors within the firm's control and factors outside the firm's control. The two long-term viable price positioning strategies are the market ruler (low price/high customer benefits) and the thriver (low price/medium benefits or medium price/high benefits). The chancer position (low price/low benefits or high price/high benefits) is a short-term viable position although it is dominated by the thriver and market ruler positions.

- Many different departments have an input into the pricing process, and members of different departments tend to have different pricing priorities. For example, the finance department may insist that all products should always make a profit, while the marketing department may see strategic advantage in occasionally taking a loss on one or more products. The role of the sales force in pricing is particularly problematic – the key question being how much pricing latitude should be given to the individual salesperson. The best advice seems to be that salespeople should have considerable pricing authority in market segments where selling is either particularly difficult or particularly easy, but only limited authority in market segments that fall between these categories.

- Buyer–supplier relationships in business markets influence pricing decisions. Suppliers that are involved in long-term relationships with customers benefit from higher sales growth and lower inventory costs, but also have to deliver lower prices than suppliers that do not engage in long-term partnering. It would be rational for the firms involved in a supply chain to co-ordinate their pricing strategies in order to maximize their collective profitability, although in practice this will be difficult to achieve.

- Bid pricing (competitive tendering) is common in business markets. The Internet has facilitated business-to-business auctions. When offered the opportunity to bid, a firm must first decide whether it is worthwhile taking part at all (since there are substantial costs associated with bidding), and subsequently decide on a bidding strategy. The likelihood of success in a bidding process depends on the cost base of the bidder, the desired profit margin and the number of other bidders taking part. As the number of other bidders increases, the probability of success declines.

- Pricing is an aspect of business marketing that often raises ethical concerns, such as anti-competitive pricing, price fixing, price collusion, price discrimination, predatory pricing (dumping) and price gouging. Both ethical and legal issues are relevant. Price fixing is illegal in all major economies of the world, while under the GATT countries are allowed to take action where overseas companies are proved to be dumping (selling below the normal price in the home market) goods in their markets.

Questions for discussion

1. Discourse Products makes electrical components that have multiple uses in industrial manufacturing. The Marketing Director is considering whether or not to implement a price cut, and has asked for your advice. You have been provided with the following data:

    Current price = £2.50
    Variable costs = £1.00
    Fixed costs = £12,500

What is the break-even sales volume at the current price of £2.50 per unit? If Discourse Products cut the price to £2.25 per unit, by how much would sales need to increase for profits to be maintained at the current level? Given the further information that Discourse Products believe demand for their products is inelastic with respect to price, do you think that they should proceed with a price cut?

2. What are the characteristics that differentiate an oligopoly from a perfectly competitive market and from a monopoly? What difference does this make to pricing strategy?

3. Explain why, in an oligopolistic industry that faces inelastic demand and in which there is no acknowledged price leader, it is inadvisable for a firm to pursue a price-cutting strategy aimed at increasing market share.

4. What are the arguments for and against giving salespeople a high level of price discretion during their negotiations with customers?

5. From the point of view of costs, prices, revenues and profitability, what are the pros and cons of engaging in long-term partnerships with major customers?

6. A business colleague to whom you have shown Nagle and Holden's (2002) 'five ethical levels' (see the final section of this chapter) simply cannot understand why any of them is relevant except for the first – 'pricing is ethical where the buyer voluntarily pays the agreed price'. What arguments can you provide in favour of going beyond level 1? What is your own view on the five ethical levels?

References

Avila, R., Dodds, W., Chapman, J., Mann, K. and Wahlers, R. (1993) 'Importance of price in industrial buying', *Review of Business*, 15 (2): 34–48.

Buzzell, R.D. and Gale, B.T. (1987) *The PIMS Principles: Linking Strategy to Performance*. New York: Free Press.

Christopher, M. and Gattorna, J. (2005) 'Supply chain cost management and value-based pricing', *Industrial Marketing Management*, 34: 115–21.

Cravens, D. (1997) *Strategic Marketing*. New York: Irwin-McGraw Hill.

Daly, S.P. and Nath, P. (2005) 'Reverse auctions for relationship marketers', *Industrial Marketing Management*, 34: 157–66.

Delener, N. (1998) 'An ethical and legal synthesis of dumping: growing concerns in international marketing', *Journal of Business Ethics*, 17: 1747–53.

Hinterhuber, A. (2004) 'Towards value-based pricing – An integrative framework for decision making', *Industrial Marketing Management*, 33: 765–78.

Jackson, B.B. (1985) *Winning and Keeping Industrial Customers: The Dynamics of Customer Relationships*. Lexington, MA: Lexington Books.

Joseph, K. (2001) 'On the optimality of delegating pricing authority to the sales force', *Journal of Marketing*, 65 (January): 62–70.

Kalwani, M.U. and Narayandas, N. (1995) 'Long-term manufacturer–supplier relationships: do they pay off for supplier firms', *Journal of Marketing*, 59: 1–16.

Laczniak, G.R. and Murphy, P.E. (1993) *Ethical Marketing Decisions: The Higher Road*. New Jersey: Prentice Hall.

Lancioni, R.A. (2004) 'A strategic approach to industrial product pricing: the pricing plan', *Industrial Marketing Management*, 34: 177–83.

Lancioni, R. A. (2005) 'A strategic approach to industrial product pricing', *Industrial Marketing Management*, 34: 177–83.

Lucking-Reiley, D. (1999) 'Using field experiments to test equivalence between auction formats: magic on the Internet', *The American Economic Review*, 89 (5): 1063–80.

Malhotra, N. (1996) 'The impact of the academy of marketing science on marketing scholarship – an analysis of the research published in *JAMS*', *Journal of the Academy of Marketing Science*, 24 (4): 291–8.

Nagle, T.T. and Holden, R.K. (2002) *The Strategy and Tactics of Pricing: A Guide to Profitable Decision Making* (3rd edn). Upper Saddle River, NJ: Prentice Hall.

Sashi, C.M. and O' Leary, B. (2002) 'The role of Internet auctions in the expansion of B2B markets', *Industrial Marketing Management*, 31: 103–10.

Schlegelmilch, B. (1998) *Marketing Ethics: An International Perspective*. London: International Thompson Business Press.

Shipley, D. and Jobber, D. (2001) 'Integrative pricing via the pricing wheel', *Industrial Marketing Management*, 30: 301–14.

Smith, N.C. and Quelch, J.A. (1993). *Ethics in Marketing*. Homewood, IL: Irwin.

Stephenson, R.P., Cron, W.L. and Frazier, G.L. (1979) 'Delegating pricing authority to the salesforce: the effects on sales and profit performance', *Journal of Marketing*, 43 (Spring): 21–8.

Stohs, J.H. and Brannick, T. (1999) 'Codes and conduct: predictors of Irish managers' ethical reasoning', *Journal of Business Ethics*, 22: 311–26.

Timmers, P. (1999) *Electronic Commerce*. Chichester: Wiley.

US Department of Justice (1996) 'Delaware explosives company agrees to plead guilty and pay $950,000 for rigging bids on commercial explosives contracts to Alaska customers', online source: www.usdoj.gov/atr/public/press_releases/1996/0559.htm

Voeth, M. and Herbst, U. (2005) 'Supply-chain pricing – a new perspective on pricing in industrial markets', *Industrial Marketing Management*, 35 (1).

Wilson, S.G. and Abel, I. (2002) 'So you want to get involved in e-commerce', *Industrial Marketing Management*, 31: 85–94.

World Trade Organization (WTO) (1994) '*Multilateral agreements on trade in goods: anti-dumping (Article VI of GATT 1994)*', online source: www.wto.org/english/docs_e/legal_e/19-adp_01_e.htm, accessed 28 December 2005.

Zarkada-Fraser, A. (2000) 'A classification of factors influencing participating in collusive tendering arrangements', *Journal of Business Ethics*, 23: 269–82.

Index